# BLACK REDISCOVERY

## A SERIES EDITED BY PHILIP S. FONER
### PROFESSOR OF HISTORY, LINCOLN UNIVERSITY

# ADVENTURES
# OF AN AFRICAN SLAVER

MANDINGO CHIEF AND HIS SWORD BEARER.

# ADVENTURES
# OF AN AFRICAN SLAVER

## CAPTAIN THEODORE CANOT

———◆———

*An Account of the Life of
Captain Theodore Canot, Trader in Gold,
Ivory and Slaves on the Coast of Guinea.
Written out and edited from the Captain's
Journals, Memoranda and Conversations
by Brantz Mayer.*

*With an Introduction by
Malcolm Cowley*

DOVER PUBLICATIONS, INC.
NEW YORK

Published in Canada by General Publishing Company, Ltd.,
30 Lesmill Road, Don Mills, Toronto, Ontario.
Published in the United Kingdom by Constable and Company, Ltd.,
10 Orange Street, London WC 2.


This Dover edition, first published in 1969, is an
unabridged and unaltered republication of the work
first published in 1854 by D. Appleton & Co., New
York. The "Introduction" by Malcolm Cowley is
taken from the edition published in 1928 by Garden
City Publishing Co. Inc., Garden City.


Standard Book Number: 486-22456-2
Library of Congress Catalog Card Number: 77-92390

Manufactured in the United States of America
Dover Publications, Inc.
180 Varick Street
New York, N.Y. 10014

# INTRODUCTION

On July 27, 1807, a ship of three hundred tons burthen, mounting eighteen guns on her deck and carrying letters-of-marque against French and Spanish vessels—the *Kitty's Amelia*, Captain Hugh Crow, having assembled her crew of sixty from the Liverpool jails and crimping houses; having signed on two surgeons and three mates, of whom only the eldest was a navigator; having filled the slave-deck and the hold with Manchester cottons, Birmingham muskets, Sheffield cutlery, in addition to handcuffs, shackles, horse-beams, lead, Peruvian bark, chain-shot, gunpowder, rum, and water-casks—dropped with an ebb tide past the Black Rock of Liverpool and set her course for the Guinea coast. She was the last legal slaver to leave an English port.

Having lasted nearly four centuries, the great days of the slave trade were drawing to their close. They had begun in 1442, if a date must be chosen, when the explorer Antam Gonsalvez had carried ten blackamoors to Lisbon. His purpose was to save their souls. Columbus, who opened two continents to slavery, himself shipped home five hundred Indians, suggesting that they be sold in the markets of Seville. Sir John Hawkins made three slaving voyages from Guinea to the West Indies. Sir Francis Drake and John Paul Jones, the sea heroes of two nations, had helped to carry black cargoes. Great sovereigns, as capitalists, had engaged in the same commerce: among others they were Henry the Navigator, Ferdinand the Catholic, the Emperor Charles V, Elizabeth and her rival Philip II, Charles II of England (who first coined *guineas* to celebrate the trade), Philip V of Spain, Queen Anne. . . . The traffic in slaves had been a cause of war between England and Holland, between England and Spain; it had passed from one nation to another with the treaties of peace. Now, abandoned by governments, forbidden to Liverpool merchants since the first of May, it was about to fall into the hands of outlaws.

The *Kitty's Amelia*, an honest trading vessel, had received her clearance papers before the law went into effect. She had waited three months in the harbour to complete her crew. Armed with legality and eighteen guns, she was now driving southward, past Ushant, the Biscay fogs, Corunna, and the headland of Finisterre, toward the eternally pleasant belt of the northeast trades.

Her crew, on several occasions, sighted distant sails. Chase was made, but the Frenchmen, if such they were, showed a clean pair of heels. In 27° of north latitude, they passed the high peak of Teneriffe, floating in the air between two bands of cloud. These coasting sailors and wharfingers, most of whom had never been south of the Channel, now watched through the still nights as the familiar stars of Lancashire were lost beneath the horizon. Reaching the fifteenth parallel, their vessel entered the belt of storms and calms, where the sea, a dead grey, was hammered like iron by the vertical rains. A few days later, advancing with fitful breezes, they rounded Cape Palmas and sailed eastward along the Ivory Coast—composed, so it seemed, of three interminable lines, a white line of surf, a yellow line of beach, a green line of jungle. As they crept past the castles of the Gold Coast, timid canoes came forth to meet them, decided they were slavers, then paddled desperately for the beach. The Slave Coast was a tangle of lagoons and mangrove trees. Finally, after a passage of seven weeks, they reached the Coast of Calbary and anchored in Bonny River . . . in Bonny River, where the slavers lay below the town, in seven fathoms of water; where fifteen vessels, English and French, had sometimes waited for black ivory; where the war canoes of the natives, with sixty men at the paddles and thirty bound captives in the bilge, came slipping down the silent waters from the interior; where the marine cemetery, on a sandy spit, was stubbed with crosses to the memory of sailors who had died of scurvy, dysentery, ague; where fever rose from the mangrove swamps and the air was almost solid with mosquitoes; in Bonny River, the haunt of crocodiles, sea-cows, sharks, grey parrots, where the bodies of slaves washed backwards and forwards with the tide, the women floating, it is said, face downwards; the men, on their backs, staring into perpetual clouds which were almost the colour of their eyes. Here Captain Crow ordered his gig to be lowered, and was grandly rowed ashore to hold a palaver with King Holiday over the price of slaves.

Even before his arrival, the abolition of the slave trade had been announced at Bonny. The natives heard the news without enthusiasm. Because of the trade, they had been carried by millions across the Atlantic; their path could be traced by the skeletons which paved the sea; but they had been enriched by thousands, and these fortunate thousands were the kings, the traders and cabosheers, the men in power. Slavery was their economic system and their justice. Their work was performed by slaves; their wealth was estimated in slaves; their gunpowder, rum, and cotton were purchased by slaves. At law, slavery was almost the only punishment for crime. King Holiday's arguments were easy to understand, when he said in his pidgin English:

"Crow, you an me sabby each other long time, and me know you tell me true mouth (the truth); for all captains come to river tell me you (your) King and you big mans stop we trade, and s'pose dat true, what we do? For, you sabby me have too much wife, it be we country fash (custom of the country), and too much child, and some may turn big rogue man, all same time we see some bad white man. . . . "

The King, I imagined, stopped to take a deep swig of the rum which he had just received as a *dash*, or present. Then he continued:

"We law is, s'pose some of we child go bad and we no can sell 'em, we father must kill dem own child. And s'pose trade be done, we must kill too much child same way. But we tink trade no stop, for all we juju-man (priests) tell us so—for, dem say you country no can nibber pass God A'mighty."*

Captain Crow agreed with him that the British Parliament could never pass God Almighty. The other slaving captains were of the same opinion. And yet, for a few years at least, the trade was practically wiped out. Two months before the British law went into effect, a bill outlawing the slave trade had passed both houses of Congress. The Danish commerce in Negroes, once extensive, had been made illegal in 1802. The Swedes abolished the trade in 1813; the Dutch in the following year. Meanwhile all these prohibitions were being enforced by the

---

*Quoted from the *Memoirs of the late Captain H. Crow of Liverpool . . . with descriptive sketches of the Western Coast of Africa*, London, 1830.

British navy, which, in the last years of the Napoleonic wars, kept watch in every sea.

Napoleon also abolished the trade, but not until his liberal administration of the Hundred Days. On their return, the Bourbons respected his decree. Spain, in return for a British gift of £400,000, prohibited the slave trade after 1820. By the end of that year, it was legal only in Portuguese vessels, and only on condition that their cruise be south of the equator. By the same year, however, the new age of slaving had begun—the harsh, daring, and picturesque age which is described in the present volume.

This new slave trade, which developed after the Napoleonic wars, bore much resemblance to the rum-running which followed the great wars of our own century. In both forms of smuggling one finds the swift vessels, the desperate crews, the dash to load or unload a cargo, and the carouse at the end of the voyage when profits were divided. In both, one discovers that the headquarters of the smugglers are in Cuba or on the Florida keys; the capital for their venture is generally obtained from New York. Hijacking, so often mentioned in the present narrative under a different name, was a development of both. One form of smuggling depended; the other still depends, on strong local sympathies for the smugglers—because of which officials were easy to bribe and cargoes easy to sell.

Stories of bribery, some of them very amusing, occur by the dozen in *The Adventures of an African Slaver*. First, before the vessel could sail for the African coast, it was necessary to bribe the port authorities of Havana. Another bribe was offered the governor of the Cape Verde Islands for permission to use the Portuguese flag. Should the vessel be captured, the captain gave a bribe for his release. Then, on the return to Cuba, there were bribes for the Captain-General, for his secretary, and for several of the local officials. Sometimes all the profits of the voyage were eaten up in bribes.

In order to make the venture pay, the slaves were packed as tightly as cases of Scotch whiskey. The *Volador*, mentioned at the end of this narrative, was the size of a small coasting schooner; she carried 747 Negroes, of whom 136 died in the middle passage. The degree of mortality was not unusual; neither was the overcrowding. The slaves were laid on their sides, spoon-fashion, the bent knees of one fitting into the hamstrings of his neighbour. On some vessels, they could not even lie down; they spent the voyage sitting in each other's laps. The stench was terrific. A British officer testified that one could smell a slaver "five miles down wind."

No vessel could be confiscated for slaving unless Negroes were found on board to serve as evidence. This ruling, to which the courts adhered during a period of thirty years, was similar to a more recent ruling with regard to whiskey runners. It suggested an admirably simple method of avoiding capture. Many smugglers have adopted the plan, but none with more grandiose cruelty than Captain Homans of the *Brillante*.

This slaving brig was trapped, late in the afternoon, by four cruisers approaching from different quarters. There was no chance for escape. However, the light breeze died away, and night crept over the sea before the first of the British vessels came within gunshot.

Hidden by darkness, Captain Homans made his preparations for saving the vessel. He set his largest anchor ready for dropping. He hauled the chain-cable out through the hawse pipe, and stretched it round the ship outside the rail. He brought the slaves on deck, to the number of six hundred. Piling them up at the rail, he bound them to the anchor chain by strong cords attached to their manacles. Soon the boats of the four cruisers were heard approaching through the night. There was the grind of oar-locks, the splashing of oar-blades in the still water. Homans cast loose the anchor. Through the night rose a confused wail of voices as the chain, with its load of bodies, sank into the calm sea.

The cries of the slaves had been heard by the British sailors; the smell of the slaves clung heavily to the vessel; the huge kettles for cooking their food, and the food itself, and some of their manacles, were still on board; but there was no slave left to serve as evidence. Homans, jeering in the faces of the boarders, went free.

The illegal slave trade was a hothouse in which cruelty flourished, like some cancerous plant of the tropics. Every consideration seemed to favour its growth: the unlimited power of the captain, the unlimited subjection of the slaves, their colour and strange ways of speech, the desperate life of the crew, the dread of fever, imprisonment, or the gallows. With four hundred black men crowded between the decks, there was continual danger of mutiny. Two hundred women, naked and shining, swarmed in the cabin and on the after-deck. During such a voyage, lechery and fear, the red rose and the brier, were twined together as in some ancient ballad. Yet few of the captains were as cruel as Homans of the *Brillante*. They were held in check, some by their natural humanity, some by sound principles of trade. There was no profit in corpses. In order to deliver their cargoes in good health, fat, not too dejected, ready for the auction block, most smugglers treated their slaves with the same consideration they would have offered to a shipload of sheep, monkeys, or steers—with rather more kindliness, that is, than honest sailors of the same period showed to Irish or German immigrants, whose lives were of value only to themselves.

The hero of this narrative, who is not unprejudiced, speaks of the middle passage as a sort of Atlantidean idyll. He describes the plentiful food, the strict cleanliness, and the pains taken to secure good ventilation. There were even entertainments, he tells us, on afternoons of serene weather, when "men, women, girls, and boys are allowed to unite in African melodies, which they always enhance by an extemporaneous tom-tom on the bottom of a tub or tin kettle." He adds that the lash was rarely used—though from reading his own narrative, one doubts the statement.

Cruel or merciful, the trade went on. It was encouraged by economic forces which were even more powerful than the British navy. Since the close of the Napoleonic wars, there had been a revival of commerce in the tropical products which could profitably be produced by slave labour. Once more the continent of Europe was open to importations of cane sugar, rice, and coffee. The demand for cotton seemed unlimited. Slaves were scarce, and, by 1819, prime field hands were selling for $1100 in the markets of New Orleans. Even in Cuba, the paradise of smugglers, they brought $350. On the Guinea coast they could be purchased for a few yards of cloth, a keg of gunpowder, and a cask of rum—for goods, that is, worth $25 to $50. It was an old maxim of the British excise men that no trade could be prohibited when its profits were more than thirty per cent. The profits of a successful slaving voyage were a hundred and fifty, two hundred, two hundred and fifty per cent.

The slave trade also was stimulated by other forces, not of the economic order. Thousands of young soldiers, trained to adventure, had been robbed of a profession by the Congress of Vienna. They sought for new fields of enterprise. Some of them volunteered in the South American wars of independence. Some of them served on Colombian privateers, with a general license to plunder Spanish shipping. Some, like the hero's Uncle Rafael, were honest pirates on the coast of Cuba. In Spain itself, they became guerilla chieftains in the troubles which led into the Carlist wars.

This generation of young adventurers, privates in the army of Fortune, enlisted by hundreds in the new slave trade. Their love of danger helped to make it possible. In return, the slave trade satisfied their thirst for the unknown; it led them, over new horizons, toward battles, disease, strange lands, strange women, long cruises over forbidden waters, rivers of champagne, rum, brandy, and, at the end of the voyage, a last carouse on the *paseo* of Havana, while the dull-eyed wenches listened to their stories and coasting sailors watched them with hate and admiration. Besides, the slave trade offered them a career—the opportunity of rising to a sort of distinction. Da Souza, on the seacoast of Dahomey, amassed a considerable fortune and several hundred wives. After twenty years on the Windward Coast, Pedro Blanco retired with a million dollars—some say a million pounds. Our own African Slaver, the protagonist of this story, was somewhat less successful than his two great rivals, but for many years his name was equally notorious.

The life of Theodore Canot was an international episode. Brought up in Florence by his Italian mother, who was the widow of a Frenchman, he was educated by the captain of an American vessel, and served indifferently under the Dutch, English, Portuguese, Spanish, Brazilian, and Colombian flags. He could easily be considered an American, for he commanded several American ships, spent his last years in this country, and contributed not a little to the spread of slavery in the Southern states. However, his character was that of an Italian *condottiere*, born four centuries out of his time. Like his great prototypes, he was wily, suave, ambitious, politic, and unforgiving. He had no religion, many vices, and few weaknesses. His feelings, usually repressed, broke forth in terrible rages. The natives called him Mr. Gunpowder.

In the days of Galeazzo Visconti or of Francesco Sforza, a man like this would have won a little cisalpine dukedom. During the Napoleonic wars, he might have been a cavalry general, harrying the Austrians; or he might have commanded one of those frigates which inflicted such damage on British shipping. Even in the slave trade, Theodore Canot rose to a place of much importance. He commanded large vessels; he owned rich factories along the Windward Coast, and always he planned still greater ventures. Though few of them succeeded, his failures were due to no lack of ability. There was a poison in the slave trade, a sort of miasma like the slow mist that rose from African lagoons. With Theodore Canot, as with most of the other traders, every voyage led him nearer to disaster; and in 1853, after thirty years of adventure, he was lounging about the wharves of Baltimore, cadging for drinks, "a perfect wreck."

There he renewed his acquaintance with James Hall, a prominent member of the African Colonization Society. They had met ten years before, on the Guinea coast. Hall, a philanthropist, was establishing a colony of free Negroes in the low-lands near Cape Palmas. Canot, having temporarily abandoned the slave trade, was failing to prosper as an honest planter. Always courteous to strangers, he rendered several small services to the Cape Palmas colonists, which Hall was now prepared to return. Probably he gave Canot a small sum of money. He asked him to write his memoirs, and was interested to learn that his diaries and papers had been preserved. He introduced him to Brantz Mayer, then prominent as a journalist.

Mayer was one of those admirable nonentities who had learnt the art of being important. He was a friend of many editors, including the powerful Nat Willis, to whom this volume is dedicated. He had written a silly and rather successful book on Mexico. He had founded, or was about to found, the Maryland Historical Society. In politics he was one of those moderates who believed that the Abolitionists were insane and dangerous; he liked to think that the problem of slavery could gradually be solved by shipping the Negroes to Africa; and he was always ready to support this compromise in his luxuriant prose.

The story of Theodore Canot, the slaver who lived in peace with the Liberian colonists, seemed to advance his thesis. Mayer became his too-willing scribe. Over a bottle of port and a box of havanas, the work went forward—Canot supplying the background, the humour, the characters, the adventures; Mayer unfolding the majestic sentences which curl their length like serpents over the page. Always he found a moral to adorn their tails. His style is turgid, bombastic, sometimes ungrammatical, and generally euphuistic. It has led me to omit some passages, and to shorten several others. And yet, it has a dignity which is not unappealing in these days of mountebank writers and simple declarative sentences. It has balance, leisure, and the rhythms of fine speech. But chiefly I value it as a translucent medium through which shine the wild adventures and wilder character of Theodore Canot—that soldier of fortune, brave, treacherous, and obliging, honest only in his rages, who went seeking danger and fortune in the African trade.

M. C.

*January 1, 1928*

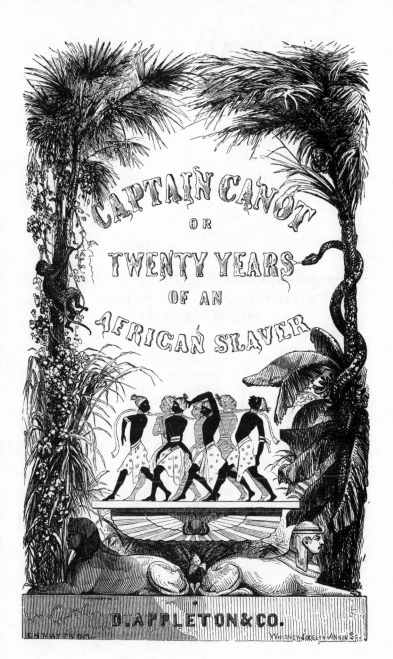

CAPTAIN CANOT

OR

TWENTY YEARS

OF AN

AFRICAN SLAVER

D. APPLETON & CO.

# CAPTAIN CANOT;

OR,

# TWENTY YEARS OF AN AFRICAN SLAVER

BEING AN ACCOUNT OF

## HIS CAREER AND ADVENTURES ON THE COAST, IN THE INTERIOR, ON SHIPBOARD, AND IN THE WEST INDIES.

WRITTEN OUT AND EDITED FROM THE

Captain's Journals, Memoranda and Conversations.

BY

# BRANTZ MAYER.

NEW YORK:
D. APPLETON AND COMPANY,
346 & 348 BROADWAY.
LONDON: 16 LITTLE BRITAIN.
M.DCCC.LIV.

TO

# N. P. WILLIS,

OF IDLEWILD.

———

MY DEAR WILLIS,

WHILE inscribing this work with your name, as a testimonial
of our long, unbroken friendship, you will let me say, I am sure,
not only how, but why I have written it.

About a year ago I was introduced to its hero, by Dr. James
Hall, the distinguished founder and first governor of our colony
at Cape Palmas. While busy with his noble task in Africa,
Dr. Hall accidentally became acquainted with Captain Canot,
during his residence at Cape Mount, and was greatly impressed
in his favor by the accounts of all who knew him. Indeed,—
setting aside his career as a slaver,—Dr. Hall's observation
convinced him that Canot was a man of unquestionable integrity.
The zeal, moreover, with which he embraced the first opportunity, after his downfall, to mend his fortunes by honorable
industry in South America, entitled him to respectful confidence.
As their acquaintance ripened, my friend gradually drew from
the wanderer the story of his adventurous life, and so striking
were its incidents, so true its delineations of African character,

that he advised the captain to prepare a copious memorandum, which I should write out for the public.

Let me tell you why I undertook this task; but first, let me assure you that, entertaining as the story might have been for a large class of readers, I would not have composed a line for the mere gratification of scandalous curiosity. My conversations with Canot satisfied me that his disclosures were more thoroughly candid than those of any one who has hitherto related his connection with the traffic. I thought that the evidence of one who, for twenty years, played the chief part in such a drama, was of value to society, which is making up its mind, not only about a great political and domestic problem, but as to the nature of the race itself. I thought that a true picture of aboriginal Africa,—unstirred by progress,—unmodified by reflected civilization,—full of the barbarism that blood and tradition have handed down from the beginning, and embalmed in its prejudices, like the corpses of Egypt,—could not fail to be of incalculable importance to philanthropists who regard no people as beyond the reach of enlightenment.

The completed task rises before me like a moving panorama whose scenery and background are the ocean and tropics, and whose principal actor combines the astuteness of Fouché with the dexterity of Gil Blas. I have endeavored to set forth his story as plainly as possible, letting events instead of descriptions develope a chequered life which was incessantly connected with desperate men of both colors. As he unmasked his whole career, and gave me leave to use the incidents, I have not dared to hide what the actor himself displayed no wish to conceal. Besides the sketches of character which familiarize us with the aboriginal negro in Africa, there is a good moral in the resultless life, which, after all its toils, hazards, and successes leaves the adventurer a stranded wreck in the prime of manhood. One half the natural capacity, employed industriously in lawful commerce, would have made the captain comfortable and independent. Nor is there much to attract in the singular abnegation of civilized happiness in a slaver's career. We may not be surprised, that such an *animal* as Da Souza, who is portrayed in these pages, should revel in the sensualities of Dahomey; but we must wonder at the passive endurance that could chain a superior order of man, like Don Pedro Blanco, for fifteen unbroken years, to his pestilential hermitage, till the avaricious anchorite went forth from the marshes of Gallinas, laden with gold. I do not think this story is likely to seduce or educate a race of slavers!

The frankness of Canot's disclosures may surprise the more reserved and timid classes of society; but I am of opinion that there is an ethnographic value in the account of his visit to the Mandingoes and Fullahs, and especially in his narrative of the wars, jugglery, cruelty, superstition, and crime, by which one sixth of Africa subjects the remaining five sixths to servitude.

As the reader peruses these characteristic anecdotes, he will ask himself how,—in the progress of mankind,—such a people is to be approached and dealt with? Will the Mahometanism of the North which is winning its way southward, and infusing itself among the crowds of central Africa, so as, in some degree, to modify their barbarism, prepare the primitive tribes to receive a civilization and faith which are as true as they are divine? Will our colonial fringe spread its fibres from the coast to the interior, and, like veins of refreshing blood, pour new currents into the mummy's heart? Is there hope for a nation which, in three thousand years, has hardly turned in its sleep? The identical types of race, servitude, occupation, and character that are now extant in Africa, may be found on the Egyptian monuments built forty centuries ago; while a Latin poem, attributed to **Vir-**

gil, describes a menial negress who might unquestionably pass
for a slave of our Southern plantations :

> "Interdum clamat Cybalen ; erat unica custos ;
> Afra genus, tota patriam testante figura ;
> Torta comam, labroque tumens, et fusca colorem ;
> Pectore lata, jacens mammis, compressior alvo,
> Cruribus exilis, spatiosa prodiga planta ;
> Continuis rimis calcanea scissa rigebant."[1]

It will be seen from these hints that our memoir has nothing
to do with slavery as a North American institution, except so far
as it is an inheritance from the system it describes ; yet, in proportion as the details exhibit an innate or acquired inferiority of
the negro race *in its own land*, they must appeal to every generous heart in behalf of the benighted continent.

It has lately become common to assert that Providence permits *an exodus through slavery*, in order that the liberated
negro may in time return, and, with foreign acquirements, become the pioneer of African civilization. It is attempted to
reconcile us to this " good from evil," by stopping inquiry with
the " inscrutability of God's ways ! " But we should not suffer
ourselves to be deceived by such imaginary irreverence ; for, in
God's ways, there is nothing *less* inscrutable than his *law of right*.
That law is never qualified in this world. It moves with the
irresistible certainty of organized nature, and, while it makes
man free, in order that his responsibility may be unquestionable,
it leaves mercy, even, for the judgment hereafter. Such a system of divine law can never palliate *the African slave trade*,
and, in fact, it is the basis of that human legislation which converts the slaver into a pirate, and awards him a felon's doom.

For these reasons, we should discountenance schemes like
those proposed not long ago in England, and sanctioned by the

[1] MORETUM,—Carm. Virg. Wagner's ed. vol. 4, p. 301.

British government, for the encouragement of spontaneous emigration from Africa under the charge of *contractors*. The plan was viewed with fear by the colonial authorities, and President Roberts at once issued a proclamation to guard the natives. No one, I think, will read this book without a conviction that the idea of *voluntary expatriation* has not dawned on the African mind, and, consequently, what might begin in laudable philanthropy would be likely to end in practical servitude.

Intercourse, trade, and colonization, in slow but steadfast growth, are the providences intrusted to us for the noble task of civilization. They who are practically acquainted with the colored race of our country, have long believed that gradual colonization was the only remedy for Africa as well as America. The repugnance of the free blacks to *emigration from our shores* has produced a tardy movement, and thus the African population has been thrown back grain by grain, and not wave by wave. Every one conversant with the state of our colonies, knows how beneficial this languid accretion has been. It moved many of the most enterprising, thrifty, and independent. It established a social nucleus from the best classes of American colored people. Like human growth, it allowed the frame to mature in muscular solidity. It gave immigrants time to test the climate ; to learn the habit of government in states as well as in families ; to acquire the bearing of freemen ; to aban don their imitation of the whites among whom they had lived , and thus, by degrees, to consolidate a social and political system which may expand into independent and lasting nationality. Instead, therefore, of lamenting the slowness with which the colonies have reached their vigorous promise, we should consider it a blessing that the vicious did not rush forth in turbulent crowds with the worthy, and impede the movements of better folks, who were still unused to the task of self-reliance.

Men are often too much in a hurry to do good, and mar by excessive zeal what patience would complete. " Deus quies quia æternus," saith St. Augustine. The cypress is a thousand years in growth, yet its limbs touch not the clouds, save on a mountain top. Shall the regeneration of a continent be quicker than its ripening ? That would be miracle—not progress.

Accept this offering, my dear Willis, as a token of that sincere regard, which, during an intimacy of a quarter of a century, has never wavered in its friendly trust.

Faithfully, yours,

BRANTZ MAYER.

BALTIMORE, 1st July, 1854.

# CONTENTS.

# THEODORE CANOT.

## CHAPTER I.

Whilst Bonaparte was busy conquering Italy, my excellent father, Louis Canot, a captain and paymaster in the French army, thought fit to pursue his fortunes among the gentler sex of that fascinating country, and luckily won the heart and hand of a blooming Piedmontese, to whom I owe my birth in the capital of Tuscany.

My father was faithful to the Emperor as well as the Consul. He followed his sovereign in his disasters as well as glory ; nor did he falter in allegiance until death closed his career on the field of Waterloo.

Soldiers' wives are seldom rich, and my mother was no exception to the rule. She was left in very moderate circumstances, with six children to support; but the widow of an old campaigner, who had partaken the sufferings of many a long and dreary march with her husband, was neither disheartened by the calamity, nor at a loss for thrifty expedients to educate her younger offspring. Accordingly, I was kept at school, studying geography, arithmetic, history and the languages, until near twelve years old, when it was thought time for me to choose a profession. At school, and in my leisure hours, I had always been a greedy devourer of books of travel, or historical narratives full of stirring incidents, so that when I avowed my preference for a sea-faring life, no one was surprised. Indeed, my fancy was rather applauded, as two of my mother's brothers had served in the Neapolitan navy, under Murat. Proper inquiries were quickly made at Leghorn; and, in a few weeks, I found myself on the *mole* of that noble seaport, comfortably equipped, with a liberal outfit, ready to embark, as an apprentice, upon the American ship Galatea, of Boston.

It was in the year 1819, that I first saluted the element upon which it has been my destiny to pass so much of my life. The reader will readily imagine the discomforts to which I was subjected on this voyage. Born and bred in the interior of Italy, I had only the most romantic ideas of the sea. My opinions had been formed from the lives of men in loftier rank and under more interesting circumstances. My career was necessarily one of great hardship; and, to add to my misfortunes, I had neither companion nor language to vent my grief and demand sympathy. For the first three months, I was the butt of every joker in the ship. I was the scape-goat of every accident and of every one's sins or carelessness. As I lived in the cabin, each plate, glass, or utensil that fell to leeward in a gale, was charged to my negligence. Indeed, no one seemed to compassionate my lot save a fat, lubberly negro cook, whom I could not endure. He was the *first* African my eye ever fell on, and I must confess that he was the only friend I possessed during my early adventures.

Besides the officers of the Galatea, there was a clerk on board, whom the captain directed to teach me English, so that, by the time we reached Sumatra, I was able to stand up for my rights, and plead my cause. As we could not obtain a cargo of pepper on the island, we proceeded to Bengal; and, on our arrival at Calcutta, the captain, who was also supercargo, took apartments on shore, where the clerk and myself were allowed to follow him.

According to the fashion of that period, the house provided for our accommodation was a spacious and elegant one, equipped with every oriental comfort and convenience, while fifteen or

twenty servants were always at the command of its inmates.
For three months we lived like nabobs, and sorry, indeed, was I
when the clerk announced that the vessel's loading was completed,
and our holiday over.

On the voyage home, I was promoted from the cabin, and
sent into the steerage to do duty as a " light hand," in the chief
mate's watch.  Between this officer and the captain there was
ill blood, and, as I was considered the master's pet, I soon began
to feel the bitterness of the subordinate's spite.  This fellow
was not only cross-grained, but absolutely malignant.  One day,
while the ship was skimming along gayly with a five-knot breeze,
he ordered me out to the end of the jib-boom to loosen the sail;
yet, without waiting until I was clear of the jib, he suddenly
commanded the men who were at the halliards to hoist the canvas aloft.  A sailor who stood by pointed out my situation, but
was cursed into silence.  In a moment I was jerked into the air,
and, after performing half a dozen involuntary summersets, was
thrown into the water, some distance from the ship's side.
When I rose to the surface, I heard the prolonged cry of the
anxious crew, all of whom rushed to the ship's side, some with
ropes' ends, some with chicken coops, while others sprang to the
stern boat to prepare it for launching.  In the midst of the
hurly-burly, the captain reached the deck, and laid the ship to;
the sailor who had remonstrated with the mate having, in the
meantime, clutched that officer, and attempted to throw him
over, believing I had been drowned by his cruelty.  As the sails
of the Galatea flattened against the wind, many an anxious eye
was strained over the water in search of me ; but I was nowhere
seen !  In truth, as the vessel turned on her heel, the movement
brought her so close to the spot where I rose, that I clutched a
rope thrown over for my rescue, and climbed to the lee channels
without being perceived.  As I leaped to the deck, I found one
half the men in tumultuous assemblage around the struggling
mate and sailor ; but my sudden apparition served to divert the
mob from its fell purpose, and, in a few moments, order was perfectly restored.  Our captain was an intelligent and just man,
as may be readily supposed from the fact that he exclusively

controlled so valuable an enterprise. Accordingly, the matter was examined with much deliberation ; and, on the following day, the chief mate was deprived of his command. I should not forget to mention that, in the midst of the excitement, my sable friend the cook leaped overboard to rescue his *protegé*. Nobody happened to notice the darkey when he sprang into the sea ; and, as he swam in a direction quite contrary from the spot where I fell, he was nigh being lost, when the ship's sails were trimmed upon her course. Just at that moment a faint call was heard from the sea, and the woolly skull perceived in time for rescue.

This adventure elevated not only "little Theodore," but our "culinary artist" in the good opinion of the mess. Every Saturday night my African friend was allowed to share the cheer of the forecastle, while our captain presented him with a certificate of his meritorious deed, and made the paper more palatable by the promise of a liberal bounty in current coin at the end of the voyage.

I now began to feel at ease, and acquire a genuine fondness for sea life. My aptitude for languages not only familiarized me with English, but enabled me soon to begin the scientific study of navigation, in which, I am glad to say, that Captain Solomon Towne was always pleased to aid my industrious efforts.

We touched at St. Helena for supplies, but as Napoleon was still alive, a British frigate met us within five miles of that rock-bound coast, and after furnishing a scant supply of water, bade us take our way homeward.

I remember very well that it was a fine night in July, 1820, when we touched the wharf at Boston, Massachusetts. Captain Towne's family resided in Salem, and, of course, he was soon on his way thither. The new mate had a young wife in Boston, and he, too, was speedily missing. One by one, the crew sneaked off in the darkness. The second mate quickly found an excuse for a visit in the neighborhood ; so that, by midnight, the Galatea, with a cargo valued at about one hundred and twenty thousand dollars, was intrusted to the watchfulness of a stripling cabin-boy.

I do not say it boastfully, but it is true that, whenever I

have been placed in responsible situations, from the earliest period of my recollection, I felt an immediate stirring of that pride which always made me equal, or at least willing, for the required duty. All night long I paced the deck. Of all the wandering crowd that had accompanied me nearly a year across many seas, I alone had no companions, friends, home, or sweetheart, to seduce me from my craft ; and I confess that the sentiment of loneliness, which, under other circumstances, might have unmanned me at my American greeting, was stifled by the mingled vanity and pride with which I trod the quarter-deck as temporary captain.

When dawn ripened into daylight, I remembered the stirring account my shipmates had given of the beauty of Boston, and I suddenly felt disposed to imitate the example of my fellow-sailors. Honor, however, checked my feet as they moved towards the ship's ladder ; so that, instead of descending her side, I closed the cabin door, and climbed to the main-royal yard, to *see* the city at least, if I could not mingle with its inhabitants. I expected to behold a second Calcutta ; but my fancy was not gratified. Instead of observing the long, glittering lines of palaces and villas I left in India and on the Tuscan shore, my Italian eyes were first of all saluted by dingy bricks and painted boards. But, as my sight wandered away from the town, and swept down both sides of the beautiful bay, filled with its lovely islands, and dressed in the fresh greenness of summer, I confess that my memory and heart were magically carried away into the heart of Italy, playing sad tricks with my sense of duty, when I was abruptly restored to consciousness by hearing the heavy footfall of a stranger on deck.

The intruder—as well as I could see from aloft—seemed to be a stout, elderly person. I did not delay to descend the ratlins, but slid down a back-stay, just in time to meet the stranger as he approached our cabin. My notions of Italian manners did not yet permit me to appreciate the greater freedom and social liberty with which I have since become so familiar in America, and it may naturally be supposed that I was rather peremptory in ordering the inquisitive Bostonian to leave the ship. I was in command—in my *first* command; and so unceremonious a visit was peculiarly annoying. Nor did the conduct of the intruder lessen my anger, as, quietly smiling at my order, he continued moving around the ship, and peered into every nook and corner. Presently he demanded whether I was alone? My self-possession was quite sufficient to leave the question unanswered ; but I ordered him off again, and, to enforce my command, called a dog that did not exist. My *ruse*, however, did not succeed. The Yankee still continued his examination, while I followed closely on his heels, now and then twitching the long skirts of his surtout to enforce my mandate for his departure.

During this promenade, my unwelcome guest questioned me about the captain's health,—about the mate,—as to the cause of his dismissal,—about our cargo,—and the length of our voyage. Each new question begot a shorter and more surly answer. I was perfectly satisfied that he was not only a rogue, but a most impudent one ; and my Franco-Italian temper strained almost to bursting.

By this time, we approached the house which covered the steering-gear at the ship's stern, and in which were buckets containing a dozen small turtles, purchased at the island of Ascension, where we stopped to water after the refusal at St. Helena. The turtle at once attracted the stranger's notice, and he promptly offered to purchase them. I stated that only half the lot belonged to me, but that I would sell the whole, provided he was able to pay. In a moment, my persecutor drew forth a well-worn pocket-book, and handing me six dollars, asked whether I was satisfied with the price. The dollars were unquestionable gleams, if not absolute proofs, of honesty, and I am sure my heart would have melted had not the purchaser insisted on taking one of the buckets to convey the turtles home. Now, as these charming implements were part of the ship's pride, as well as property, and had been laboriously adorned by our marine artists with a spread eagle and the vessel's name, I resisted the demand, offering, at the same time, to return the money. But my turtle-dealer was not to be repulsed so easily ; his ugly smile still sneered in my face as he endeavored to push me aside and **drag** the bucket from my hand.  I soon found that he was the stronger of the two, and that it would be impossible for me to rescue my bucket fairly; so, giving it a sudden twist and shake, I contrived to upset both water and turtles on the deck, thus sprinkling the feet and coat-tails of the veteran with a copious ablution.  To my surprise, however, the tormentor's cursed grin not only continued but absolutely expanded to an immoderate laugh, the uproariousness of which was increased by another suspicious Bostonian, who leaped on deck during our dispute.  By this time I was in a red heat.  My lips were white, my cheeks in a blaze, and my eyes sparks.  Beyond myself with ferocious rage, I gnashed my teeth, and buried them in the hand which I could not otherwise release from its grasp on the bucket.  In the scramble, I either lost or destroyed part of my bank notes; yet, being conqueror at last, I became clement, and taking up my turtles, once more insisted upon the departure of my annoyers.  There is no doubt that I larded my language with certain epithets, very current among sailors, most of which are learned more rapidly by foreigners than the politer parts of speech.

Still the abominable monster, nothing daunted by my onslaught, rushed to the cabin, and would doubtless have descended, had not I been nimbler than he in reaching the doors, against which I placed my back, in defiance.  Here, of course, another battle ensued, enlivened by a chorus of laughter from a crowd of laborers on the wharf.  This time I could not bite, yet I kept the apparent thief at bay with my feet, kicking his shins unmercifully whenever he approached, and swearing in the choicest Tuscan.

He who knows any thing of Italian character, especially when it is additionally spiced by French condiments, may imagine the intense rage to which so volcanic a nature as mine was, by this time, fully aroused.  Language and motion were nearly exhausted.  I could neither speak nor strike.  The mind's passion had almost produced the body's paralysis.  Tears began to fall from my eyes: but still he laughed!  At length, I suddenly flung wide the cabin doors, and leaping below at a bound, seized from the rack a loaded musket, with which I rushed upon deck.  As soon as the muzzle appeared above the hatchway, my tormentor sprang over the ship, and by the time I reached the ladder, I found him on the wharf, surrounded by a laughing and shouting crowd. I shook my head menacingly at the group; and shouldering my firelock, mounted guard at the gangway. It was fully a quarter of an hour that I paraded (occasionally ramming home my musket's charge, and varying the amusement by an Italian defiance to the jesters), before the tardy mate made his appearance on the wharf. But what was my consternation, when I beheld him advance deferentially to my pestilent visitor, and taking off his hat, respectfully offer to conduct him on board! This was a great lesson to me in life on the subject of " appearances." The shabby old individual was no less a personage than the celebrated William Gray, of Boston, owner of the Galatea and cargo, and proprietor of many a richer craft then floating on every sea.

But Mr. Gray was a forgiving enemy. As he left the ship that morning, he presented me fifty dollars, "in exchange," he said, "for the six destroyed in protection of his property;" and, on the day of my discharge, he not only paid the wages of my voyage, but added fifty dollars more to aid my schooling in scientific navigation.

Four years after, I again met this distinguished merchant at the Marlborough Hotel, in Boston. I was accompanied, on that occasion, by an uncle who visited the United States on a commercial tour. When my relative mentioned my name to Mr. Gray, that gentleman immediately recollected me, and told my venerable kinsman that he never received such abuse as I bestowed on him in July, 1820! The sting of my teeth, he declared, still tingled in his hand, while the kicks I bestowed on his ankles, occasionally displayed the scars they had left on his limbs. He seemed particularly annoyed, however, by some caustic remarks I had made about his protuberant stomach, and forgave the blows but not the language.

My uncle, who was somewhat of a tart disciplinarian, gave me an extremely black look, while, in French, he demanded an explanation of my conduct. I knew Mr. Gray, however, better than my relative; and so, without heeding his reprimand, I answered, in English, that if I cursed the ship's owner on that occasion, it was my *debut* in the English language on the American continent; and as my Anglo-Saxon education had been finished in a forecastle, it was not to be expected I should be select in my vocabulary. "Nevertheless," I added, "Mr. Gray was so delighted with my *accolade*, that he valued my defence of his property and our delicious *tête-à-tête* at the sum of a hundred dollars!"

# CHAPTER II.

THE anecdote told in the last chapter revived my uncle's recollection of several instances of my early impetuosity; among which was a rencounter with Lord Byron, while that poet was residing at his villa on the slope of Monte Negro near Leghorn, which he took the liberty to narrate to Mr. Gray.

A commercial house at that port, in which my uncle had some interest, was the noble lord's banker;—and, one day, while my relative and the poet were inspecting some boxes recently arrived from Greece, I was dispatched to see them safely deposited in the warehouse. Suddenly, Lord Byron demanded a pencil. My uncle had none with him, but remembering that I had lately been presented one in a handsome silver case, requested the loan of it. Now, as this was my first *silver* possession, I was somewhat reluctant to let it leave my possession even for a moment, and handed it to his lordship with a bad grace. When the poet had made his memorandum, he paused a moment, as if lost in thought, and then very unceremoniously—but, doubtless, in a fit of abstraction—put the pencil in his pocket. If I had already visited America at that time, it is likely that I would have warned the Englishman of his mistake on the spot; but, as children in the Old World are rather more curbed in their intercourse with elders than on this side of the Atlantic, I bore the forgetfulness as well as I could until next morning. Summoning all my resolution, I repaired without my uncle's knowledge to the poet's house at an early hour, and after much difficulty was admitted to his room. He was still in bed. Every body has heard of Byron's peevishness, when disturbed or intruded on. He demanded my business in a petulant and offensive tone. I replied, respectfully, that on the preceding day I loaned him a *silver* pencil,—strongly emphasizing and repeating the word *silver*, —which, I was grieved to say, he forgot to return. Byron reflected a moment, and then declared he had restored it to me on the spot! I mildly but firmly denied the fact; while his lordship as sturdily reasserted it. In a short time, we were both in such a passion that Byron commanded me to leave the room. I edged out of the apartment with the slow, defying air of angry boyhood; but when I reached the door, I suddenly turned, and looking at him with all the bitterness I felt for his nation, called him, in French, " an English hog!" Till then our quarrel had been waged in Italian. Hardly were the words out of my mouth when his lordship leaped from the bed, and in the scantiest drapery imaginable, seized me by the collar, inflicting such a shaking as I would willingly have exchanged for a tertian ague from the Pontine marshes. The sudden air-bath probably cooled his choler, for, in a few moments, we found ourselves in a pacific explanation about the luckless pencil. Hitherto I had not mentioned my uncle; but the moment I stated the relationship, Byron became pacified and credited my story. After searching his pockets once more ineffectually for the lost *silver*, he presented me his own *gold* pencil instead, and requested me to say why I " cursed him *in French?*"

" My father was a Frenchman, my lord," said I.

" And your mother?"

" She is an Italian, sir."

" Ah! no wonder, then, you called me an ' English hog.' The hatred runs in the blood; you could not help it."

After a moment's hesitation, he continued,—still pacing the apartment in his night linen,—" You don't like the English, do you, my boy?"

" No," said I, " I don't.'

" Why?" returned Byron, quietly.

" Because my father died fighting them," replied I.

" Then, youngster, you have *a right* to hate them," said the poet, as he put me gently out of the door, and locked it on the inside.

A week after, one of the porters of my uncle's warehouse offered to sell, at an exorbitant price, what he called " Lord Byron's pencil," declaring that his lordship had presented it to him. My uncle was on the eve of bargaining with the man, when he perceived his own initials on the silver. In fact, it was my lost gift. Byron, in his abstraction, had evidently mistaken the porter for myself; so the servant was rewarded with a trifling gratuity, while my *virtuoso* uncle took the liberty to appropriate the golden relic of Byron to himself, and put me off with the humbler remembrance of his honored name.

These, however, are episodes. Let us return once more to the Galatea and her worthy commander.

Captain Towne retired to Salem after the hands were discharged, and took me with him to reside in his family until he was ready for another voyage. In looking back through the vista of a stormy and adventurous life, my memory lights on no happier days than those spent in this seafaring emporium. Salem, in 1821, was my paradise. I received more kindness, enjoyed more juvenile pleasures, and found more affectionate hospitality in that comfortable city than I can well describe. Every boy was my friend. No one laughed at my broken English, but on the contrary, all seemed charmed by my foreign accent. People thought proper to surround me with a sort of romantic mystery, for, perhaps, there was a flavor of the dashing dare-devil in my demeanor, which imparted influence over homelier companions Besides this, I soon got the reputation of a scholar. I was considered a marvel in languages, inasmuch as I spoke French, Italian, Spanish, English, and *professed* a familiarity with Latin. I remember there was a wag in Salem, who, determining one day to test my acquaintance with the latter tongue, took me into a neighboring druggist's, where there were some Latin volumes, and handed me one with the request to translate a page, either verbally or on paper. Fortunately, the book he produced was Æsop, whose fables had been so thoroughly studied by me two years before, that I even knew some of them by heart. Still, as I was not very well versed in the niceties of English, I thought it prudent to make my version of the selected fable in French; and, as there was a neighbor who knew the latter language perfectly, my translation was soon rendered into English, and the proficiency of the " Italian boy " conceded.

I sailed during five years from Salem on voyages to various parts of the world, always employing my leisure, while on shore and at sea, in familiarizing myself minutely with the practical and scientific details of the profession to which I designed devoting my life. I do not mean to narrate the adventures of those early voyages, but I cannot help setting down a single anecdote of that fresh and earnest period, in order to illustrate the changes that time and " *circumstances* " are said to work on human character.

In my second voyage to India, I was once on shore with the captain at Quallahbattoo, in search of pepper, when a large *proa*, or Malay canoe, arrived at the landing crammed with prisoners, from one of the islands. The unfortunate victims were to be sold *as slaves*. They were the *first slaves* I had seen ! As the human cargo was disembarked, I observed one of the Malays dragging a handsome young female by the hair along the beach. Cramped by long confinement in the wet bottom of the canoe, the shrieking girl was unable to stand or walk. My blood was up quickly. I ordered the brute to desist from his cruelty ; and, as he answered with a derisive laugh, I felled him to the earth with a single blow of my boat-hook. This impetuous vindication of humanity forced us to quit Quallahbattoo in great haste ; but, at the age of seventeen, my feelings in regard to slavery were very different from what this narrative may disclose them to have become in later days.

When my apprenticeship was over, I made two or three successful voyages as mate, until—I am ashamed to say,—that a " disappointment " caused me to forsake my employers, and to yield to the temptations of reckless adventure. This sad and early blight overtook me at Antwerp,—a port rather noted for the backslidings of young seamen. My hard-earned pay soon diminished very sensibly, while I was desperately in love with a Belgian beauty, who made a complete fool of me—for at least three months! From Antwerp, I betook myself to Paris to vent my second " disappointment." The pleasant capital of *la belle France* was a cup that I drained at a single draught. Few young men of eighteen or twenty have lived faster. The gaming tables at Frascati's and the Palais Royal finished my consumptive purse; and, leaving an empty trunk as a recompense for my landlord, I took " French leave" one fine morning, and hastened to sea.

The reader will do me the justice to believe that nothing but the direst necessity compelled me to embark on board a *British* vessel, bound to Brazil. The captain and his wife who accompanied him, were both stout, handsome Irish people, of equal age, but addicted to fondness for strong and flavored drinks.

My introduction on board was signalized by the ceremonious bestowal upon me of the key of the spirit-locker, with a strict injunction from the commander to deny more than three glasses daily either to his wife or himself. I hardly comprehended this singular order at first, but, in a few days, I became aware of its propriety. About eleven o'clock her ladyship generally approached when I was serving out the men's ration of gin, and requested me to fill her tumbler. Of course, I gallantly complied. When I returned from deck below with the bottle, she again required a similar dose, which, with some reluctance, I furnished. At dinner the dame drank *porter*, but passed off the gin on her credulous husband as water. This system of deception continued as long as the malt liquor lasted, so that her ladyship received and swallowed daily a triple allowance of capital grog. Indeed, it is quite astonishing what quantities of the article can sometimes be swallowed by seafaring *women*. The oddness of their appetite for the cordials is not a little enhanced by the well-known aversion the sex have to spirituous fluids, in every shape, on shore. Perhaps the salt air may have something to do with the acquired relish; but, as I am not composing an essay on temperance, I shall leave the discussion to wiser physiologists.

My companions' indulgence illustrated another diversity between the sexes, which I believe is historically true from the earliest records to the present day. *The lady* broke her rule, but *the captain* adhered faithfully to his. Whilst on duty, the allotted three glasses completed his potations. But when we reached Rio de Janeiro, and there was no longer need of abstinence, save for the sake of propriety, both my shipmates gave loose to their thirst and tempers. They drank, quarrelled, and kissed, with more frequency and fervor than any creatures it has been my lot to encounter throughout an adventurous life. After we got the vessel into the inner harbor,—though not without a mishap, owing to the captain's drunken stubbornness,—my Irish friends resolved to take lodgings for a while on shore. For two days they did not make their appearance; but toward the close of the third, they returned, " fresh," as they said, " from the theatre." It was very evident that the jolly god had been their companion; and, as I was not a little scandalized by the conjugal scenes which usually closed these frolics, I hastened to order tea under the awning on deck, while I betook myself to a hammock which was slung on the main boom. Just as I fell off into pleasant dreams, I was roused from my nap by a prelude to the opera. Madame gave her lord the lie direct. A loaf of bread, discharged against her head across the table, was his reply. Not content with this harmless demonstration of rage, he seized the four corners of the table cloth, and gathering the tea-things and food in the sack, threw the whole overboard into the bay. In a flash, the tigress fastened on his scanty locks with one hand, while, with the other, she pummelled his eyes and nose. Badly used as he was, I must confess that the captain proved too generous to retaliate on that portion of his spouse where female charms are most bewitching and visible; still, I am much mistaken if the sound spanking she received did not elsewhere leave marks of physical vigor that would have been creditable to a pugilist.

It was remarkable that these human tornados were as violent

and brief as those which scourge tropical lands as well as tropical characters. In a quarter of an hour there was a dead calm. The silence of the night, on those still and star-lit waters, was only broken by a sort of chirrup, that might have been mistaken for a cricket, but which I think was *a kiss*. Indeed, I was rapidly going off again to sleep, when I was called to give the key of the spirit-locker,—a glorious resource that never failed as a solemn seal of reconciliation and bliss.

Next morning, before I awoke, the captain went ashore, and when his wife, at breakfast, inquired my knowledge of the night's affray, my gallantry forced me to confess that I was one of the soundest sleepers on earth or water, and, moreover, that I was surprised to learn there had been the least difference between such happy partners. In spite of my simplicity, the lady insisted on confiding her griefs, with the assurance that she would not have been half so angry had not her spouse foolishly thrown her silver spoons into the sea, with the bread and butter. She grew quite eloquent on the pleasures of married life, and told me of many a similar reproof she had been forced to give her husband during their voyages. It did him good, she said, and kept him wholesome. In fact, she hoped, that if ever I married, I would have the luck to win a guardian like herself. Of course, I was again most gallantly silent. Still, I could not help reserving a decision as to the merits of matrimony; for present appearances certainly did not demonstrate the bliss I had so often read and heard of. At any rate, I resolved, that if ever I ventured upon a trial of love, it should, at least, in the first instance, be love *without* liquor!

On our return to Europe we called at Dover for orders, and found that Antwerp was our destination. We made sail at sunset, but as the wind was adverse and the weather boisterous, we anchored for two days in the Downs. At length, during a lull of the gale, we sailed for the mouth of the Scheldt; but, as we approached the coast of Holland, the wind became light and baffling, so that we were unable to enter the river. We had not taken a pilot at Ramsgate, being confident of obtaining one off Flushing. At sundown, the storm again arose in all its fury from the northwest; but all attempts to put back to England were unavailing, for we dared not show a rag of sail before the howling tempest. It was, indeed, a fearful night of wind, hail, darkness, and anxiety. At two o'clock in the morning, we suddenly grounded on one of the numerous banks off Flushing. Hardly had we struck when the sea made a clean sweep over us, covering the decks with sand, and snapping the spars like pipe-stems. The captain was killed instantly by the fall of a top-gallant yard, which crushed his skull; while the sailors, who in such moments seem possessed by utter recklessness, broke into the spirit-room and drank to excess. For awhile I had some hope that the stanchness of our vessel's hull might enable us to cling to her till daylight, but she speedily bilged and began to fill.

After this it would have been madness to linger. The boats were still safe. The long one was quickly filled by the crew, under the command of the second mate—who threw an anker of gin into the craft before he leaped aboard,—while I reserved the jolly-boat for myself, the captain's widow, the cook, and the steward. The long-boat was never heard of.

All night long that dreadful nor'wester howled along and lashed the narrow sea between England and the Continent; yet I kept our frail skiff before it, hoping, at daylight, to descry the lowlands of Belgium. The heart-broken woman rested motionless in the stern-sheets. We covered her with all the available garments, and, even in the midst of our own griefs, could not help feeling that the suddenness of her double desolation had made her perfectly unconscious of our dreary surroundings.

Shortly after eight o'clock a cry of joy announced the sight of land within a short distance. The villagers of Bragden, who soon descried us, hastened to the beach, and rushing knee-deep into the water, signalled that the shore was safe after passing the surf. The sea was churned by the storm into a perfect foam. Breakers roared, gathered, and poured along like avalanches. Still, there was no hope for us but in passing the line of these angry sentinels. Accordingly, I watched the swell, and pulling firmly, bow on, into the first of the breakers, we spun with such arrowy swiftness across the intervening space, that I recollect nothing until we were clasped in the arms of the brawny Belgians on the beach.

But, alas! the poor widow was no more. I cannot imagine when she died. During the four hours of our passage from the wreck to land, her head rested on my lap; yet no spasm of pain or convulsion marked the moment of her departure.

That night the parish priest buried the unfortunate lady, and afterwards carried round a plate, asking alms,—not for masses to insure the repose of her soul,—but to defray the expenses of *the living* to Ostend.

## CHAPTER III.

I HAD no time or temper to be idle.   In a week, I was on board
a Dutch galliot, bound to Havana; but I soon perceived that I
was again under the command of two captains—male and female.
The regular master superintended the navigation, while the
*bloomer* controlled the whole of us.   Indeed, the dame was the
actual owner of the craft, and, from skipper to cabin-boy, governed not only our actions but our stomachs.   I know not
whether it was piety or economy that swayed her soul, but I
never met a person who was so rigid as this lady in the obser-
vance of the church calendar, especially whenever a day of abstinence allowed her to deprive us of our beef.   Nothing but my
destitution compelled me to ship in this craft; still, to say the
truth, I had well-nigh given up all idea of returning to the
United States, and determined to engage in any adventurous expedition that my profession offered.   In 1824, it will be remembered, Mexico, the Spanish main, Peru, and the Pacific coasts,
were renowned for the fortunes they bestowed on enterprise;
and, as the galliot was bound to Havana, I hailed her as a sort
of floating bridge to my EL DORADO.

On the seventh night after our departure, while beating out
of the bay of Biscay with a six-knot breeze, in a clear moonlight,
we ran foul of a vessel which approached us on the opposite tack.
Whence she sprang no one could tell.   In an instant, she appear-

ed and was on us with a dreadful concussion. Every man was prostrated on deck and all our masts were carried away. From the other vessel we heard shrieks and a cry of despair; but the ill-omened miscreant disappeared as rapidly as she approached, and left us floating a helpless log, on a sea proverbial for storms.

We contrived, however, to reach the port of Ferrol, in Spain, where we were detained four months, in consequence of the difficulty of obtaining the materials for repairs, notwithstanding this place is considered the best and largest ship yard of Castile.

It was at Ferrol that I met with a singular adventure, which was well-nigh depriving me of my personal identity, as Peter Schlemhil was deprived of his shadow. I went one afternoon in my boat to the other side of the harbor to obtain some pieces of leather from a tannery, and, having completed my purchase, was lounging slowly towards the quay, when I stopped at a house for a drink of water.. I was handed a tumbler by the trim-built, black-eyed girl, who stood in the doorway, and whose rosy lips and sparkling eyes were more the sources of my thirst than the water; but, while I was drinking, the damsel ran into the dwelling, and hastily returned with her mother and another sister, who stared at me a moment without saying a word, and simultaneously fell upon my neck, smothering my lips and cheeks with repeated kisses!

"*Oh! mi querido hijo*," said the mother.

"*Carissimo Antonio*," sobbed the daughter.

"*Mi hermano!*" exclaimed her sister.

"Dear son, dear Antonio, dear brother! Come into the house; where have you been? Your grandmother is dying to see you once more! Don't delay an instant, but come in without a word! *Por dios!* that we should have caught you at last, and in such a way: *Ave Maria! madrecita, aqui viene Antonito!*"

In the midst of all these exclamations, embraces, fondlings, and kisses, it may easily be imagined that I stood staring about me with wide eyes and mouth, and half-drained tumbler in hand, like one in a dream. I asked no questions, but as the dame was buxom, and the girls were fresh, I kissed in return, and followed unreluctantly as they half dragged, half carried me into their domicil. On the door sill of the inner apartment I found myself locked in the skinny arms of a brown and withered crone, who was said to be my grandmother, and, of course, my youthful *moustache* was properly bedewed with the moisture of her toothless mouth.

As soon as I was seated, I took the liberty to say,—though without any protest against this charming assault, — that I fancied there might possibly be some mistake; but I was quickly silenced. My *madrecita* declared at once, and in the presence of my four shipmates, that, six years before, I left her on my first voyage in a Dutch vessel; that my *querido padre*, had gone to bliss two years after my departure; and, accordingly, that now, I, Antonio Gomez y Carrasco, was the only surviving male of the family, and, of course, would never more quit either her, my darling sisters, or the old *pobrecita*, our grandmother. This florid explanation was immediately closed like the pleasant air of an opera by a new chorus of kisses, nor can there be any doubt that I responded to the embraces of my sweet *hermanas* with the most gratifying fraternity.

Our charming *quartette* lasted in all its harmony for half an hour, during which volley after volley of family secrets was discharged into my eager ears. So rapid was the talk, and so quickly was its thread taken up and spun out by each of the three, that I had no opportunity to interpose. At length, however, in a momentary lull and in a jocular manner,—but in rather bad Spanish,—I ventured to ask my loving and talkative mamma, " what amount of property my worthy father had deemed proper to leave on earth *for his son* when he took his departure to rest *con Dios?* " I thought it possible that this agreeable drama was a Spanish joke, got up *al' improvista*, and that I might end it by exploding the dangerous mine of money : besides this, it was growing late, and my return to the galliot was imperative.

But alas ! my question brought tears in an instant into my mother's eyes, and I saw that the scene was *not* a jest. Accordingly, I hastened, in all seriousness, to explain and insist on their error.

I protested with all the force of my Franco-Italian nature and Spanish rhetoric, against the assumed relationship. But all was unavailing; they argued and persisted; they brought in the neighbors; lots of old women and old men, with rusty cloaks or shawls, with cigars or *cigarillos* in mouth, formed a jury of inquest; so that, in the end, there was an unanimous verdict in favor of my Galician nativity!

Finding matters had indeed taken so serious a turn, and knowing the impossibility of eradicating an impression from the female mind when it becomes imbedded with so much apparent conviction, I resolved to yield; and, assuming the manner of a penitent prodigal, I kissed the girls, embraced my mother, passed my head over both shoulders of my grand-dame, and promised my progenitors a visit next day.

As I did not keep my word, and two suns descended without my return, the imaginary " mother " applied to the ministers of law to enforce her rights over the truant boy. The *Alcalde*, after hearing my story, dismissed the claim; but my dissatisfied relatives summoned me, on appeal, before the governor of the district, nor was it without infinite difficulty that I at last succeeded in shaking off their annoying consanguinity.

I have always been at a loss to account for this queer mistake. It is true that my father was in Spain with the French army during Napoleon's invasion, but that excellent gentleman was a faithful spouse as well as valiant soldier, and I do not remember that he ever sojourned in the pleasant port of Ferrol!

At length, we sailed for Havana, and nothing of importance occurred to break the monotony of our hot and sweltering voyage, save a sudden flurry of jealousy on the part of the captain, who imagined I made an attempt to conquer the pious and economical heart of his wife! In truth, nothing was further from my mind or taste than such an enterprise; but as the demon had complete possession of him, and his passion was stimulated by the lies of a cabin boy, I was forced to undergo an inquisitorial examination, which I resisted manfully but fruitlessly. The Bloomer-dame, who knew her man, assumed such an air of outraged innocence and calumniated virtue, interlarded with sobs, tears, and hysterics, that her perplexed husband was quite at his wit's end, but terminated the scene by abruptly ordering me to my state-room.

This was at nightfall. I left the cabin willingly but with great mortification; yet the surly pair eyed each other with so much anger that I had some fear for the *denouement*. I know not what passed during the silent watches of that night; but doubtless woman's witchcraft had much to do in pouring oil on the seared heart of the skipper. At daylight he emerged from his cabin with orders to have the tell tale cabin boy soundly thrashed; and, when Madame mounted the deck, I saw at a glance that her influence was completely restored. Nor was I neglected in this round of reconciliation. In the course of the day, I was requested to resume my duty on board, but I stubbornly refused. Indeed, my denial caused the captain great uneasiness, for he was a miserable navigator, and, now that we approached the Bahamas, my services were chiefly requisite. The jealous scamp was urgent in desiring me to forget the past and resume duty; still I declined, especially as his wife informed me in private that there would perhaps be peril in my compliance.

The day after we passed the " Hole in the Wall" and steered for Salt Key, we obtained no meridian observation, and no one on board, except myself, was capable of taking a lunar, which in our position, among unknown keys and currents, was of the greatest value. I knew this troubled the skipper, yet, after his wife's significant warning, I did not think it wise to resume my functions. Nevertheless, I secretly made calculations and watched the vessel's course. Another day went by without a noontide observation; but, at midnight, I furtively obtained a lunar, by the result of which I found we were drifting close to the Cuba reefs, about five miles from the CRUZ DEL PADRE.

As soon as I was sure of my calculation and sensible of imminent danger, I did not hesitate to order the second officer,— whose watch it was,—to call all hands and tack ship. At the same time, I directed the helmsman to luff the galliot close into the wind's eye.

But the new mate, proud of his command, refused to obey until the captain was informed; nor would he call that officer, inasmuch as no danger was visible ahead on the allotted course. But time was precious. Delay would lose us. As I felt confident of my opinion, I turned abruptly from the disobedient mariners, and letting go the main brace, brought the vessel to with the topsail aback. Quickly, then, I ordered the watch as it rushed aft, to clew up the mainsail;—but alas! no one would obey; and, in the fracas, the captain, who rushed on deck ignorant of the facts or danger, ordered me back to my state-room with curses for my interference in his skilful navigation.

With a shrug of my shoulders, I obeyed. Remonstrance was useless. For twenty minutes the galliot cleft the waters on her old course, when the look-out screamed: " Hard up!—rocks and breakers dead a-head!"

" Put down the helm!" yelled the confused second-mate;—but the galliot lost her headway, and, taken aback, shaved the edge of a foam-covered rock, dropping astern on a reef with seven feet water around her.

All was consternation;—sails flapping; breakers roaring; ropes snapping and beating; masts creaking; hull thumping; men shouting! The captain and his wife were on deck in the wink of an eye. Every one issued an order and no one obeyed. At last, *the lady* shouted—"let go the anchor!"—the worst command that could be given,— and down went the best bower and the second anchor, while the vessel swung round, and dashed flat on both of them. No one seemed to think of clewing up the sails, and thereby lessening the impetuous surges of the unfortunate galliot.

Our sad mishap occurred about one o'clock in the morning. Fortunately there was not much wind and the sea was tolerably calm, so that we could recognize, and, in some degree, control our situation;—yet, every thing on board appeared given over to Batavian stupidity and panic.

My own feelings may be understood by those who have calmly

passed through danger, while they beheld their companions unmanned by fear or lack of coolness. There was no use of my interference, for no one would heed me. At last the captain's wife,
who was probably the most collected individual on board, called
my name loudly, and in the presence of officers and crew, who,
by this time were generally crowded on the quarter-deck, entreated me to save her ship!

Of course, I sprang to duty. Every sail was clewed up,
while the anchors were weighed to prevent our thumping on
them. I next ordered the boats to be lowered; and, taking a
crew in one, directed the captain to embark in another to seek an
escape from our perilous trap. At daylight, we ascertained that
we had crossed the edge of the reef at high water, yet it would
be useless to attempt to force her back, as she was already half a
foot buried in the soft and mushy outcroppings of coral.

Soon after sunrise, we beheld, at no great distance, one of
those low sandy keys which are so well known to West Indian
navigators; while, further in the distance, loomed up the blue
and beautiful outline of the highlands of Cuba. The sea was
not much ruffled by swell or waves; but as we gazed at the key,
which we supposed deserted, we saw a boat suddenly shoot from
behind one of its points and approach our wreck. The visitors
were five in number; their trim, beautiful boat was completely
furnished with fishing implements, and four of the hands spoke
Spanish only, while the *patron*, or master, addressed us in French.
The whole crew were dressed in flannel shirts, the skirts of which
were belted by a leather strap over their trowsers, and when the
wind suddenly dashed the flannel aside, I saw they had long
knives concealed beneath it.

The *patron* of these fellows offered to aid us in lightening the
galliot and depositing the cargo on the key; where, he said, there
was a hut in which he would guarantee the safety of our merchandise until, at the full of the moon, we could float the vessel from
the reef. He offered, moreover, to pilot us out of harm's way;
and, for all his services in salvage, we were to pay him a thousand dollars.

While the master was busy making terms, his companions were

rummaging the galliot in order to ascertain our cargo and armament. It was finally agreed by the captain and his petticoat
commodore, that if, by evening and the return of tide, our galliot would not float, we would accept the wreckers' offer; and,
accordingly, I was ordered to inform them of the resolution.

As soon as I stated our assent, the *patron*, suddenly assumed an air of deliberation, and insisted that the money should be
paid in hard cash on the spot, and not by drafts on Havana, as
originally required. I thought the demand a significant one, and
hoped the joint partners would neither yield nor admit their
ability to do so; but, unfortunately, they assented at once. The
nod and wink I saw the *patron* immediately bestow on one of
his companions, satisfied me of the imprudence of the concession
and the justice of my suspicions.

The fishermen departed to try their luck on the sea, promising to be back at sunset, on their way to the island. We
spent the day in fruitless efforts to relieve the galliot or to find
a channel, so that when the Spaniards returned in the afternoon
with a rather careless reiteration of their proposal, our captain,
with some eagerness, made his final arrangements for the cargo's
discharge early next morning. Our skipper had visited the key
in the course of the day, and finding the place of deposit apparently safe, and every thing else seemingly honest, he was anxious that the night might pass in order that the disembarkation
might begin.

The calm quiet of that tropic season soon wore away, and,
when I looked landward, at day-dawn, I perceived two strange
boats at anchor near the key. As this gave me some uneasiness,
I mentioned it to the captain and his wife, but they laughed at
my suspicions. After an early meal we began to discharge our
heaviest cargo with the fishermen's aid, yet we made little progress towards completion by the afternoon. At sunset, accounts
were compared, and finding a considerable difference *in favor*
of the wreckers, I was dispatched ashore to ascertain the error.
At the landing I was greeted by several new faces. I particularly observed a Frenchman whom I had not noticed before. He
addressed me with a courteous offer of refreshments. His man-

ners and language were evidently those of an educated person, while his figure and physiognomy indicated aristocratic habits or birth, yet his features and complexion bore the strong imprint of that premature old age which always marks a dissipated career.

After a delightful chat in my mother-tongue with the pleasant stranger, he invited me to spend the night on shore. I declined politely, and, having rectified the cargo's error, was preparing to re-embark, when the Frenchman once more approached and insisted on my remaining. I again declined, asserting that duty forbade my absence. He then remarked that orders had been left by my countryman the *patron* to detain me; but if I was so obstinate as to go, *I might probably regret it.*

With a laugh, I stepped into my boat, and on reaching the galliot, learned that our skipper had imprudently avowed the rich nature of our cargo.

Before leaving the vessel that night, the *patron* took me aside, and inquired whether I received the invitation to pass the night on the key, and why I had not accepted it ? To my great astonishment, he addressed me in pure Italian; and when I expressed gratitude for his offer, he beset me with questions about my country, my parents, my age, my objects in life, and my prospects. Once or twice he threw in the ejaculation of, "poor boy! poor boy!" As he stepped over the taffrail to enter his boat, I offered my hand, which he first attempted to take,—then suddenly stopping, rejected the grasp, and, with an abrupt— "*No! addio!*" he spun away in his boat from the galliot's side.

I could not help putting these things together in my mind during the glowing twilight. I felt as if walking in a cold shadow; an unconquerable sense of impending danger oppressed me. I tried to relieve myself by discussing the signs with the captain, but the phlegmatic Hollander only scoffed at my suspicions, and bade me sleep off my nervousness.

When I set the first night watch, I took good care to place every case containing valuables *below*, and to order the look-out to call all hands at the first appearance or sound of a boat. Had we been provided with arms, I would have equipped the crew with weapons of defence, but, unluckily, there was not on board even a rusty firelock or sabre.

How wondrously calm was all nature that night! Not a breath of air, or a ripple on the water! The sky was brilliant with stars, as if the firmament were strewn with silver dust. The full moon, with its glowing disc, hung some fifteen or twenty degrees above the horizon. The intense stillness weighed upon my tired limbs and eyes, while I leaned with my elbows on the taffrail, watching the roll of the vessel as she swung lazily from side to side on the long and weary swell. Every body but the watch had retired, and I, too, went to my state-room in hope of burying my sorrows in sleep. But the calm night near the land had so completely filled my berth with annoying insects, that I was obliged to decamp and take refuge in the stay-sail netting, where, wrapped in the cool canvas, I was at rest in quicker time than I have taken to tell it.

Notwithstanding my nervous apprehension, a sleep more like the torpor of lethargy than natural slumber, fell on me at once. I neither stirred nor heard any thing till near two o'clock, when a piercing shriek from the deck aroused me. The moon had set, but there was light enough to show the decks abaft filled with men, though I could distinguish neither their persons nor movements. Cries of appeal, and moans as of wounded or dying, constantly reached me. I roused myself as well and quickly as I could from the oppression of my deathlike sleep, and tried to shake off the nightmare. The effort assured me that it was reality and not a dream! In an instant, that presence of mind which has seldom deserted me, suggested escape. I seized the gasket, and dropping by aid of it as softly as I could in the water, struck out for shore. It was time. My plunge into the sea, notwithstanding its caution, had made some noise, and a rough voice called in Spanish to return or I would be shot.

When I began to go to sea, I took pains to become a good swimmer, and my acquired skill served well on this occasion. As soon as the voice ceased from the deck, I lay still on the water until I saw a flash from the bow of the *galliot*, to which I immediately made a complaisant bow by diving deeply. This operation I repeated several times, till I was lost in the distant darkness; nor can I pride myself much on my address in escaping the musket balls, as I have since had my own aim similarly eluded by many a harmless duck.

After swimming about ten minutes, I threw myself on my back to rest and "take a fresh departure." It was so dark that I could not see the key, yet, as I still discerned the galliot's masts relieved against the sky, I was enabled by that beacon to steer my way landward. Naked, with the exception of trowsers, I had but little difficulty in swimming, so that in less than half an hour, I touched the key, and immediately sought concealment in a thick growth of mangroves.

I had not been five minutes in this dismal jungle, when such a swarm of mosquitoes beset me, that I was forced to hurry to the beach and plunge into the water. In this way was I tormented the whole night. At dawn, I retreated once more to the bushes; and climbing the highest tree I found,—whose altitude, however, was not more than twelve feet above the sand,—I beheld, across the calm sea, the dismantled hull of my late home, surrounded by a crowd of boats, which were rapidly filling with plundered merchandise. It was evident that we had fallen a prey to pirates; yet I could not imagine why _I_ had been singled from this scene of butchery, to receive the marks of anxious sympathy that were manifested by the _patron_ and his French companion on the key. All the morning I continued in my comfortless position, watching their movements,—occasionally refreshing my parched lips by chewing the bitter berries of the thicket. Daylight, with its heat, was as intolerable as night, with its venom. The tropical sun and the glaring reflection from a waveless sea, poured through the calm atmosphere upon my naked flesh, like boiling oil. My thirst was intense. As the afternoon wore away, I observed several boats tow the lightened hull of our galliot southeast of the key till it disappeared behind a point of the island. Up to that moment, my manhood had not forsaken me; but, as the last timber of my vessel was lost to sight, nature resumed its dominion. Every hope of seeing my old companions was gone; I was utterly

alone. If this narrative were designed to be a sentimental confession, the reader might see unveiled the ghastly spectacle of a
" troubled conscience," nor am I ashamed to say that no consolation cheered my desolate heart, till I prayed to my Maker that
the loss of so many lives might not be imputed to the wilful
malice of a proud and stubborn nature.

## CHAPTER IV.

So passed the day.  As the sun sank in the west, I began to re-flect about obtaining the rest for mind and body I so much needed.  My system was almost exhausted by want of food and water, while the dreadful tragedy of the preceding night shat-tered my nerves far more than they ever suffered amid the try-ing scenes I have passed through since.  It was my *first* adven-ture of peril and of blood; and my soul shrank with the natural recoil that virtue experiences in its earliest encounter with fla-grant crime.

In order to escape the incessant torment of insects, I had just determined to bury my naked body in the sand, and to cover my head with the only garment I possessed, when I heard a noise in the neighboring bushes, and perceived a large and sav-age dog rushing rapidly from side to side, with his nose to the ground, evidently in search of game or prey.  I could not mistake the nature of his hunt.  With the agility of a harlequin, I sprang to my friendly perch just in time to save myself from his fangs. The foiled and ferocious beast, yelling with rage, gave an alarm which was quickly responded to by other dogs, three of which— followed by two armed men—promptly made their appearance beneath my tree.  The hunters were not surprised at finding me, as, in truth, I was the game they sought.  Ordering me down, I was commanded to march slowly before them, and especially warned to make no attempt at flight, as the bloodhounds would tear me to pieces on the spot.  I told my guard that I should of course manifest no such folly as to attempt an escape from *caballeros* like themselves,—upon a desolate sand key half a mile wide,—especially when my alternative refuge could only be found among the fish of the sea. The self-possession and good humor with which I replied, seemed somewhat to mollify the cross-grained savages, and we soon approached a habitation, where I was ordered to sit down until the whole party assembled. After a while, I was invited to join them in their evening meal.

The piquant stew upon which we fed effectually loosened their tongues, so that, in the course of conversation, I discovered my pursuers had been in quest of me since early morning, though it was hardly believed I had either escaped the shot, or swam fully a mile amid sharks during the darkness. Upon this, I ventured to put some ordinary questions, but was quickly informed that inquisitiveness was considered very unwholesome on the sand keys about Cuba!

At sunset, the whole piratical community of the little isle was assembled. It consisted of two parties, each headed by its respective chief. Both gangs were apparently subject to the leadership of the *rancho's* proprietor ; and in this man I recognized the *patron* who inquired so minutely about my biography and prospects. His companions addressed him either as " El señor patron " or " Don Rafael." I was surveyed very closely by the picturesque group of bandits, who retired into the interior of the *rancho*,— a hut made of planks and sails rescued from wrecks. My guard or sentinel consisted of but a single vagabond, who amused himself by whetting a long knife on a hone, and then trying its sharpness on a single hair and then on his finger. Sometimes the scoundrel made a face at me, and drew the back of his weapon across his throat.

The conversation within, which I felt satisfied involved my fate, was a long one. I could distinctly overhear the murmuring roar of talk, although I could not distinguish words. One sentence, however, did not escape me, and its signification proved particularly interesting :—" *Los muertos*," said the French dandy, —" *no hablan*,"—Dead men tell no tales !

It is hard to imagine a situation more trying for a young, hearty, and hopeful man. I was half naked ; my skin was excoriated by the sun, sand, and salt water; four bloodhounds were at my feet ready to fasten on my throat at the bidding of a *desperado ;* a piratical sentry, knife in hand, kept watch over me, while a jury of *buccaneers* discussed my fate within earshot. Dante's Inferno had hardly more torments.

The *filibustero* conclave lasted quite an hour without reaching a conclusion. At length, after an unusual clamor, the *patron* Rafael rushed from the *rancho* with a horseman's pistol, and, calling my name, whirled me behind him in his strong and irresistible grasp. Then facing both bands, with a terrible imprecation, he swore vengeance if they persisted in requiring the death of HIS NEPHEW !

At the mention of the word "*nephew*," every one paused with a look of surprise, and drawing near the excited man with expressions of interest, agreed to respect his new-found relative, though they insisted I should swear never to disclose the occurrence of which I had been an unwilling witness. I complied with the condition unhesitatingly, and shook hands with every one present except the sentry, of whom I shall have occasion to speak hereafter.

It is astonishing what revulsions of manner, if not of feeling, take place suddenly among the class of men with whom my lot had now been cast. Ten minutes before, they were greedy for my blood, not on account of personal malice, but from utter recklessness of life whenever an individual interfered with their personal hopes or tenure of existence. Each one of these outlaws now vied with his companions in finding articles to cover my nakedness and make me comfortable. Ac soon as I was clothed, supper was announced and I was given almost a seat of honor at a table plentifully spread with fresh fish, sardines, olives, ham, cheese, and an abundance of capital claret.

The chat naturally turned upon me, and some sly jokes were uttered at the expense of Rafael, concerning the kinsman who had suddenly sprung up like a mushroom out of this pool of blood.

"*Caballeros !* " interposed Rafael, passionately, " you seem inclined to doubt my word. Perhaps you are no longer disposed to regard me as your chief ? We have broken bread together during four months; we have shared the same dangers and divided our spoils fairly : am I *now* to be charged to my face with a lie ? " " Ha ! " said he, rising from the table and striding through the apartment with violent gestures, " who dares doubt my word, and impute to me the meanness of a lie ? Are ye drunk ? Can this wine have made you mad ? " and seizing a bottle, he dashed it to the ground, stamping with rage. Has the blood of last night unsettled your nerves and made you delirious ? *Basta ! basta !* Let me not hear another word of doubt as to this youth. The first who utters a syllable of incredulity shall kill me on the spot or fall by my hand ! "

This sounds, I confess, very melo-dramatically, yet, my experience has taught me that it is precisely a bold and dashing tone of bravado, adopted at the right moment, which is always most successful among *such* ruffians as surrounded my preserver. The speech was delivered with such genuine vehemence and resolution that no one could question his sincerity or suppose him acting. But, as soon as he was done, the leader of the other gang, who had been very unconcernedly smoking his cigar, and apparently punctuating Don Rafael's oration with his little puffs, advanced to my new uncle, and laying his hand on his arm, said :—

" *Amigo*, you take a joke too seriously. No one here certainly desires to harm the boy or disbelieve you. Take my advice,— calm yourself, light a cigarillo, drink a tumbler of claret, and drop the subject."

But this process of pacification was too rapid for my excited uncle. Men of his quality require to be let down gradually from their wrath, for I have frequently noticed that when their object is too easily gained, they interpose obstacles and start new subjects of controversy, so that the most amiable and yielding temper may at last become inflamed to passionate resistance.

" No, *caballeros !* " exclaimed Don Rafael, " I will neither light a *cigarillo*, drink claret, calm myself, nor accept satisfaction for this insult, short of the self-condemnation you will all experience for a mean suspicion, when I *prove* the truth of my assertions about this boy. A doubted man has no business at the head of such fellows as you are. Begone out of my hearing, Theodore," continued he, pointing to the canvas door, "begone till I convince these people that I am your uncle!"

As soon as I was out of the chamber, I afterwards learned, that Rafael announced my name, place of birth, and parentage to the wreckers, and desired the other *patron*, Mesclet, who spoke Italian, to follow and interrogate me as to his accuracy.

Mesclet performed the service in a kind manner, opening the interview by asking the names of my father and mother, and then demanding how many uncles I had on my mother's side? My replies appeared satisfactory.

"Was one of your uncles a navy officer?" inquired Mesclet. "and where is he at present?" The only uncle I had in the navy, I declared, had long been absent from his family. But once in my life had I seen him, and that was while on his way to Marseilles, in 1815, to embark for the Spanish main; since then no intelligence of the wanderer had reached my ears. Had I been a French *scholar* at that time, my adventures of consanguinity at Ferrol and on this key might well have brought Molière's satire to my mind:

> "De moi je commence à douter tout de bon;
> Pourtant, quand je me tâte et que je me rapelle,
> *Il me semble que je suis moi!*"

Mesclet's report gave perfect satisfaction to the scoffers, and the mysterious drama at once established me in a position I could not have attained even by desperate services to the *filibusteros*. A bumper, all round, closed the night; and each slunk off to his cot or blanket beneath a mosquito bar, while the bloodhounds were chained at the door to do double duty as sentinels and body guard.

I hope there are few who will deny me the justice to believe that when I stretched my limbs on the hard couch assigned me that night, I remembered my God in heaven, and my home in Tuscany. It was the first night that an ingenuous youth had spent among outcasts, whose hands were still reeking with the blood of his companions. At that period of manhood we are grateful for the mere boon of *life*. It is pleasant to live, to breathe, to have one's being, on this glorious earth, even though that life may be cast among felons. There is still a *future* before us; and Hope, the bright goddess of health and enthusiasm, inspires our nerves with energy to conquer our present ills.

I threw myself down thankfully, but I could not rest. Sore and tired as I was, I could not compose my mind to sleep. The conduct of Rafael surprised me. I could not imagine how he became familiar with my biography, nor could I identify his personal appearance with my uncle who went so long before to South America. A thousand fancies jumbled themselves in my brain, and, in their midst, I fell into slumber. Yet my self-oblivion was broken and short. My pulse beat wildly, but my skin did not indicate the heat of fever. The tragedy of the galliot was reacted before me. Phantoms of the butchered wife and men, streaming with blood, stood beside my bed, while a chorus of devils, in the garb of sailors, shouted that *I* was the cause of the galliot's loss, and of their murder. Then the wretched woman would hang round my neck, and crawl on my breast, besprinkling me with gore that spouted from her eyeless sockets, imploring me to save her;—till, shrieking and panting, I awoke from the horrible nightmare. Such were the dreams that haunted my pillow nearly all the time I was forced to remain with these desperadoes.

I thanked God that the night of the tropics was so brief. The first glimmer of light found me up, and as soon as I could find a companion to control the hounds, I ran to the sea for refreshment by a glorious surf-bath. I was on a miserable sandbar, whose surface was hardly covered with soil; yet, in that prolific land of rain and sunshine, nature seems only to require the slightest footing to assert her magnificent power of vegetation. In spots, along the arid island, were the most beautiful groves of abundant undergrowth, matted with broad-leaved vines, while, within their shadow, the fresh herbage sprang up, sparkling with morning dew. In those climates, the blaze of noon is a season of oppressive languor, but morning and evening, with their dawn and twilight,—their lengthened shadows and declining sun, are draughts of beauty that have often intoxicated less enthusiastic tempers than mine. The bath, the breeze, the renewed nature, aroused and restored a degree of tone to my shattered nerves, so that when I reached the *rancho*, I was ready for any duty that might be imposed. The twin gangs had gone off in their boats soon after daylight, with saws and axes; but Rafael left orders with my brutal sentry that I should assist him in preparing breakfast, which was to be ready by eleven o'clock.

I never knew the real patronymic of this fellow, who was a Spaniard, and passed among us by the nickname of Gallego. Gallego possessed a good figure,—symmetrical and strong, while it was lithe and active. But his head and face were the most repulsive I ever encountered. The fellow was not absolutely ugly, so far as mere contour of features was concerned; but there was so dropsical a bloat in his cheeks, such a stagnant sallowness in his complexion, such a watching scowl in his eyes, such a drawling sullenness of speech, such sensuality in the turn of his resolute lips, that I trembled to know he was to be my daily companion. His dress and skin denoted slovenly habits, while a rude and growling voice gave token of the bitter heart that kept the enginery of the brute in motion.

With this wretch for *chèf de cuisine*, I was exalted to the post of " cook's mate."

I found that a fire had been already kindled beneath some dwarf trees, and that a kettle was set over it to boil. Gallego beckoned me to follow him into a thicket some distance from the *rancho*, where, beneath the protection of a large tarpaulin, we found the *filibustero's* pantry amply provided with butter, onions, spices, salt-fish, bacon, lard, rice, coffee, wines, and all the requisites of comfortable living. In the corners, strewn at random on the ground, I observed spy-glasses, compasses, sea-charts, books, and a quantity of choice cabin-furniture. We obtained a sufficiency of water for cookery and drinking from holes dug in the sand, and we managed to cool the beverage by suspending it in a draft of air in porous vessels, which are known throughout the West Indies by the mischievous name of "monkeys." Our copious thickets supplied us with fuel, nor were we without a small, rough garden, in which the gang cultivated peppers, tomatoes and mint. The premises being reviewed, I returned with my ill-favored guard to take a lesson in piratical cookery.

It is astonishing how well these wandering vagabonds know how to toss up a savory mess, and how admirably they understand its enjoyment. A tickled palate is one of the great objects of their mere animal existence, and they are generally prepared with a mate who might pass muster in a second-rate restaurant. The *déjeuner* we served of codfish stewed in claret, snowy and granulated rice, delicious tomatoes and fried ham, was irreproachable. Coffee had been drunk at day dawn ; so that my comrades contented themselves during the meal with liberal potations of claret, while they finished the morning with brandy and cigars.

By two o'clock the breakfast was over, and most of the gorged scamps had retired for a *siesta* during the sweltering heat. A few of the toughest took muskets and went to the beach to shoot gulls or sharks. Gallego and myself were dispatched to our grove-kitchen to scullionize our utensils ; and, finally, being the youngest, I was intrusted with the honorable duty of feeding the blood-hounds.

As soon as my duties were over, I was preparing to follow the siesta-example of my betters, when I met Don Rafael coming out of the door, and, without a word, was beckoned to follow towards the interior of the island. When we reached a solitary spot, two or three hundred yards from the *rancho*, Rafael drew me down beside him in the shade of a tree, and said gently with a smile, that he supposed I was at least *surprised* by the events of the last four days. I must confess that I saw little for any thing else but astonishment in them, and I took the liberty to concede that fact to the Don.

" Well," continued he, " I have brought you here to explain a part of the mystery, and especially to let you understand why it was that I passed myself off last night as your uncle, in order to save your life. I was obliged to do it, boy; and, *voto à Dios!*

I would have fought the *junta*,—bloodhounds and all,—before they should have harmed a limb of your body ! "

Don Rafael explained that as soon as he caught a glimpse of my face when he boarded the *galliot* on the morning of our disaster, he recognized the lineaments of an old companion in arms. The resemblance caused him to address me as particularly as he had done on the night of the piracy, the consequence of which was that his suspicions ripened into certainty.

If I were writing the story of Don Rafael's life, instead of my own, I might give an interesting and instructive narrative, which showed,—as he alleged,—how those potent controllers of outlaws,—" circumstances,"—had changed him from a very respectable soldier of fortune into a genuine buccaneer. He asserted that my uncle had been his schoolmate and professional companion in the old world. When the war of South American independence demanded the aid of certain Dugald Dalgettys to help its fortune, Don Rafael and my uncle had lent the revolutionists of Mexico their swords, for which they were repaid in the coin that " patriots " commonly receive for such amiable self-sacrifice. *Republics* are proverbially ungrateful, and Mexico, alas ! was a republic.

After many a buffet of fortune, my poor uncle, it seems, perished in a duel at which Don Rafael performed the professional part of " his friend." My relation died, of course, like a " man of honor," and soon after, Don Rafael, himself, fell a victim to the " circumstances " which, in the end, enabled him to slaughter my shipmates and save my life.

I must admit that I use this flippant tone with a twinge of sorrow, for I think I perceived certain spasms of conscience during our interview, which proved that, among the lees of that withered heart, there were some rich drops of manhood ready to mantle his cheek with shame at our surroundings. Indeed, as he disclosed his story, he exhibited several outbursts of passionate agony which satisfied me that if Don Rafael were in Paris, Don Rafael would have been a most respectable *bourgeois ;* while, doubtless, there were many estimable citizens at that moment in Paris, who would have given up their shops in order to become Don Rafaels in Cuba! Such is life—and "circum·stances!"

Our chat wasted a large portion of the afternoon. It was terminated by a counsel from my friend to be wary in my deportment, and a direction to console myself with the idea that he did not mean I should tarry long upon the island.

"You see," said he, "that I do not lack force of eye, voice, and personal influence over these ruffians; yet I do not know that I can always serve or save a friend, so your fate hangs very much on your circumspection. Men in our situation are Ishmaelites. Our hands are not only against all, and all against us, but we do not know the minute when we may be all against each other. The power of habitual control may do much for a leader among such men; but such an one must neither quail nor *deceive*. Therefore, *beware!* Let none of your actions mar my projects. Let them never suspect the truth of our consanguinity. Call me "uncle;" and in my mouth you shall always be "Theodore." Ask no questions; be civil, cheerful, and serviceable about the *rancho;* never establish an intimacy, confidence, or friendship with any *one* of the band; stifle your feelings and your tears if you ever find them rising to your lips or eyes; talk as little as you possibly can; avoid that smooth-tongued Frenchman; keep away from our revels, and refrain entirely from wine.

"I charge you to be specially watchful of Gallego, the cook. He is our man of dirty work,—a shameless coward, though revengeful as a cat. If it shall ever happen that you come in collision with him, *strike first and well;* no one cares for him; even his death will make no stir. Take this *cuchillo,*—it is sharp and reliable; keep it near you day and night; and, *in self-defence,* do not hesitate to make good use of it. In a few days, I may say more to you; until then,—*corragio figlio, è addio!*"

We returned to the *rancho* by different paths.

# CHAPTER V.

The life of men under the ban of society, on a desolate sand key, whose only visitors are land-crabs and sea-gulls, is a dull and dreary affair. The genuine pirate, properly equipped for a desperate lot, who has his swift keel beneath him and is wafted wheresoever he lists on canvas wings, encounters, it is true, an existence of peril; yet there is something exhilarating and romantic in his dashing career of incessant peril: he is ever on the wing, and ever amid novelty; there is something about his life that smacks of genuine warfare, and his existence becomes as much more respectable as the old-fashioned highwayman on his mettlesome steed was superior to the sneaking footpad, who leaped from behind a thicket and bade the unarmed pedestrian stand and deliver. But the wrecker-pirate takes his victim at a disadvantage, for he is not a genuine freebooter of the sea. He shuns an able foe and strikes the crippled. Like the shark and the eagle, he delights to prey on the carcass, rather than to strike the living quarry.

The companionship into which misfortune had thrown me was precisely of this character, and I gladly confess that I was never tempted for a moment to bind up my fate with the sorry gang. I confided, it is true, in Rafael's promise to liberate me; yet I never abandoned the hope of escape by my own tact and energy.

Meanwhile, I became heartily tired of my scullion duties as the subordinate of Gallego. Finding one day a chest of carpen-

ters' tools among the rubbish, I busied myself in making a rudder for one of the boats, and so well did I succeed, that when
my companions returned to breakfast from their daily "fishing,"
my mechanical skill was lauded to such a degree that Rafael
converted the general enthusiasm to my advantage by separating
me from the cook. I was raised to the head of our "naval
bureau" as boatbuilder in chief. Indeed, it was admitted on
all hands that I was abler with the adze than the ladle and
spoiled fewer boards than broths.

A few days passed, during which I learned that our unfortunate galliot was gradually emptied and destroyed. This
was the usual morning occupation of the whole gang until
the enterprise ended. When the job was over Don Rafael told
me that he was about to depart hurriedly on business with the
whole company, to the main-land of Cuba, so that, during his
absence, the island and its property would be left in custody of
Gallego, myself, and the bloodhounds. He specially charged the
cook to keep sober, and to give a good account of himself at the
end of *five days*, which would terminate his absence.

But no sooner was the *patron* away, than the lazy scamp neglected his duties, skulked all day among the bushes, and refused
even to furnish my food or supply the dogs. Of course, I speedily attended to the welfare of myself and the animals; but, at
night, the surly Galician came home, prepared his own supper,
drank till he was completely drunk, and retired without uttering
a word.

I was glad that he yielded to the temptation of liquor, as I
hoped he would thereby become incapable of harming me during
the watches of the night, if weariness compelled me to sleep.
He was a malignant wretch, and his taciturnity and ill-will appeared so ominous now that I was left utterly alone, that I
resolved, if possible, to keep awake, and not to trust to luck or
liquor. The galliot's tragedy and anxiety stood me in stead, so
that I did not close my eyes in sleep the whole of that dreary
vigil. About midnight, Gallego stealthily approached my cot,
and pausing a moment to assure himself that I was in the profound repose which I admirable feigned, he turned on tip-toe to

the door of our cabin, and disappeared with a large bundle in his hand. He did not return until near day dawn; and, next night, the same act was exactly repeated.

The mysterious sullenness of this vagabond not only alarmed, but increased my nervousness, for I can assure the reader that, on a desolate island, without a companion but a single outcast, one would rather hear the sound of that wretch's voice than be doomed to the silence of such inhuman solitude. During the day he kept entirely aloof,—generally at sea fishing,—affording me time for a long *siesta* in a nook near the shore, penetrated by a thorny path, which Gallego could not have traced without hounds. On the fourth night, when the pirate left our hut for his accustomed excursion, I resolved to follow; and taking a pistol with renewed priming, I pursued his steps at a safe distance, till I saw him enter a thick shrubbery, in which he was lost. I marked the spot and returned to the cabin. Next morning, after coffee, Gallego departed in his canoe to fish. I watched him anxiously from the beach until he anchored about two miles from the reef, and then calling the dogs, retraced my way to the thicket. The hounds were of great service, for, having placed them on the track, they instantly traced the path of the surly scoundrel.

After some trouble in passing the dense copse of underwood, I entered a large patch of naked sand, broken by heaps of stones, which appeared to cover graves. One heap bore the form of a cross, and was probably the sepulchre of a wrecker. I stopped awhile and reflected as to further explorations. On entering this arid graveyard, I observed a number of land-crabs scamper away; but, after awhile, when I sat down in a corner and became perfectly quiet, I noticed that the army returned to the field and introduced themselves into all the heaps of stones or graves *save one*. This struck me as singular; for, when people are so hopelessly alone as I was, they become minute observers, and derive infinite happiness from the consideration of the merest trifles. Accordingly, I ventured close to the abandoned heap, and found at once that the neighboring sand had been freshly smoothed. I was on Gallego's track! In dread of detection, I stealthily climbed a tree, and, screening myself behind the foliage, peered out towards the sea till I beheld the cook at work beyond the reef. My musket and pistols were again examined and found in order. With these precautions, I began to remove the stones, taking care to mark their relative positions so that I might replace them exactly; and, in about ten minutes work at excavation, I came upon two barrels, one of which was filled with bundles of silk, linens, and handkerchiefs, while the other contained a chronometer, several pieces of valuable lace, and a beautifully bound, gilt, and ornamented *Bible*. One bundle, tied in a Madras handkerchief, particularly attracted my attention, for I thought I recognized the covering. Within it I found a number of trinkets belonging to the wife of my Dutch captain, and a large hairpin, set with diamonds, which I remember she wore the last day of her life. Had this wretch torn it from her head, as he imbrued his hands in her blood on that terrible night? The painful revelation brought all before me once more with appalling force. I shuddered and became sick. Yet, I had no time for maudlin dalliance with my feelings. Replacing every thing with precision, and smoothing the sand once more with my flannel shirt, I returned to the *rancho*, where I indulged in the boyish but honest outburst of nature which I could no longer restrain. I was not then—and, thank God, I am not now—a stranger to tears! To the world, the human heart and the human eye, like the coral isle of the Atlantic, may be parched and withered; yet, beneath the seared and arid surface, the living water still flows and gushes, when the rock and the heart alike are stricken!

Just before sunset of this day, the deep baying of our hounds gave notice of approaching strangers; and, soon after, four boats appeared in the cove. The two foremost belonged to Don Rafael and his crew, while the others were filled with strangers whose appearance was that of landsmen rather than mariners. As Rafael received them on the beach, he introduced them to me as his especial pets, the " AMPHIBIOUS JEWS."

Our delicious supper of that night was augmented by a fine store of beef, pork and fowls, brought from shore. I lingered at table as long as the company maintained a decent sobriety, and learned that these saltwater Hebrews were, in truth, speculators from Cardenas, who accompanied Rafael in the guise of fisher- men, to purchase the plundered cargo of my galliot.

During his visit to Cuba, Don Rafael was apprised that the Cuban authorities were about sending an Inspector among the islands off the coast, and accordingly took precaution to furnish himself in advance with a regular "fishing license." All hands were forthwith set to work to make our key and *rancho* conform to this calling, and, in a few days, the canvas roof of our hut was replaced by a thatch of leaves, while every dangerous article or implement was concealed in the thicket of a labyrinthine creek. In fact, our piscatory character could not be doubted. In our persons and occupation, we looked as innocent and rustic as a pic-nic party on a summer bivouac for fresh air and salt bathing. Nor was the transformation less real in regard to our daily tasks. We became, in reality, most industrious fishermen ; so that we had more than a thousand of the finny tribe piled up and dried, when the hounds signalled the arrival of the expected officials.

Breakfast was on the table when they landed, but it was the *banyan* meal of humble men, whose nets were never filled with aught but the *scaly* products of the sea. Our inspector was regaled with a scant fish-feast, and allowed to digest it over the genuine license. Rafael complained sadly of hard times and poverty ;—in fact, the drama of humility was played to perfec- tion, and, finally, the functionary signed our license, with a cer- tificate of our loyalty, and pocketed a moderate " gratification of *five ounces !*

Six long, hot, and wretched weeks passed over my head before any striking occurrence relieved the monotony of my life. During the whole of this period, our fishing adventure was steadily pursued, when information was mysteriously brought to the key that a richly-laden French vessel had run ashore on the Cayo Verde, an islet some forty miles east of the Cruz del Padre. That afternoon, both of our large boats were filled with armed men, and, as they departed with *every* wrecker

aboard, I alone was left on the islet to guard our property with
the dogs.

The thought and hope of escape both swelled in my breast
as I saw the hulls dwindle to a dot and disappear behind the
horizon. In a moment, my plan was conceived and perfected.
The sea was perfectly smooth, and I was expert in the use of oars.
That very night I launched our canoe,—the only vessel left in
the cove,—and placing the sail, scullers, and grappling-hook
within it, returned to the *rancho* for clothing. As it was dark,
I lighted a candle, when, on looking into the clothes-chest
beneath my bed, I found inscribed on the lid, in fresh chalk-
marks, the words " PATIENCE ! WAIT ! "

This discovery made me pause in my preparations. Was it
the warning—as it was certainly the handwriting—of Rafael ?
Had he purposely and honorably left me alone, in order to escape
this scene of blood ? Did he anticipate my effort to fly, and endeavor to save me from the double risk of crossing to the mainland, and of future provision for my comfort ? I could not doubt
its being the work of my friend ; and, whether it was superstition
or prudence, I cannot say, but I resolved, unhesitatingly, to
abandon a scheme in regard to which I hesitated. Instead,
therefore, of attempting to pass the strait between the key and
Cuba, I went to bed, and slept more comfortably in my utter
abandonment than I had done since I was on the island.

Next day, at noon, I descried a small pilot-boat sailing inside
the reef, with all the confidence of a perfect master of the channel. Two persons speedily landed, with provisions from the
mainland, and stated that, on his last visit to Cuba, Don Rafael
engaged them to take me to Havana. This, however, was to be
done with much caution, inasmuch as his men would not assent
to my departure until they had compromised my life with theirs
by some act of desperate guilt. The pilots declined taking me
then without my guardian's assent ;—and, in truth, so fully was
I convinced of his intention to liberate me in the best and speediest way, that I made up my mind to abide where I was till he
returned.

For three days more I was doomed to solitude. On the

fourth, the boats came back, with the pilot's cutter, and I quickly saw that a serious encounter had taken place. The pilot-boat appeared to be deeply laden. Next day, she was taken to the mazes of the winding and wooded creek, where, I learned, the booty was disembarked and hidden. While the party had gone to complete this portion of their enterprise, the Frenchman, who was wounded in the head and remained behind, took that opportunity to enlighten me on passing events. When the wreckers reached Cayo Verde, they found the French vessel already taken possession of by "fishermen" of that quarter. Anticipated in their dirty work, our comrades were in no mood to be sociable with the fortunate party. An affray was the natural result, in which knives had been freely used, while Mesclet himself had been rescued by Rafael, pistol in hand, after receiving the violent blow on his head from which he was now suffering. Having secured a retreat to their boats, they were just beginning to think of a rapid departure, when the friendly pilot-boat hove in sight. So fortunate a reinforcement renerved our gang. A plan of united action was quickly concerted. The French vessel was again boarded and carried. Two of the opposite party were slain in the onslaught; and, finally, a rich remnant of the cargo was seized, though the greater part of the valuables had, no doubt, been previously dispatched ashore by the earlier band of desperadoes.

"Thank God !" added the narrator, "we have now the boat and the assistance of Bachicha, who is as brave as Rafael : with his "*Baltimore clipper*," we shall conduct our affairs on a grander scale than heretofore. *Sacre-bleu !* we may now cruise under the Columbian flag, and rob Peter to pay Paul !"

In fact, the "clipper" had brought down an ample store of ammunition, under the innocent name of "provisions," while she carried in her bowels a long six, which she was ready to mount amidships at a moment's notice.

But poor Mesclet did not live to enjoy the fruits of the larger piracy, which he hoped to carry on in a more elegant way with Bachicha. The *roué* could not be restrained from the favorite beverages of his beautiful France. His wound soon mastered him; and, in a month, all that was mortal of this gallant Gaul, who, in earlier years, had figured in the best saloons of his country, rested among sand-graves of a Cuban key.

"Ah!" growled Gallego, as they came home from his burial, "there is one less to share our earnings; and, what is better, claret and brandy will be more plentiful now that this sponge is under the sand!"

In a few days, the boats were laden with fish for the mainland, in order to cover the real object of our *patron's* visit to Cuba, which was to dispose of the booty. At his departure, he repeated the cherished promise of liberty, and privately hinted that I had better continue fishing on good terms with Señor Gallego.

It required some time to repair the nets, for they had been rather neglected during our late fishing, so that it was not, in fact, until Rafael had been three days gone that I took the canoe with Gallego, and dropped anchor outside the reef, to take breakfast before beginning our labor.

We had hardly begun a frugal meal when, suddenly, a large schooner shot from behind a bend of the island, and steered in our direction. As the surly Spaniard never spoke, I had become accustomed to be equally silent. Unexpectedly, however, he gave a scowling glance from beneath his shaggy brows at the vessel, and exclaimed with unusual energy: "A Columbian privateer!"

"We had best up anchor, and get inside the reef," continued he, "or our sport will be spoiled for the day."

"Pshaw!" returned I, "she's not making for us, and, even if she were, I wouldn't be such a coward as to run!" Indeed, I had heard so much of "Columbian privateers" and the patriot service, that I rather longed to be captured, that I might try my hand at lawful war and glory. The impulse was sudden and silly.

Still Gallego insisted on retreating; until, at length, we got into an angry controversy, which the cook, who was in the bow of the boat, attempted to end by cutting the anchor-rope. As he was drawing his knife to execute this purpose, I swiftly lifted an oar, and, with a single blow, laid him senseless in the bottom of the canoe. By this time the schooner was within pistol-shot; and, as she passed with a three-knot breeze, the captain, who had witnessed the scene, threw a grappling-iron into our skiff, and taking us in tow, dragged the boat from its moorings.

As soon as we got into deeper water, I was ordered on deck, while Gallego, still quite insensible, was hoisted carefully on board. I told the truth as to our dispute, reserving, however, the important fact that I had been originally urged into the quarrel by my anxiety " to ship " on board a privateer.

" I want a pilot for Key West," said the master, hurriedly, " and I have no time to trifle with your stupid quarrels. Can either of you perform this service ? "

By this time Gallego had been somewhat roused from his stupor, and pointing feebly towards me, uttered a languid :— " Yes, and an *excellent* one."

Mistaking the word "*pilote*," which in Spanish signifies " navigator," the French captain, who spoke the Castilian very badly, translated it into the more limited meaning attached to that peculiar profession, one of whose ministers he was anxious to secure.

" *Bon !* " said the master, " put the other fellow back into his skiff, and make sail at once under charge of this youngster."

I remonstrated, protested, declaimed, swore, that I knew nothing of Key West and its approaches ; but all my efforts were vain. I was a pilot in spite of myself.

The malicious cook enjoyed the joke of which I had so hastily become the victim. As they lowered him again into the boat, he jeered at my incredulity, and in ten minutes was towed to the edge of the reef, where the scamp was turned adrift to make for the island.

When the schooner was once more under full sail, I was ordered to give the course for Key West. I at once informed the captain, whose name I understood to be Laminé, that he really labored under a mistake in translating the Spanish word *pilote* into *port guide,* and assured him that Gallego had been prompted by a double desire to get rid of him as well as me by fostering his pernicious error. I acknowledged that I was a "*pilot*," or "navigator," though not a "*practico*," or harbor-pilot; yet I urged that I could not, without absolute foolhardiness, undertake to conduct his schooner into a port of which I was utterly igno- rant, and had never visited. Hereupon the first lieutenant or mate interposed. This fellow was a short, stout-built person of thirty-five, with reddish whiskers and hair, a long-projecting un- der-jaw, and eye-teeth that jutted out like tusks. To add to his ugliness, he was sadly pitted by small-pox, and waddled about on short duck legs, which were altogether out of proportion to his long body, immense arms, and broad, massive shoulders. I do not remember a more vulgarly repulsive person than this pri- vateering lieutenant.

"He is a liar, Captain Laminé, and only wants to extort money for his services," interjected the brute. "Leave him to me, sir; I'll find a way to refresh his memory of Key West that will open the bottom of the gulf to his eyes as clearly as the pathway to his piratical hut on the sand-key! To the helm, sir—to the helm!"

What possible object or result could I gain by resistance amid the motley assemblage that surrounded me on the deck of the "CARA-BOBO?" She was a craft of about 200 tons; and, with her crew of seventy-five, composed of the scourings of all nations, castes, and colors, bore a commission from the author- ities of Carthagena to burn, sink and destroy all Spanish prop- erty she was strong enough to capture. Laminé was born in the isle of France, while Lasquetti, the lieutenant, was a creole of Pensacola. The latter spoke French and Spanish quite well, but very little English; while both master and mate were almost entirely ignorant of navigation, having intrusted that task to the third lieutenant, who was then ill with yellow fever. The second lieutenant was absent on board a prize.

Thus forced to take charge of a privateer without a moment's warning, I submitted with the best grace, and, calling for charts and instruments, I shaped my way for the destined port. All day we steered west-north-west, but at sunset, as we had run along smartly, I ordered the schooner to be "laid to" for the night. The wind and weather were both charmingly fair, and objections were of course made to my command. But, as the most difficult part of our navigation was to be encountered during the night, if I kept on my course, I resolved to persist to the last in my resolution, and I was fortunate enough to carry my point.

"D—n you," said Lasquetti, as the vessel was brought to the wind and made snug for the night, "d—n you, Master Téodore; this laying-to shall give *you* no rest, at least, if you thought to dodge work, and get into a hammock by means of it! You shall march the deck all night to see that we don't drift on a reef, if I have to sit up, or stand up till day-dawn to watch you!"

Obedience, alas! had been the order of the day with me for a long while ; so I promenaded the lee quarter till nearly midnight, when, utterly exhausted by fatigue, I sat down on a long brass chaser, and almost instantly fell asleep.

I know not how long I rested, but a tremendous shock knocked me from the cannon and laid me flat on the deck, bleeding from mouth, nose and ears. Lasquetti stood beside me, cigar in hand, laughing immoderately, blaspheming like a demon, and kicking me in the ribs with his rough wet-weather boots. He had detected me asleep, and touched off the gun with his *havanna!*

The explosion aroused all hands, and brought the commander on deck. My blood flowed, but it did not pour fast enough to relieve my agonizing rage. As soon as I recovered consciousness, I seized the first heavy implement I could grasp, and rushed at my aggressor, whose skull was saved from the blow by descending beneath the combings of the hatchway, which, the instant after, were shivered by the descent of my heavy weapon. Laminé was a man of some sensibility, and, though selfish, as usual with his set, could not avoid at once reprimanding Lasquetti with uncommon severity in presence of his men.

That afternoon, I was fortunate enough, by the aid of a good chart, and a sort of *navigating instinct*, to anchor the "Carabobo" in the narrow harbor of Key West. When Laminé went ashore, he ordered me not to leave the schooner, while sentries were placed to prevent boats from boarding or even approaching us. Hardly was the master out of the vessel before two men seized me as I looked at the shore through a telescope. In the twinkling of an eye, I was hurried below and double-ironed; nor would I have received a morsel of food save bread and water during our detention, had I not been secretly fed by some good fellows from the forecastle, who stole to me after dark with the remnant of their rations. This was the cowardly revenge of Lasquetti.

On the third day, Laminé returned, bringing an American pilot for the coast and islands. I was set at liberty as he was seen approaching; and when we got under way on another cruise, I was commanded to do duty as sailing-master, which I promptly refused with spirited indignation, until I received satisfaction from the dastard lieutenant. But this fellow had taken care to forestall me, by assuring Laminé that he never dreamed of securing me until I was caught in the very act of escaping from the schooner!

During a week's cruise of indifferent success with these "patriots," I won the kind heart of the American pilot, who heard the story of my late adventures with patience; and, through his influence with the commander, my lot was mitigated, notwithstanding my refusal to do duty. By this time, the third lieutenant was restored to sufficient health to resume the deck. He was a native of Spain and a gallant sailor. Many an hour did he pass beside me, recounting his adventures or listening to mine, until I seemed to win his sympathy, and insure his assistance for relief from this miserable tyranny.

At length, the schooner's course was shaped for the Cruz del Padre, while I was summoned to the cabin. I perceived at once a singular change for the better in Monsieur Laminé's manner. He requested me to be seated; pressed me to accept a tumbler of claret; inquired about my health, and ended this harmonious overture by saying, that if I would sign a document exonerating him from all charges of compulsory detention or ill-treatment, he would pay me two hundred dollars for my service, and land me again on the key.

I promptly saw that his object in replacing me on the island was to prevent my complaints against his conduct from reaching the ears of a tribunal in a neutral port; and, accordingly, I declined the proposition,—demanding, however, to be put on board of any vessel we met, no matter what might be her nationality. I sternly refused his money, and insisted that my only desire was to be free from his brutal officer.

But Laminé was in power and I was not. In the end, I discovered that worse consequences might befall me among these ruffians, if I hesitated to take the recompense and sign the paper. In fact, I began to be quite satisfied that, in reality, it was an *escape* to be freed from the privateer, even if I took refuge once more among pirates !

So, after a good deal of claret and controversy had been wasted, I signed the document and pocketed the cash.

As the first bars of saffron streaked the east next morning, the reef of the Cruz del Padre hove in sight dead ahead. The third lieutenant presented me at my departure with a set of charts, a spy-glass, a quadrant, and a large bag of clothes; while, in the breast of a rich silk waistcoat, he concealed three ounces and a silver watch, which he desired me to wear in honor of him, if ever I was fortunate enough to tread the streets of Havana. Several of the white sailors also offered me useful garments ; and a black fellow, who had charge of the boat in which I was sent ashore, forced on me two sovereigns, which he considered a small gratuity to " *a countryman* " in distress. He hailed from Marblehead, and protested that he knew me in Salem when I was a lad.

As the boat approached the *rancho's* cove, I perceived every body under arms, and heard Don Rafael command my boatmen, in a loud, imperious voice, to begone, or he would fire. Standing on the thwarts of the boat, I ordered the oarsmen to back water, and leaping into the sea, waist-deep, struggled alone to the beach, calling " mi tio ! mi tio ! "—"*my uncle ! Don Rafael !* "—who, recognizing my voice and gestures, promptly rushed forward to

embrace me. Our boat was then allowed to approach the landing and disburthen itself of the gifts. I thought it best to
request my sable ally from Marblehead to narrate, in as good
Spanish or *lingua-franca* as he could press into his service, the
whole story of my capture and the conduct of Gallego. This
being done, the boat and its crew were dispatched aboard with a
multitude of Spanish courtesies and the substantial gift of some
*Chateau Margaux.*

After an early supper, I became the lion of the evening, and
was requested to give a narrative of my cruise in the "patriot
service." I noticed that some of the gang looked on me askance
with an incredulous air, while others amused themselves by
smoking and spitting in a very contemptuous way whenever I
reached what I conceived to be a thrilling portion of my story.
At its conclusion, I arose and deposited in the hands of Don
Rafael my gifts of two hundred dollars and the two sovereigns.
This evidence of reciprocity seemed to restore the good temper
of my impatient hearers, so that, by the time the *patron* went
round the circle, giving each man his share of my earnings,—not
even omitting Gallego,—my credit was almost restored among
the gang.

"As for these two pieces of gold, these charts, instruments
and clothes," said Don Rafael, "they are the property of the
youth, and I am sure none of you are mean enough to divide
them. The money was another thing. That was *his* earning, as
the 'fishing *revenue*' is ours; and as he is entitled to a share
of what *we* gain, we are entitled to participate in whatever *he*
wins. Yet, *amigos*, this is not all. My nephew, *caballeros*, has
been accused, by one of this party, *during his absence*, of being
not only a contemptible thief, but a traitor and coward. Now,
as these are three 'blasphemous vituperations' which are not to
be found under any head in my prayer-book, and never were
chargeable on the blood of our family, I insist on immediate justice to my kinsman. Let that cowardly scoundrel repeat and
*prove* his accusation of Teodore, face to face ! You, *señores*,
shall stand judges. Every thing shall be fair. To-night, my
boy shall be found guilty or purged of the baseness imputed to

him; and, moreover, I apprise you now, that if he is innocent, I shall to-morrow restore him to liberty. His voluntary return was a voucher of honesty; and I doubt whether there is a clever man among you who does not agree with me. Stand forth, Gallego, and charge this youth again with the infamy you heaped on him while he was away."

But the sullen wretch bowed his head, with a hang-dog look, and rolled his black and bushy skull slowly from side to side, with an air of bullying defiance. Still he remained perfectly silent.

"Stand forth, Gallego, once more, I say!" shouted Don Rafael, stamping with fury and foaming at the mouth; "stand forth, imp of the devil, and make good your charge, or I'll trice you up to these rafters by your thumbs, and lash you with a cow-hide till your stretched skin peels off in ribbons!"

The threat restored Gallego's voice; but he could only say that there was no use in repeating the charges, because the case was prejudged, and all feared Don Rafael and his parasite to such a degree that it was impossible to treat him with justice. "Yet, look ye, señores, if I can't talk, I can fight. If Don Rafael is ready to meet me, knife in hand, in support of my cause, why, all I have to say is, that I am ready for him and his bastard to boot!"

In a moment, Rafael's knife was out of his belt, and the two sprang forward in a death-struggle, which would doubtless have been a short affair, had not the whole party interposed between the combatants and forbidden the fight. In the hurly-burly, Gallego took to his heels and departed.

The scoundrel's escape caused some alarm in the camp, as it was feared he might leave the island, and, turning king's evidence, make the waters of Cuba too hot for the band. Accordingly, all the canoes and boats that night were drawn up on the beach and kept under double watch.

When order was restored in the *rancho*, I asked Don Rafael to explain the "three accusations" that had been made against my fair fame; when I learned that I was charged by Gallego with having felled him in the boat, with having shipped voluntarily in the privateer, and with returning in the Cara-bobo's boats *to rob the rancho of its valuables !*

The first of the allegations I admitted to be true; the second had been disproved by the privateer's boatmen; and, as to the third, I at once insisted upon the party's taking torches and accompanying me to the graveyard, where, I told them, they would find—as, in truth, they did—the valuables this villain had charged me with stealing. On our way thither, I recounted the manner in which I detected his infamy.

Next morning we divided into two parties, and taking the dogs, proceeded in chase of the dastard Galician. He was quickly tracked by the hounds and caught asleep, with two empty flasks beside him.

A drum-head court-martial at once convened for his trial, and it was unanimously resolved to chain him to a tree, where he was to be left exposed to the elements until he starved to death. The passive and silent fit had again come over Gallego. I implored that the sentence might be softened, but I was laughed at for my childish pity, and ordered home to the *rancho*. The command to chain him having been executed, the Spanish outcast was left to his terrible fate. One of the men, out of compassion, as he said, secretly conveyed a case of gin to the doomed man, and left it within reach, either to solace his departure from the world, or to render him insensible. But his end was speedy. Next morning the guard found him dead, with six empty bottles out of the case. His body was denied the rites of sepulture. It was left lying in chains as he perished, to rot in the sun and be devoured by the insects generated from his decay.

## CHAPTER VI.

WHEN these dreadful scenes were over, Don Rafael took me aside with the pleasant news that the time for my liberation was indeed arrived. He handed me one hundred and twenty-five dollars, which were my share of the proceeds of our lawful fishing. "Take the money," said Rafael, with a good deal of feeling; "take it, young man, with *perfect* confidence;—*there is no blood on it!*"

My preparations for departure were quickly made, as Bachicha was in the cove with his craft ready to take me to the mainland. I bade a hasty adieu to the gang; and perhaps it is rare that any one ever abandoned the companions of several months' intimacy with so little pain. Rafael's solicitude for my character touched me. He had done all in his power to preserve my self-respect, and I was, therefore, well disposed to regard the good counsel he gave me at parting, and to believe in his sincerity when he pictured a bright future, and contrasted it with his own desolation and remorse.

"I have recommended you, *hijo mio*, to a friend in Regla, on the opposite side of the harbor at Havana, who will take care of you. He is a *paisano* of ours. Take these additional ten ounces, which are the fruit of honest labor. They will help you to appear properly in Havana; so that, with the care of Bachicha and our Regla countryman, I don't despair of your welfare. ADIOS! *para siempre!*"

And so we parted ;—and it was, indeed, an adieu for ever. We never met again, but I heard of Don Rafael and his fortunes. The new enterprise with the pilot-boat turned out successfully, and the band acquired considerable property on the island before the piratical nests along the coast of Cuba were broken up by cruisers. Rafael had some narrow escapes from the noose and the yard-arm; but he eluded the grasp of his pursuers, and died a respectable *ranchero* on a comfortable farm in the interior of the Queen of the Antilles.

The light winds of summer soon brought us inside the Moro Castle, past the frowning batteries of the Cabanas, and at anchor near Regla, within the beautiful harbor of Havana. I shall never forget the impression made on my mind by this delicious scene as it first broke on my sight at sunrise, in all the cool freshness of morning. The grand amphitheatre of hills swept down to the calm and lake-like water with gentle slopes, lapped in the velvet robes of richest green, and embroidered, as it were, with lace-like spots of castle, fort, dwelling, and villa, until the seaward points were terminated on the left, by the brilliant city, and on the right by a pile of majestic batteries.

This grand and lasting impression was made almost at a glance, for, at my time of life, I was more concerned with man than nature, and rarely paused to dwell on the most fascinating scenery. Accordingly, I hastened to Regla with my letter of introduction, which was *interpreted* by Bachicha to the Italian grocer, the friend of Rafael, to whom I was confided. *Il signore Carlo Cibo* was an illiterate man of kind heart, who had adventurously emigrated from Italy to furnish the Havanese with good things; while, in return, the Havanese had been so pleased with his provender, that Carlo may be said to have been a man "very well to do in the world" for a foreigner. He received me with unbounded kindness;—welcomed me to his bachelor home;—apologized for its cold cheerlessness, and ordered me to consider himself and his "*casa*" entirely at my disposal as long as I chose to remain.

I was content to accept this unstinted hospitality for a few days, while I ran over the town, the hills, and the *paseos ;* but I could not consent to dally long eating the bread of idleness and charity. I observed that my friend Carlo was either the most prudent or least inquisitive man I knew, for he never asked me a question about my early or recent history. As he would not lead the conversation to my affairs, I one day took the liberty to inquire whether there was a vessel in port bound to the Pacific Ocean or Mexico, in which my protector could possibly find a situation for me as an officer, or procure me permission to work my way even as a common sailor.

The kind grocer instantly divined my true motive, and while he honored me for it, deprecated the idea of my departure. He said that my visit, instead of being a burden, was a pleasure he could not soon replace. As to the expenses of his house, he declared they were, in fact, *not* increased. What fed five, fed half a dozen ; and, as to my proposal to go to Mexico, or any other place in Spanish America on the Continent, with a view of "making my fortune," he warmly protested against it, in consequence of his own experience.

" They can never conquer their jealousy of *foreigners*," said Carlo ; " you may live with them for years, and imagine yourself as intimate as brothers ; but, at last, *carramba*, you will find something turn up, that marks you an alien and kindles nationality against you. Take my advice, Don Téodore, stay where you are ; study Spanish carefully ; get the hang of the people ; and, my life on it, before long, you'll have your hands full of trump cards and the game in your power."

I did as he desired, and was presented to a corpulent old quiz of a *padre*, who pretended to instruct me in classical Castilian. Two lessons demonstrated his incapacity ; but as he was a jolly gossip of my grocer, and hail-fellow with the whole village of Regla, I thought it good policy to continue his pupil in appearance, while I taught myself *in private*. Besides this, the *padre* was a *bon vivant* and devoted lover of fish. Now, as I happened to be a good sportsman, with a canoe at my command, I managed to supply his kitchen with an abundance of the finny tribe, which his cook was an adept in preparing. It may be supposed that our " fast days " were especial epochs of delicious reunion.   A fine dinner smoked on the table ; a good bottle was added by the grocer ; and, while my entertainer discussed the viands, I contrived to keep him in continual chat, which, in reality, was the best practical lesson a man in my circumstances could receive.

It is strange how our lives and destinies are often decided by trifles.   As I sailed about the harbor in idleness, my nautical eye and taste were struck by the trim rig of the sharp built " slavers," which, at that time, used to congregate at Havana. There was something bewitching to my mind in their race-horse beauty.   A splendid vessel has always had the same influence on my mind, that I have heard a splendid woman has on the minds of other men.   These dashing *slavers*, with their arrowy hulls and raking masts, got complete possession of my fancy.   There was hardly a day that I did not come home with a discovery of added charms.   Signor Carlo listened in silence and nodded his head, when I was done, with an approving smile and a " *bueno !* "

I continued my sailing peregrinations for a month around the harbor, when my kind entertainer invited me to accompany him aboard a vessel of which, he said, he owned two shares—*she was bound to Africa !*  The splendid clipper was one of the very craft that had won my heart ; and my feverish soul was completely upset by the gala-scene as we drifted down the bay, partaking of a famous breakfast, and quaffing bumpers of Champagne to the schooner's luck.   When she passed the Moro Castle we leaped into our boats, and gave the voyagers three hearty and tipsy cheers.   My grocer was a " slaver ! "

I had a thousand questions for the Italian in regard to the trade, now that I found *he* belonged to the fraternity.   All my inquiries were gratified in his usually amiable manner ; and that night, in my dreams, I was on board of a coaster chased by John Bull.

My mind was made up.   Mexico, Peru, South American independence, patriotism, and all that, were given to the breezes of the gulf. I slept off my headache and nightmare; and next morning announced to Cibo my abandonment of the Costa Firma, and my anxiety to get a situation in a vessel bound to Africa.

In a few days I was told that my wishes would perhaps be gratified, as a fast vessel from the Canaries was about to be sold; and if she went off a bargain, Signor Carlo had resolved to purchase her, with a friend, to send to Africa.

Accordingly, the Canary "GLOBO" was acquired for $3000; and after a perfect refitting at the Casa-Blanca of Havana, loomed in the harbor as a respectable pilot-boat of forty tons. Her name, in consequence of reputed speed, was changed to "El Areostatico;" a culverine was placed amidships; all the requisites for a slave cargo were put on board; fifteen sailors, the refuse of the press-gang and jail-birds, were shipped; powder, ammunition, and small arms, were abundantly supplied; and, last of all, four kegs, ballasted with specie, were conveyed into the cabin to purchase our return cargo.

It was on the 2d of September, 1826, after a charming *dejeuner*, that I bade farewell to my friend Carlo on the deck of the Areostatico, cleared for the Cape de Verd isles, but, in truth, bound for the Rio Pongo. Our crew consisted of twenty-one scamps—Spaniards, Portuguese, Frenchmen, and mongrels. The Majorcan captain was an odd character to intrust with such an enterprise, and probably nowhere else, save in Havana at that period, would he have been allowed to command a slaver. He was a scientific navigator, but no sailor;—afraid of his shadow, he had not a particle of confidence in his own judgment; every body was listened to, and he readily yielded his opinions without argument or controversy. Our chief officer, a Catalonian cousin of the captain, made no pretensions to seamanship, yet he was a good mathematician. I still remember the laughs I had at the care he took of his lily-white hands, and the jokes we cracked upon his girl-like manners, voice, and conversation. The boatswain, who was in his watch, assured me that he rarely gave an order without humming it out to a tune of some favorite opera.

In this fantastic group, I occupied the position of supernumerary officer and interpreter; but accustomed, as I had been, to wholesome *American* seamanship and discipline, I trembled not a little when I discovered the amazing ignorance of the master, and observed the utter worthlessness of our crew. These things made me doubly vigilant; and sometimes I grieved that I was not still in Regla, or on the *paseo.* On the tenth day out, a northwester began to pipe and ripen to a gale as the sea rose with it. Sail had been soon diminished on the schooner; but when I was relieved in my watch by the first officer, I hinted to the captain that it would be best to lay the vessel to as soon as possible. We had been scudding before the tempest for some hours under a close-reefed foresail, and I feared if we did not bring our craft to the wind at once, we would either run her under, or be swamped in attempting the manœuvre when the waves got higher. The captain, however, with his usual submission to the views of the wrong person, took the advice of the helmsman, who happened to be older than I, and the schooner was allowed to dash on either through or over the seas, at the speed of a racer.

By this time the forward deck was always under water, and the men gathered abaft the trunk to keep as dry as possible. Officers and crew were huddled together pell-mell, and, with our usual loose discipline, every body joined in the conversation and counsel. Before sundown I again advised the laying to of the schooner; but the task had now become so formidable that the men, who dreaded the job, assured the captain that the wind would fall as the moon arose. Yet, when the dim orb appeared above the thick, low-drifting scud, the gale *increased.* The light rather hinted than revealed the frightful scene around that egg-shell on the lashed and furious sea. Each wave swept over us, but our buoyant craft rose on the succeeding swell, and cleft its crest with her knife-like prow. It was now too late to attempt bringing her to the wind; still it became more urgent to do something to prevent us from being submerged by the huge seas, which came thundering after us like avalanches on our quarters.

The perilous dilemma of our doubtful captain and his dainty mate, may be easily imagined. Every body had an opinion, and of course they vied with each other in absurdity;—at last some one proposed to cut away the foresail, and bring her to the wind under bare poles.

I was " conning " the schooner when this insane scheme was broached, and fearing that the captain might adopt it, I leaped on the hatch, after calling the boatswain to my place, and assured the crew that if they severed the sail, we would lose command of the vessel, so that with impaired headway, the next wave that struck her would show her keel to the skies and her deck to the fishes. I exhorted them to drive her *faster* if possible rather than stop. To turn out the " balance reef," I said, was our only salvation;—and I alleged that I had seen a vessel saved before in precisely the same way. Cowards, with death clutching their throats, were soon convinced by a man of nerve. I availed myself of the instantaneous silence that followed my act, and before the captain could think or speak, I leaped to the boom with my sharp knife, cutting the reef-points slowly and carefully, so as not to allow the foresail to be inflated and torn by a single blast.

My judgment was correct. Our increased canvas immediately sent us skimming over the waves ; the rollers no longer combed dangerously over our quarter; we scudded steadily throughout the remnant of the gale ; and, next night, at sundown, we rested on a quiet, lake-like ocean, taughtening the strained rigging, and priding ourselves mightily on the hazards we encountered and overcame. The Minorcan skipper was satisfied that no man ever before performed so daring an exploit. He was, moreover, convinced, that no one but himself could have carried the schooner through so frightful a storm, or would have invented the noble expedient of driving instead of stripping her !

From this hour all semblance of regular discipline was abandoned. Sailors, who are suffered to tread the quarter-deck familiarly and offer their opinions, never get over the permitted freedom. Our ragamuffins of the Aerostatico could never abide the idea that the youngest seaman aboard,—and he, too, a *foreigner*,—should have proved the best sailor. The skilful performance of my duty was the source of a rankling grudge. As I would not mix with the scamps, they called me arrogant. My orders were negligently obeyed; and, in fact, every thing in the schooner became as comfortless as possible.

Forty-one days, however, brought us to the end of our voyage at the mouth of the Rio Pongo. No one being acquainted with the river's entrance or navigation, the captain and four hands went ashore for a pilot, who came off in the afternoon, while our master ascended in a boat to the slave-factory at Bangalang. Four o'clock found us entering the Rio Pongo, with tide and wind in our favor, so that before the sun sank into the Atlantic Ocean we were safe at our anchorage below the settlement.

While we were slowly drifting between the river banks, and watching the gorgeous vegetation of Africa, which, that evening, first burst upon my sight, I fell into a chat with the native pilot, who had been in the United States, and spoke English remarkably well. Berak very soon inquired whether there was any one else on board who spoke the language besides myself, and when told that the cabin-boy alone knew it, he whispered a story which, in truth, I was not in the least surprised to hear.

That afternoon one of our crew had attempted the captain's life, while on shore, by snapping a carabine behind his back! Our pilot learned the fact from a native who followed the party from the landing, along the beach; and its truth was confirmed, in his belief, by the significant boasts made by the *tallest* of the boatmen who accompanied him on board. He was satisfied that the entire gang contemplated our schooner's seizure.

The pilot's story corroborated some hints I received from our cook during the voyage. It struck me instantly, that if a crime like this were really designed, no opportunity for its execution could be more propitious than the present. I determined, therefore, to omit no precaution that might save the vessel and the lives of her honest officers. On examining the carabines brought back from shore, which I had hurriedly thrown into the arm-chest on deck, I found that the lock of this armory had been forced, and several pistols and cutlasses abstracted.

Preparations had undoubtedly been made to assassinate us. As night drew on, my judgment, as well as *nervousness*, convinced me that the darkness would not pass without a murderous attempt. There was an unusual silence. On reaching port, there is commonly fun and merriment among crews; but the usual song and invariable guitar were omitted from the evening's entertainment. I searched the deck carefully, yet but two mariners were found above the hatches apparently asleep. Inasmuch as I was only a subordinate officer, I could not command, nor had I any confidence in the nerve or judgment of the chief mate, if I trusted my information to him. Still I deemed it a duty to tell him the story, as well as my discovery about the missing arms. Accordingly, I called the first officer, boatswain, and cook, as quietly as possible, into the cabin; leaving our English cabin-boy to watch in the companion way. Here I imparted our danger, and asked their assistance in *striking the first blow*. My plan was to secure the crew, and give them battle. The mate, as I expected, shrank like a girl, declining any step till the captain returned. The cook and boatswain, however, silently approved my movement; so that we counselled our cowardly comrade to remain below, while we assumed the responsibility and risk of the enterprise.

It may have been rather rash, but I resolved to begin the rescue, by shooting down, like a dog and without a word, the notorious Cuban convict who had attempted the captain's life. This, I thought, would strike panic into the mutineers; and end the mutiny in the most bloodless way. Drawing a pair of large horse-pistols from beneath the captain's pillow, and examining the load, I ordered the cook and boatswain to follow me to the deck. But the craven officer would not quit his hold on my person. He besought me not to commit murder. He clung to me with the panting fear and grasp of a woman. He begged me, with every term of endearment, to desist; and, in the midst of my scuffle to throw him off, one of the pistols accidentally exploded. A moment after, my vigilant watch-boy screamed from the starboard, a warning "look-out!" and, peering forward in the blinding darkness as I emerged from the lighted cabin, I beheld the stalwart form of the ringleader, brandishing a cutlass within a stride of me. I aimed and fired. We both fell: the mutineer with two balls in his abdomen, and I from the recoil of an overcharged pistol.

My face was cut, and my eye injured by the concussion; but as neither combatant was deprived of consciousness, in a moment we were both on our feet. The Spanish felon, however, pressed his hand on his bowels, and rushed forward exclaiming he was slain; but, in his descent to the forecastle, he was stabbed in the shoulder with a bayonet by the boatswain, whose vigorous blow drove the weapon with such tremendous force that it could hardly be withdrawn from the scoundrel's carcass.

I said I was up in a minute; and, feeling my face with my hand, I perceived a quantity of blood on my cheek, around which I hastily tied a handkerchief, below my eyes. I then rushed to the arm-chest. At that moment, the crack of a pistol, and a sharp, boyish cry, told me that my pet was wounded beside me. I laid him behind the hatchway, and returned to the charge. By this time I was blind with rage, and fought, it seems, like a *madman*. I confess that I have no personal recollection whatever of the following events, and only learned them from the subsequent report of the cook and boatswain.

I stood, they said, over the arm chest like one spell-bound. My eyes were fixed on the forecastle; and, as head after head loomed out of the darkness above the hatch, I discharged carabine after carabine at the mark. Every thing that moved fell by my aim. As I fired the weapons, I flung them away to grasp fresh ones; and, when the battle was over, the cook aroused me from my mad stupor, still groping wildly for arms in the emptied chest.

As the smoke cleared off, the fore part of our schooner seemed utterly deserted; yet we found two men dead, one in mortal agony on the deck, while the ringleader and a colleague were gasping in the forecastle. Six pistols had been fired against us from forward; but, strange to say, the only efficient ball was the one that struck my English boy's leg.

When I came to my senses, my first quest was for the gallant boatswain, who, being unarmed on the forecastle when the unexpected discharge took place, and seeing no chance of escape from my murderous carabines, took refuge over the bows.

Our cabin-boy was soon quieted. The mutineers needed but little care for their hopeless wounds, while the felon chief, like all such wretches, died in an agony of despicable fear, shrieking for pardon. My shriving of his sins was a speedy rite !

Such was my *first* night in Africa !

# CHAPTER VII.

There are casual readers who may consider the scene described in the last chapter unnatural. It may be said that a youth, whose life had been checquered by trials and disasters, but who preserved a pure sensibility throughout them, is sadly distorted when portrayed as expanding, at a leap, into a desperado. I have but little to say in reply to these objections, save that *the occurrences are perfectly true as stated*, and, moreover, that I am satisfied they were only the natural developments of my character.

From my earliest years I have adored nobility of soul, and detested dishonor and treachery. I have passed through scenes which will be hereafter told, that the world may qualify by harsh names ; yet I have striven to conduct myself throughout them, not only with the ideas of fairness current among reckless men, but with the truth that, under all circumstances, characterizes an honorable nature.

Now, the tragedy of my first night on the Rio Pongo was my transition from pupilage to responsible independence. I do not allege in a boastful spirit that I was a man of courage ; because courage, or the want of it, are things for which a person is no more responsible than he is for the possession or lack of physical strength. I was, moreover, always a man of what I may style *self-possessed passion*. I was endowed with something more than cool energy ; or, rather, cool energy was heightened and sublimated by the fire of an ardent nature. Hitherto, I had been tempered down by the habitual obedience to which I was subjected as a sailor under lawful discipline. But the events of the last six months, and especially the gross relaxation on the voyage to Africa, the risks we had run in navigating the vessel, and the outlaws that surrounded me, not only kept my mind for ever on the alert, but aroused my dormant nature to a full sense of duty and self-protection.

Is it unnatural, then, for a man whose heart and nerves have been laid bare for months, to quiver with agony and respond with headlong violence, when imperilled character, property and life, hang upon the fiat of his courageous promptitude? The doubters may cavil over the philosophy, but I think I may remain content with the fact. *I did my duty*—dreadful as it was.

Let me draw a veil over our gory decks when the gorgeous sun of Africa shot his first rays through the magnificent trees and herbage that hemmed the placid river. Five bodies were cast into the stream, and the traces of the tragedy obliterated as well as possible. The recreant mate, who plunged into the cabin at the report of the first pistol from the forecastle, reappeared with haggard looks and trembling frame, to protest that *he* had no hand in what he called "the murder." The cook, boatswain, and African pilot, recounted the whole transaction to the master, who inserted it in the log-book, and caused me to sign the narrative with unimplicated witnesses. Then the wound of the cabin-boy was examined and found to be trifling, while mine, though not painful, was thought to imperil my sight. The flint lock of a rebounding pistol had inflicted three gashes, just beneath the eye on my cheek.

There was but little appetite for breakfast that day. After the story was told and recorded, we went sadly to work unmooring the vessel, bringing her slowly like a hearse to an anchorage in front of Bangalang, the residence and factory of Mr. Ormond, better known by the country-name of "Mongo John." This personage came on board early in the morning with our returned captain, and promised to send a native doctor to cure both my eye and the boy's leg, making me pledge him a visit as soon as the vessel's duties would permit.

That evening the specie was landed, and the schooner left in my charge by the master, with orders to strip, repair, and provide for the voyage home. Before night, Mongo John fulfilled his promise of a physician, who came on board with his prescription,—not in his pocket, but by his side! He ordered my torn cheek to be bathed, every half hour, *with human milk fresh from the breast*; and, in order to secure a prompt, pure, and plentiful supply, a stout negress and her infant were sent, with orders to remain as long as her lacteal services might be required! I cannot say whether nature or the remedy healed my wound, but in a short time the flesh cicatrized, and all symptoms of inflammation disappeared entirely.

It required ten days to put the Areostatico in ship-shape and supply her with wood and water. Provisions had been brought from Havana, so that it was only necessary we should stow them in an accessible manner. As our schooner was extremely small, we possessed no slave-deck; accordingly, mats were spread over the fire-wood which filled the interstices of the water casks, in order to make an even surface for our cargo's repose.

When my tiresome task was done, I went ashore—almost for the first time—to report progress to the master; but he was still unprepared to embark his living freight. Large sums, far in advance of the usual market, were offered by him for a cargo of *boys*; still we were delayed full twenty days longer than our contract required before a supply reached Bangalang.

As I had promised *Mongo John*, or John the Chief, to visit his factory, I took this opportunity to fulfil my pledge. He received me with elaborate politeness; showed me his town, barracoons, and stores, and even stretched a point, to honor me by an introduction to the *penetralia* of his *harem*. The visit paid, he insisted that I should dine with him; and a couple of choice bottles were quickly disposed of. Ormond, like myself, had been a sailor. We spoke of the lands, scenes, and adventures, each had passed through, while a fresh bottle was called to fillip our memories. There is nothing so nourishing to friendship as wine! Before sundown our electric memories had circled the globe, and our intimacy culminated.

While the rosy fluid operated as a sedative on the Mongo, and glued him to his chair in a comfortable nap, it had a contrary effect on my exhilarated nerves. I strolled to the verandah to get a breath of fresh air from the river, but soon dashed off in the darkness to the sacred precincts of the *harem!* I was not detected till I reached nearly the centre of the sanctuary where Ormond confined his motley group of black, mulatto, and quarteroon wives. The first dame who perceived me was a bright mulatto, with rosy cheeks, sloe-like eyes, coquettish turban, and most voluptuous mouth, whom I afterwards discovered to be second in the chief's affections. In an instant the court resounded with a chattering call to her companions, so that, before I could turn, the whole band of gabbling parrots hemmed me in with a deluge of talk. Fame had preceded me! My sable nurse was a servant of the harem, and her visit to the schooner, with the tale of the tragedy, supplied anecdotes for a lifetime. Every body was on the *qui vive* to see the "white fighter." Every body was crazy to feel the "white skin" she had healed. Then, with a sudden, childish freak of caprice, they ran off from me as if afraid, and at once rushed back again like a flock of glib-tongued and playful monkeys. I could not comprehend a word they said; but the bevy squealed with quite as much pleasure as if I did, and peered into my eyes for answers, with impish devilry at my wondering ignorance.

At last, my sable friends seemed not only anxious to amuse themselves but to do something for my entertainment also. A chatter in a corner settled what it should be. Two or three brought sticks, while two or three brought coals. A fire was quickly kindled in the centre of the court; and as its flames lit up the area, a whirling circle of half-stripped girls danced to the monotonous beat of a *tom-tom*. Presently, the formal ring was broken, and each female stepping out singly, danced according to her individual fancy. Some were wild, some were soft, some were tame, and some were fiery. After so many years I have no distinct recollection of the characteristic movements of these semi-savages, especially as the claret and champagne rather fermented in my brain, and possessed me with the idea that it was my duty to mingle in the bounding throng. I resolved that the barbarians should have a taste of Italian quality !

Accordingly, I leaped from the hammock where I had swung idly during the scene, and, beginning with a *balancez* and an *avant-deux*, terminated my terpsichorean exhibition by a regular "double shuffle" and sailor's hornpipe. The delirious laughter, cracked sides, rollicking fun, and outrageous merriment, with which my feats were received, are unimaginable by sober-sided people. Tired of my single exhibition, I seized the prettiest of the group by her slim, shining waist, and whirled her round and round the court in the quickest of waltzes, until, with a kiss, I laid her giddy and panting on the floor. Then, grasping another,—another,—another,—and another,—and treating each to the same dizzy swim, I was about waltzing the whole *seraglio* into quiescence, when who should rise before us but the staring and yawning *Mongo !*

The apparition sobered me. A quarteroon pet of Ormond,— just spinning into fashionable and luscious insensiblility,—fell from my arms into those of her master; and while I apologized for the freak, I charged it altogether to the witchcraft of his wit and wine.

"Ha!" said the Mongo, "St. Vitus is in your Italian heels the moment you are within hail of music and dancing; and, by Jove, it seems you can scent a petticoat as readily as a hound tracks runaways. But there's no harm in *dancing*, Don Téodore; only hereafter I hope you will enjoy the amusement in a less uproarious manner. In Africa we are fond of a *siesta* after dinner; and I recommend you to get, as soon as possible, under the lee of another bottle."

We retired once more to his mahogany; and, under the spell of my chieftain's claret and sea-yarns, I was soon lapped in delicious sleep.

———

Next day the captain of the Areostatico drew me aside confidentially, and hinted that Ormond had taken such a decided fancy for me, and *insinuated* so warm a wish for my continuance *as his clerk* at Bangalang, that he thought it quite a duty, though a sad one, to give his advice on the subject.

" It may be well for your purse, Don Téodore, to stay with so powerful a trader ; but beside the improvement of your fortunes, there are doubts whether it will be *wholesome* for you to revisit Havana, at least at present. It may be said, *amigo mio*, that you *commenced* the warfare on board the schooner ;—and as five men were slain in the affray, it will be necessary for me to report the fact to the *commandante* as soon as I arrive. Now it is true, *hijo mio*, that you saved the vessel, cargo, specie, and my cousin; yet, God knows what may be the result of Havana justice. You will have a rigid examination, and I rather think you will be *imprisoned* until the final decision is made. When that consummation shall occur is quite uncertain. If you have friends, they will be bled as long as possible before you get out ; if you have none, no one will take pains to see you released without recompense. When you see daylight once more, the rest of these ragamuffins and the felon friends of the dead men, will begin to dog your steps, and make Havana uncomfortable as well as dangerous ; so that I have no hesitation in recommending you to stay where you are, and take the doubloons of the Mongo."

I thought I saw at a glance the drift of this hypocritical *fanfaronade*, and was satisfied he only desired to get rid of me in order to reinstate the chief mate in a situation which he surely could not occupy as long as I was on board. As I meant to stay in Africa, I told him at once that I grieved because he had not spoken his wishes openly, boldly, and honestly, like a man, but had masked an ungrateful cowardice by hypocritical solicitude for my welfare. I departed abruptly with a scowl of contempt ; and as he hastened to hide his blanched face in the cabin, I called a boat, and throwing my sea chest, bedding, and arms, aboard, committed my fate to the African continent. *A half-hour turned and decided my fate !*

Mr. Ormond received me very cordially, and, installing me in my new secretaryship, promised a private establishment, a seat at his table, and a negro per month,—or its value at the rate of forty dollars,—for my services.

When the runners returned from the interior with the slaves required to complete the Areostatico's cargo, I considered it my duty to the Italian grocer of Regla to dispatch his vessel personally. Accordingly, I returned on board to aid in stowing *one hundred and eight boys and girls, the eldest of whom did not exceed fifteen years!* As I crawled between decks, I confess I could not imagine how this little army was to be packed or draw breath in a hold but *twenty-two inches high!* Yet the experiment was promptly made, inasmuch as it was necessary to secure them below in descending the river, in order to prevent their leaping overboard and swimming ashore. I found it impossible to adjust the whole in a sitting posture; but we made them lie down in each other's laps, like *sardines* in a can, and in this way obtained space for the entire cargo. Strange to tell, when the Areostatico reached Havana, but *three* of these "passengers" had paid the debt of nature.

As I left the schooner a few miles outside the bar, I crossed her side without an adieu save for the English cabin boy, whose fate I was pained to intrust to these stupid Spaniards. Indeed, the youth almost belonged to me, for I may say he owed his life to my interference.

Previous to the voyage, while waiting in the harbor of Havana for a crew, our vessel was anchored near the wharves, next to an English merchantman. One afternoon I heard a scream from the neighboring craft, and perceived a boy rush from the cabin with his face dyed in blood. He was instantly pursued by a burly seaman, inflicting blows with his fist. I implored the brute to desist, but my interference seemed to augment his choler to such a degree, that he seized a handspike to knock the stripling down. Upon this I called the child to leap overboard, at the same time commanding a hand to lower my boat and scull in the direction of his fall. The boy obeyed my voice; and in a few minutes I had him on board blessing me for his safety. But the drunken Briton vented his rage in the most indecent language; and had his boat been aboard, I doubt not a summary visit would have terminated in a fight on my deck.

However, as good luck would have it, his skiff was at the

landing, so that there was ample time, before he could reach the Areostatico, to tie up the bruised face and broken rib of the child, and to conceal him in the house of a Spanish crone in Havana, who cured the maladies of credulous seamen by witchcraft!

After nightfall the master of the British vessel came aboard to claim his boy; but as he was petulant and seemed disposed to carry matters with a high hand, my temper rose in resistance, and I refused to release the child until he sealed with an oath his promise to treat him better in future.   But the cruel scoundrel insisted on *unconditional* surrender; and to end the controversy, I was compelled to order him off the schooner.

British pluck of course would not allow a captain to be deprived so easily of his property, so the British consul was invoked to appeal to the captain of the port.   This personage summoned me before him, and listened calmly to a story which added no honor to English mariners.   In my last interview with the boy he implored my continued protection and concealment; so that when the Spanish official declared—notwithstanding the officer's conduct—that the vessel was entitled to her crew, and that I must surrender the child, I excused myself from complying by pleading utter ignorance of his whereabout.   In view of this contingency, I directed the woman to hide him in a place of which I should be ignorant.   So I told no lie, and saved the boy from his tyrant.

The inquiry was dropped at this stage of proceedings.   When the British vessel sailed a few days after, I caused the youth to be brought from his concealment; and, with our captain's consent, brought him aboard to serve in our cabin.

I have narrated this little episode in consequence of my love for the boy, and because *he was the only English subject I ever knew to ship in a slaver*.

I requested the Areostatic's owners to pay him liberally for his fidelity when he got back to Havana; and I was happy to learn next year, that they not only complied with my request, but sent him home to his friends in Liverpool.

# CHAPTER VIII.

WHEN I got back to Bangalang, my first movement was to take possession of the quarters assigned me by the Mongo, and to make myself as comfortable as possible in a land whose chief requirements are shade and shelter. My house, built of cane plastered with mud, consisted of two earthen-floored rooms and a broad verandah. The thatched roof was rather leaky, while my furniture comprised two arm-chests covered with mats, a deal table, a bamboo settle, a tin-pan with palm-oil for a lamp, and a German looking-glass mounted in a paper frame. I augmented these comforts by the addition of a trunk, mattress, hammock and pair of blankets; yet, after all this embellishment, I confess my household was rather a sorry affair.

It is time I should make the reader acquainted with the individual who was the presiding genius of the scene, and, in some degree, a type of his peculiar class in Africa.

Mr. Ormond was the son of an opulent slave-trader from Liverpool, and owed his birth to the daughter of a native chief on the Rio Pongo. His father seems to have been rather proud of his mulatto stripling, and dispatched him to England to be educated. But Master John had made little progress in belles-lettres, when news of the trader's death was brought to the British agent, who refused the youth further supplies of money. The poor boy soon became an outcast in a land which had not yet become fashionably addicted to philanthropy; and, after drifting about awhile in England, he shipped on board a merchantman. The press-gang soon got possession of the likely mulatto for the service of his Britannic Majesty. Sometimes he played the part of dandy waiter in the cabin; sometimes he swung a hammock with the hands in the forecastle. Thus, five years slipped by, during which the wanderer visited most of the West Indian and Mediterranean stations.

At length the prolonged cruise was terminated, and Ormond paid off. He immediately determined to employ his hoarded cash in a voyage to Africa, where he might claim his father's property. The project was executed; his mother was still found alive; and, fortunately for the manly youth, she recognized him at once as her first born.

The reader will recollect that these things occurred on the west coast of Africa in the early part of the present century, and that the tenure of property, and the interests of foreign traders, were controlled entirely by such *customary* laws as prevailed on the spot. Accordingly, a "grand palaver" was appointed, and all Mr. Ormond's brothers, sisters, uncles, and cousins,—many of whom were in possession of his father's slaves or their descendants,—were summoned to attend. The "talk" took place at the appointed time. The African mother stood forth stanchly to assert the identity and rights of her first-born, and, in the end, all of the Liverpool trader's property, in houses, lands, and negroes, that could be ascertained, was handed over, according to coast-law, to the returned heir.

When the mulatto youth was thus suddenly elevated into comfort, if not opulence, in his own country, he resolved to augment his wealth by pursuing his father's business. But the whole country was then desolated by a civil war, occasioned, as most of them are, by family disputes, which it was necessary to terminate before trade could be comfortably established.

To this task Ormond steadfastly devoted his first year. His efforts were seconded by the opportune death of one of the warring chiefs. A tame opponent,—a brother of Ormond's mother,—was quickly brought to terms by a trifling present; so that the sailor boy soon concentrated the family influence, and declared himself "Mongo," or, Chief of the River.

Bangalang had long been a noted factory among the English traders. When war was over, Ormond selected this post as his permanent residence, while he sent runners to Sierra Leone and Goree with notice that he would shortly be prepared with ample cargoes. Trade, which had been so long interrupted by hostilities, poured from the interior. Vessels from Goree and Sierra Leone were seen in the offing, responding to his invitation. His stores were packed with British, French, and American fabrics; while hides, wax, palm-oil, ivory, gold, and slaves, were the native products for which Spaniards and Portuguese hurried to proffer their doubloons and bills.

It will be readily conjectured that a very few years sufficed to make Jack Ormond not only a wealthy merchant, but a popular Mongo among the great interior tribes of Foulahs and Mandingoes. The petty chiefs, whose territory bordered the sea, flattered him with the title of king; and, knowing his *Mormon taste*, stocked his *harem* with their choicest children as the most valuable tokens of friendship and fidelity.

When I was summoned to act as secretary or clerk of such a personage, I saw immediately that it would be well not only to understand my duties promptly, but to possess a clear estimate of the property I was to administer and account for. Ormond's easy habits satisfied me that he was not a man of business originally, or had become sadly negligent under the debasing influence of wealth and voluptuousness. My earliest task, therefore, was to make out a *minute inventory* of his possessions, while I kept a watchful eye on his stores, never allowing any one to enter them unattended. When I presented this document, which exhibited a large deficiency, the Mongo received it with indifference, begging me not to "annoy him with accounts." His manner indicated so much petulant fretfulness, that I augured from it the conscious decline or disorder of his affairs.

As I was returning to the warehouse from this mortifying interview, I encountered an ancient hag,—a sort of superintendent Cerberus or manager of the Mongo's *harem*,—who, by signs, intimated that she wanted the key to the " cloth-chest," whence she immediately helped herself to several fathoms of calico The crone could not speak English, and, as I did not understand the Soosoo dialect, we attempted no oral argument about the propriety of her conduct; but, taking a pencil and paper, and making signs that she should go to the Mongo, who would write an order for the raiment, I led her quietly to the door. The wrath of the virago was instantly kindled, while her horrid face gleamed with that devilish ferocity, which, in some degree is lost by Africans who dwell on our continent. During the reign of my predecessors, it seems that she had been allowed to control the store keys, and to help herself unstintedly. I knew not, of course, what she *said* on this occasion ; but the violence of her gestures, the nervous spasms of her limbs, the flashing of her eyes, the scream of her voluble tongue, gave token that she swelled with a rage which was augmented by my imperturbable quietness. At dinner, I apprised Mr. Ormond of the negro's conduct ; but he received the announcement with the same laugh of indifference that greeted the account of his deficient in-ventory.

That night I had just stretched myself on my hard pallet, and was revolving the difficulties of my position with some de-gree of pain at my forced continuance in Africa, when my ser-vant tapped softly at the door, and announced that some one demanded admittance, but begged that I would first of all ex-tinguish the light. I was in a country requiring caution ; so I felt my pistols before I undid the latch. It was a bright, star-light night; and, as I opened the door sufficiently to obtain a glance beyond,—still maintaining my control of the aperture,— I perceived the figure of a female, wrapped in cotton cloth from head to foot, except the face, which I recollected as that of the beautiful *quarteroon* I was whirling in the waltz, when sur-prised by the Mongo. She put forth her hands from the folds of her garment, and laying one softly on my arm, while she touched her lips with the other, looked wistfully behind, and glided into my apartment.

This poor girl, the child of a mulatto mother and a white

parent, was born in the settlement of Sierra Leone, and had acquired our language with much more fluency than is common among her race.  It was said that her father had been originally a missionary from Great Britain, but abandoned his profession for the more lucrative traffic in slaves, to which he owed an abundant fortune.  It is probable that the early ecclesiastical turn of her delinquent progenitor induced him, before he departed for America, to bestow on his child the biblical name of ESTHER.

I led my trembling visitor to the arm-chest, and, seating her gently by my side, inquired why I was favored by so stealthy a visit from the *harem*.  My suspicions were aroused; for, though a novice in Africa, I knew enough of the discipline maintained in these slave factories, not to allow my fancy to seduce me with the idea that her visit was owing to mad-cap sentimentality.

The manner of these *quarteroon* girls, whose complexion hardly separates them from our own race, is most winningly graceful; and Esther, with abated breath, timidly asked my pardon for intruding, while she declared I had made so bitter an enemy of Unga-golah,—the head-woman of the seraglio,—that, in spite of danger, she stole to my quarters with a warning.  Unga swore revenge.  I had insulted and thwarted her; I was able to thwart her at all times, if I remained the Mongo's " book-man; "—I must soon " go to another country; " but, if I did not, I would quickly find the food of Bangalang excessively unwholesome!  " Never eat any thing that a Mandingo offers you," said Esther.  " Take your meals exlusively from the Mongo's table.  Unga-golah knows all the Mandingo *ju-jus*, and she will have no scruple in using them in order to secure once more the control of the store keys.  Good night! "

With this she rose to depart, begging me to be silent about her visit, and to believe that a poor slave could feel true kindness for a white man, or even expose herself to save him.

If an unruly passion had tugged at my heartstrings, the soft appeal, the liquid tones, the tenderness of this girl's humanity, would have extinguished it in an instant.  It was the first time for many a long and desolate month that I had experienced the gentle touch of a woman's hand, or felt the interest of mortal solicitude fall like a refreshing dew upon my heart ! Who will censure me for halting on my door-sill as I led her forth, retaining her little hand in mine, while I cast my eyes over the lithe symmetry of those slender and rounded limbs; while I feasted on the flushed magnolia of those beautiful cheeks, twined my fingers in the trailing braids of that raven hair, peered into the blackness of those large and swimming orbs, felt a tear trickle down my hardening face, and left, on those coral lips, the print of a kiss that was fuller of gratitude than passion !

Nowadays that Mormonism is grafting a " celestial wifery " upon the civilization of the nineteenth century, I do not think it amiss to recall the memory of those African establishments which formed so large a portion of a trader's homestead. It is not to be supposed that the luxurious *harem* of Turkey or Egypt was transferred to the Guinea coast, or that its lofty walls were barricaded by stout gates, guarded by troops of sable eunuchs. The " wifery " of my employer was a bare inclosure, formed by a quadrangular cluster of mud-houses, the entrance to whose courtyard was never watched save at night. Unga-golah, the eldest and least delectable of the dames, maintained the establishment's police, assigned gifts or servants to each female, and distributed her master's favors according to the bribes she was cajoled by.

In early life and during his gorged prosperity, Ormond,—a stout, burly, black-eyed, broad-shouldered, short-necked man,— ruled his *harem* with the rigid decorum of the East. But as age and misfortunes stole over the sensual voluptuary, his mental and bodily vigor became impaired, not only by excessive drink, but by the narcotics to which he habitually resorted for excite- ment. When I became acquainted with him, his face and figure bore the marks of a worn-out *debauché*. His harem now was a fashion of the country rather than a domestic resort. His wives ridiculed him, or amused themselves as they pleased. I learned from Esther that there was hardly one who did not " flirt " with a lover in Bangalang, and that Unga-golah was blinded by gifts, while the stupor of the Mongo was perpetuated by liquor.

It may be supposed that in such a *seraglio*, and with such a master, there were but few matrimonial jealousies; still, as it would be difficult to find, even in our most Christian society, two females without some lurking bitterness towards rivals, so it is not to be imagined that the Mongo's mansion was free from womanly quarrels. These disputes chiefly occurred when Ormond distributed gifts of calico, beads, tobacco, pipes and looking-glasses. If the slightest preference or inequality was shown, adieu to order. Unga-golah descended below zero! The favorite wife, outraged by her neglected authority, became furious; and, for a season, pandemonium was let loose in Bangalang.

One of these scenes of passion occurs to me as I write. I was in the store with the Mongo when an aggrieved dame, not remarkable either for delicacy of complexion or sweetness of odor, entered the room, and marching up with a swagger to her master, dashed a German looking-glass on the floor at his feet. She wanted a larger one, for the glass bestowed on her was half an inch smaller than the gifts to her companions.

When Ormond was sober, his pride commonly restrained him from allowing the women to molest his leisure; so he quietly turned from the virago and ordered her out of the store.

But my lady was not to be appeased by dignity like this. " Ha!" shrieked the termagant, as she wrenched off her handkerchief. " Ha!" yelled she, tearing off one sleeve, and then the other. " Ha!" screamed the fiend, kicking a shoe into one corner, and the other shoe into another corner. " Ha! Mongo!" roared the beldame, as she stripped every garment from her body and stood absolutely *naked* before us, slapping her wool, cheeks, forehead, breasts, arms, stomach and limbs, and appealing to Ormond to say where she was deficient in charms, that she should be slighted half an inch on a looking-glass?

As the Mongo was silent, she strode up to me for an opinion; but, scarlet with blushes, I dived behind the cloth-chest, and left the laughing Ormond to gratify the whim of the " *model artiste.*"

Years afterwards, I remember seeing an infuriate Ethiopian fling her infant into the fire because its white father preferred the child of another spouse.   Indeed, I was glad my station at Bang-alang did not make it needful for the preservation of my respect-ability that I should indulge in the luxury of *African matri-mony!*

But these exhibitions of jealous passion were not excited alone by the unequal distribution of presents from the liege lord of Bangalang.   I have observed that Ormond's wives took advantage of his carelessness and age, to seek congenial compan-ionship outside the *harem*.   Sometimes the preference of two of these sable *belles* alighted on the same lover, and then the battle was transferred from a worthless looking glass to the darling *beau*.   When such a quarrel arose, a meeting between the rivals was arranged out of the Mongo's hearing; when, throwing off their waist-cloths, the controversy was settled between the female gladiators without much damage.   But, now and then, the matter was not left to the ladies.   The sable lovers them-selves took up the conflict, and a regular challenge passed between the gay Othellos.

At the appointed time, the duellists appeared upon " the field of honor " accompanied by friends who were to witness their victory or sympathize in their defeat.   Each stalwart savage leaped into the arena, armed with a cow-hide cat, whose sharp and triple thongs were capable of inflicting the harshest blows. They stripped, and tossed three *cowries* into the air to determine which of the two should receive the first lashing.   The unfortu-nate loser immediately took his stand, and received, with the firmness of a martyr, the allotted number of blows.   Then came the turn of the whipper, who, with equal constancy, offered his back to the scourge of the enraged sufferer.   Thus they alter-nated until one gave in, or until the bystanders decreed victory to him who bore the punishment longest without wincing.   The flayed backs of these " chivalrous men of honor " were ever after displayed in token of bravery ; and, doubtless, their Dulcineas devoted to their healing the subtlest ointment and tenderest affection recognized among Africans.

# CHAPTER IX.

My business habits and systematic devotion to the Mongo's interests soon made me familiar with the broad features of "country trade;" but as I was still unable to speak the coast dialects,
Mr. Ormond—who rarely entered the warehouse or conversed
about commerce—supplied an adroit interpreter, who stood
beside me and assisted in the retail of foreign merchandise, for
rice, ivory, palm-oil, and domestic provisions. The purchase of
slaves and gold was conducted exclusively by the Mongo, who
did not consider me sufficiently initiated in native character and
tricks to receive so delicate a trust.

Long and dreary were the days and nights of the apparently
interminable "wet season." Rain in a city, rain in the country, rain in a village, rain at sea, are sufficiently wearying, even
to those whose mental activity is amused or occupied by books or
the concerns of life; but who can comprehend the insufferable
lassitude and despondency that overwhelm an African resident,
as he lies on his mat-covered arm-chest, and listens to the endless
deluge pouring for days, weeks, months, upon his leaky thatch?

At last, however, the season of rain passed by, and the "dry
season" set in. This was the epoch for the arrival of caravans
from the interior; so that we were not surprised when our runners appeared, with news that Ahmah-de-Bellah, son of a noted

Fullah chief, was about to visit the Rio Pongo with an imposing train of followers and merchandise. The only means of communication with the interior of Africa are, for short distances, by rivers, and, for longer ones, by " paths " or " trails " leading through the dense forest and among the hills, to innumerable " towns " that stud this prolific land. Stephenson and McAdam have not been to Africa, and there are neither turnpikes nor railways. Now, when the coast-traders of the west are apprised that caravans are threading their way towards the Atlantic shores, it is always thought advisable to make suitable preparations for the chiefs, and especially to greet them by messages, before their arrival at the beach. Accordingly, "*barkers*" are sent forth on the forest "paths " to welcome the visitors with gifts of tobacco and powder. " *Barkers* " are colored gentlemen, with fluent tongues and flexible consciences, always in the train of factories on the coast, who hasten to the wilderness at the first signal of a caravan's approach, and magnify the prosperity and merchandise of their patrons with as much zeal and veracity as the " drummers" of more Christian lands.

A few days after our band of travelling agents had departed on their mission, the crack of fire-arms was heard from the hills in our rear, signifying that the Mongo's " *barkers* " had been successful with the caravan in tow. A prompt response to the joyous signal was made by our cannons ; so that, after half an hour's firing, Ahmah-de-Bellah and his party emerged from the smoke, marshalled by our band of singers, who preceded him, chanting with loud voices the praise of the youthful chieftain. Behind the master came the principal traders and their slaves laden with produce, and followed by forty captive negroes, secured by bamboo withes. These were succeeded by three-score bullocks, a large flock of sheep or goats, and the females of the party ; while the procession was closed by the demure tread of a tame and stately OSTRICH !

It was the first time I had seen so odd an assemblage of beasts and humanity. Indeed, had the troupe been accompanied by a bevy of ourang-outangs, I confess I might, at times, have had difficulty in deciding the grade of animal life to which the object in front of me belonged.

Mr. Ormond, when put upon his mettle, was one of the ablest traders in Africa, and received the Mahometan strangers with becoming state. He awaited Ahmah-de-Bellah and his committee of head-traders on the piazza of his receiving-house, which was a rather stately edifice, one hundred and fifty feet in length, built to be fire-proof for the protection of our stores. When each Fullah stranger was presented, he shook hands and "snapped fingers" with the Mongo several times; and, as every petty peddler in the train wanted to *salaam* the "white man for good luck," the process of presentation occupied at least an hour.

According to coast-custom, as soon as these compliments were over, the caravan's merchandise was deposited within our walls, not only for security, but in order that we might gauge the *value of the welcome* the owners were entitled to receive. This precaution, though ungallant, is extremely necessary, inasmuch as many of the interior dealers were in the habit of declaring, on arrival, the value of their gold and ivory to be much greater than it was in fact, in order to receive a more liberal "present." Even savages instinctively acquire the tricks of trade!

When the goods were stored, a couple of fat bullocks, with an abundant supply of rice, were given to the visitors, and the chiefs of the caravan were billeted upon our townspeople. The *canaille* built temporary huts for themselves in the outskirts; while Ahmah-de-Bellah, a strict Mahometan, accompanied by two of his wives, was furnished with a pair of neat houses that had been hastily fitted up with new and elegant mats.*

While the merchandise of these large caravans is unpaid for, their owners, by the custom of the country, remain a costly burden upon the factories. We were naturally anxious to be free from this expense as soon as possible, and gave notice next morning that "trade would begin forthwith." Ahmah-de-Bellah, the chiefs of the caravans, and Mr. Ormond, at once entered into negotiations, so that by nightfall a bargain had been struck, not

---

* As it may be interesting to learn the nature of trade on this coast,— *which is commonly misunderstood as consisting in slaves alone,*—I thought it well to set down the inventory I made out of the caravan's stock and its result, as the various items were intrusted to my guardianship. The body

only for their presents, but for the price of merchandise, and the percentage to be retained as "native duty." Such a preliminary liquidation with *the heads* of a caravan is ever indispensable, for, without their assistance, it would be out of the question to traffic with the ragamuffins who hang on the skirts of opulent chieftains.

of the caravan itself consisted of seven hundred persons, principally men; while the produce was as follows:

| | |
|---|---|
| 3,500 hides . . . . . . . . . | $1,750 |
| 19 large and prime teeth of ivory, . . . | 1,560 |
| Gold, . . . . . . . . . | 2,500 |
| 600 pounds small ivory, . . . . | 320 |
| 15 tons of rice, . . . . . . . | 600 |
| 40 slaves, . . . . . . . . | 1,600 |
| 36 bullocks, . . . . . . . | 360 |
| Sheep, goats, butter, vegetables, . . | 100 |
| 900 pounds bees-wax, . . . . . | 95 |

Total value of the caravan's merchandise, . . $8,885.

Our profits on this speculation were very flattering, both as regards sales and acquisitions. Rice cost us one cent per pound; hides were delivered at eighteen or twenty cents each; a bullock was sold for twenty or thirty pounds of tobacco; sheep, goats or hogs, cost two pounds of tobacco, or a fathom of common cotton, each; ivory was purchased at the rate of a dollar the pound for the best, while inferior kinds were given at half that price. In fact, the profit on our merchandise was, at least, one hundred and fifty per cent. As gold commands the very best fabrics in exchange, and was paid for at the rate of sixteen dollars an ounce, we made but seventy per cent. on the article. The slaves were delivered at the rate of one hundred "*bars*" each. The "*bar*" is valued on the coast at half a dollar; but a pound and a half of tobacco is also a "bar," as well as a fathom of ordinary cotton cloth, or a pound of powder, while a common musket is equal to twelve "bars." Accordingly, where slaves were purchased for one hundred and fifty pounds of tobacco, only eighteen dollars were, in reality, paid; and when one hundred pounds of powder were given, we got them for twenty dollars each. Our *British* muskets cost us but three dollars a-piece; yet we seldom purchased negroes for this article alone. If the women, offered in the market, exceeded twenty-five years of age, we made a deduction of twenty per cent.; but if they were stanchly-built, and gave promising tokens for the future, we took them at the price of an able-bodied man. The same estimate was made for youths over four feet four inches high; but children were rarely purchased at the factories, though they might be advantageously traded in the native towns.

Each morning, at daylight, a crier went through the town, announcing the character of the specific trade which would be carried on during hours of business. One day it was in hides; another, rice; another, cattle. When these were disposed of, a time was specially appointed for the exchange of gold, ivory and slaves; and, at the agreed hour, Mr. Ormond, Ahmah-de-bellah, and myself, locked the doors of the warehouse, and traded through a window, while our "barkers" distributed the goods to the Africans, often using their whips to keep the chattering and disputatious scamps in order. Ahmah-de-bellah pretended to inspect the measurement of cloth, powder and tobacco, to insure justice to his compatriots; but, in reality, like a true tax-gatherer, he was busy ascertaining his lawful percentage on the sale, in return for the protection from robbery he gave the petty traders on their pilgrimage to the coast.

At length the market was cleared of sellers and merchandise—except the ostrich, which, when all was over, reached the Mongo's hands as a royal gift from the Ali-mami of Footha Yallon, the pious father of Ahmah-de-Bellah. The bird, it is true, was presented as a free offering; yet it was hinted that the worthy Ali stood in need of reliable muskets, which his son would take charge of on the journey home. As twenty of those warlike instruments were dispatched by Ahmah-de-Bellah, the ostrich became rather a costly as well as characteristic gift. Each of the traders, moreover, expected a "bungee" or "dash" of some sort, in token of good will, and in proportion to his sales; so that we hastened to comply with all the common-law customs of the country, in order to liberate Bangalang from the annoying crowd. They dropped off rapidly as they were paid; and in a short time Ahmah-de-Bellah, his wives, and immediate followers, were all that remained of the seven hundred Fullahs.

Ahmah-de-Bellah was a fine specimen of what may be considered "Young Africa," though he can hardly be classed among the progressives or revolutionary propagandists of the age. In person he was tall, graceful, and commanding. As the son of an important chief, he had been free from those menial toils which, in that climate, soon obliterate all intellectual characteristics. His face was well formed for an African's. His high and broad brow arched over a straight nose, while his lips had nothing of that vulgar grossness which gives so sensual an expression to his countrymen. Ahmah's manners to strangers or superiors were refined and courteous in a remarkable degree; but to the mob of the coast and inferiors generally, he manifested that harsh and peremptory tone which is common among the savages of a fiery clime.

Ahmah-de-Bellah was second son of the Ali-mami, or King of Footha-Yallon, who allowed him to exercise the prerogative of leading for the first time, a caravan to the seaboard, in honor of attaining the discreet age of " twenty four rainy seasons." The privilege however, was not granted without a view to profit by the courage of his own blood; for the Ali-mami was never known to suffer a son or relative to depart from his jurisdiction without a promise of *half* the products of the lucrative enter prise.

The formation of a caravan, when the king's permission has been finally secured, is a work of time and skill. At the beginning of the " dry season," the privileged chieftain departs with power of life and death over his followers, and " squats " in one of the most frequented " paths " to the sea, while he dispatches small bands of daring retainers to other trails throughout the neighborhood, to blockade every passage to the beach. The siege of the highways is kept up with vigor for a month or more, by these black Rob Roys and Robin Hoods, until a sufficient number of traders may be trapped to constitute a valuable caravan, and give importance to its leader. While this is the main purpose of the forest-adventure, the occasion is taken advantage of to collect a local tribute, due by small tribes to the Ali, which could not be obtained otherwise. The despotic officer, moreover, avails himself of the blockade to stop malefactors and absconding debtors. Goods that are seized in the possession of the latter may be sequestrated to pay his creditors; but if their value is not equal to the debt, the delinquent, if a pagan, is sold as a slave, but is let off with a *bastinado*, if he proves to be " one of the faithful."

It is natural to suppose that every effort is made by the small traders of the interior to avoid these savage press-gangs. The poor wretches are not only subjected to annoying vassalage by ruffian princes, but the blockade of the forest often diverts them from the point they originally designed to reach,—forces them to towns or factories they had no intention of visiting,— and, by extreme delay, wastes their provisions and diminishes their frugal profits. It is surprising to see how admirably even savages understand and exercise the powers of sovereignty and the rights of transit !

While Ahmah-de-Bellah tarried at Bangalang, it was my habit to visit him every night to hear his interesting chat, as it was translated by an interpreter. Sometimes, in return, I would recount the adventures of my sea-faring life, which seemed to have a peculiar flavor for this child of the wilderness, who now gazed for the first time on the ocean. Among other things, I strove to convince him of the world's rotundity ; but, to the last, he smiled incredulously at my daring assertion, and closed the argument by asking me to prove it from the Koran ? He allowed me the honors due a traveller and " book-man ; " but a mind that had swallowed, digested, and remembered every text of Mahomet's volume, was not to be deceived by such idle fantasies. He kindly undertook to conquer my ignorance of his creed by a careful exposition of its mysteries in several long-winded lectures, and I was so patient a listener, that I believe Ahmah was entirely satisfied of my conversion.

My seeming acquiescence was well repaid by the Fullah's confidence. He returned my nightly calls with interest; and, visiting me in the warehouse during hours of business, became so fervently wrapped up in my spiritual salvation, that he would spout Mahometanism for hours through an interpreter. To get rid of him, one day, I promised to follow the Prophet with pleasure if he consented to receive me; but I insisted on entering the " fold of the faithful " *without* submitting to the peculiar rite of Mussulman baptism !

Ahmah-de-Bellah took the jest kindly, laughing like a good

fellow, and from that day forward, we were sworn cronies. The Fullah at once wrote down a favorite prayer in Arabic, requiring as my spiritual guide, that I should commit it to memory for constant and ready use. After a day or two, he examined me in the ritual; but, finding I was at fault after the first sentence, reproached me pathetically upon my negligence and exhorted me to repentance,—much to the edification of our interpreter, who was neither Jew, Christian, nor Mussulman.

But the visit of the young chieftain, which began in trade and tapered off in piety, drew to a close. Ahmah-de-Bellah began to prepare for his journey homeward. As the day of departure approached, I saw that my joke had been taken seriously by the Fullah, and that he *relied* upon my apostasy. At the last moment, Ahmah tried to put me to a severe test, by suddenly producing the holy book, and requiring me to seal our friendship by an oath that I would never abandon Islamism. I contrived, however, adroitly to evade the affirmation by feigning an excessive anxiety to acquire more profound knowledge of the Koran, before I made so solemn a pledge.

It came to pass that, out of the forty slaves brought in the caravan, the Mongo rejected eight. After some altercation, Ahmah-de-Bellah consented to discard seven; but he insisted that the remaining veteran should be shipped, as he could neither *kill* nor send him back to Footha-Yallon.

I was somewhat curious to know the crime this culprit had committed, which was so heinous as to demand his perpetual exile, though it spared his life. The chief informed me that the wretch had slain his son; and, as there was no punishment for such an offence assigned by the Koran, the judges of his country condemned him to be sold *a slave to Christians*,—a penalty they considered worse than death.

Another curious feature of African law was developed in the sale of this caravan. I noticed a couple of women drawn along with ropes around their necks, while others of their sex and class were suffered to wander about without bonds. These females, the chief apprised us, would have been burnt in his father's domains for witchcraft, had not his venerable ancestor been so much distressed for powder that he thought their lives would be more valuable to his treasury than their carcasses to outraged law.

It was a general complaint among the companions of Ahmah-de-Bellah that the caravan was scant of slaves in consequence of this unfortunate lack of powder. The young chieftain promised better things in future. Next year, the Mongo's barracoons should teem with his conquests. When the "rainy season" approached, the Ali-mami, his father, meant to carry on a "great war" against a variety of small tribes, whose captives would replenish the herds, that, two years before, had been carried off by a sudden blight.

I learned from my intelligent Fullah, that while the Mahometan courts of his country rescued by law the people of their own faith from slavery, they omitted no occasion to inflict it, as a penalty, upon the African "unbelievers" who fell within their jurisdiction. Among these unfortunates, the smallest crime is considered capital, and a "capital crime" merits the profitable punishment of slavery. Nor was it difficult, he told me, for a country of "true believers" to acquire a multitude of bondsmen. They detested the institution, it is true, among themselves, and among their own caste, but it was both right and reputable among the unorthodox. The Koran commanded the "subjugation of the tribes to the true faith," so that, to enforce the Prophet's order against infidels, they resorted to the white man's cupidity, which authorized its votaries to enslave the negro! My inquisitiveness prompted me to demand whether these holy wars spoken of in the Koran were not somewhat stimulated, in our time, at least, by the profits that ensued; and I even ventured to hint that it was questionable whether the mighty chief of Footha-Yallon would willingly storm a Kaffir fortification, were he not prompted by the booty of slaves!

Ahmah-de-Bellah was silent for a minute, when his solemn face gradually relaxed into a quizzical smile, as he replied that, in truth, Mahometans were no worse than Christians, so that it was quite likely,—if the white elect of heaven, who knew how to make powder and guns, did not tempt the black man with their weapons,—the commands of Allah would be followed with less zeal, and implements not quite so dangerous !

I could not help thinking that there was a good deal of quiet satire in the gossip of this negro prince.  According to the cus- tom of his country, we " exchanged names " at parting ;  and, while he put in my pocket the gift of a well-thumbed *Koran*, I slung over his shoulder a *double-barrelled gun*.  We walked side by side for some miles into the forest, as he went forth from Bangalang ;  and as we " cracked fingers " for farewell, I prom- ised, with my hand on my heart, that the " next dry season " I would visit his father, the venerable Ali-mami, in his realm of Footha-Yallon.

# CHAPTER X.

I WAS a close watcher of Mongo John whenever he engaged in the purchase of slaves. As each negro was brought before him, Ormond examined the subject, without regard to sex, from head to foot. A careful manipulation of the chief muscles, joints, arm-pits and groins was made, to assure soundness. The mouth, too, was inspected, and if a tooth was missing, it was noted as a defect liable to deduction. Eyes, voice, lungs, fingers and toes were not forgotten; so that when the negro passed from the Mongo's hands without censure, he might' have been readily adopted as a good " life " by an insurance company.

Upon one occasion, to my great astonishment, I saw a stout and apparently powerful man discarded by Ormond as utterly worthless. His full muscles and sleek skin, to my unpractised eye, denoted the height of robust health. Still, I was told that he had been medicated for the market with bloating drugs, and sweated with powder and lemon-juice to impart a gloss to his skin. Ormond remarked that these jockey-tricks are as common in Africa as among horse-dealers in Christian lands; and desiring me to feel the negro's pulse, I immediately detected disease or excessive excitement. In a few days I found the poor wretch, abandoned by his owner, a paralyzed wreck in the hut of ˙ villager at Bangalang.

When a slave becomes useless to his master in the interior, or exhibits signs of failing constitution, he is soon disposed of to a peddler or broker. These men call to their aid a quack, familiar with drugs, who, for a small compensation, undertakes to refit an impaired body for the temptation of green-horns. Sometimes the cheat is successfully effected; but experienced slavers detect it readily by the yellow eye, swollen tongue, and feverish skin.

After a few more lessons, I was considered by the Mongo sufficiently learned in the slave traffic to be intrusted with the sole management of his stores. This exemption from commerce enabled him to indulge more than ever in the use of ardent spirits, though his vanity to be called "king," still prompted him to attend faithfully to all the "country palavers;"—and, let it be said to his credit, his decisions were never defective in judgment or impartiality.

After I had been three months occupied in the multifarious intercourse of Bangalang and its neighborhood, I understood the language well enough to dispense with the interpreter, who was one of the Mongo's confidential agents. When my companion departed on a long journey, he counselled me to make up with Unga-golah, the *harem's* cerberus, as she suspected my intimacy with Esther, who would doubtless be denounced to Ormond, unless I purchased the beldame's silence.

Indeed, ever since the night of warning, when the beautiful *quarteroon* visited my hovel, I had contrived to meet this charming girl, as the only solace of my solitude. Amid all the wild, passionate, and savage surroundings of Bangalang, Esther—the Pariah—was the only golden link that still seemed to bind me to humanity and the lands beyond the seas. On that burning coast, I was not excited by the stirring of an adventurous life, nor was my young heart seduced and bewildered by absorbing avarice. Many a night, when the dews penetrated my flesh, as I looked towards the west, my soul shrank from the selfish wretches around me, and went off in dreams to the homes I had abandoned. When I came back to myself,—when I was forced to recognize my doom in Africa,—when I acknowledged that my lot had been cast, perhaps unwisely, by myself, my spirit turned, like the worm from the crushing heel, and found nothing that kindled for me with the light of human sympathy, save this outcast girl. Esther was to me as a sister, and when the hint of her harm or loss was given, I hastened to disarm the only hand that could inflict a blow. Unga-golah was a woman, and a rope of sparkling coral for her neck, smothered all her wrongs.

The months I had passed in Africa without illness,—though I went abroad after dark, and bathed in the river during the heat of the day,—made me believe myself proof against malaria. But, at length, a violent pain in my loins, accompanied by a swimming head, warned me that the African fever held me in its dreaded gripe. In two days I was delirious. Ormond visited me; but I knew him not, and in my madness, called on Esther, accompanying the name with terms of endearment. This, I was told, stirred the surprise and jealousy of the Mongo, who forthwith assailed the matron of his harem with a torrent of inquiries and abuse. But Unga-golah was faithful. The beads had sealed her tongue; so that, with the instinctive adroitness peculiar to ladies of her color, she fabricated a story which not only quieted the Mongo, but added lustre to Esther's character.

The credulous old man finding Unga so well disposed towards his watchful clerk, restored the warehouse to her custody. This was the height of her avaricious ambition; and, in token of gratitude for my profitable malady, she contrived to let Esther become the nurse and guardian of my sick bed.

As my fever and delirium continued, a native doctor, renowned for his skill, was summoned, who ordered me to be cupped in the African fashion by scarifying my back and stomach with a hot knife, and applying plaintain leaves to the wounds. The operation allayed my pulse for a few hours; but as the fever came back with new vigor, it became necessary for my attendants to arouse the Mongo to a sense of my imminent danger. Yet Ormond, instead of springing with alacrity to succor a friend and retainer in affliction, sent for a young man, named Edward Joseph, who had formerly been in his employment, but was now settled on his own account in Bangalang.

Joseph proved a good Samaritan. As soon as he dared venture upon my removal, he took me to his establishment at Kambia, and engaged the services of another Mandingo doctor, in whose absurdities he believed. But all the charms and incantations of the savage would not avail, and I remained in a state of utter prostration and apparent insensibility until morning. As soon as day dawned, my faithful Esther was again on the field of action ; and this time she insisted upon the trial of her judgment, in the person of an old white-headed woman, who accompanied her in the guise of the greatest enchantress of the coast. A slave, paid in advance, was the fee for which she undertook to warrant my cure.

No time was to be lost. The floor of a small and close mud hut was intensely heated, and thickly strewn with moistened lemon leaves, over which a cloth was spread for a couch. As soon as the bed was ready, I was borne to the hovel, and, covered with blankets, was allowed to steam and perspire, while my medical attendant dosed me with half a tumbler of a green disgusting juice which she extracted from herbs. This process of drinking and barbecuing was repeated during five consecutive days, at he end of which my fever was gone. But my convalescence was not speedy. For many a day, I stalked about, a useless skeleton, quivering with ague, and afflicted by an insatiable appetite, until a French physician restored me to health by the use of cold baths at the crisis of my fever.

When I was sufficiently recovered to attend to business, Mongo John desired me to resume my position in his employment. I heard, however, from Esther, that during my illness, Unga-golah used her opportunities so profitably in the warehouse, that there would be sad deficiencies, which, doubtless, might be thrown on me, if the crone were badly disposed at any future period. Accordingly, I thought it decidedly most prudent to decline the clerkship, and requested the Mongo to recompense me for the time and attention I had already bestowed on him. This was refused by the indolent voluptuary ; so we parted with coolness, and I was once more adrift in the world.

In these great outlying colonies and lodgments of European nations in the East Indies and Africa, a stranger is commonly welcome to the hospitality of every foreigner. I had no hesitation, therefore, in returning to the house of Joseph, who, like myself, had been a clerk of Ormond, and suffered from the pilferings of the matron.

My host, I understood, was a native of London, where he was born of continental parents, and came to Sierra Leone with Governor Turner. Upon the death or return of that officer,—I do not recollect which,—the young adventurer remained in the colony, and, for a time, enjoyed the post of harbor master. His first visit to the Rio Pongo was in the capacity of supercargo of a small coasting craft, laden with valuable merchandise. Joseph succeeded in disposing of his wares, but was not equally fortunate in collecting their avails. It was, perhaps, an ill judged act of the supercargo, but he declined to face his creditors with a deficient balance-sheet; and quitting Sierra Leone for ever, accepted service with Ormond. For a year he continued in this employment; but, at the end of that period, considering himself sufficiently informed of the trade and language of the river, he sent a message to his creditors at the British settlement that he could promptly pay them in full, if they would advance him capital enough to commence an independent trade. The terms were accepted by an opulent Israelite, and in a short time Edward Joseph was numbered among the successful factors of Rio Pongo.

As I had nothing to do but get well and talk, I employed my entire leisure in acquiring the native language perfectly. The Soosoo is a dialect of the Mandingo. Its words, ending almost universally in vowels, render it as glibly soft and musical as Italian; so that, in a short time, I spoke it as fluently as my native tongue.

## CHAPTER XI.

THE 15th of March, 1827, was an epoch in my life. I remember it well, because it became the turning point of my destiny. A few weeks more of indolence might have forced me back to Europe or America, but the fortune of that day decided my residence and dealings in Africa.

At dawn of the 15th, a vessel was descried in the offing, and, as she approached the coast, the initiated soon ascertained her to be a Spanish slaver. But, what was the amazement of the river grandees when the captain landed and consigned his vessel *to me!*

"LA FORTUNA," the property, chiefly, of my old friend the Regla grocer, was successor of the Areostatico, which she exceeded in size as well as comfort. Her captain was charged to pay me my wages in full for the round voyage in the craft I had abandoned, and handed me, besides, a purse of thirty doubloons as a testimonial from his owners for my defence of their property on the dreadful night of our arrival. The "Fortuna" was dispatched to me for an "assorted cargo of slaves," while 200,000 cigars and 500 ounces of Mexican gold, were on board for their purchase. My commission was fixed at ten per cent., and I was promised a command whenever I saw fit to abandon my residence on the African coast.

Having no factory, or *barracoon* of slaves, and being elevated to the dignity of "a trader" in so sudden a manner, I thought it best to summon all the factors of the river on board the schooner, with an offer to divide the cargo, provided they would pledge the production of the slaves within thirty days. Dispatch was all-important to the owners, and, so anxious was I to gratify them, that I consented to pay fifty dollars for every slave that should be accepted.

After some discussion my offer was taken, and the cargo apportioned among the residents. They declined, however, receiving any share of the cigars in payment, insisting on liquidation in gold alone.

As this was my first enterprise, I felt at a loss to know how to convert my useless tobacco into merchantable doubloons. In this strait, I had recourse to the Englishman Joseph, who hitherto traded exclusively in produce; but, being unable to withstand the temptation of gold, had consented to furnish a portion of my required negroes. As soon as I stated the difficulty to Don Edward, he proposed to send the Havanas to his Hebrew friend in Sierra Leone, where, he did not doubt, they would be readily exchanged for Manchester merchandise. That evening a canoe was dispatched to the English colony with the cigars; and, on the tenth day after, the trusty Israelite appeared in the Rio Pongo, with a cutter laden to the deck with superior British fabrics. The rumor of five hundred doubloons disturbed his rest in Sierra Leone! So much gold could not linger in the hands of natives as long as Manchester and Birmingham were represented in the colony; and, accordingly, he coasted the edge of the surf, as rapidly as possible, to pay me a profit of four dollars a thousand for the cigars, and to take his chances at the exchange of my gold for the sable cargo! By this happy hit I was enabled to pay for the required balance of negroes, as well as to liquidate the schooner's expenses while in the river. I was amazingly rejoiced and proud at this happy result, because I learned from the captain that the invoice of cigars was a malicious trick, palmed off on the Areostatico's owners by her captain, in order to thwart or embarrass me, when he heard I was to be intrusted with the purchase of a cargo on the coast.

At the appointed day, La Fortuna sailed with 220 human beings packed in her hold. Three months afterwards, I received advices that she safely landed 217 in the bay of Matanzas, and that their sale yielded a clear profit on the voyage of forty-one thousand four hundred and thirty-eight dollars.*

* As the reader may scarcely credit so large a profit, I subjoin an account of the fitting of a slave vessel from Havana in 1827, and the liquidation of her voyage in Cuba:—

### 1.—EXPENSES OUT.

| | |
|---|---:|
| Cost of LA FORTUNA, a 90 ton schooner, . . . | $3,700 00 |
| Fitting out, sails, carpenter and cooper's bills, . | 2,500 00 |
| Provisions for crew and slaves, . . . . | 1,115 00 |
| Wages advanced to 18 men before the mast, . | 900 00 |
| "      "      to captain, mates, boatswain, cook, and steward, . . . . } | 440 00 |
| 200,000 cigars and 500 doubloons, cargo, . . | 10,900 00 |
| Clearance and hush-money, . . . . . | 200 00 |
| | $19,755 00 |
| Commission at 5 per cent,, . . . . . | 987 00 |
| Full cost of voyage out, . . . . | $20,742 00 |

### 2.—EXPENSES HOME.

| | |
|---|---:|
| Captain's head-money, at $8 a head, . . . | 1,746 00 |
| Mate's      "      $4   "   . . . . | 873 00 |
| Second mate and boatswain's head-money, at $2 each a head, . . . . . . . . } | 873 00 |
| Captain's wages, . . . . . . | 219 78 |
| First mate's wages, . . . . . . | 175 56 |
| Second mate and boatswain's wages, . . . | 307 12 |
| Cook and steward's wages, . . . . . | 264 00 |
| Eighteen sailors' wages, . . . . . . | 1,972 00 |
| | $27,172 46 |

### 3.—EXPENSES IN HAVANA.

| | |
|---|---:|
| Government officers, at $8 per head, . . . | 1,736 00 |
| My commission on 217 slaves, expenses off, . . | 5,565 00 |
| Consignees' commissions, . . . . . | 3,873 00 |
| 217 slave dresses, at $2 each, . . . . | 634 00 |
| Extra expenses of all kinds, say, . . . | 1,000 00 |
| Total expenses, . . . . . | $39,980 46 |

### 4.—RETURNS.

| | |
|---|---:|
| Value of vessel at auction, . . . . . | $3,950 00 |
| Proceeds of 217 slaves, . . . . . | 77,469 00 |
| | $81,419 00 |

### RESUMÉ.

| | |
|---|---:|
| Total Returns, . . . . . | $81,419 00 |
| "    Expenses, . . . . . | 39,980 46 |
| Nett profit, . . . | $41,438 54 |

As I am now fairly embarked in a trade which absorbed so many of my most vigorous years, I suppose the reader will not be loth to learn a little of my experience in the alleged " cruelties " of this commerce ; and the first question, in all likelihood, that rises to his lips, is a solicitation to be apprised of the embarkation and treatment of slaves on the dreaded voyage.

An African factor of fair repute is ever careful to select his human cargo with consummate prudence, so as not only to supply his employers with athletic laborers, but to avoid any taint of disease that may affect the slaves in their transit to Cuba or the American main. Two days before embarkation, the head of every male and female is neatly shaved; and, if the cargo belongs to several owners, each man's *brand* is impressed on the body of his respective negro. This operation is performed with pieces of silver wire, or small irons fashioned into the merchant's initials, heated just hot enough to blister without burning the skin. When the entire cargo is the venture of but one proprietor, the branding is always dispensed with.

On the appointed day, the *barracoon* or slave-pen is made joyous by the abundant " feed " which signalizes the negro's last hours in his native country. The feast over, they are taken alongside the vessel in canoes ; and as they touch the deck, they are entirely stripped, so that women as well as men go out of Africa as they came into it—*naked*. This precaution, it will be understood, is indispensable; for perfect nudity, during the whole voyage, is the only means of securing cleanliness and health. In this state, they are immediately ordered below, the men to the hold and the women to the cabin, while boys and girls are, day and night, kept on deck, where their sole protection from the elements is a sail in fair weather, and a *tarpaulin* in foul.

At meal time they are distributed in messes of ten. Thirty years ago, when the Spanish slave trade was lawful, the captains were somewhat more ceremoniously religious than at present, and it was then a universal habit to make the gangs say grace before meat, and give thanks afterwards. In our days, however, they dispense with this ritual, and content themselves with a " *Viva la Habana*," or " hurrah for Havana," accompanied by a clapping of hands.

BRANDING A NEGRESS.

This over, a bucket of salt water is served to each mess, by way of " finger glasses " for the ablution of hands, after which a *kidd*,—either of rice, farina, yams, or beans,—according to the tribal habit of the negroes, is placed before the squad. In order to prevent greediness or inequality in the appropriation of nourishment, the process is performed by signals from a monitor, whose motions indicate when the darkies shall dip and when they shall swallow.

It is the duty of a guard to report immediately whenever a slave refuses to eat, in order that his abstinence may be traced to stubbornness or disease. Negroes have sometimes been found in slavers who attempted voluntary starvation; so that, when the watch reports the patient to be "shamming," his appetite is stimulated by the medical antidote of a "cat." If the slave, however, is truly ill, he is forthwith ticketed for the sick-list by a bead or button around his neck, and dispatched to an infirmary in the forecastle.

These meals occur twice daily,—at ten in the morning and four in the afternoon,—and are terminated by another ablution. Thrice in each twenty-four hours they are served with half a pint of water. Pipes and tobacco are circulated economically among both sexes; but, as each negro cannot be allowed the luxury of a separate bowl, boys are sent round with an adequate supply, allowing a few whiffs to each individual. On regular days,— probably three times a week,—their mouths are carefully rinsed with vinegar, while, nearly every morning, a dram is given as an antidote to scurvy.

Although it is found necessary to keep the sexes apart, they are allowed to converse freely during day while on deck. Corporal punishment is *never* inflicted save by order of an officer, and, even then, not until the culprit understands exactly why it is done. Once a week, the ship's barber scrapes their chins without assistance from soap; and, on the same day, their nails are closely pared, to insure security from harm in those nightly battles that occur, when the slave contests with his neighbor every inch of plank to which he is glued. During afternoons of serene weather, men, women, girls, and boys are allowed to unite in African melodies, which they always enhance by an extemporaneous *tom-tom* on the bottom of a tub or tin kettle.

These hints will apprise the reader that the greatest care, compatible with safety, is taken of a negro's health and cleanliness on the voyage. In every well-conducted slaver, the captain, officers, and crew, are alert and vigilant to preserve the cargo. It is their personal interest, as well as the interest of humanity to do so. The boatswain is incessant in his patrol of purification, and disinfecting substances are plenteously distributed. The upper deck is washed and swabbed daily; the slave deck is scraped and holy-stoned; and, at nine o'clock each morning, the captain inspects every part of his craft; so that no vessel, except a man-of-war, can compare with a slaver in systematic order, purity, and neatness. I am not aware that the ship-fever, which sometimes decimates the emigrants from Europe, has ever prevailed in these African traders.

At sundown, the process of stowing the slaves for the night is begun. The second mate and boatswain descend into the hold, whip in hand, and range the slaves in their regular places; those on the right side of the vessel facing forward, and lying in each other's lap, while those on the left are similarly stowed with their faces towards the stern. In this way each negro lies on his right side, which is considered preferable for the action of the heart. In allotting places, particular attention is paid to size, the taller being selected for the greatest breadth of the vessel, while the shorter and younger are lodged near the bows. When the cargo is large and the lower deck crammed, the supernumeraries are disposed of on deck, which is securely covered with boards to shield them from moisture. The *strict* discipline of nightly stowage is, of course, of the greatest importance in slavers, else every negro would accommodate himself as if he were a passenger.

In order to insure perfect silence and regularity during night, a slave is chosen as constable from every ten, and furnished with a "cat" to enforce commands during his appointed watch. In remuneration for his services, which, it may be believed, are admirably performed whenever the whip is required, he is adorned with an old shirt or tarry trowsers. Now and then, billets of wood are distributed among the sleepers, but this luxury is never granted until the good temper of the negroes is ascertained, for slaves have often been tempted to mutiny by the power of arming themselves with these pillows from the forest.

It is very probable that many of my readers will consider it barbarous to make slaves lie down naked upon a board, but let me inform them that native Africans are not familiar with the use of feather-beds, nor do any but the free and rich in their mother country indulge in the luxury even of a mat or raw-hide. Among the Mandingo chiefs,—the most industrious and civilized of Africans,—the beds, divans, and sofas, are heaps of mud, covered with untanned skins for cushions, while logs of wood serve for bolsters ! I am of opinion, therefore, that emigrant slaves experience very slight inconvenience in lying down on the deck.

But *ventilation* is carefully attended to. The hatches and bulkheads of every slaver are grated, and apertures are cut about the deck for ampler circulation of air. Wind-sails, too, are constantly pouring a steady draft into the hold, except during a chase, when, of course, every comfort is temporarily sacrificed for safety. During calms or in light and baffling winds, when the suffocating air of the tropics makes ventilation impossible, the gratings are always removed, and portions of the slaves allowed to repose at night on deck, while the crew is armed to watch the sleepers.

Handcuffs are rarely used on shipboard. It is the common custom to secure slaves in the *barracoons*, and while shipping, by chaining *ten* in a gang ; but as these platoons would be extremely inconvenient at sea, the manacles are immediately taken off and replaced by leg-irons, which fasten them in pairs by the feet. Shackles are never used but for *full-grown men*, while *women* and *boys* are set at liberty as soon as they embark. It frequently happens that when the behavior of *male* slaves warrants their freedom, they are released from all fastenings long before they arrive. Irons are altogether dispensed with on many *Brazilian* slavers, as negroes from Anjuda, Benin, and Angola, are mild; and unaddicted to revolt like those who dwell east of the Cape or north of the Gold Coast. Indeed, a knowing trader will never use chains but when compelled, for the longer a slave is ironed the more he deteriorates ; and, as his sole object is to land a healthy cargo, pecuniary interest, as well as natural feeling, urges the sparing of metal.

My object in writing this palliative description is not to exculpate the slavers or their commerce, but to correct those exaggerated stories which have so long been current in regard to the *usual* voyage of a trader. I have always believed that the cause of humanity, as well as any other cause, was least served by over-statement; and I am sure that if the narratives given by Englishmen are true, the voyages they detail must either have occurred before my day, or were conducted in British vessels, while her majesty's subjects still considered the traffic lawful.*

* The treaty with Spain, which was designed by Great Britain to end the slave trade, failed utterly to produce the desired result.

All *profitable* trade,—illicit, contraband, or what not,—*will* be carried on by avaricious men, as long as the temptation continues. Accordingly, whenever a trade becomes *forced*, the only and sure result of violent restriction is to imperil still more both life and cargo.

1st.—The treaty with Spain, it is said, was enforced some time before it was properly promulgated or notified ; so that British cruisers seized over eighty vessels, one third of which certainly were not designed for slave-trade.

2d.—As the compact condemned slave vessels to be broken up, the sailing qualities of craft were improved to facilitate escape, rather than insure human comfort.

3d.—The Spanish slavers had recourse to Brazilians and Portuguese to cover their property ; and, as slavers could not be fitted out in Cuba, other nations sent their vessels ready equipped to Africa, and (under the jib-booms of cruisers) Sardinians, Frenchmen and Americans, transferred them to slave traders, while the captains and parts of the crew took passage home in regular merchantmen.

4th.—As the treaty created greater risk, every method of economy was resorted to ; and the crowding and cramming of slaves was one of the most prominent results. Water and provisions were diminished; and every thing was sacrificed for gain.

# CHAPTER XII.

In old times, before treaties made slave-trade piracy, the landing of human cargoes was as comfortably conducted as the disembarkation of flour. But now, the enterprise is effected with secrecy and hazard. A wild, uninhabited portion of the coast, where some little bay or sheltering nook exists, is commonly selected by the captain and his confederates. As soon as the vessel is driven close to the beach and anchored, her boats are packed with slaves, while the craft is quickly dismantled to avoid detection from sea or land. The busy skiffs are hurried to and fro incessantly till the cargo is entirely ashore, when the secured gang, led by the captain, and escorted by armed sailors, is rapidly marched to the nearest plantation. There it is safe from the rapacity of local magistrates, who, if they have a chance, imitate their superiors by exacting "*gratifications.*"

In the mean time, a *courier* has been dispatched to the owners in Havana, Matanzas, or Santiago de Cuba, who immediately post to the plantation with clothes for the slaves and gold for the crew. Preparations are quickly made through brokers for the sale of the blacks; while the vessel, if small, is disguised, to warrant her return under the coasting flag to a port of clearance. If the craft happens to be large, it is considered perilous to attempt a return with a cargo, or "*in distress,*" and, accordingly, she is either sunk or burnt where she lies.

When the genuine African reaches a plantation for the first time, he fancies himself in paradise. He is amazed by the generosity with which he is fed with fruit and fresh provisions. His new clothes, red cap, and roasting blanket (a civilized superfluity he never dreamed of), strike him dumb with delight, and, in his savage joy, he not only forgets country, relations, and friends, but skips about like a monkey, while he dons his garments wrongside out or hind-part before! The arrival of a carriage or cart creates no little confusion among the Ethiopian groups, who never imagined that beasts could be made to work. But the climax of wonder is reached when that paragon of oddities, a Cuban *postilion*, dressed in his sky-blue coat, silver-laced hat, white breeches, polished jack-boots, and ringing spurs, leaps from his prancing quadruped, and bids them welcome in their mother tongue. Every African rushes to " snap fingers " with his equestrian brother, who, according to orders, forthwith preaches an edifying sermon on the happiness of being a white man's slave, taking care to jingle his spurs and crack his whip at the end of every sentence, by way of *amen*.

Whenever a cargo is owned by several proprietors, each one takes his share at once to his plantation; but if it is the property of speculators, the blacks are sold to any one who requires them before removal from the original depot. The sale is, of course, conducted as rapidly as possible, to forestall the inter-ference of British officials with the Captain-General.

Many of the Spanish Governors in Cuba have respected treaties, or, at least, promised to enforce the laws. Squadrons of dragoons and troops of lancers have been paraded with convenient delay, and ordered to gallop to plantations designated by the representative of England. It generally happens, however, that when the hunters arrive the game is gone. Scandal declares that, while brokers are selling the blacks at the depot, it is not unusual for their owner or his agent to be found knocking at the door of the Captain-General's secretary. It is often said that the Captain-General himself is sometimes present in the sanctuary, and, after a familiar chat about the happy landing of " the contraband,"—as the traffic is amiably called,

the requisite *rouleaux* are insinuated into the official desk under
the intense smoke of a fragrant *cigarillo*.   The metal is always
considered the property of the Captain-General, but his scribe
avails himself of a lingering farewell at the door, to hint an
immediate and pressing need for " a very small darkey ! "   Next
day, the diminutive African does not appear; but, as it is believed that Spanish officials prefer gold even to mortal flesh, his
algebraic equivalent is unquestionably furnished in the shape of
shining ounces !

The prompt dispatch I gave the schooner Fortuna, started
new ideas among the traders of the Rio Pongo, so that it was
generally agreed my method of dividing the cargo among different factors was not only most advantageous for speed, but prevented monopoly, and gave all an equal chance.   At a " grand
palaver " or assemblage of the traders on the river, it was resolved that this should be the course of trade for the future.
All the factors, except Ormond, attended and assented ; but
we learned that the Mongo's people, with difficulty prevented
him from sending an armed party to break up our deliberations.

The knowledge of this hostile feeling soon spread throughout
the settlement and adjacent towns, creating considerable excitement against Ormond.   My plan and principles were approved
by the natives as well as foreigners, so that warning was sent
the Mongo, if any harm befell Joseph and Theodore, it would
be promptly resented.   Our native landlord, Ali-Ninpha, a
Foulah by descent, told him boldly, in presence of his people,
that the Africans were " tired of a mulatto Mongo ; " and, from
that day, his power dwindled away visibly, though a show of
respect was kept up in consequence of his age and ancient importance.

During these troubles, the Areostatico returned to my consignment, and in twenty-two days was dispatched with a choice
cargo of Mandingos,—a tribe, which had become fashionable for
house servants among the Havanese.   But the luckless vessel
was never heard of, and it is likely she went down in some of
the dreadful gales that scourged the coast immediately after her
departure.

## CHAPTER XIII.

I HAD now grown to such sudden importance among the natives, that the neighboring chiefs and kings sent me daily messages of friendship, with trifling gifts that I readily accepted. One of these bordering lords, more generous and insinuating than the rest, hinted several times his anxiety for a closer connection in affection as well as trade, and, at length, insisted upon becoming my father-in-law!

I had always heard in Italy that it was something to receive the hand of a princess, even after long and tedious wooing; but now that I was surrounded by a mob of kings, who absolutely thrust their daughters on me, I confess I had the bad taste not to leap with joy at the royal offering. Still, I was in a difficult position, as no graver offence can be given a chief than to reject his child. It is so serious an insult to refuse a wife, that, high born natives, in order to avoid quarrels or war, accept the tender boon, and as soon as etiquette permits, pass it over to a friend or relation. As the offer was made to me personally by the king, I found the utmost difficulty in escaping. Indeed, he would receive no excuse. When I declined on account of the damsel's youth, he laughed incredulously. If I urged the feebleness of my health and tardy convalescence, he insisted that a regular life of matrimony was the best cordial for an impaired constitution. In fact, the paternal solicitude of his majesty for my doubloons

was so urgent that I was on the point of yielding myself a
patient sacrifice, when Joseph came to my relief with the offer
of his hand as a substitute.

The Gordian knot was cut. Prince Yungee in reality did not
care so much who should be his son-in-law as that he obtained
one with a white skin and plentiful purse. Joseph or Theodore,
Saxon or Italian, made no difference to the chief; and, as is the
case in all Oriental lands, the opinion of the lady was of no importance whatever.

I cannot say that my partner viewed this matrimonial project with the disgust that I did. Perhaps he was a man of
more liberal philosophy and wider views of human brotherhood;
at any rate, his residence in Africa gave him a taste not only for
its people, habits, and superstitions, but he upheld practical
amalgamation with more fervor and honesty than a regular
abolitionist. Joseph was possessed by Africo-mania. He admired the women, the men, the language, the cookery, the music.
He would fall into philharmonic ecstasies over the discord of a
bamboo *tom-tom*. I have reason to believe that even African
barbarities had charms for the odd Englishman; but he was
chiefly won by the *dolce far niente* of the natives, and the Oriental
license of polygamy. In a word, Joseph had the same taste for a
full-blooded *cuffee*, that an epicure has for the *haut gout* of a
stale partridge, and was in ecstasies at my extrication. He neglected his *siestas* and his accounts; he wandered from house to
house with the rapture of an impatient bridegroom; and, till
every thing was ready for the nuptial rites, no one at the factory
had a moment's rest.

As the bride's relations were eminent folks on the upper part
of the river, they insisted that the marriage ceremony should be
performed with all the honorable formalities due to the lady's
rank. Esther, who acted as my mentor in every " country-ques-
tion," suggested that it would be contrary to the Englishman's
interest to ally himself with a family whose only motive was sor-
did. She strongly urged that if he persisted in taking the girl,
he should do so without a " *colungee*," or ceremonial feast. But
Joseph was obstinate as a bull; and as he doubted whether he

would ever commit matrimony again, he insisted that the nuptials should be celebrated with all the fashionable splendor of
high life in Africa.

When this was decided, it became necessary, by a fiction
of etiquette, to ignore the previous offer of the bride, and to
begin anew, as if the damsel were to be sought in the most delicate way by a desponding lover. She must be demanded formally, by the bridegroom from her reluctant mother; and accordingly, the most respectable matron in our colony was chosen by
Joseph from his colored acquaintances to be the bearer of his
valentine. In the present instance, the selected Cupid was the
principal wife of our native landlord, Ali-Ninpha; and, as Africans as well as Turks love by the pound, the dame happened to
be one of the fattest, as well as most respectable, in our parish.
Several female *attachés* were added to the suite of the ambassadress, who forthwith departed to make a proper "*dantica.*"
The gifts selected were of four kinds. First of all, two demijohns of *trade*-rum were filled to gladden the community of Mongo-Yungee's town. Next, a piece of blue cotton cloth, a musket,
a keg of powder, and a demijohn of *pure* rum, were packed for
papa. Thirdly, a youthful virgin dressed in a white "tontongee,"[1] a piece of white cotton cloth, a white basin, a white sheep,
and a basket of white rice, were put up for mamma, in token of her
daughter's purity. And, lastly, a German looking-glass, several
bunches of beads, a coral necklace, a dozen of turkey-red handkerchiefs, and a spotless white country-cloth, were presented to
the bride; together with a decanter of white palm oil for the
anointment of her ebony limbs after the bath, which is never neglected by African *belles*.

While the missionary of love was absent, our sighing swain
devoted his energies to the erection of a bridal palace; and the
task required just as many days as were employed in the creation of the world. The building was finished by the aid of bam-

---

[1] A *tontongee* is a strip of white cotton cloth, three inches wide and
four feet long, used as a *virgin African's only dress*. It is wound round
the limbs, and, hanging partly in front and partly behind, is supported
from the maiden's waist by strands of *showee-beads*.

boos, straw, and a modicum of mud; and, as Joseph imagined that love and coolness were secured in such a climate by utter darkness, he provided an abundance of that commodity by omitting windows entirely. The furnishing of the domicil was completed with all the luxury of native taste. An elastic four-poster was constructed of bamboos; some dashing crockery was set about the apartment for display; a cotton quilt was cast over the matted couch; an old trunk served for bureau and wardrobe; and, as negresses adore looking-glasses, the largest in our warehouse was nailed against the door, as the only illuminated part of the edifice.

At last all was complete, and Joseph snapped his fingers with delight, when the corpulent dame waddled up asthmatically, and announced with a wheeze that her mission was prosperous. If there had ever been doubt, there was now no more. The oracular " *feitich* " had announced that the delivery of the bride to her lord might take place " on the tenth day of the new moon."

As the planet waxed from its slender sickle to the thicker quarter, the impatience of my Cockney waxed with it; but, at length, the firing of muskets, the twang of horns, and the rattle of tom-toms, gave notice from the river that COOMBA, the bride, was approaching the quay. Joseph and myself hastily donned our clean shirts, white trousers, and glistening pumps; and, under the shade of broad *sombreros* and umbrellas, proceeded to greet the damsel. Our fat friend, the matron; Ali-Ninpha, her husband; our servants, and a troop of village ragamuffins, accompanied us to the water's brink, so that we were just in time to receive the five large canoes bearing the escort of the king and his daughter. Boat after boat disgorged its passengers; but, to our dismay, they ranged themselves apart, and were evidently displeased. When the last canoe, decorated with flags, containing the bridal party, approached the strand, the chief of the escort signalled it to stop and forbade the landing.

In a moment there was a general row—a row, conceivable only by residents of Africa, or those whose ears have been regaled with the chattering of a " wilderness of monkeys." Our lusty *factotum* was astonished. The Cockney aspirated his *h's* with uncommon volubility. We hastened from one to the other to inquire the cause ; nor was it until near half an hour had been wasted in palaver, that I found they considered themselves slighted, first of all because we had not fired a salvo in their honor, and secondly because we failed to spread mats from the beach to the house, upon which the bride might place her virgin feet without defilement ! These were indispensable formalities among the " upper ten ; " and the result was that COOMBA could not land unless the etiquette were fulfilled.

Here, then, was a sad dilemma. The guns could be fired instantly ;—but where, alas ! at a moment's notice, were we to obtain mats enough to carpet the five hundred yards of transit from the river to the house ? The match must be broken off !

My crest-fallen cockney immediately began to exculpate himself by pleading ignorance of the country's customs,—assuring the strangers that he had not the slightest inkling of the requirement. Still, the stubborn " master of ceremonies " would not relax an iota of his rigorous behests.

At length, our bulky dame approached the master of the bridal party, and, squatting on her knees, confessed her neglectful fault. Then, for the first time, I saw a gleam of hope. Joseph improved the moment by alleging that he employed this lady patroness to conduct every thing in the sublimest style imaginable, because it was presumed no one knew better than she all that was requisite for so admirable and virtuous a lady as COOMBA. Inasmuch, however, as he had been disappointed by her unhappy error, he did not think the blow should fall on *his* shoulders. The negligent matron ought to pay the penalty; and, as it was impossible now to procure the mats, she should forfeit the value of a slave to aid the merry-making, *and carry the bride on her back from the river to her home !*

A clapping of hands and a quick murmur of assent ran through the crowd, telling me that the compromise was accepted. But the porterage was no sinecure for the delinquent elephant, who found it difficult at times to get along over African sands even without a burden. Still, no time was lost in further parley or remonstrance. The muskets and cannon were brought down and exploded; the royal boat was brought to the landing; father, mother, brothers, and relations were paraded on the strand; tom-toms and horns were beaten and blown; and, at last, the suffering missionary waddled to the canoe to receive the veiled form of the slender bride.

The process of removal was accompanied by much merriment. Our corpulent porter groaned as she "larded the lean earth" beneath her ponderous tread; but, in due course of labor and patience, she sank with her charge on the bamboo couch of Master Joseph.

As soon as the bearer and the burden were relieved from their fatigue, the maiden was brought to the door, and, as her long concealing veil of spotless cotton was unwrapped from head and limbs, a shout of admiration went up from the native crowd that followed us from the quay to the hovel. As Joseph received the hand of COOMBA, he paid the princely fee of a slave to the matron.

COOMBA had certainly not numbered more than sixteen years, yet, in that burning region, the sex ripen long before their pallid sisters of the North. She belonged to the Soosoo tribe, but was descended from Mandingo ancestors, and I was particularly struck by the uncommon symmetry of her tapering limbs. Her features and head, though decidedly African, were not of that coarse and heavy cast that marks the lineaments of her race. The grain of her shining skin was as fine and polished as ebony. A melancholy languor subdued and deepened the blackness of her large eyes, while her small and even teeth gleamed with the brilliant purity of snow. Her mouth was rosy and even delicate; and, indeed, had not her ankles, feet, and wool, manifested the unfortunate types of her kindred, COOMBA, the daughter of Mongo-Yungee, might have passed for a *chef d'œuvre in black marble.*

The scant dress of the damsel enabled me to be so minute in this catalogue of her charms; and, in truth, had I not inspected them closely, I would have violated matrimonial etiquette as much as if I failed to admire the *trousseau* and gifts of a bride at home. Coomba's costume was as innocently primitive as Eve's after the expulsion. Like all maidens of her country, she had beads round her ankles, beads round her waist, beads round her neck, while an abundance of bracelets hooped her arms from wrist to elbow. The white *tontongee* still girdled her loins; but Coomba's climate was her mantuamaker, and indicated more necessity for ornament than drapery. Accordingly, Coomba was obedient to Nature, and troubled herself very little about a supply of useless garments, to load the presses and vex the purse of her bridegroom.

As soon as the process of unveiling was over, and time had been allowed the spectators to behold the damsel, her mother led her gently to the fat ambassadress, who, with her companions, bore the girl to a bath for ablution, anointment, and perfuming. While Coomba underwent this ceremony at the hands of our matron, flocks of sable dames entered the apartment; and, as they withdrew, shook hands with her mother, in token of the maiden's purity, and with the groom in compliment to his luck.

As soon as the bath and *oiling* were over, six girls issued from the hut, bearing the glistening bride on a snow-white sheet to the home of her spouse. The transfer was soon completed, and the burden deposited on the nuptial bed. The dwelling was then closed and put in charge of sentinels; when the plump plenipotentiary approached the Anglo-Saxon, and handing him the scant fragments of the bridal dress, pointed to the door, and, in a loud voice, exclaimed : " White man, this authorizes you to take possession of your wife ! "

It may naturally be supposed that our radiant cockney was somewhat embarrassed by so public a display of matrimonial happiness, at six o'clock in the afternoon, on the thirtieth day of a sweltering June. Joseph could not help looking at me with a blush and a laugh, as he saw the eyes of the whole crowd fixed on his movements ; but, nerving himself like a man, he made a profound *salaam* to the admiring multitude, and shaking my hand with a convulsive grip, plunged into the darkness of his abode. A long pole was forthwith planted before the door, and a slender strip of white cotton, about the size of a "*tontongee*," was hoisted in token of privacy, and floated from the staff like a pennant, giving notice that the commodore is aboard.

No sooner were these rites over, than the house was surrounded by a swarm of women from the adjacent villages, whose incessant songs, screams, chatter, and *tom-tom* beatings, drowned every mortal sound. Meanwhile, the men of the party—whose merriment around an enormous *bonfire* was augmented by abundance of liquor and provisions—amused themselves in dancing, shouting, yelling, and discharging muskets in honor of the nuptials.

Such was the ceaseless serenade that drove peace from the lovers' pillow during the whole of that memorable night. At dawn, the corpulent matron again appeared from among the wild and reeling crowd, and concluding her functions by some mysterious ceremonies, led forth the lank groom from the dark cavity of his hot and sleepless oven, looking more like a bewildered wretch rescued from drowning, than a radiant lover fresh from his charmer. In due time, the bride also was brought forth by the matrons for the bath, where she was anointed from head to foot with a vegetable butter,—whose odor is probably more agreeable to Africans than Americans,—and fed with a bowl of broth made from a young and tender pullet.

The marriage *fêtes* lasted three days, after which I insisted that Joseph should give up nonsense for business, and sobered his ecstasies by handing him a wedding-bill for five hundred and fifty dollars.

There is hardly a doubt that he considered COOMBA very *dear*, if not absolutely adorable!

# CHAPTER XIV.

I AM sorry to say that my colleague's honeymoon did not last long, although it was not interrupted by domestic discord. One of his malicious Sierra Leone creditors, who had not been dealt with quite as liberally as the rest, called on the colonial governor of that British establishment, and alleged that a certain Edward Joseph, an Englishman, owned a factory on the Rio Pongo, in company with a Spaniard, and was engaged in the slave trade!

At this the British lion, of course, growled in his African cage, and bestirred himself to punish the recreant cub. An expedition was forthwith fitted out to descend upon our little establishment; and, in all likelihood, the design would have been executed, had not our friendly Israelite in Sierra Leone sent us timely warning. No sooner did the news arrive than Joseph embarked in a slaver, and, packing up his valuables, together with sixty negroes, fled from Africa. His disconsolate bride was left to return to her parents.

As the hostile visit from the British colony was hourly expected, I did not tarry long in putting a new face on Kambia. Fresh books were made out in my name exclusively; their dates were carefully suited to meet all inquiries; and the townspeople were prepared to answer impertinent questions; so that, when Lieutenant Findlay, of Her Britannic Majesty's naval service, made his appearance in the river, with three boats bearing the cross of St. George, no man in the settlement was less anxious than Don Téodore, the *Spaniard*.

When the lieutenant handed me an order from the governor of Sierra Leone and its dependencies, authorizing him to burn or destroy the property of Joseph, as well as to arrest that personage himself, I regretted that I was unable to facilitate his patriotic projects, inasmuch as the felon was afloat on salt water, while all his property had long before been conveyed to me by a regular bill of sale. In proof of my assertions, I produced the instrument and the books; and when I brought in our African landlord to sustain me in every particular, the worthy lieutenant was forced to relinquish his hostility and accept an invitation to dinner. His conduct during the whole investigation was that of a gentleman; which, I am sorry to say, was not always the case with his professional countrymen.

During the rainy season, which begins in June and lasts till October, the stores of provisions in establishments along the Atlantic coast often become sadly impaired. The Foulah and Mandingo tribes of the interior are prevented by the swollen condition of intervening streams from visiting the beach with their produce. In these straits, the factories have recourse by canoes to the smaller rivers, which are neither entered by sea-going vessels, nor blockaded for the caravans of interior chiefs.

Among the tribes or clans visited by me in such seasons, I do not remember any whose intercourse afforded more pleasure, or exhibited nobler traits, than the BAGERS, who dwell on the solitary margins of these shallow rivulets, and subsist by boiling salt in the dry season and making palm oil in the wet. I have never read an account of these worthy blacks, whose civility, kindness, and honesty will compare favorably with those of more civilized people.

The Bagers live very much apart from the great African tribes, and keep up their race by intermarriage. The language is peculiar, and altogether devoid of that Italian softness that makes the Soosoo so musical.

Having a week or two of perfect leisure, I determined to set out in a canoe to visit one of these establishments, especially as no intelligence had reached me for some time from one of my country traders who had been dispatched thither with an invoice of goods to purchase palm oil. My canoe was comfortably fitted with a water-proof awning, and provisioned for a week.

A tedious pull along the coast and through the dangerous surf, brought us to the narrow creek through whose marshy mesh of *mangroves* we squeezed our canoe to the bank. Even after landing, we waded a considerable distance through marsh before we reached the solid land. The Bager town stood some hundred yards from the landing, at the end of a desolate savanna, whose lonely waste spread as far as the eye could reach. The village itself seemed quite deserted, so that I had difficulty in finding " the oldest inhabitant," who invariably stays at home and acts the part of chieftain. This venerable personage welcomed me with great cordiality ; and, having made my *dantica*, or, in other words, declared the purpose of my visit, I desired to be shown the trader's house. The patriarch led me at once to a hut, whose miserable thatch was supported by four posts. Here I recognized a large chest, a rum cask, and the grass hammock of my agent. I was rather exasperated to find my property thus neglected and exposed, and began venting my wrath in no seemly terms on the delinquent clerk, when my conductor laid his hand gently on my sleeve, and said there was no need to blame him. " This," continued he, "is his house ; here your property is sheltered from sun and rain ; and, among the Bagers, whenever your goods are protected from the elements, they are safe from every danger. Your man has gone across the plain to a neighboring town for oil ; to-night he will be back ;—in the mean time, look at your goods ! "

I opened the chest, which, to my surprise, was unlocked, and found it nearly full of the merchandise I had placed in it. I shook the cask, and its weight seemed hardly diminished. I turned the spiggot, and lo ! the rum trickled on my feet,

Hard-by was a temporary shed, filled to the roof with hides and casks of palm oil, all of which, the gray-beard declared was my property.

Whilst making this inspection, I have no doubt the expression of my face indicated a good deal of wonder, for I saw the old man smile complacently as he followed me with his quiet eye.

" Good!" said the chief, " it is all there,—is it not? We Bagers are neither Soosoos, Mandingoes, Foulahs, nor *Whitemen*, that the goods of a stranger are not safe in our towns! We work for a living; we want little; big ships never come to us, and we neither steal from our guests nor go to war to sell one another!"

The conversation, I thought, was becoming a little personal; and, with a gesture of impatience, I put a stop to it. On second thoughts, however, I turned abruptly round, and shaking the noble savage's hand with a vigor that made him wince, presented him with a piece of cloth. Had Diogenes visited Africa in search of his man, it is by no means unlikely that he might have extinguished his lamp among the Bagers!

It was about two o'clock in the afternoon when I arrived in the town, which, as I before observed, seemed quite deserted, except by a dozen or two ebony antiquities, who crawled into the sunshine when they learned the advent of a stranger. The young people were absent gathering palm nuts in a neighboring grove. A couple of hours before sundown, my trader returned; and, shortly after, the merry gang of villagers made their appearance, laughing, singing, dancing, and laden with fruit. As soon as the gossips announced the arrival of a white man during their absence, the little hut that had been hospitably assigned me was surrounded by a crowd, five or six deep, of men, women, and children. The pressure was so close and sudden that I was almost stifled. Finding they would not depart until I made myself visible, I emerged from concealment and shook hands with nearly all. The women, in particular, insisted on gratifying themselves with a *sumboo* or smell at my face,—which is the native's kiss,—and folded their long black arms in an embrace of my neck, threatening peril to my shirt with their oiled and dusty flesh. However, I noticed so much *bon-hommie* among the happy crew that my heart would not allow me to repulse them; so I kissed the youngest and shunned the crones. In token of my good-will, I led a dozen or more of the prettiest to the rum-barrel, and made them happy for the night.

When the townsfolks had comfortably nestled themselves in their hovels, the old chief, with a show of some formality, presented me a heavy ram-goat, distinguished for its formidable head-ornaments, which, he said, was offered as a *bonne-bouche*, for my supper. He then sent a crier through the town, informing the women that a white stranger would be their guest during the night; and, in less than half an hour, my hut was visited by most of the village dames and damsels. One brought a pint of rice; another some roots of *cassava;* another, a few spoonfuls of palm oil; another a bunch of peppers; while the oldest lady of the party made herself particularly remarkable by the gift of a splendid fowl. In fact, the crier had hardly gone his rounds, before my mat was filled with the voluntary contributions of the villagers; and the wants, not only of myself but of my eight rowers, completely supplied.

There was nothing peculiar in this exhibition of hospitality, on account of my nationality. It was the mere fulfilment of a Bager law; and the poorest *black stranger* would have shared the rite as well as myself. I could not help thinking that I might have travelled from one end of England or America to the other, without meeting a Bager *welcome*. Indeed, it seemed somewhat questionable, whether it were better for the English to civilize Africa, or for the Bagers to send missionaries to their brethren in Britain!

These reflections, however, did not spoil my appetite, for I confess a feeling of unusual content and relish when the patriarch sat down with me before the covered bowls prepared for our supper. But, alas! for human hopes and tastes! As I lifted the lid from the vessel containing the steaming stew, its powerful fragrance announced the remains of that venerable quadruped with which I had been welcomed.  It was probably not quite in etiquette among the Bagers to decline the stew, yet, had starvation depended on it, I could not have touched a morsel.  Accordingly, I forbore the mess and made free with the rice, seasoning it well with salt and peppers.  But my amiable landlord was resolved that I should not go to rest with such penitential fare, and ordered one of his wives to bring her supper to my lodge.  A taste of the dish satisfied me that it was edible, though intensely peppered.  I ate with the appetite of an alderman, nor was it till two days after that my trader informed me I had supped so heartily on the spareribs of an alligator !  It was well that the hours of digestion had gone by, for though partial to the chase, I had never loved " water fowl " of so wild a character.

When supper was over, I escaped from the hut to breathe a little fresh air before retiring for the night.  Hardly had I put my head outside when I found myself literally inhaling the mosquitoes that swarmed at nightfall over these marshy flats.  I took it for granted that there was to be no rest for me in darkness among the Bagers ; but, when I mentioned my trouble to the chief, he told me that another hut had already been provided for my sleeping quarters, where my bed was made of certain green and odorous leaves which are antidotes to mosquitoes.  After a little more chat, he offered to guide me to the hovel, a low, thickly matted bower, through whose single aperture I crawled on hands and knees.  As soon as I was in, the entrance was closed, and although I felt very much as if packed in my grave, I slept an unbroken sleep till day dawn.*

* These Bagers are remarkable for their honesty, as I was convinced by several anecdotes related, during my stay in this village, by my trading clerk.  He took me to a neighboring lemon-tree, and exhibited an English brass steelyard hanging on its branches, which had been left there by a mulatto merchant from Sierra Leone, who died in the town on a trading trip.  This article, with a chest half full of goods, deposited in the "palaver house," had been kept securely more than twelve years in expectation that some of his friends would send for them from the colony.  The Bagers,

My return to the Rio Pongo was attended with considerable danger, yet I did not regret the trial of my spirit, as it enabled me to see a phase of African character which otherwise might have been missed.

After passing two days among the Bagers, I departed once more in my canoe, impelled by the stout muscles of the Kroomen. The breeze freshened as we passed from the river's mouth across the boiling surf of the bar, but, when we got fairly to sea, I found the Atlantic so vexed by the rising gale, that, in spite of waterproof awning and diligent bailing, we were several times near destruction. Still, I had great confidence in the native boatmen, whose skill in their skiffs is quite as great as their dexterity when naked in the water. I had often witnessed their agility as they escaped from capsized boats on the surf of our bar; and often had I rewarded them with a dram, when they came, as from a frolic, dripping and laughing to the beach.

When night began to fall around us the storm increased, and

I was told, have no *jujus, feitiches,* or *gregrees;*—they worship no god or evil spirit;—their dead are buried without tears or ceremony;—and their hereafter is eternal oblivion.

The males of this tribe are of middling size and deep black color; broad shouldered, but neither brave nor warlike. They keep aloof from other tribes, and by a Fullah law, are protected from foreign violence in consequence of their occupation as salt-makers, which is regarded by the interior natives as one of the most useful trades. Their fondness for palm oil and the little work they are compelled to perform, make them generally indolent. Their dress is a single handkerchief, or a strip of country cloth four or five inches wide, most carefully put on.

The young women have none of the sylphlike appearance of the Mandingoes or Soosoos. They work hard and use palm oil plentifully both internally and externally, so that their relaxed flesh is bloated like blubber. Both sexes shave their heads, and adorn their noses and lower lips with rings, while they penetrate their ears with porcupine quills or sticks. *They neither sell nor buy each other,* though they acquire children of both sexes from other tribes, and adopt them into their own, or dispose of them if not suitable. Their avails of work are commonly divided; so the Bagers may be said to resemble the Mormons in polygamy, the Fourierites in community, but to exceed both in honesty!

I am sorry that their nobler characteristics have so few imitators among the other tribes of Africa.

I could detect, by the low chatter and anxious looks of the rowers, that they were alarmed.  As far as my eye reached landward, I could descry nothing but a continuous reef on which the chafed sea was dashing furiously in columns of the densest spray.  Of course I felt that it was not my duty, nor would it be prudent, to undertake the guidance of the canoe in such circumstances.  Yet, I confess that a shudder ran through my nerves when I saw my "head-man" suddenly change our course and steer the skiff directly towards the rocks.  On she bounded like a racer.  The sea through which they urged her foamed like a caldron with the rebounding surf.  Nothing but wave-lashed rock was before us.  At last I could detect a narrow gap in the iron wall, which was filled with surges in the heaviest swells.  We approached it, and paused at the distance of fifty feet.  A wave had just burst through the chasm like a storming army.  We waited for the succeeding lull.  All hands laid still,—not a word was spoken or paddle dipped.  Then came the next enormous swell under our stern ;—the oars flew like lightning ;—the canoe rose as a feather on the crest of the surf ;—in a moment she shot through the cleft and reposed in smooth water near the shore.  As we sped through the gap, I might have touched the rocks on both sides with my extended arms !

Such is the skill and daring of Kroomen.

# CHAPTER XV.

WHEN the rains began to slacken, a petty caravan now and then straggled towards the coast; but, as I was only a new-comer in the region, and not possessed of abundant means, I enjoyed a slender share of the trade. Still I consoled myself with the hope of better luck in the dry season.

In the mean time, however, I not only heard of Joseph's safe arrival at Matanzas, but received a clerk whom he dispatched to dwell in Kambia while I visited the interior. Moreover, I built a boat, and sent her to Sierra Leone with a cargo of palm oil, to be exchanged for British goods; and, finally, during my perfect leisure, I went to work with diligence *to study* the trade in which fortune seemed to have cast my lot.

It would be a task of many pages if I attempted to give a full account of the origin and causes of *slavery in Africa*. As a national institution, it seems to have existed always. Africans have been bondsmen every where: and the oldest monuments bear their images linked with menial toils and absolute servitude. Still, I have no hesitation in saying, that three fourths of the slaves *sent abroad* from Africa are the fruit of native wars, fomented by the avarice and temptation of our own race. I cannot exculpate any commercial nation from this sweeping censure. We stimulate the negro's passions by the introduction of wants and fancies never dreamed of by the simple native, while slavery was an institution of domestic need and comfort alone. But what was once a luxury has now ripened into an absolute necessity; so that MAN, *in truth, has become the coin of Africa, and the " legal tender " of a brutal trade.*

England, to-day, with all her philanthropy, sends, under the cross of St. George, to convenient magazines of *lawful commerce* on the coast, her Birmingham muskets, Manchester cottons, and Liverpool lead, all of which are righteously swapped at Sierra Leone, Acra, and on the Gold coast, for Spanish or Brazilian bills on London. Yet, what British merchant does not know the traffic on which those bills are founded, and for whose support his wares are purchased? France, with her *bonnet rouge* and fraternity, dispatches her Rouen cottons, Marseilles brandies, flimsy taffetas, and indescribable variety of tinsel gewgaws. Philosophic Germany demands a slice for her looking-glasses and beads; while multitudes of our own worthy traders, who would hang a slaver as a pirate *when caught*, do not hesitate to supply him indirectly with tobacco, powder, cotton, Yankee rum, and New England notions, in order to bait the trap in which he *may* be caught! It is the temptation of these things, I repeat, that feeds the slave-making wars of Africa, and forms the human basis of those admirable bills of exchange.

I did not intend to write a homily on Ethiopian commerce when I begun this chapter; but, on reviewing the substantial motives of the traffic, I could not escape a statement which tells its own tale, and is as unquestionable as the facts of verified history.

Such, then, may be said to be the *predominating* influence that supports the African slave trade; yet, if commerce of all kinds were forbidden with that continent, the customs and laws of the natives would still encourage slavery as a domestic affair, though, of course, in a very modified degree. The rancorous family quarrels among tribes and parts of tribes, will always promote conflicts that resemble the forays of our feudal ancestors, while the captives made therein will invariably become serfs.

Besides this, the financial genius of Africa, instead of devising bank notes or the precious metals as a circulating medium, has from time immemorial, declared that a human creature,—*the true representative and embodiment of labor*,—is the most valuable article on earth. A man, therefore, becomes the standard of prices. A slave is a note of hand, that may be discounted or pawned; he is a bill of exchange that carries himself to his destination and pays a debt bodily; he is a tax that walks corporeally into the chieftain's treasury. Thus, slavery is not likely to be surrendered by the negroes themselves as a national institution. Their social interests will continue to maintain hereditary bondage; they will send the felon and the captive to foreign *barracoons*; and they will sentence to domestic servitude the orphans of culprits, disorderly children, gamblers, witches, vagrants, cripples, insolvents, the deaf, the mute, the barren, and the faithless. Five-sixths of the population is in chains.[1]

To facilitate the sale of these various unfortunates or malefactors, there exists among the Africans a numerous class of brokers, who are as skilful in their traffic as the jockeys of civilized lands. These adroit scoundrels rove the country in search of objects to suit different patrons. They supply the body-guard of princes; procure especial tribes for personal attendants; furnish laborers for farms; fill the *harems* of debauchees; pay or collect debts in flesh; and in cases of emergency take the place of bailiffs, to kidnap under the name of sequestration. If a native king lacks cloth, arms, powder, balls, tobacco, rum, or salt, and does not trade personally with the factories on the beach, he employs one of these dexterous gentry to effect the barter; and thus both British cotton and Yankee rum ascend the rivers from the second hands into which they have passed, while the slave approaches the coast to become the ebony basis of a bill of exchange!

It has sometimes struck me as odd, how the extremes of society almost meet on similar principles; and how much some African short-comings resemble the conceded civilizations of other lands!

---

[1] Dr. Lugenbeel's "Sketches of Liberia.": 1853. p. 45, 2d ed.

# CHAPTER XVI.

THE month of November, 1827, brought the wished-for "dry season;" and with it came a message from the leader of a caravan, that, at the full of the moon, he would halt in my village with all the produce he could impress. The runner represented his master as bearing a missive from his beloved nephew Amah-de-Bellah, and declared that he only lingered on the path to swell his caravan for the profit of my coffers.

I did not let the day pass before I sent an interpreter to greet my promised guest with suitable presents; while I took advantage of his delay to build a neat cottage for his reception, inasmuch as no Fullah Mahometan will abide beneath the same roof with an infidel. I furnished the establishment, according to their taste, with green hides and several fresh mats.

True to his word, Mami-de-Yong made known his arrival in my neighborhood on the day when the planet attained its full diameter. The moment the pious Mussulman, from the high hills in the rear of my settlement, espied the river winding to the sea, he turned to the east, and raising his arms to heaven, and extending them towards Mecca, gave thanks for his safe arrival on the beach. After repeated genuflections, in which the earth was touched by his prostrate forehead, he arose, and taking the path towards Kambia, struck up a loud chant in honor of the prophet in which he was joined by the interminable procession.

It was quite an imposing sight—this Oriental parade and barbaric pomp. My native landlord, proud of the occasion, as well as of his Mahometan progenitors, joined in the display. As the train approached my establishment, I ordered repeated salutes in honor of the stranger, and as I had no minstrels or music to welcome the Fullah, I commanded my master of ceremonies to conceal the deficiency by plenty of smoke and a dozen more rounds of rattling musketry.

This was the first caravan and the first leader of absolutely royal pretensions that visited my settlement; so I lined my piazza with mats, put a body-guard under arms behind me, decorated the front with fancy flags, and opposite the stool where I took my seat, caused a pure white sheepskin of finest wool to be spread for the accommodation of the noble savage. Advancing to the steps of my dwelling, I stood uncovered as the Fullah approached and tendered me a silver-mounted gazelle-horn snuff-box—the credential by which Amah-de-Bellah had agreed to certify the mission. Receiving the token with a *salaam*, I carried it reverently to my forehead, and passed it to Ali-Ninpha, who, on this occasion, played the part of my scribe. The ceremony over, we took him by the hands and led him to his allotted sheepskin, while, with a bow, I returned to my stool.

According to " country custom," Mami-de-Yong then began the *dantica*, or exposition of purposes, first of all invoking ALLAH to witness his honor and sincerity. " Not only," said the Mussulman, " am I the bearer of a greeting from my dear nephew Amah-de-Bellah, but I am an envoy from my royal master the Ali-mami, of Footha-Yallon, who, at his son's desire, has sent me with an escort to conduct you on your promised visit to Timbo. During your absence, my lord has commanded us to dwell in your stead at Kambia, so that your property may be safe from the Mulatto Mongo of Bangalang, whose malice towards your person has been heard of even among our distant hills ! "

The latter portion of this message somewhat surprised me, for though my relations with Mongo John were by no means amicable, I did not imagine that the story of our rupture had spread so far, or been received with so much sympathy.

Accordingly, when Mami-de-Yong finished his message, I approached him with thanks for his master's interest in my welfare; and, placing Amah-de-Bellah's Koran—which I had previously wrapped in a white napkin—in his hands, as a token of the nephew's friendship, I retired once more to my seat. As soon as the holy book appeared from the folds, Mami-de-Yong drew a breath of surprise, and striking his breast, fell on his knees with his head on the ground, where he remained for several minutes apparently in rapt devotion. As he rose—his forehead sprinkled with dust, and his eyes sparkling with tears—he opened the volume, and pointed out to me and his people his own handwriting, which he translated to signify that " Mami-de-Yong gave this word of God to Amah-de-Bellah, his kinsman." At the reading of the sentence, all the Fullahs shouted, " Glory to Allah and Mahomet his Prophet! " Then, coming forward again to the chief, I laid my hand on the Koran, and swore by the help of God, to accept the invitation of the great king of Footha-Yallon.

This terminated the ceremonial reception, after which I hastened to conduct Mami-de-Yong to his quarters, where I presented him with a sparkling new kettle and an inkstand, letting him understand, moreover, I was specially anxious to know that all the wants of his attendants in the caravan were completely satisfied.

Next morning early, I remembered the joy of his nephew Amah-de-Bellah, when I first treated him to *coffee;* and determined to welcome the chief, as soon as he came forth from his ablutions to prayers, with a cup distilled from the fragrant berry. I could not have hit upon a luxury more gratifying to the old gentleman. Thirty years before had he drank it in Timbuctoo, where it is used, he said, by the Moses-people (meaning the Hebrews), with milk and honey; and its delicous aroma brought the well-remembered taste to his lips ere they touched the sable fluid.

Long before Mami-de-Yong's arrival, his fame as a learned " book-man " and extensive traveller preceded him, so that when he mentioned his travel to Timbuctoo, I begged him to give me some account of that " capital of capitals," as the Africans call it. The royal messenger promised to comply as soon as he fin-ished the morning lessons of the caravan's children. His quar-ters were filled with a dozen or more of young Fullahs and Mandingoes squatted around a fire, while the prince sat apart in a corner with inkstand, writing reeds, and a pile of old manu-scripts. Ali-Ninpha, our backsliding Mahometan, stood by, pre-tending devoted attention to Mami's precepts and the Prophet's verses. The sinner was a scrupulous follower in the presence of the faithful; but when their backs were turned, I know few who relished a porker more lusciously, or avoided water with more scrupulous care. Yet why should I scoff at poor Ali? Jo seph and I had done our best to *civilize* him!

Mami-de-Yong apologized for the completion of his daily task in my presence, and went on with his instruction, while the pupils wrote down notes, on wooden slabs, with reeds and a fluid made of powder dissolved in water.

I am sorry to say that these Ethiopian Mahometans are but poor scholars. Their entire instruction amounts to little more than the Koran, and when they happen to write or receive a letter, its interpretation is a matter over which many an hour is toilsomely spent. Mami-de-Yong, however, was superior to most of his countrymen; and, in fact, I must record him in my nar-rative as the most erudite Negro I ever encountered.

### HIS TRIP TO TIMBUCTOO.

True to his promise, the envoy came to my piazza, as soon as school was over, and squatting sociably on our mats and sheep-skins, with a plentiful supply of pipes and tobacco, we formed as pleasant a little party as was assembled that day on the banks of the Rio Pongo. Ali-Ninpha acted as interpreter, having pre-pared himself for the long-winded task by a preliminary dram from my private locker, out of sight of the noble Mahometan.

Invoking the Lord's name,—as is usual among Mussulmen,—Mami-de-Yong took a long whiff at his pipe, and, receiving from his servant a small bag of fine sand, spread it smoothly on the floor, leaving the mass about a quarter of an inch in thickness. This was his black-board, designed to serve for the delineation of his journey. On the westernmost margin of his sand, he dotted a point with his finger for the starting at Timbo. As he proceeded with his track over Africa towards the grand capital, he marked the outlines of the principal terri- tories, and spotted the remarkable towns through which he passed. By a thick or thin line, he denoted the large rivers and small streams that intercepted his path, while he heaved up the sand into heaps to represent a mountain, or smoothed it into per- fect levels to imitate the broad prairies and savannas of the in- terior. When he came to a dense forest, his snuff-box was called in requisition, and a pinch or two judiciously sprinkled, stood for the monarchs of the wood.

Like all Oriental story-tellers, Mami proved rather prolix. His tale was nearly as long as his travel. He insisted on de- scribing his reception at every village. At each river he had his story of difficulty and danger in constructing rafts or building bridges. He counted the minutes he lost in awaiting the diminu- tion of floods. Anon, he would catalogue the various fish with which a famous river teemed; and, when he got fairly into the woods, there was no end of adventures and hairbreadth escapes from alligators, elephants, anacondas, vipers, and the fatal tape snake, whose bite is certain death. In the mountains he encoun- tered wolves, wild-asses, hyænas, zebras, and eagles.

In fact, the whole morning glided away with a geographical, zoological, and statistical overture to his tour; so that, when the hour of prayer and ablution arrived, Mami-de-Yong had not yet reached Timbuctoo! The double rite of cleanliness and faith required him to pause in his narrative; and, apologizing for the interruption, he left a slave to guard the map while he retired to perform his religious services.

When the noble Fullah got back, I had a nice lunch prepared on a napkin in the neighborhood of his diagram, so that he could munch his biscuits and sugar without halting on his path. Before he began, however, I took the liberty to offer a hint about the precious value of time in this brief life of ours, whilst I asked a question or two about the " capital of capitals," to indicate my eagerness to enter the walls of Timbuctoo.  Mami-de-Yong, who was a man of tact as well as humor, smiled at my insinuation, and apologizing like a Christian for the natural tediousness of all old travellers, skipped a degree or two of the wilderness, and at once stuck his buffalo-horn snuff-box into the eastern margin of the sand, to indicate that he was at his journey's end.

Mami had visited many of the European colonies and Moorish kingdoms on the north coast of Africa, so that he enjoyed the advantage of comparison, and, of course, was not stupefied by the untravelled ignorance of Africans who consider Timbuctoo a combination of Paris and paradise.  Indeed, he did not presume, like most of the Mandingo chiefs, to prefer it to Senegal or Sierra Leone.  He confessed that the royal palace was nothing but a vast inclosure of mud walls, built without taste or symmetry, within whose labyrinthine mesh there were numerous buildings for the wives, children, and kindred of the sovereign.  If the royal palace of Timbuctoo was of *such* a character, —"What," said he, "were the dwellings of nobles and townsfolk?"  The streets were paths;—the stores were shops;—the suburb of an European colony was *superior* to their best display!  The markets of Timbuctoo, alone, secured his admiration.  Every week they were thronged with traders, dealers, peddlers and merchants, who either dwelt in the neighboring kingdoms, or came from afar with slaves and produce.  Moors and Israelites, from the northeast, were the most eminent and opulent merchants; and among them he counted a travelling class, crowned with peculiar turbans, whom he called "Joseph's-people," or, in all likelihood, Armenians.

The prince had no mercy on the government of this influential realm.  Strangers, he said, were watched and taxed.  Indeed, he spoke of it with the peculiar love that we would suppose a Hungarian might bear towards Austria, or a Milanese to the inquisitorial powers of Lombardy.  In fact, I found that, despite of its architectural meanness, Timbuctoo was a great central mart for exchange, and that commercial men as well as the innumerable petty kings, frequented it not only for the abundant mineral salt in its vicinity, *but because they could ex-*

*change their slaves for foreign merchandise.* I asked the Fullah why he preferred the markets of Timbuctoo to the well-stocked stores of regular European settlements on a coast which was reached with so much more ease than this core of Africa? " Ah ! " said the astute trafficker, " no market is a good one for the genuine African, in which he cannot openly exchange his *blacks* for whatever the original owner or importer can sell without fear ! *Slaves, Don Téodore, are our money !* "

The answer solved in my mind one of the political problems in the question of African civilization, which I shall probably develope in the course of this narrative.

## CHAPTER XVII.

HAVING completed the mercantile negotiations of the caravan, and made my personal arrangements for a protracted absence, I put the noble Fullah in charge of my establishment, with special charges to my retainers, clerks, runners, and villagers, to regard the Mami as my second self. I thought it well, moreover, before I plunged into the wilderness,—leaving my worldly goods and worldly prospects in charge of a Mussulman stranger,—to row down to Bangalang for a parting chat with Mongo John, in which I might sound the veteran as to his feeling and projects. Ormond was in trouble as soon as I appeared. He was willing enough that I might perish by treachery on the road side, yet he he was extremely reluctant that I should penetrate Africa and make alliances which should give me superiority over the monopolists of the beach. I saw these things passing through his jealous heart as we talked together with uncordial civility. At parting I told the Mongo, for the first time, that I was sure my establishment would not go to decay or suffer harm in my absence, inasmuch as that powerful Fullah, the Ali-Mami of Footha-Yallon had deputed a lieutenant to watch Kamba while I travelled, and that he would occupy my village with his chosen warriors. The mulatto started with surprise as I finished, and abruptly left the apartment in silence.

I slept well that night, notwithstanding the Mongo's displeasure. My confidence in the Fullah was perfect. Stranger as he was, I had an instinctive reliance on his protection of my home, and his guardianship of my person through the wilderness.

At day-dawn I was up. It was a fresh and glorious morning. As nature awoke in the woods of that primitive world, the mists stole off from the surface of the water; and, as the first rays shot through the glistening dew of the prodigious vegetation, a thousand birds sent forth their songs as if to welcome me into their realm of unknown paths.

After a hearty breakfast my Spanish clerk was furnished with minute instructions in writing, and, at the last moment, I presented the Fullah chief to my people as a temporary master to whom they were to pay implicit obedience for his generous protection. By ten o'clock, my caravan was in motion. It consisted of thirty individuals deputed by Amah-de-Bellah, headed by one of his relations as captain. Ten of my own servants were assigned to carry baggage, merchandise, and provisions; while Ali-Ninpha, two interpreters, my body servant, a waiter, and a hunter, composed my immediate guard. In all, there were about forty-five persons.

When we were starting, Mami-de-Yong approached to " snap fingers;" and put in my hands a verse of the Koran in his master's handwriting,—" hospitality to the wearied stranger is the road to heaven,"—which was to serve me as a passport among all good Mahometans. If I had time, no doubt I would have thought how much more Christian this document was than the formal paper with which we are fortified by " foreign offices " and " state departments," when we go abroad from civilized lands ;—but, before I could summon so much sentiment, the Fullah chief stooped to the earth, and filling his hands with dust, sprinkled it over our heads, in token of a prosperous journey. Then, prostrating himself with his head on the ground, he bade us " go our way ! "

I believe I have already said that even the best of African roads are no better than goat-paths, and barely sufficient for the passage of a single traveller. Accordingly, our train marched off in single file. Two men, cutlass in hand, armed, besides, with loaded muskets, went in advance not only to scour the way and warn us of danger, but to cut the branches and briers that soon impede an untravelled path in this prolific land. They marched within hail of the caravan, and shouted whenever we approached bee-trees, ant-hills, hornet-nests, reptiles, or any of the Ethiopian perils that are unheard of in our American forests. Behind these pioneers, came the porters with food and luggage; the centre of the caravan was made up of women, children, guards, and followers; while the rear was commanded by myself and the chiefs, who, whips in hand, found it sometimes beneficial to stimulate the steps of stragglers. As we crossed the neighboring Soosoo towns, our imposing train was saluted with discharges of musketry, while crowds of women and children followed their "*cupy*," or "white-man," to bid him farewell on the border of the settlement.

For a day or two our road passed through a rolling country, interspersed with forests, cultivated fields, and African villages, in which we were welcomed by the generous chiefs with *bugnees*, or trifling gifts, in token of amity. Used to the scant exercise of a lazy dweller on the coast, whose migrations are confined to a journey from his house to the landing, and from the landing to his house, it required some time to habituate me once more to walking. By degrees, however, I overcame the foot-sore weariness that wrapped me in perfect lassitude when I sank into my hammock on the first night of travel. However, as we became better acquainted with each other and with wood-life, we tripped along merrily in the shadowy silence of the forest,—singing, jesting, and praising Allah. Even the slaves were relaxed into familiarity never permitted in the towns; while masters would sometimes be seen relieving the servants by bearing their burdens. At nightfall the women brought water, cooked food, and distributed rations; so that, after four days pleasant wayfaring in a gentle trot, our dusty caravan halted at sunset before the closed gates of a fortified town belonging to Ibrahim Ali, the Mandingo chief of Kya.

It was some time before our shouts and beating on the gates aroused the watchman to answer our appeal, for it was the hour of prayer, and Ibrahim was at his devotions. At last, pestered by their dalliance, I fired my double-barrelled gun, whose loud report I knew was more likely to reach the ear of a praying Mussulman. I did not reckon improperly, for hardly had the echoes died away before the great war-drum of the town was rattled, while a voice from a loophole demanded our business. I left the negotiation for our entry to the Fullah chief, who forthwith answered that "the *Ali-Mami's* caravan, laden with goods, demanded hospitality;" while Ali-Ninpha informed the questioner, that Don Téodore, the "white man of Kambia," craved admittance to the presence of Ibrahim the faithful.

In a short time the wicket creaked, and Ibrahim himself put forth his head to welcome the strangers, and to admit them, one by one, into the town. His reception of myself and Ali-Ninpha was extremely cordial; but the Fullah chief was addressed with cold formality, for the Mandingoes have but little patience with the well-known haughtiness of their national rivals.

Ali-Ninpha had been Ibrahim's playmate before he migrated to the coast. Their friendship still existed in primitive sincerity, and the chieftain's highest ambition was to honor the companion and guest of his friend. Accordingly, his wives and females were summoned to prepare my quarters with comfort and luxury. The best house was chosen for my lodging. The earthen floor was spread with mats. Hides were stretched on *adobe* couches, and a fire was kindled to purify the atmosphere. Pipes were furnished my companions; and, while a hammock was slung for my repose before supper, a chosen henchman was dispatched to seek the fattest sheep for that important meal.

Ibrahim posted sentinels around my hut, so that my slumbers were uninterrupted, until Ali-Ninpha roused me with the pleasant news that the bowls of rice and stews were smoking on the mat in the chamber of Ibrahim himself. Ninpha knew my tastes and superintended the cook. He had often jested at the "white man's folly," when my stomach turned at some disgusting dish of the country; so that the pure roasts and broils of well-known pieces slipped down my throat with the appetite of a trooper  While these messes were under discussion, the savory steam of a rich stew with a creamy sauce saluted my nostrils, and, without asking leave, I plunged my spoon into a dish that stood before my entertainers, and seemed prepared exclusively for themselves. In a moment I was invited to partake of the *bonne-bouche ;* and so delicious did I find it, that, even at this distance of time, my mouth waters when I remember the forced-meat balls of mutton, minced with roasted ground-nuts, that I devoured that night in the Mandingo town of Kya.

But the best of feasts is dull work without an enlivening bowl. Water alone—pure and cool as it was in this hilly region —did not quench our thirst. Besides this, I recollected the fondness of my landlord, Ali-Ninpha, for strong distillations, and I guessed that his playmate might indulge, at least privately, in a taste for similar libations. I spoke, therefore, of " cordial bitters,"—(a name not unfamiliar even to the most temperate Christians, in defence of flatulent stomachs,)—and at the same time producing my travelling canteen of Otard's best, applied it to the nostrils of the pair.

I know not how it happened, but before I could warn the Mahometans of the risk they incurred, the lips of the bottle slid from their noses to their mouths, while upheaved elbows long sustained in air, gave notice that the flask was relishing and the draft " good for their complaints." Indeed, so appetizing was the liquor, that another ground-nut stew was demanded ; and, of course, another bottle was required to allay its dyspeptic qualities.

By degrees, the brandy did its work on the worthy Mahometans. While it restored Ali-Ninpha to his early faith, and brought him piously to his knees with prayers to Allah, it had a contrary effect on Ibrahim, whom it rendered wild and generous. Every thing was mine ;—house, lands, slaves, and children. He dwelt rapturously on the beauty of his wives, and kissed Ali-Ninpha in mistake for one of them. This only rendered the apostate more devout than ever, and set him roaring invocations like a muezzin from a minaret. In the midst of these orgies, I stole off at midnight, and was escorted by my servant to a delicious hammock.

It was day-dawn when the caravan's crier aroused me, as he stood on a house-top calling the faithful to prayer previous to our departure. Before I could stir, Ali-Ninpba, haggard, sick, and crest-fallen, from his debauch, rolled into my chamber, and begged the postponement of our departure, as it was impossible for *Ibrahim Ali* to appear, being perfectly vanquished by—"the bitters!" The poor devil hiccoughed between his words, and so earnestly and with so many bodily gyrations implored my interference with the Fullah guide, that I saw at once he was in no condition to travel.

As the caravan was my personal escort and designed exclusively for my convenience, I did not hesitate to command a halt, especially as I was in some measure the cause of my landlord's malady. Accordingly, I tied a kerchief round my head, covered myself with a cloak, and leaning very lackadaisically on the edge of my hammock, sent for the Fullah chief.

I moaned with pain as he approached, and, declaring that I was prostrated by sudden fever, hoped he would indulge me by countermanding the order for our march. I do not know whether the worthy Mussulman understood my case or believed my fever, but the result was precisely the same, for he assented to my request like a gentleman, and expressed the deepest sympathy with my sufferings. His next concern was for my cure. True to the superstition and bigotry of his country, the good-natured Fullah insisted on taking the management of matters into his own hands, and forthwith prescribed a dose from the Koran, diluted in water, which he declared was a specific remedy for my complaint. I smiled at the idea of making a drug of divinity, but as I knew that homœopathy was harmless under the circumstances, I requested the Fullah to prepare his physic on the spot. The chief immediately brought his Koran, and turning over the leaves attentively for some time, at last hit on the appropriate verse, which he wrote down on a board with gunpowder ink, which he washed off into a bowl with clean water. This was given me to swallow, and the Mahometan left me to the operation of his religious charm, with special directions to the servant to allow no one to disturb my rest.

I have no doubt that the Fullah was somewhat of a quiz, and thought a chapter in his Bible a capital lesson after a reckless debauch; so I ordered my door to be barricaded, and slept like a dormouse, until Ibrahim and Ali-Ninpha came thundering at the portal long after mid-day. They were sadly chopfallen. Penitence spoke from their aching brows; nor do I hesitate to believe they were devoutly sincere when they forswore " *bitters* " for the future. In order to allay suspicion, or quiet his conscience, the Fullah had been presented with a magnificent ram-goat, flanked by baskets of choicest rice.

When I sallied forth into the town with the suffering sinners, I found the sun fast declining in the west, and, although my fever had left me, it was altogether too late to depart from the village on our journey. I mentioned to Ibrahim a report on the coast that his town was bordered by a sacred spring known as the DEVIL's FOUNTAIN, and inquired whether daylight enough still remained to allow us a visit. The chief assented; and as in his generous fit last night, he had offered me a horse, I now claimed the gift, and quickly mounted in search of the aqueous demon.

## CHAPTER XVIII.

Ah! what joy, after so many years, to be once more in the saddle in an open country, with a steed of fire and spirit bounding beneath my exhilarated frame! It was long before I could consent to obey the summons of our guide to follow him on the path. When the gates of Kya were behind, and the wider roads opened invitingly before me, I could not help giving rein to the mettlesome beast, as he dashed across the plain beneath the arching branches of magnificent cotton woods. The solitude and the motion were both delightful. Never, since I last galloped from the *paseo* to Atares, and from Atares to El Principe, overlooking the beautiful bay of Havana, and the distant outline of her purple sea, had I felt so gloriously the rush of joyous blood that careered through my veins like electric fire. Indeed, I know not how long I would have traversed the woods had not the path suddenly ended at a town, where my Arabian turned of his own accord, and dashed back along the road till I met my wondering companions.

Having sobered both our bloods, I felt rather better prepared for a visit to the Satanic personage who was the object of our excursion. About two miles from Kya, we struck the foot of a steep hill, some three hundred feet in height, over whose shoulder we reached a deep and tangled dell, watered by a slender stream which was hemmed in by a profusion of shrubbery. Crossing the brook, we ascended the opposite declivity for a short distance till we approached a shelving precipice of rock, along whose slippery side the ledgelike path continued. I passed it at a bound, and instantly stood within the arched aperture of a deep cavern, whence a hot and sulphurous stream trickled slowly towards the ravine. This was the fountain, and the demon who presided over its source dwelt within the cave.

Whilst I was examining the rocks to ascertain their quality, the guide apprised me that the impish proprietor of these waters was gifted with a " multitude of tongues," and, in all probability, would reply to me in my own, if I thought fit to address him. " Indeed," said the savage, " he will answer you *word for word* and that, too, almost before you can shape your thought in language. Let us see if he is at home ? "

I called, in a loud voice, " KYA ! " but as no reply followed, I perceived at once the wit of the imposture, and without waiting for him to place me, took my own position at a spot inside the cavern, where I knew the *echoes* would be redoubled. " Now," said I, " I know the devil is at home, as well as you do ;"—and, telling my people to listen, I bellowed, with all my might— " *caffra fure !* " " infernal black one ! "—till the resounding rocks roared again with demoniac responses. In a moment the cavern was clear of every African ; so that I amused myself letting off shrieks, howls, squeals, and pistols, until the afrighted natives peeped into the mouth of the cave, thinking the devil in reality had come for me in a double-breasted garment of thunder and lightning. I came forth, however, with a whole skin and so hearty a laugh, that the Africans seized my hands in token of congratulation, and looked at me with wonderment, as some-thing greater than the devil himself. Without waiting for a commentary, I leaped on my Arab and darted down the hill.

" And so," said I, when I got back to Kya, " dost thou in truth believe, beloved Ibrahim, that the devil dwells in those rocks of the sulphur stream ? "

" Why not, brother Theodore ? Isn't the water poison ? If you drink, will it not physic you? When animals lick it in the dry season, do they not die on the margin by scores? Now, a 'book-man' like you, my brother, knows well enough that *water* alone can't kill; so that whenever it does, the devil *must* be in it; and, moreover, is it not he who speaks in the cavern?"

"Good," replied I; "but, pry'thee, dear Ibrahim, read me this riddle: if the devil gets into *water* and kills, why don't he kill when he gets into '*bitters?*'"

"Ah!" said the Ali—"you white men are infidels and scoffers!" as he laughed like a rollicking trooper, and led me, with his arm round my neck, into supper. "And yet, Don Téodore, don't forget the portable imp that you carry in that Yankee flask in your pocket!"

We did not dispute the matter further. I had been long enough in Africa to find out that white men made themselves odious to the natives and created bitter enemies, by despising or ridiculing their errors; and as I was not abroad on a mission of civilization, I left matters just as I found them. When I was among the Mahometans, I was an excellent Mussulman, while, among the heathen, I affected considerable respect for their *jujus*, *gree-grees*, *feitiches*, *snakes*, *iguanas*, *alligators*, and wooden images.

Ere we set forth next morning, my noble host caused a generous meal to be dispensed among the caravan. The breakfast consisted of boiled rice dried in the sun, and then boiled again with milk or water after being pounded finely in a mortar. This nutritive dish was liberally served; and, as a new Mongo, I was tendered an especial platter, flanked by copious bowls of cream and honey.

It is true Mandingo etiquette, at the departure of an honored friend, for the Lord of the Town to escort him on his way to the first brook, drink of the water with the wayfarer, toast a prompt return, invoke Allah for a prosperous voyage, shake hands, and snap fingers, in token of friendly adieu. The host who tarries then takes post in the path, and, fixing his eyes on the departing guest, never stirs till the traveller is lost in the folds of the forest, or sinks behind the distant horizon.

Such was the conduct of my friend Ibrahim on this occasion; nor was it all. It is a singular habit of these benighted people, to keep their word whenever they make a promise! I dare say it is one of the marks of their faint civilization; yet I am forced to record it as a striking fact. When I sallied forth from the gate of the town, I noticed a slave holding the horse I rode the day before to the Devil's fountain, ready caprisoned and groomed as for a journey. Being accompanied by Ibrahim on foot, I supposed the animal was designed for his return after our complimentary adieus. But when we had passed at least a mile beyond the parting brook, I *again* encountered the beast, whose leader approached Ali-Ninpha, announcing the horse as a gift from his master to help me on my way. Ere I backed the blooded animal, an order was directed to my clerk at Kambia for two muskets, two kegs of powder, two pieces of blue cotton, and one hundred pounds of tobacco. I advised my official, moreover, to inclose in the core of the tobacco the stoutest flask he could find of our fourth proof " bitters ! "

# CHAPTER XIX.

THE day was cloudy, but our trotting caravan did not exceed twenty miles in travel. In Africa things are done leisurely, for neither life, speculation, nor ambition is so exciting or exacting as to make any one in a hurry. I do not recollect to have ever seen an individual *in haste* while I dwelt in the torrid clime. The shortest existence is long enough, when it is made up of sleep, slave-trade, and mastication.

At sunset no town was in sight; so it was resolved to bivouac in the forest on the margin of a beautiful brook, where rice, tea, and beef, were speedily boiled and smoking on the mats. When I was about to stretch my weary limbs for the night on the ground, my boy gave me another instance of Ibrahim's true and heedful hospitality, by producing a grass hammock he had secretly ordered to be packed among my baggage. With a hammock and a horse I was on velvet in the forest!

Delicious sleep curtained my swinging couch between two splendid cotton-woods until midnight, when the arm of our Fullah chief was suddenly laid on my shoulder with a whispered call to prepare for defence or flight. As I leaped to the ground the caravan was already afoot, though the profoundest silence prevailed throughout the wary crowd. The watch announced strangers in our neighborhood, and two guides had been despatched immediately to reconnoitre the forest. This was all the information they could give me.

The native party was fully prepared and alert with spears, lances, bows and arrows. I commanded my own men to re-prime their muskets, pistols, and rifles; so that, when the guides returned with a report that the intruders were supposed to form a party of fugitive slaves, we were ready for our customers.

Their capture was promptly determined. Some proposed we should delay till daylight; but Ali-Ninpha, who was a sagacious old fighter, thought it best to complete the enterprise by night, especially as the savages kept up a smouldering fire in the midst of their sleeping group, which would serve to guide us.

Our little band was immediately divided into two squads, one under the lead of the Fullah, and the other commanded by Ali-Ninpha. The Fullah was directed to make a circuit until he got in the rear of the slaves, while Ali-Ninpha, at a concerted signal, began to advance towards them from our camp. Half an hour probably elapsed before a faint call, like the cry of a child, was heard in the distant forest, upon which the squad of my landlord fell on all-fours, and crawled cautiously, like cats, through the short grass and brushwood, in the direction of the sound. The sleepers were quickly surrounded. The Mandingo gave the signal as soon as the ends of the two parties met and completed the circle; and, in an instant, every one of the runaways, except two, was in the grasp of a warrior, with a cord around his throat. Fourteen captives were brought into camp. The eldest of the party alleged that they belonged to the chief of Tamisso, a town on our path to Timbo, and were bound to the coast for sale. On their way to the *foreign* factories, which they were exceedingly anxious to reach, their owner died, so that they came under the control of his brother, who threatened to change their destination, and sell them in the interior. In consequence of this they fled; and, as their master would surely slay them if restored to Tamisso, they besought us with tears not to take them thither.

Another council was called, for we were touched by the earnest manner of the negroes. Ali-Ninpha and the Fullah were of opinion that the spoil was fairly ours, and should be divided in proportion to the men in both parties. Yet, as our road passed by the objectionable town, it was impossible to carry the slaves along, either in justice to ourselves or them. In this strait, which puzzled the Africans sorely, I came to their relief, by suggesting their dispatch to my factory with orders for the payment of their value in merchandise.

The proposal was quickly assented to as the most feasible, and our fourteen captives were at once divided into two gangs, of seven each. Hoops of bamboo were soon clasped round their waists, while their hands were tied by stout ropes to the hoops. A long tether was then passed with a slip-knot through each rattan belt, so that the slaves were firmly secured to each other, while a small coil was employed to link them more securely in a band by their necks. These extreme precautions were needed, because we dared not diminish our party to guard the gang. Indeed, Ali-Ninpha was only allowed the two interpreters and four of my armed people as his escort to Kya, where, it was agreed, he should deliver the captives to Ibrahim, to be forwarded to my factory, while he hastened to rejoin us at the river Sanghu, where we designed tarrying.

For three days we journeyed through the forest, passing occasionally along the beds of dried-up streams and across lonely tracts of wood which seemed never to have been penetrated, save by the solitary path we were treading. As we were anxious to be speedily reunited with our companions, our steps were not hastened; so that, at the end of the third day, we had not advanced more than thirty miles from the scene of capture, when we reached a small *Mandingo* village, recently built by an upstart trader, who, with the common envy and pride of his tribe, gave our *Fullah* caravan a frigid reception. A single hut was assigned to the chief and myself for a dwelling, and the rage of the Mahometan may readily be estimated by an insult that would doom him to sleep beneath the same roof with a Christian !

I endeavored to avert an outburst by apprising the Mandingo that I was a bosom friend of Ali-Ninpha, his countryman and superior, and begged that he would suffer the " head man " of our caravan to dwell in a house *alone*. But the impudent *parvenu* sneered at my advice; "he knew no such person as Ali-Ninpha, and cared not a snap of his finger for a Fullah chief, or a beggarly white man!"

My body servant was standing by when this tart reply fell from the Mandingo's lips, and, before I could stop the impetuous youth, he answered the trader with as gross an insult as an African can utter. To this the Mandingo replied by a blow over the boy's shoulders with the flat of a cutlass; and, in a twinkling, there was a general shout for "rescue" from all my party who happened to witness the scene. Fullahs, Mandingoes, and Soosoos dashed to the spot, with spears, guns, and arrows. The Fullah chief seized my double-barrelled gun and followed the crowd; and when he reached the spot, seeing the trader still waving his cutlass in a menacing manner, he pulled both triggers at the inhospitable savage. Fortunately, however, it was always my custom on arriving in *friendly* towns, to remove the copper caps from my weapons, so that, when the hammers fell, the gun was silent. Before the Fullah could club the instrument and prostrate the insulter, I rushed between them to prevent murder. This I was happy enough to succeed in; but I could not deter the rival tribe from binding the brute, hand and foot, to a post in the centre of his town, while the majority of our caravan cleared the settlement at once of its fifty or sixty inhabitants.

Of course, we appropriated the dwellings as we pleased, and supplied ourselves with provisions. Moreover, it was thought preferable to wait in this village for Ali-Ninpha, than to proceed onwards towards the borders of the Sanghu. When he arrived, on the second day after the sad occurrence, he did not hesitate to exercise the prerogative of judgment and condemnation always claimed by superior chiefs over inferiors, whenever they consider themselves slighted or wronged. The process in this case was calmly and humanely formed. A regular trial was allowed the culprit. He was arraigned on three charges:—1. Want of hospitality; 2. Cursing and maltreating a Fullah chief and a white Mongo; 3. Disrespect to the name and authority of his country-

man and superior, Ali Ninpha.   On all these articles the prisoner
was found guilty ; but, as there were neither slaves nor personal
property by which the ruffian could be mulcted for his crimes,
the tribunal adjudged him to be scourged with fifty lashes, and
to have his " town-fence or stockade destroyed, never to be
rebuilt." The blows were inflicted for the abuse, but the perpetual demolition of his defensive barrier was in punishment for
refused hospitality.   Such is the summary process by which
social virtues are inculcated and enforced among these interior
tribes of Africa !

---

It required three days for our refreshed caravan to reach the
dry and precipitous bed of the Sanghu, which I found impossible
to pass with my horse, in consequence of jagged rocks and immense boulders that covered its channel.   But the men were
resolved that my convenient animal should not be left behind.
Accordingly, all hands went to work with alacrity on the trees,
and in a day, they bridged the ravine with logs bound together
by ropes made from twisted bark.   Across this frail and sway-
ing fabric I urged the horse with difficulty ; but hardly had he
reached the opposite bank, and recovered from his nervous
tremor, when I was surprised by an evident anxiety in the beast
to return to his swinging pathway.   The guides declared it to be
an instinctive warning of danger from wild beasts with which the
region is filled ; and, even while we spoke, two of the scouts who
were in advance selecting ground for our camp, returned with the
carcasses of a deer and leopard.   Though meat had not passed
our lips for five days, we were in no danger of starvation ; the
villages teemed with fruits and vegetables.   Pineapples, bananas, and a pulpy globe resembling the peach in form and flavor,
quenched our thirst and satisfied our hunger.

Besides these, our greedy natives foraged in the wilderness
for nourishment unknown, or at least unused, by civilized folks.
They found comfort in barks of various trees, as well as in buds,
berries, and roots, some of which they devoured raw, while
others were either boiled or made into palatable decoctions with

water that gurgled from every hill.   The broad valleys and open country supplied  animal  and  vegetable  " delicacies "  which a white man would  pass unnoticed.   Many a  time, when I was as hungry as a wolf, I found my vagabonds in a nook of the woods, luxuriating  over  a  mess  with  the  unctuous  lips  of  aldermen ; but when I  came  to  analyze  the stew, I  generally found  it  to consist  of  a  " witch's  cauldron,"  copiously  filled  with  snails, lizards, iguanas, frogs and alligators !

# CHAPTER XX.

A JOURNEY to the interior of Africa would be a rural jaunt, were it not so often endangered by the perils of war. The African may fairly be characterized as a shepherd, whose pastoral life is varied by a little agriculture, and the conflicts into which he is seduced, either by family quarrels, or the natural passions of his blood. His country, though uncivilized, is not so absolutely wild as is generally supposed. The gradual extension of Mahometanism throughout t₁e interior is slowly but evidently modifying the Negro. An African Mussulman is *still* a warrior, for the dissemination of faith as well as for the gratification of avarice; yet the Prophet's laws are so much more genial than the precepts of paganism, that, within the last half century, the humanizing influence of the Koran is acknowledged by all who are acquainted with the interior tribes.

But in all the changes that may come over the spirit of *man* in Africa, her magnificent external *nature* will for ever remain the same. A little labor teems with vast returns. The climate exacts nothing but shade from the sun and shelter from the storm. Its oppressive heat forbids a toilsome industry, and almost enforces indolence as a law. With every want supplied, without the allurements of social rivalry, without the temptations of national ambition or personal pride, what has the African to do in his forest of palm and cocoa,—his grove of orange, pomegranate and fig,—on his mat of comfortable repose, where the fruit stoops to his lips without a struggle for the prize,—save to brood over, or gratify, the electric passions with which his soul seems charged to bursting!

It is an interesting task to travel through a continent filled with such people, whose minds are just beginning, here and there, to emerge from the vilest heathenism, and to glimmer with a faith that bears wrapped in its unfolded leaves, the seeds of a modified civilization.

As I travelled in the "dry season," I did not encounter many of the discomforts that beset the African wayfarer in periods of rain and tempest. I was not obliged to flounder through lagoons, or swim against the current of perilous rivers. We met their traces almost every day; and, in many places, the soil was worn into parched ravines or the tracks of dried-up torrents. Whatever affliction I experienced arose from the wasting depression of heat. We did not suffer from lack of water or food, for the caravan of the ALI-MAMI commanded implicit obedience throughout our journey.

In the six hundred miles I traversed, whilst absent from the coast, my memory, after twenty-six years, leads me, from beginning to end, through an almost continuous forest-path. We struck a trail when we started, and we left it when we came home. It was rare, indeed, to encounter a cross road, except when it led to neighboring villages, water, or cultivated fields. So dense was the forest foliage, that we often walked for hours in shade without a glimpse of the sun. The emerald light that penetrated the wood, bathed every thing it touched with mellow refreshment. But we were repaid for this partial bliss by intense suffering when we came forth from the sanctuary into the bare valleys, the arid *barrancas*, and marshy *savannas* of an open region. There, the red eye of the African sun glared with merciless fervor. Every thing reflected its rays. They struck us like lances from above, from below, from the sides, from the rocks, from the fields, from the stunted herbage, from the bushes. All was glare! Our eyes seemed to simmer in their sockets.

Whenever the path followed the channel of a brook, whose dried torrents left bare the scorched and broken rocks, our feet fled from the ravine as from heated iron. Frequently we entered extensive *prairies*, covered with blades of sword-grass, tall as our heads, whose jagged edges tore us like saws, though we protected our faces with masks of wattled willows. And yet, after all these discomforts, how often are my dreams haunted by charming pictures of natural scenery that have fastened themselves for ever in my memory!

As the traveller along the coast turns the prow of his canoe through the surf, and crosses the angry bar that guards the mouth of an African river, he suddenly finds himself moving calmly onward between sedgy shores, buried in mangroves. Presently, the scene expands in the unruffled mirror of a deep, majestic stream. Its lofty banks are covered by innumerable varieties of the tallest forest trees, from whose summits a trailing network of vines and flowers floats down and sweeps the passing current. A stranger who beholds this scenery for the first time is struck by the immense size, the prolific abundance, and gorgeous verdure of every thing. Leaves, large enough for garments, lie piled and motionless in the lazy air. The bamboo and cane shake their slender spears and pennant leaves as the stream ripples among their roots. Beneath the massive trunks of forest trees, the country opens; and, in vistas through the wood, the traveller sees innumerable fields lying fallow in grass, or waving with harvests of rice and *cassava*, broken by golden clusters of Indian corn. Anon, groups of oranges, lemons, coffee-trees, plantains and bananas, are crossed by the tall stems of cocoas, and arched by the broad and drooping coronals of royal palm. Beyond this, capping the summit of a hill, may be seen the conical huts of natives, bordered by fresh pastures dotted with flocks of sheep and goats, or covered by numbers of the sleekest cattle. As you leave the coast, and shoot round the river-curves of this fragrant wilderness teeming with flowers, vocal with birds, and gay with their radiant plumage, you plunge into the interior, where the rising country slowly expands into hills and mountains.

The forest is varied. Sometimes it is a matted pile of tree vine, and bramble, obscuring every thing, and impervious save with knife and hatchet. At others, it is a Gothic temple. The sward spreads openly for miles on every side, while, from its even surface, the trunks of straight and massive trees rise to a prodigious height, clear from every obstruction, till their gigantic limbs, like the capitals of columns, mingle their foliage in a roof of perpetual verdure.

At length the hills are reached, and the lowland heat is tempered by mountain freshness. The scene that may be beheld from almost any elevation, is always beautiful, and sometimes grand. Forest, of course, prevails; yet, with a glass, and often by the unaided eye, gentle hills, swelling from the wooded landscape, may be seen covered with native huts, whose neighborhood is checkered with patches of sward and cultivation, and inclosed by massive belts of primeval wildness. Such is commonly the westward view; but north and east, as far as vision extends, noble outlines of hill and mountain may be traced against the sky, lapping each other with their mighty folds, until they fade away in the azure horizon.

When a view like this is beheld at morning, in the neighborhood of rivers, a dense mist will be observed lying beneath the spectator in a solid stratum, refracting the light now breaking from the east. Here and there, in this lake of vapor, the tops of hills peer up like green islands in a golden sea. But, ere you have time to let fancy run riot, the " cloud compelling " orb lifts its disc over the mountains, and the fogs of the valley, like ghosts at cock-crow, flit from the dells they have haunted since nightfall. Presently, the sun is out in his terrible splendor. Africa unveils to her master, and the blue sky and green forest blaze and quiver with his beams.

# CHAPTER XXI.

I FELT so much the lack of scenery in my narrative, that I thought it well to group in a few pages the African pictures I have given in the last chapter.  My story had too much of the bareness of the Greek stage, and I was conscious that landscape, as well as action, was required to mellow the subject and relieve it from tedium.  After our dash through the wilderness, let us return to the slow toil of the caravan.

Four days brought us to Tamisso from our last halt.  We camped on the copious brook that ran near the town-walls, and while Ali-Ninpha thought proper to compliment the chief, Mohamedoo, by a formal announcement of our arrival, the caravan made ready for reception by copious, but *needed*, ablutions of flesh and raiment.  The women, especially, were careful in adorning and heightening their charms.  Wool was combed to its utmost rigidity; skins were greased till they shone like polished ebony; ankles and arms were restrung with beads; and loins were girded with snowy waistcloths.  Ali-Ninpha knew the pride of his old Mandingo companions, and was satisfied that Mohamedoo would have been mortified had we surprised him within the precincts of his court, squatted, perhaps, on a dirty mat with a female scratching his head!  Ali-Ninpha was a prudent gentleman, and knew the difference between the private and public lives of his illustrious countrymen!

In the afternoon our interpreters returned to camp with Mohamedoo's son, accompanied by a dozen women carrying platters of boiled rice, calabashes filled with delicate sauce, and abundance of *ture*, or vegetable butter. A beautiful horse was also despatched for my triumphal entry into town.

The food was swallowed with an appetite corresponding to our recent penitential fare; the tents were struck; and the caravan was forthwith advanced towards Tamisso. All the noise we could conveniently make, by way of *music*, was, of course, duly attempted. Interpreters and guides went ahead, discharging guns. Half a dozen tom-toms were struck with uncommon rapidity and vigor, while the unctuous women set up a chorus of melody that would not have disgraced a band of " Ethiopian Minstrels."

Half-way to the town our turbulent mob was met by a troop of musicians sent out by the chief to greet us with song and harp. I was quickly surrounded by the singers, who chanted the most fulsome praise of the opulent Mongo, while a court-fool or buffoon insisted on leading my horse, and occasionally wiping my face with his filthy handkerchief!

Presently we reached the gates, thronged by pressing crowds of curious burghers. Men, women, and children, had all come abroad to see the immense *Furtoo*, or white man, and appeared as much charmed by the spectacle as if I had been a banished patriot. I was forced to dismount at the low wicket, but here the *empressement* of my inquisitive hosts became so great, that the " nation's guest " was forced to pause until some amiable bailiffs modified the amazement of their fellow-citizens by staves and whips.

I lost no time in the lull, while relieved from the mob, to pass onward to "the palace" of Mohamedoo, which, like all royal residences in Africa, consisted of a mud-walled quadrangular inclosure, with a small gate, a large court, and a quantity of *adobe* huts, surrounded by shady verandahs. The furniture, mats, and couches were of cane, while wooden platters, brass kettles, and common wash-basins, were spread out in every direction for show and service.

On a couch, covered with several splendid leopard skins, re-clined Mohamedoo, awaiting my arrival with as much stateliness as if he had been a scion of civilized royalty. The chief was a man of sixty at least. His corpulent body was covered with short Turkish trousers, and a large Mandingo shirt profusely embroidered with red and yellow worsted. His bald or shaved head was concealed by a light turban, while a long white beard stood out in relief against his tawny skin, and hung down upon his breast. Ali-Ninpha presented me formally to this personage, who got up, shook hands, " snapped fingers," and welcomed me thrice. My Fullah chief and Mandingo companion then pro-ceeded to "*make their dantica*," or declare the purpose of their visit; but when they announced that I was the guest of the Fullah Ali-Mami, and, accordingly, was *entitled* to free pas-sage every where without expense, I saw that the countenance of the veteran instantly fell, and that his welcome was dashed by the loss of a heavy duty which he designed exacting for my transit.

The sharp eye of Ali-Ninpha was not slow in detecting Mo-hamedoo's displeasure ; and, as I had previously prepared him in private, he took an early opportunity to whisper in the old man's ear, that Don Téodore knew he was compelled to jour-ney through Tamisso, and, of course, had not come empty-handed. My object, he said, in visiting this region and the territory of the Fullah king, was not idle curiosity alone ; but that I was prompted by a desire for liberal trade, and especially for the purchase of slaves to load the numerous vessels I had lingering on the coast, with immense cargoes of cloth, muskets, and pow-der.

The clouds were dispersed as soon as a hint was thrown out about traffic. The old sinner nodded like a mandarin who knew what he was about, and, rising as soon as the adroit whisperer had finished, took me by the hand, and in a loud voice, presented me to the people as his "*beloved son!*" Besides this, the best house within the royal inclosure was fitted with fresh comforts for my lodging. When the Fullah chief withdrew from the audience, Ali-Ninpha brought in the mistress of Mohamedoo's harem, who acted as his confidential clerk, and we speedily handed over the six pieces of cotton and an abundant supply of tobacco with which I designed to propitiate her lord and master.

Tired of the dust, crowd, heat, confinement and curiosity of an African town, I was glad to gulp down my supper of broiled chickens and milk, preparatory to a sleepy attack on my couch of rushes spread with mats and skins. Yet, before retiring for the night, I thought it well to refresh my jaded frame by a bath, which the prince had ordered to be prepared in a small court behind my chamber. But I grieve to say, that my modesty was put to a sore trial, when I began to unrobe. Locks and latches are unknown in this free-and-easy region. It had been noised abroad among the dames of the harem, that the *Furtoo* would probably perform his ablutions before he slept; so that, when I entered the yard, my tub was surrounded by as many inquisitive eyes as the dinner table of Louis the Fourteenth, when sovereigns dined in public. As I could not speak their language, I made all the pantomimic signs of graceful supplication that commonly soften the hearts of the sex on the stage, hoping, by dumb show, to secure my privacy. But gestures and grimace were unavailing. I then made bold to take off my shirt, leaving my nether garments untouched. Hitherto, the dames had seen only my bronzed face and hands, but when the snowy pallor of my breast and back was unveiled, many of them fled incontinently, shouting to their friends to " come and see the *peeled Furtoo !* " An ancient crone, the eldest of the crew, ran her hand roughly across the fairest portion of my bosom, and looking at her fingers with disgust, as if I reeked with leprosy, wiped them on the wall. As displeasure seemed to predominate over admiration, I hoped this experiment would have satisfied the inquest, but, as black curiosity exceeds all others, the wenches continued to linger, chatter, grin and feel, until I was forced to disappoint their anxiety for further disclosures, by an abrupt " good-night."

We tarried in Tamisso three days to recruit, during which I was liberally entertained on the prince's hospitable mat, where African stews of relishing flavor, and tender fowls smothered in snowy rice, regaled me at least twice in every twenty-four hours.

Mohamedoo fed me with an European silver spoon, which, he said, came from among the effects of a traveller who, many years before, died far in the interior.   In all his life, he had seen but *four* of our race within the walls of Tamisso.   Their names escaped his memory; but the last, he declared, was a poor and clever youth, probably from Senegal, who followed a powerful caravan, and " read the Koran like a *mufti*."

Tamisso was entirely surrounded by a tall double fence of pointed posts.   The space betwixt the inclosures, which were about seven feet apart, was thickly planted with smaller spear-headed staves, hardened by fire.   If the first fence was leaped by assailants, they met a cruel reception from these impaling sentinels.   Three gates afforded admission to different sections of the town, but the passage through them consisted of zig-zags, with loopholes cut judiciously in the angles, so as to command every point of access to the narrow streets of the suburbs.

The parting between Mohamedoo and myself was friendly in the extreme.   Provisions for four days were distributed by the prince to the caravan, and he promised that my return should be welcomed by an abundant supply of slaves.

# CHAPTER XXII.

As our caravan approached the Fullah country, and got into the higher lands, where the air was invigorating, I found its pace improved so much that we often exceeded twenty miles in our daily journey. The next important place we were to approach was Jallica. For three days, our path coasted the southern edge of a mountain range, whose declivities and valleys were filled with rivers, brooks, and streamlets, affording abundant irrigation to fields teeming with vegetable wealth. The population was dense. Frequent caravans, with cattle and slaves, passed us on their way to various marts. Our supplies of food were plentiful. A leaf of tobacco purchased a fowl; a charge of powder obtained a basin of milk, or a dozen of eggs; and a large sheep cost only six cents, or a quart of salt.

Five days after quitting Tamisso, our approach to Jallica was announced; and here, as at our last resting-place, it was deemed proper to halt half a day for notice and ablution before entering a city, whose chief—SUPHIANA—was a kinsman of Ali-Ninpha.

The distance from our encampment to the town was about three miles; but an hour had hardly elapsed after our arrival, when the deep boom of the war-drum gave token that our message had been received with welcome. I was prepared, in some measure, for a display of no ordinary character at Jallica, because my Mandingo friend, Ali-Ninpha, inhabited the town in his youth, and had occupied a position which gave importance to his name throughout Soolimana. The worthy fellow had been ab-sent many years from Jallica, and wept like a child when he heard the sound of the war-drum. Its discordant beat had the same effect on the savage that the sound of their village bells has on the spirit of returning wanderers in civilized lands. When the rattle of the drum was over, he told me that for five years he controlled that very instrument in Jallica, during which it had never sounded a retreat or betokened disaster. In peace it was never touched, save for public rejoicing; and the authori-ties allowed it to be beaten *now* only because an old commander of the tribe was to be received with the honors due to his rank and service. Whilst we were still conversing, Suphiana's lance-bearer made his appearance, and, with a profound *salaam*, an-nounced that the "gates of Jallica were open to the Mandingo and his companions."

No *fanda* or refreshments were sent with the welcome; but when the caravan got within fifty yards of the walls, a band of shouting warriors marched forth, and lifting Ali-Ninpha on their shoulders, bore him through the gates, singing war-songs, accom-panied by all sorts of music and hubbub.

I had purposely lingered with my men in the rear of the great body of Africans, so that nearly the whole caravan passed the portal before my complexion—though deeply bronzed by ex-posure—made me known to the crowd as a white man.

Then, instantly, the air rang with the sound of—"Furtoo! Furtoo! Furtoo!"—and the gate was slammed in our faces, leaving us completely excluded from guide and companions. But, in the midst of his exultant reception, Ali-Ninpha did not forget the Mongo of Kambia. Hardly had he attained the end of the street, when he heard the cry of exclusion, and observed the closing portal. By this time, my Fullah friend had wrough himself into an examplary fit of Oriental rage with the inhos pitable Mandingoes, so that I doubt very much whether he would not have knocked the dust from his sandals on the gate of Jallica, had not Ali-Ninpha rushed through the wicket, and commanding the portal to be reopened, apologized contritely to the Mahometan and myself.

This unfortunate mistake, or accident, not only caused considerable delay, but rather dampened the delight of our party as it defiled in the spacious square of Jallica, and entered the open shed which was called a "*palaver-house*." Its vast area was densely packed with a fragrant crowd of old and young, armed with muskets or spears. All wore knives or cutlasses, slung by a belt high up on their necks; while, in their midst surrounded by a court of veterans, stood Suphiana, the prince, waiting our arrival.

In front marched Ali-Ninpha, preceded by a numerous band of shrieking and twanging minstrels. As he entered the apartment, Suphiana arose, drew his sword, and embracing the stranger with his left arm, waved the shining blade over his head, with the other. This peculiar *accolade* was imitated by each member of the royal council; while, in the centre of the square, the war-drum,—a hollowed tree, four feet in diameter, covered with hides,—was beaten by two savages with slung-shot, until its thundering reverberations completely deafened us.

You may imagine my joy and comfort when I saw the Mandingo take a seat near the prince, as a signal for the din's cessation. This, however, was only the commencement of another prolonged ceremonial; for now began the royal review and salute in honor of the returned commander. During two hours, an uninterrupted procession of all the warriors, chiefs, and head-men of Jallica, defiled in front of the ancient drum-major; and, as each approached, he made his obeisance by pointing a spear or weapon at my landlord's feet. During this I remained on horseback without notice or relief from the authorities. Ali-Ninpha, however, saw my impatient discomfort, and once or twice despatched a sly message to preserve my good humor. The ceremony was one of absolute compulsion, and could not be avoided without discourtesy to the prince and his countrymen. As soon as he could escape, however, he hastened over the court-yard to assist me in dismounting; and dashing the rude crowd right and left, led me to his kinsman Suphiana. The prince extended his

royal hand in token of amity; Ali-Ninphà declared me to be
his "son;" while the long string of compliments and panegyrics
he pronounced upon my personal qualities, moral virtues, and
*wealth*, brought down a roar of grunts by way of applause from
the toad-eating courtiers.

Jallica was a fairer town than any I had hitherto encountered in my travels. Its streets were wider, its houses better, its
people more civil. No one intruded on the friend of Ali-Ninpha,
and guest of Suphiana. I bathed without visits from inquisitive
females. My house was my castle; and, when I stirred abroad,
two men preceded me with rattans to keep my path clear from
women and children.

After lounging about quietly for a couple of days, wearing
away fatigue, and getting rid of the stains of travel, I thought
it advisable to drop in one morning, unannounced, after breakfast, at Suphiana's with the presents that are customary in the
east. As the guest,—during my whole journey,—of the Ali-
Mami, or King of Foota-Yallon, I was entirely exempt by customary law from this species of tax, nor would my Fullah protector have allowed me to offer a tribute had he known it;—yet,
I always took a secret opportunity to present a *voluntary gift*,
for I wished my memory to smell sweet along my track in Africa.
Suphiana fully appreciated my generosity under the circumstances, and returned the civility by an invitation to dinner
at the house of his principal wife. When the savory feast
with which he regaled me was over, female singers were introduced for a concert. Their harps were triangles of wood, cord-
ed with fibres of cane; their banjoes consisted of gourds cov-red
with skin pierced by holes, and strung like the harps; but, I
confess, that I can neither rave nor go into ecstasies over the combined effect which saluted me from such instruments or such
voices. I was particularly struck, however, by one of their in-
ventions, which slightly resembles the *harmonica* I have seen
played by children in this country. A board, about two feet
square, was bordered by a light frame at two ends, across which
a couple of cane strings were tightly stretched. On these, strips

of nicely trimmed bamboo, gradually diminishing in size from left to right, were placed; whilst beneath them, seven gourds, also gradually decreasing, were securely fastened to mellow the sound. The instrument was carried by a strap round the player's neck, and was struck by two small wooden hammers softened by some delicate substance.

One of the prettiest girls in the bevy had charge of this African piano, and was said to be renowned for uncommon skill. Her feet, hands, wrists, elbows, ankles, and knees, were strung with small silvery bells; and, as the gay damsel was dancer and singer as well as musician, she seemed to reek with sound from every pore. Many of her attitudes would probably have been, at least, more picturesque and decent for drapery; but, in Jallica, MADOO, the *ayah*, was considered a Mozart in composition, a Lind in melody, and a Taglioni on the "light fantastic toe!"

When the performance closed, Suphiana presented her a slave; and, as she made an obeisance to me in passing, I handed her my *bowie-knife*, promising to redeem it at my lodgings with *ten pounds of tobacco!*

Some superstitious notions about the state of the moon prevented my Fullah guide from departing as soon as I desired; but while we were dallying with the planet, Ali-Ninpha became so ill that he was compelled to halt and end the journey in his favorite Jallica. I rather suspected the Mandingo to feign more suffering than he really experienced, and I soon discovered that his malady was nothing but a sham. In truth, Ali-Ninpha had duped so many Fullah traders on the beach, and owed them the value of so many slaves, that he found it extremely inconvenient, if not perilous, to enter the domain of the ALI-MAMI of FOOTHA-YALLON!

# CHAPTER XXIII.

A MESSENGER was despatched from Jallica, in advance of our departure, to announce our approach to Timbo. For six days more, our path led over hill and dale, and through charming valleys, fed by gentle streamlets that nourished the vigorous vegetation of a mountain land.

As we crossed the last summits that overlooked the territory of Footha-Yallon, a broad *plateau*, whence a wide range of country might be beheld, was filled with bands of armed men, afoot and on horseback, while a dozen animals were held in tether by their gayly dressed attendants. I dashed to the head of the caravan on my jaded beast, and reached it just in time to find the sable arms of Ahmah-de-Bellah opening to greet me! The generous youth, surrounded by his friends and escorted by a select corps of soldiers and slaves, had come thus far on the path to offer the prince's welcome!

I greeted the Mahometan with the fervor of ancient love and, in a moment, we were all dismounted and on our knees; while, at a signal from the chief, profound silence reigned throughout the troop and caravan. Every eye was turned across the distant plain to the east. An air of profoundest devotion subdued the multitude, and, in a loud chant, Ahmah-de-Bellah, with outstretched arms and upraised face, sang forth a psalm of gratitude to Allah for the safety of his " brother."

The surprise of this complimentary reception was not only delightful as an evidence of African character among these more civilized tribes of the Mahometan interior, but it gave me an assurance of security and trade, which was very acceptable to one so far within the bowels of the land. We were still a day's journey from the capital. Ahmah-de-Bellah declared it impossible, with all the diligence we could muster, to reach Timbo without another halt. Nevertheless, as he was extremely solicitous to bring us to our travel's end, he not only supplied my personal attendants with fresh horses, but ordered carriers from his own guard to charge themselves with the entire luggage of our caravan.

Thus relieved of burden, our party set forth on the path in a brisk trot, and resting after dark for several hours in a village, we entered Timbo unceremoniously before daybreak while its inhabitants were still asleep.

I was immediately conducted to a house specially built for me, surrounded by a high wall to protect my privacy from intrusion. Within, I found a careful duplicate of all the humble comforts in my domicil on the Rio Pongo. Tables, sofas, plates, knives, forks, tumblers, pitchers, basins,—had all been purchased by my friend, and forwarded for this establishment, from other factories without my knowledge; while the centre of the main apartment was decorated with an "American rocking-chair," which the natives had ingeniously contrived of rattans and bamboo! Such pleasant evidences of refined attention were more remarkable and delicate, because most of the articles are not used by Mahometans. "These, I hope," said Ahmah-de Bellah, as he led me to a seat, "will make you comparatively comfortable while you please to dwell with your brother in Timbo. You have no thanks to return, because I have not treated you like a *native* Mussulman; for you were kind enough to remember all my own little nationalities when I was your guest on the beach. ALLAH be praised for your redemption and arrival;—and so, brother, take your rest in peace within the realm of the Ali-Mami, your father!"

I embraced the generous fellow with as much cordiality as if he had been a kinsman from the sweet valley of Arno. During his visit to my factory he was particularly charmed with an old dressing-gown I used for my siestas, and when I resolved on this journey, I caused an improved copy of it to be made by one of the most skilful artists on the river. A flashy pattern of calico was duly cut into rather ampler form than is usual among our dandies. This was charmingly lined with sky-blue, and set off at the edges with broad bands of glaring yellow. The effect of the whole, indeed, was calculated to strike an African fancy; so that, when I drew the garment from my luggage, and threw it, together with a fine white ruffled shirt, over the shoulders of "my brother," I thought the pious Mussulman would have gone wild with delight. He hugged me a dozen times with the gripe of a tiger, and probably would have kissed quite as lustily, had I not deprecated any further ebullitions of bodily gratitude.

A bath erased not only the dust of travel from my limbs, but seemed to extract even the memory of its toils from my bones and muscles. Ahmah-de-Bellah intimated that the Ali-Mami would soon be prepared to receive me without ceremony. The old gentleman was confined by dropsy in his lower extremities, and probably found it uncomfortable to sustain the annoyance of public life except when absolutely necessary. The burden of my entertainment and glorification, therefore, was cast on the shoulders of his younger kinsfolk, for which, I confess, I was proportionally grateful. Accordingly, when I felt perfectly refreshed, I arose from my matted sofa, and dressing for the first time in more than a month in a perfectly clean suit, I donned a snowy shirt, a pair of dashing drills, Parisian pumps, and a Turkish *fez*, tipped with a copious tassel. Our interpreters were clad in fresh Mandingo dresses adorned with extra embroidery. My body-servant was ordered to appear in a cast-off suit of my own; so that, when I gave one my double-barrelled gun to carry, and armed the others with my pistols, and a glittering regulation-sword,—designed as a gift for the Ali-Mami,—I presented a very respectable and picturesque appearance for a gentleman abroad on his travels in the East. The moment I issued with my train from the house, a crowd of Fullahs was ready to re ceive me with exclamations of chattering surprise; still I was not annoyed, as elsewhere, by the unfailing concourse that followed my footsteps or clogged my pathway.

The "palace" of the Ali-Mami of Footha-Yallon, like all African palaces in this region, was an *adobe* hovel, surrounded by its portico shed, and protected by a wall from the intrusion of the common herd. In front of the dwelling, beneath the shelter of the verandah, on a fleecy pile of sheepskin mats, reclined the veteran, whose swollen and naked feet were undergoing a cooling process from the palm-leaf fans of female slaves. I marched up boldly in front of him with my military *suite*, and, making a profound *salaam*, was presented by Ahmah-de-Bellah as his "white brother." The Ali at once extended both hands, and, grasping mine, drew me beside him on the sheepskin. Then, looking intently over my face and into the very depth of my eyes, he asked gently with a smile—"what was my name?"

"AHMAH-DE-BELLAH!" replied I, after the fashion of the country. As I uttered the Mahometan appellation, for which I had exchanged my own with his son at Kambia, the old man, who still held my hands, put one of his arms round my waist, and pressed me still closer to his side;—then, lifting both arms extended to heaven, he repeated several times,—God is great! God is great! God is great!—and Mahomet is his Prophet!"

This was followed by a grand inquest in regard to myself and history. Who was my father? Who was my mother? How many brothers had I? Were they warriors? Were they "book-men?" Why did I travel so far? What delay would I make in Footha-Yallon? Was my dwelling comfortable? Had I been treated with honor, respect and attention on my journey? And, last of all, the prince sincerely hoped that I would find it convenient to dwell with him during the whole of the "rainy season."

Several times, in the midst of these interrogations, the patriarch groaned, and I could perceive, from the pain that flitted like a shadow over the nerves and muscles of his face, that he was suffering severely, and, of course, I cut the interview as short as oriental etiquette would allow. He pressed me once more to his bosom, and speaking to the interpreter, bade him tell his master, the Furtoo, that any thing I fancied in the realm was mine. Slaves, horses, cattle, stuffs,—all were at my disposal. Then, pointing to his son, he said : " Ahmah-de-Bellah, the white man is our guest; his brother will take heed for his wants, and redress every complaint."

The prince was a man of sixty at least. His stature was noble and commanding, if not absolutely gigantic,—*being several inches over six feet*,—while his limbs and bulk were in perfect proportion. His oval head, of a rich mahogany color, was quite bald to the temples, and covered by a turban, whose ends depended in twin folds along his cheeks. The contour of his features was remarkably regular, though his lips were rather full, and his nose somewhat flat, yet free from the disgusting depression and cavities of the negro race. His forehead was high and perpendicular, while his mouth glistened with ivory when he spoke or smiled. I had frequent opportunities to talk with the king afterwards, and was always delighted by the affectionate simplicity of his demeanor. As it was the country's custom to educate the first-born of royalty for the throne, the Ali-Mami of Footha-Yallon had been brought up almost within the precincts of the mosque. I found the prince, therefore, more of a meditative " book-man " than warrior ; while the rest of his family, and especially his younger brothers, had never been exempt from military duties, at home or abroad. Like a good Mussulman, the sovereign was a quiet, temperate gentleman, never indulging in " bitters " or any thing stronger than a drink fermented from certain roots, and sweetened to resemble *mead*. His intercourse with me was always affable and solicitous for my comfort ; nor did he utter half a dozen sentences without interlarding them with fluent quotations from the Koran. Sometimes, in the midst of a pleasant chat in which he was wondering at my curiosity and taste for information about new lands, he would suddenly break off because it was his hour for prayer ; at others, he would end the interview quite as unceremoniously, because it was time for ablution. Thus, between praying, wash-ing, eating, sleeping, slave-dealing, and fanning his dropsical feet, the life of the Ali-Mami passed monotonously enough even for an oriental prince ; but I doubt not, the same childish routine is still religiously pursued, unless it has pleased Allah to sum-mon the faithful prince to the paradise of " true believers." I could never make him understand how a ship might be built large enough to hold provisions for a six months' voyage ; and, as to the *sea*, " it was a mystery that none but God and a white man could solve ! "

As I was to breakfast on the day of my arrival at the dwell-ing of Ahmah-de-Bellah's mother, after my presentation to the prince her husband, I urged the footsteps of my companion with no little impatience as soon as I got out of the royal hearing. My fast had been rather longer than comfortable, even in obedi-ence to royal etiquette. However, we were soon within the court-yard of her sable ladyship, who, though a dame of fifty at least, persisted in hiding her charms of face and bosom beneath a capacious cloth. Nevertheless, she welcomed me quite ten-derly. She called me " Ahmah-de-Bellah-Theodoree,"—and, with her own hands, mixed the dainties on which we were to breakfast while cosily squatted on the mats of her verandah. Our food was simple enough for the most dyspeptic homœopa-thist. Milk and rice were alternated with bonney-clabber and honey, seasoned by frequent words of hospitable encouragement. The frugal repast was washed down by calabashes of cool water, which were handed round by naked damsels, whose beautiful limbs might have served as models for an artist.

When the meal was finished, I hoped that the day's ceremo-nial was over, but, to my dismay, I discovered that the most formal portion of my reception was yet to come.

" We will now hasten," said Ahmah-de-Bellah, as I *salaamed* his mamma, " to the palaver-ground, where I am sure our chiefs are, by this time, impatient to see you." Had I been a feeble instead of a robust campaigner, I would not have resisted the intimation, or desired a postponement of the " palaver ; " so I " took my brother's " arm, and, followed by my *cortège*, proceeded to the interview that was to take place beyond the walls, in an exquisite grove of cotton-wood and tamarind-trees, appropriated to this sort of town-meeting. Here I found a vast assemblage of burghers ; and in their midst, squatted on sheepskins, was a select ring of *patres conscripti*, presided by Sulimani-Ali, son of the king, and brother of my companion.

As the Fullah presented me to his warrior-kinsman, he rose with a profound salutation, and taking my hand, led me to a rock, covered with a white napkin,—the seat of honor for an eminent stranger. The moment I was placed, the chiefs sprang up and each one grasped my hand, bidding me welcome *thrice*. Ahmah-de-Bellah stood patiently beside me until this ceremony was over, and each noble resumed his sheepskin. Then, taking a long cane from the eldest of the group, he stepped forward, saluted the assembly three times, thrice invoked Allah, and introduced me to the chiefs and multitude as his " brother." I came, he said, to Footha-Yallon on his invitation, and by the express consent of his beloved king and father, and of his beloved elder brother, Sulimani. He hoped, therefore, that every " head-man" present would see the rites of hospitality faithfully exercised to his white brother while he dwelt in Footha. There were many reasons that he could give why this should be done ; but he would rest content with stating only three. First of all : I was nearly as good a Mussulman as many Mandingoes, and he knew the fact, because *he had converted me himself !* Secondly : I was entitled to every sort of courtesy from Fullahs, because I was a *rich* trader from the Rio Pongo. And, thirdly : I had penetrated even to this very heart of Africa to purchase slaves for most liberal prices.

It is the custom in African " palavers," as well as among African religionists, to give token of assent by a sigh, a groan, a slight exclamation, or a shout, when any thing affecting, agreeable, or touching is uttered by a speaker. Now, when my Fullah brother informed his friends of my arrival, my name, my demand for hospitality, and my wealth, the grunts and groans of the assembly augmented in number and volume as he went on ; but when they heard of my design " to purchase *slaves*," a climax was reached at once, and, as with one voice, they shouted. " May the Lord of heaven be praised ! "

I smothered a laugh and strangled a smile as well as I could, when my interpreters expounded the "stump speech " of Ahmah-de-Bellah ; and I lost no time in directing them to display the presents which some of my retainers, in the meanwhile, had brought to the grove. They consisted of several packages of blue and white calicoes, ten yards of brilliant scarlet cloth, six kegs of powder, three hundred pounds of tobacco, two strings of amber beads, and six muskets. On a beautiful rug, I set aside the gilded sword and *a package of cantharides*, designed for the king.

When my arrangement was over, Sulimani took the cane from his brother, and stepping forward, said that the gifts to which he pointed proved the truth of Ahmah-de-Bellah's words, and that a rich man, indeed, had come to Footha-Yallon. Nay, more ;— the rich man wanted slaves ! Was I not generous ? I was their guest, and owed them no tribute or duties ; and yet, had I not *voluntarily* lavished my presents upon the chiefs ? Next day, his father would personally distribute my offering ; but, whilst I dwelt in Footha, a bullock and ten baskets of rice should daily be furnished for my caravan's support ; and, as every chief would partake my bounty, each one should contribute to my comfort.

This speech, like the former, was hailed with grunts ; but I could not help noticing that the vote of supplies was not cheered half as lustily as the announcement of my *largesse*.

The formalities being over, the inquisitive head-men crowded round the presents with as much eagerness as aspirants for office at a presidential inauguration. The merchandise was inspected, felt, smelled, counted, measured, and set aside. The rug and the sword, being royal gifts, were delicately handled. But when the vials of cantharides were unpacked, and their contents announced, each of the chieftains insisted that his majesty should not monopolize the coveted stimulant. A sharp dispute on the subject arose between the princes and the councillors , so that I was forced to interfere through the interpreters, who could only quiet the rebels by the promise of a dozen additional flasks for their private account.

In the midst of the wrangling, Sulimani and Ahmah ordered their father's slaves to carry the gifts to the Ali-Mami's palace ; and, taking me between them, we marched, arm in arm, to my domicil. Here I found Abdulmomen-Ali, another son of the king, waiting for his brothers to present him to the Mongo of Kambia. Abdulmomen was introduced as " a learned divine," and began at once to talk Koran in the most *mufti*-like manner. I had made such sorry improvement in Mahometanism since Ahmah-de-Bellah's departure from the Rio Pongo, that I thought it safest to sit silent, as if under the deepest fervor of Mussulman conviction. I soon found that Abdulmomen, like many more clergymen, was willing enough to do all the preaching, whenever he found an unresisting listener. I put on a look of very intelligent assent and thankfulness to all the arguments and commentaries of my black brother, and in this way I avoided the detection of my ignorance, as many a better man has probably done before me !

# CHAPTER XXIV.

TIMBO lies on a rolling plain.  North of it, a lofty mountain
range rises at the distance of ten or fifteen miles, and sweeps
eastwardly to the horizon.  The landscape, which declines from
these slopes to the south, is in many places bare; yet fields of
plentiful cultivation, groves of cotton-wood, tamarind and oak,
thickets of shrubbery and frequent villages, stud its surface, and
impart an air of rural comfort to the picturesque scene.

I soon proposed a gallop with my African kindred over the
neighborhood; and, one fine morning, after a plentiful breakfast
of stewed fowls, boiled to rags with rice, and seasoned with
delicious "palavra sauce," we cantered off to the distant villages.
As we approached the first brook, but before the fringe of screening bushes was passed, our cavalcade drew rein abruptly, while
Ahmah-de-Bellah cried out : " Strangers are coming ! "  A few
moments after, as we slowly crossed the stream, I noticed several
women crouched in the underwood, having fled from the bath.
This warning is universally given, and enforced by law, to guard
the modesty of the gentler sex.

In half an hour we reached the first suburban village; but
fame had preceded us with my character, and as the settlement
was cultivated either by serfs or negroes liable to be made so,
we found the houses bare.  The poor wretches had learned, on

the day of my reception, that the principal object of my journey was to obtain slaves, and, of course, they imagined that the only object of my foray in their neighborhood, was to seize the gang and bear it abroad in bondage.  Accordingly, we tarried only a few minutes in Findo, and dashed off to Furo ; but here, too, the blacks had been panic-struck, and escaped so hurriedly that they left their pots of rice, vegetables, and meat boiling in their sheds.  Furo was absolutely stripped of inhabitants ; the veteran chief of the village did not even remain to do the honors for his affrighted brethren.  Ahmah-de-Bellah laughed heartily at the terror I inspired ; but I confess I could not help feeling sadly mortified when I found my presence shunned as a pestilence.

The native villages through which I passed on this excursion manifested the great comfort in which these Africans live throughout their prolific land, when unassailed by the desolating wars that are kept up for slave-trade.  It was the height of the dry season, when every thing was parched by the sun, yet I could trace the outlines of fine plantations, gardens, and rice-fields.  Every where I found abundance of peppers, onions, garlic, tomatoes, sweet potatoes, and cassava, while tasteful fences were garlanded with immense vines and flowers.  Fowls, goats, sheep, and oxen, stalked about in innumerable flocks, and from every domicil depended a paper, inscribed with a charm from the Koran to keep off thieves and witches.

My walks through Timbo were promoted by the constant efforts of my entertainers to shield me from intrusive curiosity.  Whenever I sallied forth, two townsfolk in authority were sent forward to warn the public that the Furtoo desired to promenade without a mob at his heels.  These lusty criers stationed themselves at the corners with an iron triangle, which they rattled to call attention to the king's command ; and, in a short time, the highways were so clear of people, who feared a *bastinado*, that I found my loneliness rather disagreeable than otherwise.  *Every person I saw, shunned me.*  When I called the children or little girls,—they fled from me.  My reputation as a slaver in the villages, and the fear of a lash in the town, furnished me much more solitude than is generally agreeable to a sensitive traveller.

Towards night-fall I left my companions, and wrapping myself closely in a Mandingo dress, stole away through bye-ways to a brook which runs by the town walls. Thither the females resort at sunset to draw water; and, choosing a screened situation, where I would not be easily observed, I watched, for more than an hour, the graceful children, girls, and women of Timbo, as they performed this domestic task of eastern lands.

I was particularly impressed by the general beauty of the sex, who, in many respects, resembled the Moor rather than the negro. Unaware of a stranger's presence, they came forth as usual in a simple dress which covers their body from waist to knee, and leaves the rest of the figure entirely naked. Group after group gathered together on the brink of the brook in the slanting sunlight and lengthening shadows of the plain. Some rested on their pitchers and water vessels; some chatted, or leaned on each other gracefully, listening to the chat of friends; some stooped to fill their jars; others lifted the brimming vessels to their sisters' shoulders—while others strode homeward singing, with their charged utensils poised on head or hand. Their slow, stately, swinging movement under the burden, was grace that might be envied on a Spanish *paseo*. I do not think the forms of these Fullah girls,—with their complexions of freshest bronze,—are exceeded in symmetry by the women of any other country. There was a slender delicacy of limb, waist, neck, hand, foot, and bosom, which seemed to be the type that moulded every one of them. I saw none of the hanging breast; the flat, expanded nostrils; the swollen lips, and fillet-like foreheads, that characterize the Soosoos and their sisters of the coast. None were deformed, nor were any marked by traces of disease. I may observe, moreover, that the male Fullahs of Timbo are impressed on my memory by a beauty of form, which almost equals that of the women; and, in fact, the only fault I found with them was their minute resemblance to the feminine delicacy of the other sex. They made up, however, in courage what they lacked in form, for their manly spirit has made them

THE WOMEN OF TIMBO DRAWING WATER.

renowned among all the tribes they have so long controlled by distinguished bravery and perseverance.

The patriarchal landscape by the brook, with the Oriental girls over their water-jars, and the lowing cattle in the pastures, brought freshly to my mind many a Bible scene I heard my mother read when I was a boy at home; and I do not know what revolution might have been wrought on my spirit had I not suddenly become critical! A stately dame passed within twenty feet of my thicket, whose *coiffure* excited my mirth so powerfully that I might have been detected as a spy, had not a bitten lip controlled my laughter. Her ladyship belonged, perhaps, to the "upper-ten" of Timbo, whose heads had hitherto been hidden from my eyes by the jealous *yashmacks* they constantly wear in a stranger's presence. In this instance, however, the woman's head, like that of the younger girls, was uncovered, so that I had a full view of the stately preparation. Her lower limbs were clad in ample folds of blue and white cotton, knotted in an immense mass at the waist, while her long crisp hair had been combed out to its fullest dimensions and spliced with additional wool. The ebony fleece was then separated in strands half an inch in diameter, and plaited all over her skull in a countless number of distinct braids. This quill-like structure was then adorned with amber beads, and copiously anointed with vegetable butter, so that the points gleamed with fire in the setting sunlight, and made her look as if she had donned for a bewitching headdress a porcupine instead of a "bird of paradise."

My trip to Timbo, I confess, was one of business rather than pleasure or scientific exploration. I did not make a record, at the moment, of my "impressions de voyage," and never thought that, a quarter of a century afterwards, I would feel disposed to chronicle the journey in a book, as an interesting *souvenir* of my early life. Had I supposed that the day would come when I was to turn author, it is likely I might have been more inquisitive; but, being only "a slaver," I found Ahma, Sulimani, Abdulmomen, the Ali-Mami, and all the quality and amusements of Timbo, dull enough, *when my object was achieved*. Still, while I was there, I thought I might as well see all that was visible. I strolled repeatedly through the town. I became excessively familiar with its narrow streets, low houses, mud walls, cul-de-sacs, and mosques. I saw no fine bazaars, market-places, or shops. The chief wants of life were supplied by peddlers. Platters, jars, and baskets of fruit, vegetables, and meat, were borne around twice or thrice daily. Horsemen dashed about on beautiful steeds towards the fields in the morning, or came home at night-fall at a slower pace. *I never saw man or woman bask lazily in the sun.* Females were constantly busy over their cotton and spinning wheels when not engaged in household occupations; and often have I seen an elderly dame quietly crouched in her hovel at sunset reading the Koran. Nor are the men of Timbo less thrifty. Their city wall is said to hem in about ten thousand individuals, representing all the social industries They weave cotton, work in leather, fabricate iron from the bar, engage diligently in agriculture, and, whenever not laboriously employed, devote themselves to reading and writing, of which they are excessively fond.

These are the faint sketches, which, on ransacking my brain, I find resting on its tablets. But I was tired of Timbo; I was perfectly refreshed from my journey; and I was anxious to return to my factory on the beach. Two "moons" only had been originally set apart for the enterprise, and the third was already waxing towards its full. I feared the Ali-Mami was not yet prepared with *slaves* for my departure, and I dreaded lest objections might be made if I approached his royal highness with the flat announcement. Accordingly, I schooled my interpreters, and visited that important personage. I made a long speech, as full of compliments and blarney as a Christmas pudding is of plums, and concluded by touching the soft part in African royalty's heart—*slaves!* I told the king that a vessel or two, with abundant freights, would be waiting me on the river, and that I must hasten thither with his choicest gangs if he hoped to reap a profit.

The king and the royal family were no doubt excessively grieved to part with the Furtoo Mongo, but they were discreet persons and " listened to reason." War parties and scouts were forthwith despatched to blockade the paths, while press-gangs made recruits among the villages, and even in Timbo. Sulimani-Ali, himself, sallied forth, before daybreak, with a troop of horse, and at sundown, came back with forty-five splendid fellows, captured in Findo and Furo !

The personal dread of me in the town itself, was augmented. If I had been a Pestilence before, I was Death now ! When I took my usual morning walk the children ran from me screaming. Since the arrival of Sulimani with his victims, all who were under the yoke thought their hour of exile had come. The poor regarded me as the devil incarnate. Once or twice, I caught women throwing a handful of dust or ashes towards me, and uttering an invocation from the Koran to avert the demon or save them from his clutches. Their curiosity was merged in terror. *My popularity was over !*

It was not a little amusing that in the midst of the general dismay, caused by the court of Timbo and myself, my colored brother Ahmah-de-Bellah, and his kinsman Abdulmomen, lost no chance of lecturing me about my soul ! We kidnapped the Africans all day and spouted Islamism all night ! Our religion, however, was more speculative than practical. It was much more important, they thought, that we should embrace the faith of their peculiar theology, than that we should trouble ourselves about human rights that interfered with profits and pockets. We spared Mahometans and enslaved *only* " *the heathen ;* " so that, in fact, we were merely obedient to the behests of Mahomet when we subdued " the infidel ! "

This process of proselytism, however, was not altogether successful. As I was already a rather poor Christian, I fear that the Fullah did not succeed in making me a very good Mussulman. Still, I managed to amuse him with the hope of my *future* improvement in his creed, so that we were very good friends when the Ali-Mami summoned us for a final interview.

The parting of men is seldom a maudlin affair. The king's relations presented me bullocks, cows, goats, and sheep. His majesty sent me five slaves. Sulimani-Ali offered a splendid white charger. The king's wife supplied me with an African quilt ingeniously woven of red and yellow threads unravelled from Manchester cottons; while Ahmah-de-Bellah, like a gentleman of taste, despatched for my consolation, the two prettiest handmaidens he could buy or steal in Timbo !

## CHAPTER XXV.

I SHALL not weary the reader with a narrative of my journey homeward over the track I had followed on my way to Timbo. A grand Mahometan service was performed at my departure, and Ahmah-de-Bellah accompanied me as far as Jallica, whence he was recalled by his father in consequence of a serious family dispute that required his presence. Ali-Ninpha was prepared, in this place, to greet me with a welcome, and a copious supply of gold, wax, ivory, and slaves. At Tamisso, the worthy Mahomedoo had complied with his promise to furnish a similar addition to the caravan; so that when we set out for Kya, our troop was swelled to near a thousand strong, counting men, women, children and ragamuffins.

At Kya I could not help tarrying four days with my jolly friend Ibrahim, who received the tobacco, charged with "bitters," during my absence, and was delighted to furnish a nourishing drop after my long abstinence. As we approached the coast, another halt was called at a favorable encampment, where Ali-Ninpha divided the caravan in four parts, reserving the best portion of slaves and merchandise for me. The division, before arrival, was absolutely necessary, in order to prevent disputes or disastrous quarrels in regard to the merchantable quality of negroes on the beach.

I hoped to take my people by surprise at Kambia; but when the factory came in sight from the hill-tops back of the settlement, I saw the Spanish flag floating from its summit, and heard the cannon booming forth a welcome to the wanderer. Every thing had been admirably conducted in my absence. The Fullah and my clerk preserved their social relations and the public tranquillity unimpaired. My factory and warehouse were as neat and orderly as when I left them, so that I had nothing to do but go to sleep as if I had made a day's excursion to a neighboring village.

Within a week I paid for the caravan's produce, despatched Mami-de-Yong, and made arrangements with the captain of a slaver in the river for the remainder of his merchandise. But the Fullah chief had not left me more than a day or two, when I was surprised by a traveller who dashed into my factory, with a message from Ahmah-de-Bellah at Timbo, whence he had posted in twenty-one days.

Ahmah was in trouble. He had been recalled, as I said, from Jallica by family quarrels. When he reached the paternal mat, he found his sister Beeljie bound hand and foot in prison, with orders for her prompt transportation to my factory as a slave. These were the irrevocable commands of his royal father, and of her half-brother, Sulimani. All his appeals, seconded by those of his mother, were unheeded. She must be *shipped* from the Rio Pongo; and no one could be trusted with the task but the Ali-Mami's son and friend, the Mongo Téodor!

To resist this dire command, Ahmah charged the messenger to appeal to my heart by our brotherly love, *not* to allow the maiden to be sent over sea; but, by force or stratagem, to retain her until he arrived on the beach.

The news amazed me. I knew that African Mahometans never sold their caste or kindred into foreign slavery, unless their crime deserved a penalty severer than death. I reflected a while on the message, because I did not wish to complicate my relations with the leading chiefs of the interior; but, in a few moments, natural sensibility mastered every selfish impulse, and I told the envoy to hasten back on the path of the suffering brother, and assure him I would shield his sister, even at the risk of his kindred's wrath.

About a week afterwards I was aroused one morning by a runner from a neighboring village over the hill, who stated that a courier reached his town the night before from Sulimani-Ali,— a prince of Timbo,—conducting a Fullah girl, who was to be sold by me *immediately* to a Spanish slaver. The girl, he said, resisted with all her energy. She refused to walk. For the last four days she had been borne along in a litter. She swore never to " see the ocean ; " and threatened to dash her skull against the first rock in her path, if they attempted to carry her further. The stanch refusal embarrassed her Mahometan conductor, inasmuch as his country's law forbade him to use extraordinary compulsion, or degrade the maiden with a whip.

I saw at once that this delay and hesitation afforded an opportunity to interfere judiciously in behalf of the spirited girl, whose sins or faults were still unknown to me. Accordingly, I imparted the tale to Ali-Ninpha; and, with his consent, despatched a shrewd dame from the Mandingo's *harem*, with directions for her conduct to the village. Woman's tact and woman's sympathy are the same throughout the world, and the proud ambassadress undertook her task with pleased alacrity. I warned her to be extremely cautious before the myrmidons of Sulimani, but to seize a secret moment when she might win the maiden's confidence, to inform her that I was the sworn friend of Ahmah-de-Bellah, and would save her *if she followed my commands implicitly*. She must cease resistance at once. She must come to the river, which was fresh water, and not salt ; and she must allow her jailors to fulfil all the orders they received from her tyrannical kinsmen. Muffled in the messenger's garments, I sent the manuscript Koran of Ahmah-de-Bellah as a token of my truth, and bade the dame assure Beeljie that her brother was already far on his journey to redeem her in Kambia.

The mission was successful, and, early next day, the girl was brought to my factory, *with a rope round her neck*.

The preliminaries for her purchase were tedious and formal. As her sale was compulsory, there was not much question as to quality or price. Still, I was obliged to promise a multitude of things I did not intend to perform. In order to disgrace the poor creature as much as possible, her sentence declared she should be "sold for salt,"—the most contemptuous of all African exchanges, and used in the interior for the purchase of *cattle* alone.

Poor Beeljie stood naked and trembling before us while these ceremonies were performing. A scowl of indignation flitted like a shadow over her face, as she heard the disgusting commands. Tenderly brought up among the princely brood of Timbo, she was a bright and delicate type of the classes I described at the brookside. Her limbs and features were stained by the dust of travel, and her expression was clouded with the grief of sensible degradation: still I would have risked more than I did, when I beheld the mute appeal of her face and form, to save her from the doom of Cuban exile.

When the last tub of salt was measured, I cut the rope from Beeljie's neck, and, throwing over her shoulders a shawl,—in which she instantly shrank with a look of gratitude,—called the female who had borne my cheering message, to take the girl to her house and treat her as the sister of my Fullah brother.

As I expected, this humane command brought the emissary of Sulimani to his feet with a bound. He insisted on the restitution of the woman! He swore I had deceived him; and, in fact, went through a variety of African antics which are not unusual, even among the most civilized of the tribes, when excited to extraordinary passion.

It was my habit, during these outbursts of native ire, to remain perfectly quiet, not only until the explosion was over, but while the smoke was disappearing from the scene. I fastened my eye, therefore, silently, but intensely, on the tiger, following him in all his movements about the apartment, till he sank, subdued and panting, on the mat. I then softly told him that this excitement was not only unbecoming a Mahometan gentleman, and fit for a savage alone, but that it was altogether wasted on the present occasion, *inasmuch as the girl should be put on board a slaver in his presence.* Nevertheless, I continued, while the sister of Ahmah was under my roof, her blood must be respected, and she should be treated in every respect as a royal person.

I was quite as curious as the reader may be to know the crime of Beeljie, for, up to that moment, I had not been informed of it. Dismissing the Fullah as speedily as possible, I hastened to Ali-Ninpha's dwelling and heard the sufferer's story.

The Mahometan princess, whose age surely did not exceed eighteen, had been promised by the king and her half-brother, Sulimani, to an old relative, who was not only accused of cruelty to his harem's inmates, but was charged by Mussulmen with the heinous crime of eating " unclean flesh." The girl, who seemed to be a person of masculine courage and determination, resisted this disposal of her person; but, while her brother Ahmah was away, she was forced from her mother's arms and given to the filthy dotard.

It is commonly supposed that women are doomed to the basest obedience in oriental lands; yet, it seems there is a Mahometan law,—or, at least, a Fullah custom,—which saves the purity of an unwilling bride. The delivery of Beeljie to her brutal lord kindled the fire of an ardent temper. She furnished the old gentleman with specimens of violence to which his harem had been a stranger, save when the master himself chose to indulge in wrath. In fact, the Fullah damsel—half acting, half in reality—played the virago so finely, that her husband, after exhausting arguments, promises and supplications, sent her back to her kindred *with an insulting message.*

It was a sad day when she returned to the paternal roof in Timbo. Her resistance was regarded by the dropsical despot as rebellious disobedience to father and brother; and, as neither authority nor love would induce the outlaw to repent, her barbarous parent condemned her to be " *a slave to Christians.*"

Her story ended, I consoled the poor maiden with every assurance of protection and comfort; for, now that the excitement of sale and journey was over, her nerves gave way, and she sank on her mat, completely exhausted. I commended her to the safeguard of my landlord and the especial kindness of his women. Esther, too, stole up at night to comfort the sufferer with her fondling tenderness, for she could not speak the Fullah language;—and in a week, I had the damsel in capital condition ready for a daring enterprise that was to seal her fate.

When the Spanish slaver, whose cargo I had just completed, was ready for sea, I begged her captain to aid me in the shipment of " *a princess* " who had been consigned to my wardship by her royal relations in the interior, but whom I dared not put on board his vessel *until she was beyond the Rio Pongo's bar.* The officer assented ; and when the last boat-load of slaves was despatched from my *barracoon,* he lifted his anchor and floated down the stream till he got beyond the furthest breakers. Here, with sails loosely furled, and every thing ready for instant departure, he again laid to, awaiting the royal *bonne bouche.*

In the mean time, I hurried Beeljie with her friends and Fullah jailer to the beach, so that when the slaver threw his sails aback and brought his vessel to the wind, I lost not a moment in putting the girl in a canoe, with five Kroomen to carry her through the boiling surf.

" Allah be praised ! " sighed the Fullah, as the boat shot ahead into the sea; while the girls of the harem fell on the sand with wails of sorrow. The Kroomen, with their usual skill, drove the buoyant skiff swiftly towards the slaver ; but, as they approached the breakers south of the bar, a heavy roller struck it on the side, and instantly, its freight was struggling in the surge.

In a twinkling, the Fullah was on the earth, his face buried in the sand ; the girls screamed and tore their garments ; Ali-Ninpha's wife clung to me with the grasp of despair ; while I, stamping with rage, cursed the barbarity of the maiden's parent, whose sentence had brought her to this wretched fate.

I kicked the howling hypocrite beneath me, and bade him hasten with the news to Timbo, and tell the wicked patriarch that the Prophet himself had destroyed the life of his wretched child, sooner than suffer her to become a Christian's slave.

The Spanish vessel was under full sail, sweeping rapidly out to sea, and the Kroomen swam ashore without their boat, as the grieving group slowly and sadly retraced their way along the river's bank to Kambia.

There was wailing that night in the village, and there was wailing in Timbo when the Fullah returned with the tragic story

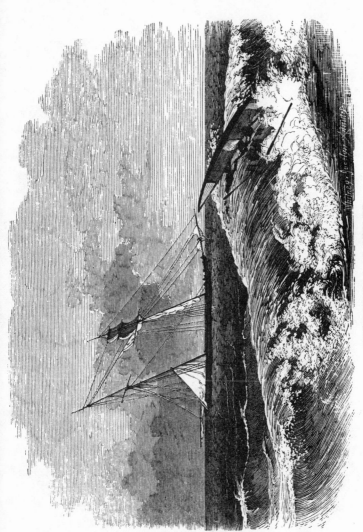

THE SHIPPING OF BEELJIE

In fact, such was the distracted excitement both on the sea-shore and in the settlement, that none of my companions had eyes to observe an episode of the drama which had been played that evening without rehearsal.

Every body who has been on the coast of Africa, or read of its people, knows that Kroomen are altogether unaware of any difference between a smooth river and the angriest wave. They would as willingly be upset in the surf as stumble against a rock. I took advantage of this amphibious nature, to station a light canoe immediately on the edge of the breakers, and to order the daring swimmers it contained to grasp the girl the moment her canoe was *purposely upset !* I promised the divers a liberal reward if they lodged her in their boat, or swam with her to the nearest point of the opposite beach ; and so well did they perform their secret task, that when they drew ashore her fainting body, it was promptly received by a trusty Bager, who was in waiting on the beach. Before the girl recovered her senses she was safely afloat in the fisherman's canoe. His home was in a village on the coast below ; and, perhaps, it still remains a secret to this day, how it was that, *for years after, a girl, the image of the lost Beeljie, followed the footsteps of Ahmah, the Fullah of Timbo !*

## CHAPTER XXVI.

AFTER my toilsome journey to the interior, my despatch of a slaver, and my adventurous enterprise in behalf of a Fullah princess, I thought myself entitled to a long *siesta ;* but my comfortable desires and anticipations were doomed to disappointment. I was suddenly stirred from this willing lethargy by a salute of twenty one guns in the offing.   Our wonder was almost insupportable as to the character of the ceremonious stranger who wasted powder so profusely, while a boy was despatched to the top of the look-out tree to ascertain his character.   He reported a schooner anchored opposite Bangalang, sporting a long pendant at the main, and a white ensign at her peak.   I took it for granted that no man-of-war would *salute* a native chief, and so concluded that it was some pretentious Frenchman, unacquainted with the prudent customs of our demure coast.

The conjecture was right.   At nightfall Mr. Ormond—whose humor had somewhat improved since my return—apprised me that a Gallic slaver had arrived to his consignment with a rich cargo, and hoped I would join him at breakfast on board, by invitation of the commander.

Next morning, at sunrise, the Mongo and myself met for the first time after our rupture with apparent cordiality on the deck of " La Perouse," where we· were welcomed with all that cordiality of grimace for which a half-bred Frenchman is so justly celebrated. Captain Brulôt could not speak English, nor could Mr. Ormond express himself in French; so we wasted the time till breakfast was served in discussing his cargo and prospects, through my interpretation. Fine samples of gaudy calicoes, French guns, and superior brandy, were exhibited and dwelt on with characteristic eloquence; but the Gaul closed his bewitching catalogue with a shout of joy that made the cabin ring, as he announced the complement of his cargo to be *five hundred doubloons*. The scent of gold has a peculiar charm to African slavers, and it will readily be supposed that our appetite for the promised *déjeuner* was not a little stimulated by the Spanish coin. As rapidly as we could, we summed up the doubloons and his merchandise; and, estimating the entire cargo at about $17,000, offered him three hundred and fifty negroes for the lot. The bid was no sooner made than accepted. Our private boats were sent ashore in search of canoes to discharge the goods, and, with a relish and spirit I never saw surpassed, we sat down to a piquant breakfast, spread on deck beneath the awning.

I will not attempt to remember the dishes which provoked our appetites and teased our thirst. We were happy already on the delightful claret that washed down the viands; but, after the substantials were gone, coffee was served, and succeeded by half a dozen various cordials, the whole being appropriately capped by the foam of champagne.

When the last bumper was quaffed in honor of " La Perouse" and " belle France," Captain Brulôt called for his writing-desk; when, at the instant, four men sprung up as if by enchantment behind the Mongo and myself, and grasping our arms with the gripe of a vice, held us in their clutches till the carpenter riveted a shackle on our feet.

The scene passed so rapidly,—the transition from gayety to outrage was so sharp and violent, that my bewildered mind cannot now declare with certainty, whether mirth or anger prevailed at the clap-trap trick of this dramatic *denouement*. I am quite sure, however, that if I laughed at first, I very soon swore; for I have a distinct recollection of dashing my fist in the poltroon's face before he could extemporize an explanation.

When our limbs were perfectly secure, the French scoundrel recommenced his shrugs, bows, grins and congées; and approaching Mr. Ormond with a sarcastic simper, apprised him that the *petite comedie* in which he took part, had been enacted for the collection of a trifling debt which his excellency the Mongo owed a beloved brother, who, alas! was no longer on earth to collect it for himself!

*Monsieur le Mongo,* he said, would have the kindness to remember that, several years ago, his brother had left some *two hundred slaves* in his hands until called for; and he would also please to take the trouble to recollect, that the said slaves had been twice sent for, and twice refused. *Monsieur le Mongo* must know, he continued, that there was not much law on the coast of Africa; and that, as he had Monsieur le Mongo's promissory note, or due-bill, for the negroes, he thought this charming little *ruse* would be the most amiable and practical mode of enforcing it! Did his friend, *le Mongo,* intend to honor this draft? It was properly endorsed, he would see, in favor of the bearer; and if the *esclaves* were quickly forthcoming, the whole affair would pass off as agreeably and quickly as the bubbles from a champagne glass.

By this time Ormond was so perfectly stupified by drink, as well as the atrocity, that he simply burst into a maudlin laugh, when I looked at him for an explanation of the charge. *I,* surely, was not implicated in it; yet, when I demanded the cause of the assault upon *my* person, in connection with the affair, Brulôt replied, with a shrug, that as I was Ormond's clerk when the note was signed, I *must* have had a finger in the pie; and, inasmuch as I now possessed a factory of my own, it would doubtless be delightful to aid my ancient patron in the liquidation of a debt that I knew to be lawful.

It was altogether useless to deny my presence in the factory, or knowledge of the transaction, which, in truth, had occurred long before my arrival on the Rio Pongo, during the clerkship of my predecessor. Still, I insisted on immediate release. An hour flew by in useless parley. But the Frenchman was firm, and swore that nothing would induce him to liberate either of us without payment of the bill. While we were talking, a crowd of canoes was seen shoving off from Bangalang, filled with armed men; whereupon the excited Gaul ordered his men to quarters, and double-shotted his guns.

As the first boat came within striking distance, a ball was fired across her bows, which not only sent back the advance, but made the entire fleet tack ship and steer homeward in dismay. Soon after, however, I heard the war-drum beating in Bangalang, and could see the natives mustering in great numbers along the river banks; yet, what could undisciplined savages effect against the skinned teeth of our six-pounders? At sunset, however, my clerk came off, with a white flag, and the captain allowed him to row alongside to receive our orders in his presence. Ormond was not yet in a state to consult as to our appropriate means of rescue from the trickster's clutches; so I directed the young man to return in the morning with changes of raiment; but, in the mean while, to desire the villagers of both settlements to refrain from interference in our behalf. An excellent meal, with abundance of claret, was served for our entertainment, and, on a capital mattress, we passed a night of patient endurance in our iron stockings.

At daylight, water and towels were served for our refreshment. After coffee and cigars were placed on the board, Brulôt put by his sarcasm, and, in an off-hand fashion, demanded whether we had come to our senses and intended to pay the debt? My Italian blood was in a fever, and I said nothing. Ormond, however,—now entirely sober, and who was enjoying a cigar with the habitual *insouciance* of a mulatto,—replied quietly that he could make no promises or arrangements whilst confined on board, but if allowed to go ashore, he would fulfil his obligation in two or three days. An hour was spent by the Frenchman in pondering on the proposal; when it was finally agreed that the Mongo should be set at liberty, provided he left, as hostages, four of his children and two of the black chiefs who visited him in my boat. The compact was sealed by the hoisting of a flag under the discharge of a blank cartridge; and, in an hour, the pledges were in the cabin, under the eye of a sentry, while the Mongo was once more in Bangalang.

These negotiations, it will be perceived, did not touch *my* case, though I was in no manner guilty; yet I assented to the proposal because I thought that Ormond would be better able than myself to find the requisite number of slaves at that moment. I ordered my clerk, however, to press all the indifferent and useless servants in my factory, and to aid the Mongo with every slave at present in my *barracoon*.

Before sunset of that day, this young man came aboard with fifty negroes from my establishment, and demanded my release. It was refused. Next day forty more were despatched by the Mongo; but still my liberty was denied. I upbraided the scoundrel with his meanness, and bade him look out for the day of retribution. But he snapped his fingers at my threat as he exclaimed: " *Cher ami, ce n'est que la fortune de guerre !* "

It was a task of difficulty to collect the remaining one hundred and ten slaves among factories which had been recently drained by Cuban vessels. Many domestic menials escaped to the forest when the story became known, as they did not wish to take the place of their betters in the " French service."

Thrice had the sun risen and set since I was a prisoner. During all the time, my blood tingled for revenge. I was tricked, humbled and disgraced. Never did I cease to pray for the arrival of some well-armed *Spanish slaver;* and, towards evening of the fourth day, lo! the boon was granted! That afternoon, a boat manned by negroes, passed with the Spanish flag; but, as there was no white man aboard, Brulôt took it for a *ruse* of the Mongo, designed to alarm him into an unconditional release of his captives.

I must do the Gaul the justice to declare, that during my confinement, he behaved like a gentleman, in supplies from the pantry and spirit room. Neither was he uncivil or unkind in his general demeanor. Indeed, he several times regretted that this was the only means in his power " to collect a promissory note on the coast of Africa; " yet, I was not Christian enough to sympathize with the sheriff, or to return his compliments with any thing but a curse. But, now that a Spaniard was within hail, I felt a sudden lifting of the weight that was on my heart.

I shouted for champagne! The steward brought it with alacrity, and poured with trembling hand the bumpers I drained to Saint Jago and old Spain. The infection soon spread. They began to believe that a rescue was at hand. The news was heard with dismay in the forecastle. Brulôt alone stood obstinate, but indecisive.

Presently, I called him to join me in a glass, and, as we drank the foaming liquid, I pledged him to another " within twenty-four hours beneath the Spanish flag." The Gaul feigned a sort of hectic hilarity as he swallowed the wine and the toast, but he could not stand the flash of revenge in my eye and burning cheek, and retired to consult with his officers.

## CHAPTER XXVII.

I SLEPT soundly that night; but the sun was not clear of the
forest when I hobbled on deck in my shackles, and was searching
the seaward horizon for my beloved Castilian. Presently the
breeze began to freshen, and the tall, raking masts of a schooner
were seen gliding above the tops of the mangroves that masked
the Rio Pongo's mouth. Very soon the light wind and tide
drifted her clear of the bends, and an anchor was let go within
musket-shot of my prison, while springs were run out to the
bushes to give range to her broadside. I saw at once, from her
manœuvres, that Ormond had communicated with the craft during the night.

Brulôt felt that his day was over. The Spaniard's decks
were crowded with an alert, armed crew; four charming little
bull-dogs showed their muzzles from port holes; while a large
brass swivel, amidships, gave token of its readiness to fight or
salute. For a minute or two the foiled Frenchman surveyed the
scene through his glass; then, throwing it over his shoulder,
ordered the mate to strike off my "darbies." As the officer
obeyed, a voice was heard from the Spaniard, commanding a
boat to be sent aboard, under penalty of a shot if not instantly
obeyed. The boat was lowered; but who would man her? The
chief officer refused; the second declined; the French sailors

objected; the creoles and mulattoes from St. Thomas went
below; so that no one was left to fulfil the slaver's order but
Brulôt or myself.

"*Bien!*" said my crest-fallen cock, "it's your turn to crow,
Don Téodore. Fortune seems on your side, and you are again
free. Go to the devil, if you please, *mon camarade*, and send
your imps for the slaves as soon as you want them!"

By this time the Spaniard had lighted his matches, levelled
his guns, and, under the aim of his musketry, repeated the order
for a boat. Seeing the danger of our party, I leaped to the bulwarks, and hailing my deliverer in Spanish, bade him desist.
The request was obeyed as I threw myself into the yawl, cut the
rope, and, alone, sculled the skiff to the slaver.

A shout went up from the deck of my deliverer as I jumped
aboard and received the cordial grasp of her commander. Ali-
Ninpha, too, was there to greet and defend me with a chosen
band of his people. While I was absorbed in the joy of welcome and liberation, the African stole with his band to the
Frenchman's boat, and was rapidly filling it to board the foe,
when my clerk apprised me of the impending danger. I was
fortunate enough to control the enraged savage, else I know not
what might have been the fate of Brulôt and the officers during
the desertion of his mongrel and cowardly crew.

The captain desired his mates to keep an eye on the Gaul
while we retired to the cabin for consultation; and here I
learned that I was on board the "Esperanza," consigned to me
from Matanzas. In turn, I confirmed the account they had
already heard of my mishap from the Mongo's messengers; but
hoped the Cuban captain would permit me to take pacific revenge
after my own fashion, inasmuch as my captor—barring the irons
—had behaved with uncommon civility. I had no trouble, of
course, in obtaining the commander's assent to this request,
though he yielded it under the evident displeasure of his crew,
whose Spanish blood was up against the Frenchman, and would
willingly have inflicted a signal punishment on this neutral
ground.

After these preliminaries, Captain Escudero and myself re-

turned to the " La Perouse " with two boat-loads of armed followers, while our approach was covered by the cannons and small
arms of the " Esperanza." Brulôt received us in moody silence
on the quarter-deck. His officers sat sulkily on a gun to leeward, while two or three French seamen walked to and fro on
the forecastle.

My first command was to spike the vessel's guns. Next, I
decreed and superintended the disembarkation of the stolen
slaves ; and, lastly, I concluded the morning call with a request
that Brulôt would *produce the five hundred doubloons and his*
*" promissory note " for two hundred slaves!*

The fatal document, duly indorsed, was quickly delivered,
but no persuasion or threat induced the angry Gaul to show
his gold, or a manifest of the cargo.

After ample indulgence, I despatched a man to seek his
writing-desk, and discovered that six hundred doubloons had
in reality been shipped in St. Thomas. Of course, their production was imperiously demanded ; but Brulôt swore they had
been landed, with his supercargo, in the neighboring Rio Nunez.
I was near crediting the story, when a slight sneer I perceived
flickering over the steward's face, put me on the *qui vive* to request
an inspection of the log-book, which, unfortunately for my captor, did not record the disembarkation of the cash. This demonstrated Brulôt's falsehood, and authorized a demand for his trunk.
The knave winced as the steward descended to bring it ; and he
leaped with rage as I split it with a hatchet, and counted two
hundred and fifty Mexican doubloons on the deck. *His cargo,*
*however, proved to be a sham of samples.*

Turning innocently to Escudero, I remarked that he must
have been put to considerable trouble in rescuing me from this
outlaw, and hoped he would suffer his men to be recompensed
for their extra toil under the rays of an African sun. I would
not venture to judge the value of such devoted services ; but
requested him to fix his own price and receive payment on the
spot.

Escudero very naturally supposed that *about* two hundred
and fifty Mexican ounces would compensate him to a fraction,

and, accordingly, the two hundred and fifty shiners, glistening on the deck, forthwith returned to their bag and went overboard into his boat.

"*Adieu! mon cher*," said I, as I followed the gold; "*la fortune de guerre* has many phases, you see; how do you like this one? The next game you play on the coast of Africa, my chicken, recollect that though a *knave* can take a trick, yet the *knave may be trumped before the hand is played out!*"

# CHAPTER XXVIII.

LA ESPERANZA discharged her cargo rapidly, but, before I was ready to send back a living freight, poor Escudero fell a victim to African fever.

I had seen much of the country; I had made some money; my clerk was a reliable fellow; I was growing somewhat anxious for a change of scene; and, in fact, I only wanted a decent excuse to find myself once more aboard a " skimmer of the seas," for a little relaxation after the oppressive monotony of a slaver's life. Escudero's death seemed to offer the desired opportunity. His mate was an inexperienced seaman; his officers were unacquainted with the management of a slave cargo; and, upon a view of the whole field of interests, I thought it best to take charge of the schooner and pay a visit to my friends in Cuba. In the mean time, however, a Danish brig arrived for negroes, so that it became necessary for me, with my multiplied duties, to bestir myself in the collection of slaves.

Whilst I was dining one afternoon at Ormond's factory with the Danish captain of the trader, the boom of a gun, followed rapidly by two or three more, announced the arrival of another craft. We drank a toast to his advent, and were beginning to condole a little over our difficulty in procuring blacks, when the look-out ran into our room with the report that my Spaniard was firing into the Dane. We rushed to the piazza whence the scene of action might be beheld, and another shot from my vessel seemed to indicate that she was the aggressor. The Dane and myself hurried aboard our respective schooners, but when I reached the Esperanza, my crew were weighing anchor, while the quarter-deck was strewn with fire-arms. The mate stood on the heel of the bowsprit, urging his men to alacrity; the sailors hove at the windlass with mingled shouts of passion and oaths of revenge; on a mattress lay the bleeding form of my second officer, while a seaman groaned beside him with a musket ball in his shoulder.

My arrival was the signal for a pause. As quickly as possible, I inquired into the affray, which had originated like many a sailor's dispute, on a question of precedence at the watering place in a neighboring brook. The Danes were seven, and we but three. Our Spaniards had been driven off, and my second mate, in charge of the yawl, received a *trenchant* blow from an oar-blade, which cut his skull and felled him senseless on the sand.

Of course, " the watering " was over for the day, and both boats returned to their vessels to tell their stories. The moment the Danes got on board, they imprudently ran up their ensign; and, as this act of apparent defiance occurred just as the Esperanza was receiving the lifeless form of her officer, my excited crew discharged a broadside in reply to the warlike token. Gun followed gun, and musketry rattled against musketry. The Dane miscalculated the range of the guns, and his grape fell short of my schooner, while our snarling sixes made sad havoc with his bulwarks and rigging.

I had hardly learned the facts of the case and thought of a truce, when the passionate Northman sent a round-shot whistling over my head. Another and another followed in its wake, but they aimed too high for damage. At twenty-four our blood is not so diplomatically pacific as in later years, and this second aggression rekindled the lava in my Italian veins. There was no longer question of a white flag or a parley. In a twinkling,

I slipped my cable and ran up the jib and mainsail, so as to swing the schooner into a raking position at short quarters; and before the Dane could counteract my manœuvre, I gave him a dose of grape and cannister which tore his ensign to ribbons and spoiled the looks of his hull materially. My second shot splintered the edge of his mast; but while I was making ready for a third, to tickle him betwixt wind and water, down tumbled his impertinent pendant and the day was won.

For a while there was a dead silence between the warriors. Neither hailed nor sent a boat on board of the other. Ormond perceived this cessation of hostilities from his piazza at Bangalang, and coming out in a canoe, rowed to the Dane after hearing my version of the battle.

I waited anxiously either for his return or a message, but as I was unadvised of the Mongo's views and temper in regard to the affray, I thought it well, before dark, to avoid treachery by quitting the river and placing my schooner in a creek with her broadside to the shore. Special charge was then given to the mate and men to be alert all night long; after which, I went on shore to protect the rear by placing my factory in a state of defence.

But my precautions were needless. At daylight the guard brought us news of the Dane's departure, and when I descended the river to Bangalang, Ormond alleged that the slaver had sailed for Sierra Leone to seek succor either from a man-of-war or the British government.

It may be supposed that I was not so " green " in Africa as to believe this story. No vessel, equipped for a slave cargo, would dare to enter the imperial colony. Yet the Northman had bitter cause for grief and anger. His vessel was seriously harmed by my grape-shot; his carpenter was slain during the action; and three of his seaman were lingering with desperate wounds. In a few days, however, he returned to the Rio Pongo from his airing on the Atlantic, where his wrath had probably been somewhat cooled by the sea-breeze. His craft was anchored higher up the river than my Spaniard, and thus our crews avoided intercourse for the future.

But this was not the case with the captains.  The Mongo's table was a sort of neutral ground, at which we met with cold salutations but without conversation.  Ormond and the Dane, however, became exceedingly intimate.  Indeed, the mulatto appeared to exhibit a degree of friendship for the Margaritan I had never seen him bestow on any one else.  This singularity, together with his well-known insincerity, put me on my guard to watch his proceedings with increased caution.

Personal observation is always a safe means of self-assurance; yet I have sometimes found it to be " a way of the world,"— not to be altogether scorned or disregarded,—to *purchase* the good will of " confidential " persons.  Accordingly, I made it " worth the while " of Ormond's body-servant to sift the secret of this sudden devotion; and in a few days the faithless slave, who spoke English remarkably well, told me that the Dane, by dint of extra pay and the secret delivery of all his spare provisions and the balance of his cargo, had induced the Mongo to promise the delivery of his slaves before mine.

Now, Ormond, by a specific contract,—made and paid for before the Dane's arrival,—owed me two hundred negroes on account of the Esperanza's cargo.  The Dane knew this perfectly, but my severe chastisement rankled in his heart, and made him seek revenge in the most effectual way on the coast of Africa.  He was bent upon depriving me of one hundred negroes, in the hands of Mr. Ormond.

I said nothing of my discovery, nor did I make any remarks on the astonishing love that existed between these Siamese twins; still, I kept my eye on Ormond's *barracoon* until I found his stock had gradually augmented to three hundred.  Thereupon, I dropped in one morning unceremoniously, and, in a gentle voice, told him of his treacherous design.  My ancient patron was so degraded by debauchery, that he not only avoided a passionate outburst when I made the charge, but actually seemed to regard it as a sort of capital joke, or recompense for the damage I had inflicted on the Dane !  We did not dream of arguing the propriety or impropriety of his conduct; nor did I think of upbraiding him with baseness, as I would have done any one who had dipped only his finger-tips in fraud. Still, ever and anon, I saw a glimmer of former spirit in the wretch, and thought I would attempt a counter-mine of interest, which Ormond might probably understand and grasp. I resolved, in fact, to *outbid* the Dane, for I thought I possessed a card that could take him. Accordingly, I offered to surrender a bond for one hundred slaves he owed me on account of the Esperanza; I promised, moreover, one hundred and fifty negroes, to be delivered that evening,—and I tendered *Brulôt's promissory note for the missing two hundred darkies,*—if he would pledge himself *to load the Dane during the succeeding night!*

Ormond took the hint like tinder, and grasped my hand on the bargain. The Dane was ordered to prepare his vessel to receive cargo without delay, and was specially desired *to drop down about fifteen miles towards the bar, so as to be off the moment his slaves were under hatches!*

For the next six hours there was not a busier bee on the Rio Pongo than Don Téodore. My schooner was put in ship-shape for cargo. The mate was ordered to have his small arms and cutlasses in perfect condition. Our pivot gun was double-loaded with chain-shot. My factory was set in order, and written direc tions given the clerk in anticipation of a four months' absence. Ali-Ninpha was put in charge of the territorial domain, while my Spaniard was intrusted with the merchandise.

It was encouraging to see, in the course of the afternoon, that my northern rival had swallowed the bait, for he borrowed a kedge to aid him, as he said, in descending the river against the tide, in order to "*get a better berth.*" He found the trees and air uncomfortable sixteen miles from the bar, and wanted to approach it to be "nearer the sea-breeze!" The adroitness of his excuse made me laugh in my sleeve, as the clumsy trickster shot past me with his sails unbent.

Well,—night came on, with as much darkness as ever robes the starlit skies of Africa when the moon is obscured. My long boat was quickly filled with ten. men, armed with pistol and cutlass; and in a short time, the canoes from Bangalang hove in sight with their sable burden. I boarded the first one myself, commanding the rowers to pull for my Spaniard. The second was seized by the mate, who followed in my wake. The third, fourth, fifth and sixth, shared the same fate in rapid succession; so that, in an hour, three hundred and seventy-five negroes were safe beneath the Esperanza's deck. Thereupon, I presented the headman of each canoe a document acknowledging the receipt of his slaves, *and wrote an order on the Mongo in favor of the Dane, for the full amount of the darkies I had borrowed!*

The land wind sprang up and the tide turned when daylight warned me it was time to be off; and, as I passed the Dane snugly at anchor just inside the bar, I called all hands to give three cheers, and to wish him happiness in the " enjoyment of his sea-breeze."

# CHAPTER XXIX.

WHEN the land breeze died away, it fell entirely calm, and the sea continued an unruffled mirror for three days, during which the highlands remained in sight, like a faint cloud in the east. The glaring sky and the reflecting ocean acted and reacted on each other until the air glowed like a furnace. During night a dense fog enveloped the vessel with its clammy folds. When the vapor lifted on the fourth morning, our look-out announced a sail from the mast-head, and every eye was quickly sweeping the landward horizon in search of the stranger. Our spies along the beach had reported the coast clear of cruisers when I sailed, so that I hardly anticipated danger from men-of-war; nevertheless, we held it discreet to avoid intercourse, and accordingly, our double-manned sweeps were rigged out to impel us slowly towards the open ocean. Presently, the mate went aloft with his glass, and, after a deliberate gaze, exclaimed: "It is only the Dane,—I see his flag." At this my crew swore they would sooner fight than sweep in such a latitude; and, with three cheers, came aft to request that I would remain quietly where I was until the Northman overhauled us.

We made so little headway with oars that I thought the difference trifling, whether we pulled or were becalmed. Perhaps, it might be better to keep the hands fresh, if a conflict proved inevitable. I passed quickly among the men, with separate inquiries as to their readiness for battle, and found all—from the boy to the mate—anxious, at every hazard, to do their duty. Our breakfast was as cold as could be served in such a climate, but I made it palatable with a case of claret.

When a sail on the coast of Africa heaves in sight of *a slaver*, it is always best for the imperilled craft, especially if gifted with swift hull and spreading wings, to take flight without the courtesies that are usual in mercantile sea-life. At the present day, fighting is, of course, out of the question, and the valuable prize is abandoned by its valueless owners. At all times, however,— and as a guard against every risk, whether the cue be to fight or fly,—the prudent slaver, as soon as he finds himself in the neighborhood of unwholesome canvas, puts out his fire, nails his forecastle, sends his negroes below, and secures the gratings over his hatches.

All these preparations were quietly made on board the Esperanza; and, in addition, I ordered a supply of small arms and ammunition on deck, where they were instantly covered with blankets. Every man was next stationed at his post, or where he might be most serviceable. The cannons were sponged and loaded with care; and, as I desired to deceive our new acquaintance, I ran up the Portuguese flag. The calm still continued as the day advanced;—indeed, I could not perceive a breath of air by our dog-vane, which veered from side to side as the schooner rolled slowly on the lazy swell. The stranger did not approach, nor did we advance. There we hung—

> "A painted ship upon a painted ocean!"

I cannot describe the fretful anxiety which vexes a mind under such circumstances. Slaves below; a blazing sun above; the boiling sea beneath; a withering air around; decks piled with materials of death; escape unlikely; a phantom in chase behind; the ocean like an unreachable eternity before; uncertainty every where; and, within your skull, a feverish mind, harassed by doubt and responsibility, yet almost craving for any act of desperation that will remove the spell. It is a living night-mare, from which the soul pants to be free.

With torments like these, I paced the deck for half an hour beneath the awning, when, seizing a telescope and mounting the rigging, I took deliberate aim at the annoyer. He was full seven or eight miles away from us, but very soon I saw, or fancied I saw, a row of ports, which the Dane had not : then sweeping the horizon a little astern of the craft, I distinctly made out three boats, fully manned, making for us with ensigns flying.

Anxious to avoid a panic, I descended leisurely, and ordered the sweeps to be spread once more in aid of the breeze, which, within the last ten minutes, had freshened enough to fan us along about a knot an hour. Next, I imparted my discovery to the officers ; and, passing once more among the men to test their nerves, I said it was likely they would have to encounter an angrier customer than the Dane. In fact, I frankly told them our antagonist was unquestionably a British cruiser of ten or twelve guns, from whose clutches there was no escape, unless we repulsed the boats.

I found my crew as confident in the face of augmented risk as they had been when we expected the less perilous Dane. Collecting their votes for fight or surrender, I learned that all *but two* were in favor of resistance. I had no doubt in regard *to the mates*, in our approaching trials.

By this time the breeze had again died away to utter calm--ness, while the air was so still and fervent that our sweltering men almost sank at the sweeps. I ordered them in, threw overboard several water-casks that encumbered the deck, and hoisted our boat to the stern-davits to prevent boarding in that quarter. Things were perfectly ship-shape all over the schooner, and I congratulated myself that her power had been increased by two twelve pound carronades, the ammunition, and part of the crew of a Spanish slaver, abandoned on the bar of Rio Pongo a week before my departure. We had in all seven guns, and abundance of musketry, pistols and cutlasses, to be wielded and managed by thirty-seven hands.

By this time the British boats, impelled by oars alone, approached within half a mile, while the breeze sprang up in cat's-paws all round the eastern horizon, but without fanning us with a single breath.  Taking advantage of one of these slants, the cruiser had followed her boats, but now, about five miles off, was again as perfectly becalmed as *we* had been all day.  Presently, I observed the boats converge within the range of my swivel, and lay on their oars as if for consultation.  I seized this opportunity, while the enemy was huddled together, to give him the first welcome ; and, slewing the schooner round with my sweeps, I sent him a shot from my swivel.  But the ball passed over their heads, while, with three cheers, they separated,—the largest boat making directly for our waist, while the others steered to cross our bow and attack our stern.

During the chase my weapons, with the exception of the pivot gun, were altogether useless, but I kept a couple of sweeps ahead and a couple astern to play the schooner, and employed that loud-tongued instrument as the foe approached.  The larger boat, bearing a small carronade, was my best target, yet we contrived to miss each other completely until my sixth discharge, when a double-headed shot raked the whole bank of starboard oar-blades, and disabled the rowers by the severe concussion.  This paralyzed the launch's advance, and allowed me to devote my exclusive attention to the other boats ; yet, before I could bring the schooner in a suitable position, a signal summoned the assailants aboard the cruiser to repair damages.  I did not reflect until this moment of reprieve, that, early in the day, I had hoisted the Portuguese ensign *to deceive the Dane*, and imprudently left it aloft in the presence of *John Bull!*  I struck the false flag at once, unfurled the Spanish, and refreshing the men with a double allowance of grog and grub, put them again to the sweeps.  When the cruisers reached their vessels, the men instantly re-embarked, while the boats were allowed to swing alongside, which convinced me that the assault would be renewed as soon as the rum and roast-beef of Old England had strengthened the heart of the adversary.  Accordingly, noon had not long passed when our pursuers again embarked.  Once more they approached, divided as before, and again we exchanged ineffectual shots.  I kept them at bay with grape and musketry until near three o'clock, when a second signal of retreat was hoisted on the cruiser, and answered by exultant *vivas* from my crew. It grieved me, I confess, not to mingle my voice with these shouts, for I was sure that the lion retreated to make a better spring, nor was I less disheartened when the mate reported that nearly all the ammunition for our cannons was exhausted. Seven kegs of powder were still in the magazine, though not more than a dozen rounds of grape, cannister, or balls, remained in the locker. There was still an abundance of cartridges for pistols and musketry, but these were poor defences against resolute Englishmen whose blood was up and who would unques- tionably renew the charge with reinforcements of vigorous men. Fore and aft, high and low, we searched for missiles. Musket balls were crammed in bags; bolts and nails were packed in cartridge paper; slave shackles were formed with rope yarns into chain-shot; and, in an hour, we were once more tolerably prepared to pepper the foe.

When these labors terminated, I turned my attention to the relaxed crew, portions of whom refused wine, and began to sulk about the decks. As yet only two had been slightly scratched by spent musket balls; but so much discontent began to appear among the passenger-sailors of the wrecked slaver, that my own hands could with difficulty restrain them from revolt. I felt much difficulty in determining how to act, but I had no time for deliberation. Violence was clearly not my *rôle*, but persuasion was a delicate game in such straits among men whom I did not command with the absolute authority of a master. I cast my eye over the taffrail, and seeing that the British boats were still afar, I followed my first impulse, and calling the whole gang to the quarter-deck, tried the effect of African palaver and Spanish gold. I spoke of the perils of capture and of the folly of sur- rendering *a slaver* while there was the slightest *hope* of escape. I painted the unquestionable result of being taken after such re- sistance as had already been made. I drew an accurate picture of a tall and dangerous instrument on which piratical gentlemen have sometimes been known to terminate their lives; and finally, I attempted to improve the rhythm of my oratory by a couple of golden ounces to each combatant, and the promise of a slave apiece at the end of our *successful* voyage

My suspense was terrible, as there,—on the deck of a slaver, amid calm, heat, battle, and mutiny, with a volcano of three hundred and seventy-five imprisoned devils below me,—I awaited a reply, which, favorable or unfavorable, I must hear without emotion. Presently, three or four came forward and accepted my offer. I shrugged my shoulders, and took half a dozen turns up and down the deck. Then, turning to the crowd, I *doubled my bounty*, and offering a boat to take the recusants on board the enemy, swore that I would stand by the Esparanza with my unaided crew in spite of the *dastards!*

The offensive word with which I closed the harangue seemed to touch the right string of the Spanish guitar, and in an instant I saw the dogged heads spring up with a jerk of mortified pride, while the steward and cabin-boy poured in a fresh supply of wine, and a shout of union went up from both divisions. •I lost no time in confirming my converts; and, ramming down my eloquence with a wad of doubloons, ordered every man to his post, for the enemy was again in motion.

But he did not come alone. New actors had appeared on the scene during my engagement with the crew. The sound of the cannonade had been heard, it seems, by a consort of his Britannic Majesty's brig * * * * ; * and, although the battle was not within her field of vision, she despatched another squadron of boats under the guidance of the reports that boomed through the silent air.

The first division of my old assailants was considerably in advance of the reinforcement; and, in perfect order, approached us in a solid body, with the apparent determination of boarding on the same side. Accordingly, I brought all my weapons and hands to that quarter, and told both gunners and musketeers not to fire without orders. Waiting their discharge, I allowed them to get close; but the commander of the launch seemed to anticipate my plan by the reservation of his fire till he could draw mine, in order to throw his other boat-loads on board under the

---

* It will be understood by the reader, hereafter, why I omit the cruiser's name.

smoke of his swivel and small arms. It was odd to witness our mutual forbearance, nor could I help laughing, even in the midst of danger, at the mutual checkmate we were trying to prepare. However, my Britons did not avoid pulling, though they omitted firing, so that they were already rather perilously close when I thought it best to give them the contents of my pivot, which I had crammed almost to the muzzle with bolts and bullets. The discharge paralyzed the advance, while my carronades flung a quantity of grape into the companion boats. In turn, however, they plied us so deftly with balls from swivels and musketry, that five of our most valuable defenders writhed in death on the deck.

The rage of battle at closer quarters than heretofore, and the screams of bleeding comrades beneath their feet, roused to its fullest extent the ardent nature of my Spanish crew. They tore their garments; stripped to their waists; called for rum; and swore they would die rather than yield !

By this time the consort's reinforcement was rapidly approaching; and, with hurrah after hurrah, the five fresh boats came on in double column. As they drew within shot, each cheer was followed with a fatal volley, under which several more of our combatants were prostrated, while a glancing musket ball lacerated my knee with a painful wound. For five minutes we met this onset with cannon, muskets, pistols, and enthusiastic shouts; but in the despairing confusion of the hour, the captain of our long gun rammed home his ball before the powder, so that when the priming burnt, the most reliable of our weapons was silent for ever ! At this moment a round shot from the launch dismounted a carronade ;—our ammunition was wasted ;—and in this disabled state, the Britons prepared to board our crippled craft. Muskets, bayonets, pistols, swords, and knives, for a space kept them at bay, even at short quarters ; but the crowded boats tumbled their enraged fighters over our forecastle like surges from the sea, and, cutlass in hand, the victorious furies swept every thing before them. The cry was to " spare no one ! " Down went sailor after sailor, struggling with the frenzied passion of despair. Presently an order went forth to split the gratings and release the slaves. I clung to my post and cheered the battle to the last; but when I heard this fatal command, which, if obeyed, might bury assailant and defender in common ruin, I ordered the remnant to throw down their arms, while I struck the flag and warned the rash and testy Englishman to beware.

The senior officer of the boarding party belonged to the division from the cruiser's consort. As he reached the deck, his clement eye fell sadly on the scene of blood, and he commanded "quarter" immediately. It was time. The excited boarders from the repulsed boats had mounted our deck brimming with revenge. Every one that opposed was cut down without mercy; and in another moment, it is likely I would have joined the throng of the departed.

All was over! There was a hushed and panting crowd of victors and vanquished on the bloody deck, when the red ball of the setting sun glared through a crimson haze and filled the motionless sea with liquid fire. For the first time that day I became sensible of personal sufferings. A stifling sensation made me gasp for air as I sat down on the taffrail of my captured schooner, and felt that I was—a prisoner!

# CHAPTER XXX.

AFTER a brief pause, the commanding officers of both divisions demanded my papers, which, while I acknowledged myself *his* prisoner, I yielded to the *senior* personage who had humanely stopped the massacre. I saw that this annoyed the other, whom I had so frequently repulsed; yet I thought the act fair as well as agreeable to my feelings, for I considered my crew competent to resist the *first division successfully*, had it not been succored by the consort's boats.

But my decision was not submitted to by the defeated leader without a dispute, which was conducted with infinite harshness, until the senior ended the quarrel by ordering his junior to tow the prize within reach of the corvette * * * * My boat, though somewhat riddled with balls, was lowered, and I was commanded to go on board the captor, with my papers and servant under the escort of a midshipman. The captain stood at the gangway as I approached, and, seeing my bloody knee, ordered me not to climb the ladder, but to be hoisted on deck and sent below for the immediate care of my wound. It was hardly more than a severe laceration of flesh, yet was quite enough to prevent me from bending my knee, though it did not deny locomotion with a stiff leg.

The dressing over,—during which I had quite a pleasant chat

with the amiable surgeon,—I was summoned to the cabin, where numerous questions were put, all of which I answered frankly and *truly*. Thirteen of my crew were slain, and nearly all the rest wounded. My papers were next inspected, and found to be Spanish. " How was it, then," exclaimed the commander, " that you fought under the Portuguese flag ? "

Here was the question I always expected, and for which I had in vain taxed my wit and ingenuity to supply a reasonable excuse ! I had nothing to say for the daring violation of nationality ; so I resolved to tell the truth boldly about my dispute with the Dane, and my desire to deceive him early in the day, but I cautiously omitted the adroitness with which I had deprived him of his darkies. I confessed that I forgot the flag when I found I had a different foe from the Dane to contend with, and I flattered myself with the hope that, had I repulsed the first unaided onset, I would have been able to escape with the usual sea-breeze.

The captain looked at me in silence a while, and, in a sorrowful voice, asked if I was aware that my defence under the Portuguese ensign, no matter what tempted its use, could only be construed as an act of *piracy !*

A change of color, an earnest gaze at the floor, compressed lips and clenched teeth, were my only replies.

This painful scrutiny took place before the surgeon, whose looks and expressions strongly denoted his cordial sympathy with my situation. " Yes," said Captain * * * *, " it is a pity for a sailor who fights as bravely as you have done, in defence of what he considers his property, to be condemned for a combination of mistakes and forgetfulness. However, let us not hasten matters ; you are hungry and want rest, and, though we are navy-men, and on the coast of Africa, we are not savages." I was then directed to remain where I was till further orders, while my servant came below with an abundant supply of provisions. The captain went on deck, but the doctor remained. Presently, I saw the surgeon and the commander's steward busy over a basket of biscuits, meat and bottles, to the handle of which a cord, several yards in length, was carefully knotted. After this was arranged, the doctor called for a lamp, and unrolling a chart, asked whether I knew the position of the vessel. I replied affirmatively, and, at his request, measured the distance, and noted the course to the nearest land, which was Cape Verga, about thirty-seven miles off.

"Now, Don Téodore, if I were in your place, with the prospect of a noose and tight-rope dancing before me, I have not the slightest hesitation in saying that I would make an attempt to know what Cape Verga is made of before twenty-four hours were over my head! And see, my good fellow, how Providence, accident, or fortune favors you! First of all, your own boat *happens* to be towing astern beneath these very cabin windows ; secondly, a basket of provisions, water and brandy, stands packed on the transom, almost ready to slip into the boat by itself; next, your boy is in the neighborhood to help you with the skiff; and, finally, it is pitch dark, perfectly calm, and there isn't a sentry to be seen aft the cabin door. Now, good night, my clever fighter, and let me never have the happiness of seeing your face again !"

As he said this, he rose, shaking my hand with the hearty grasp of a sailor, and, as he passed my servant, slipped something into his pocket, which proved to be a couple of sovereigns. Meanwhile, the steward appeared with blankets, which he spread on the locker ; and, blowing out the lamp, went on deck with a "good night."

It was very still, and unusually dark. There was dead silence in the corvette. Presently, I crawled softly to the stern window, and lying flat on my stomach over the transom, peered out into night. There, in reality, was my boat towing astern by a slack line ! As I gazed, some one on deck above me drew in the rope with softest motion, until the skiff lay close under the windows. Patiently, slowly, cautiously,—fearing the sound of his fall, and dreading almost the rush of my breath in the profound silence,—I lowered my boy into the boat. The basket followed. The negro fastened the boat-hook to the cabin window, and on this, lame as I was, I followed the basket.    Fortunately, not a plash, a crack, or a footfall disturbed the silence. I looked aloft, and no one was visible on the quarter-deck.    A slight jerk brought the boat-rope softly into the water, and I drifted away into the darkness.

# CHAPTER XXXI.

I DRIFTED without a word or motion, and almost without breath·
ing, until the corvette was perfectly obliterated against the hazy
horizon.   When every thing was dark around me, save the guid-
ing stars, I put out the oars and pulled quietly towards the east.
At day-dawn I was apparently alone on the ocean.

My appetite had improved so hugely by the night's exercise,
that my first devotion was to the basket, which I found crammed
with bologña sausages, a piece of salt junk, part of a ham, abundance of biscuit, four bottles of water, two of brandy, a pocket
compass, a jack-knife, and a large table-cloth or sheet, which the
generous doctor had no doubt inserted to serve as a sail.

The humbled *slaver* and the *slave*, for the first time in their
lives, broke bread from the same basket, and drank from the
same bottle !   Misfortune had strangely and suddenly levelled us
on the basis of common humanity.   The day before, he was the
most servile of menials ; to-day he was my equal, and, probably,
my superior in certain physical powers, without which I would
have perished !

As the sun ascended in the sky, my wound became irritated
by exercise, and the inflammation produced a feverish torment
in which I groaned as I lay extended in the stern-sheets.   By
noon a breeze sprang up from the south-west, so that the oars
and table-cloth supplied a square sail which wafted us about

three miles an hour, while my boy rigged an awning with the blankets and boat-hooks. Thus, half reclining, I steered landward till midnight, when I took in the sail and lay-to on the calm ocean till morning. Next day the breeze again favored us; and, by sundown, I came up with the coasting canoe of a friendly Mandingo, into which I at once exchanged my quarters, and falling asleep, never stirred till he landed me on the Islands de Loss.

My wound kept me a close and suffering prisoner in a hut on the isles for ten days during which I despatched a native canoe some thirty-five or forty miles to the Rio Pongo with news of my disaster, and orders for a boat with an equipment of comforts. As my clerk neglected to send a suit of clothes, I was obliged to wear the Mandingo habiliments till I reached my factory, so that during my transit, this dress became the means of an odd encounter. As I entered the Rio Pongo, a French brigantine near the bar was the first welcome of civilization that cheered my heart for near a fortnight. Passing her closely, I drifted alongside, and begged the commander for a bottle of claret. My brown skin, African raiment, and savage companions satisfied the skipper that I was a native, so that, with a sneer, he, of course, became very solicitous to know "where I drank claret *last ?*" and pointing to the sea, desired me to quench my thirst with brine!

It was rather hard for a suffering Italian to be treated so cavalierly by a Gaul; but I thanked the fellow for his civility in such excellent French, that his tone instantly changed, and he asked—" *au nom de Dieu,* where I had learned the language !" It is likely I would have rowed off without detection, had I not just then been recognized by one of his officers who visited my factory the year before.

In a moment the captain was in my boat with a bound, and grasping my hands with a thousand pardons, insisted I should not ascend the river till I had dined with him. He promised a plate of capital soup;—and where, I should like to know, is the son of France or Italy who is ready to withstand the seduction of such a provocative? Besides this, he insisted on dressing me from

his scanty wardrobe; but as he declined all subsequent remune
ration, I confined my bodily improvement to a clean shirt and his
wiry razors.

While the *bouillon* was bubbling in the coppers, I got an in-
sight into the condition of Rio Pongo concerns since my departure.
The Dane was off after a quarrel with Ormond, who gave him but a
hundred negroes for his cargo; and a Spanish brig was waiting
my arrival,—for the boy I sent home from the Isles de Loss had
reported my engagement, capture, and escape.

*La soupe sur la table,* we attacked a smoking tureen of *bouillon
gras*, while a heaping dish of toasted bread stood in the middle.
The captain loaded my plate with two slices of this sunburnt material, which he deluged with a couple of ladles of savory broth.
A long fast is a good sauce, and I need not assert that I began
*sans façon*. My appetite was sharp, and the vapor of the liquid
inviting. For a while there was a dead silence, save when
broken by smacking and relishing lips. Spoonful after spoonful
was sucked in as rapidly as the heat allowed; and, indeed, I
hardly took time to bestow a blessing on the cook. Being the
guest of the day, my plate had been the first one served, and
of course, was the first one finished. Perhaps I rather hurried
myself, for lenten diet made me greedy and I was somewhat anxious to anticipate the calls of my companions on the tureen. Accordingly, I once more ballasted my plate with toast, and, with
a charming bow and a civil " *s'il vous plait*," applied, like Oliver
Twist, " for more."

As the captain was helping me to the second ladle, he politely demanded whether I was " fond of the thick; " and as I
replied in the affirmative, he made another dive to the bottom
and brought up the instrument with a heaping mass in whose centre was a diminutive African skull, face upwards, gaping at the
guests with an infernal grin !

My plate fell from my hand at the tureen's edge. The boiling liquid splashed over the table. I stood fascinated by the horrible apparition as the captain continued to hold its dreadful
bones in view. Presently my head swam; a painful oppression

weighed at my heart; I was ill; and, in a jiffy, the appalling spectre was laid beneath the calm waters of the Rio Pongo.

Before sundown I made a speedy retreat from among the *anthropophagi;* but all their assurances, oaths, and protestations, could not satisfy me that the broth did not owe its substance to something more human than an African *baboon.*

# CHAPTER XXXII.

THERE was rejoicing that night in Kambia among my people, for it is not necessary that a despised slaver should always be a cruel master. I had many a friend among the villagers, both there and at Bangalang, and when the "barker" came from the Isles *de Loss* with the news of my capture and misery, the settlement had been keenly astir until it was known that Mongo Téodore was safe and sound among his protectors.

I had a deep, refreshing sleep after a glorious bath. Poor Esther stole over the palisades of Bangalang to hear the story from my own lips; and, in recompense for the narrative, gave me an account of the river gossip during my adventure. Next morning, bright and early, I was again in my boat, sweeping along towards the "FELIZ" from Matanzas, which was anchored within a bowshot of Bangalang. As I rounded a point in sight of her, the Spanish flag was run up, and as I touched the deck, a dozen cheers and a gun gave token of a gallant reception in consequence of my battle with the British, which had been magnified into a perfect Trafalgar.

The Feliz was originally consigned to me from Cuba, but in my absence from the river her commander thought it best not to intrust so important a charge to my clerk, and addressed her to Ormond. When my arrival at the Isles *de Loss* was announced on the river, his engagement with the Mongo had neither been entirely completed, nor had any cargo been delivered. Accordingly, the skipper at once taxed his wit for a contrivance by which he could escape the bargain. In Africa such things are sometimes done with ease on small pretexts, so that when I reached Kambia my one-hundred-and-forty-ton brig was ready for her original consignee.

I found that remittances in money and merchandise covered the value of three hundred and fifty slaves, whom I quickly ordered from different traders ;—but when I applied to the Mongo to furnish his share, the gentleman indignantly refused under the affront of his recalled assignment. I tried to pacify and persuade him ; yet all my efforts were unavailing. Still, the results of this denial did not affect the Mongo personally and alone. When a factor either declines or is unable to procure trade at an African station, the multitude of hangers-on, ragamuffins, servants and villagers around him suffer, at least, for a time. They cannot understand and are always disgusted when " trade is refused." In this case the people of Bangalang seemed peculiarly dissatisfied with their Mongo's obstinacy. They accused him of indolent disregard of their interests. They charged him with culpable neglect. Several free families departed forthwith to Kambia. His brothers, who were always material sufferers in such cases, upbraided him with arrogant conceit. His women, headed by Fatimah,—who supplied herself and her companions with abundant presents out of every fresh cargo,—rose in open mutiny, and declared they would run off unless he accepted a share of the contract. Fatimah was the orator of the harem on this as well as on all other occasions of display or grievance, and of course she did not spare poor Ormond. Age and drunkenness had made sad inroads on his constitution and looks during the last half year. His fretful irritability sometimes amounted almost to madness, when thirty female tongues joined in the chorus of their leader's assault. They boldly charged him, singly and in pairs, with every vice and fault that injured matrimony habitually denounces; and as each item of this abusive litany was screamed in his ears, the chorus responded with a deep " amen ! " They boasted of their infidelities, lauded their lovers, and producing their children, with laughs of derision, bade him note the astounding resemblance !

The poor Mongo was sorely beset by these African witches, and summoned his villagers to subdue the revolt; but many of the town-folks were pets of the girls, so that no one came forth to obey his bidding.

I visited Ormond at his request on the evening of this rebellion, and found him not only smarting with the morning's insult, but so drunk as to be incapable of business. His revengeful eye and nervous movements denoted a troubled mind. When our hands met, I found the Mongo's cold and clammy. I refused wine under a plea of illness; and when, with incoherent phrases and distracted gestures, he declared his willingness to retract his refusal and accept a share of the Feliz's cargo, I thought it best to adjourn the discussion until the following day. Whilst on the point of embarking, I was joined by the faithless servant, whom I bribed to aid me in my affair with the Dane, and was told that Ormond *had drugged the wine in anticipation of my arrival!* He bade me be wary of the Mongo, who in his presence had threatened my life. That morning, he said, while the women were upbraiding him, my name had been mentioned by one with peculiar favor,—when Ormond burst forth with a torrent of passion, and accusing me as the cause of all his troubles, felled the girl to the earth with his fist.

That night I was roused by my watchman to see a stranger, and found Esther at my gate with three of her companions. Their tale was brief. Soon after dark, Ormond entered the harem with loaded pistols, in search of Fatimah and Esther; but the wretch was so stupified by liquor and rage, that the women had little trouble to elude his grasp and escape from Bangalang. Hardly had I bestowed them for the night, when another alarm brought the watchman once more to my chamber, with the news of Ormond's death. He had shot himself through the heart!

I was in no mood for sleep after this, and the first streak of dawn found me at Bangalang. There lay the Mongo as he fell. No one disturbed his limbs or approached him till I arrived. He never stirred after the death-wound.

It seems he must have forgotten that the bottle had

been specially medicated for me, as it was found nearly drained; but the last thing distinctly known of him by the people, was his murderous entrance into the harem to despatch Esther and Fatimah. Soon after this the crack of a pistol was heard in the garden; and there, stretched among the cassava plants, with a loaded pistol grasped in his left, and a discharged one at a short distance from his right hand, laid Jack Ormond, the mulatto! His left breast was pierced by a ball, the wad of which still clung to the bloody orifice.

Bad as this man was, I could not avoid a sigh for his death. He had been my first friend in Africa, and I had forfeited his regard through no fault of mine. Besides this, there are so few on the coast of Africa in these lonely settlements among the mangrove swamps, who have tasted European civilization, and can converse like human beings, that the loss even of the worst is a dire calamity. Ormond and myself had held each other for a long time at a wary distance; yet business forced us together now and then, and during the truce, we had many a pleasant chat and joyous hour that would henceforth be lost for ever.

It is customary in this part of Africa to make the burial of a *Mongo* the occasion of a *colungee*, or festival, when all the neighboring chiefs and relations send gifts of food and beverage for the orgies of death. Messengers had been despatched for Ormond's brothers and kinsfolk, so that the native ceremony of interment was postponed till the third day; and, in the interval, I was desired to make all the preparations in a style befitting the suicide's station. Accordingly, I issued the needful orders; directed a deep grave to be dug under a noble cotton-wood tree, aloof from the village; gave the body in charge to women, who were to watch it until burial, with cries of sorrow,—and then retired to Kambia.

On the day of obsequies I came back. At noon a salute was fired by the guns of the village, which was answered by minute guns from the Feliz and my factory. Seldom have I heard a sadder sound than the boom of those cannons through the silent forest and over the waveless water.

Presently, all the neighboring chiefs, princes and kings came in with their retainers, when the body was brought out into the shade of a grove, so that all might behold it. Then the procession took up its line of march, while the thirty wives of the Mongo followed the coffin, clad in rags, their heads shaven, their bodies lacerated with burning iron, and filling the air with yells and shrieks until the senseless clay was laid in the grave.

I could find no English prayer-book or Bible in the village, from which I might read the service of his church over Ormond's remains, but I had never forgotten the *Ave Maria* and *Pater Noster* I learned when an infant, and, while I recited them devoutly over the self-murderer, I could not help thinking they were even more than sufficient for the savage surroundings.

The brief prayer was uttered; but it could not be too brief for the impatient crowd. Its *amen* was a signal for *pandemonium*. In a twinkling, every foot rushed back to the dwelling in Bangalang. The grove was alive with revelry. Stakes and racks reeked with roasting bullocks. Here and there, kettles steamed with boiling rice. Demijohn after demijohn of *rum* was served out. Very soon a sham battle was proposed, and parties were formed. The divisions took their grounds; and, presently, the scouts appeared, crawling like reptiles on the earth till they ascertained each other's position, when the armies sallied forth with guns, bows, arrows, or lances, and, after firing, shrieking and shouting till they were deaf, retired with captives, and the war was done. Then came a reinforcement of rum, and then a dance, so that the bewildering revel continued in all its delirium till rum and humanity gave out together, and reeled to the earth in drunken sleep! Such was the requiem of

THE MONGO OF BANGALANG!

## CHAPTER XXXIII.

SLAVES dropped in slowly at Kambia and Bangalang, though I still had half the cargo of the Feliz to make up. Time was precious, and there wes no foreigner on the river to aid me. In this strait, I suddenly resolved on a foray among the natives on my own account; and equipping a couple of my largest canoes with an ample armament, as well as a substantial store of provisions and merchandise, I departed for the Matacan river, a short stream, unsuitable for vessels of considerable draft. I was prepared for the purchase of fifty slaves.

I reached my destination without risk or adventure, but had the opportunity of seeing some new phases of Africanism on my arrival. Most of the coast negroes are wretchedly degraded by their superstitions and *sauvagerie*, and it is best to go among them with power to resist as well as presents to purchase. Their towns did not vary from the river and bush settlements generally. A house was given me for my companions and merchandise; yet such was the curiosity to see the " white man," that the luckless mansion swarmed with sable bees both inside and out, till I was obliged to send for his majesty to relieve my sufferings.

After a proper delay, the king made his appearance in all the paraphernalia of African court-dress. A few fathoms of check

girded his loins, while a blue shirt and red waistcoat were surmounted by a dragoon's cap with brass ornaments. His countenance was characteristic of Ethiopia and royalty. A narrow
forehead retreated rapidly till it was lost in the crisp wool, while
his eyes were wide apart, and his prominent cheek-bones formed
the base of an inverted cone, the apex of which was his braided
beard, coiled up under his chin. When earnest in talk, his gestures were mostly made with his head, by straining his eyes to
the rim of their sockets, stretching his mouth from ear to ear,
grinning like a baboon, and throwing out his chin horizontally
with a sudden jerk. Notwithstanding these personal oddities,
the sovereign was kind, courteous, hospitable, and disposed for
trade. Accordingly, I "dashed," or presented him and his
head-men a few pieces of cottons, with some pipes, beads, and
looking-glasses, by way of whet for the appetite of to-morrow.

But the division of this gift was no sportive matter. "The
spoils" were not regulated upon principles of superiority, or even
of equality; but fell to the lot of the stoutest scramblers. As
soon as the goods were deposited, the various gangs seized my
snowy cottons, dragging them right and left to their several huts,
while they shrieked, yelled, disputed, and fought in true African
fashion. Some lucky dog would now and then leap between two
combatants who had possession of the ends of a piece, and whirling himself rapidly around the middle, slashed the sides with
his jack-knife and was off to the bush. The pipes, beads, and
looking-glasses, were not bestowed more tenderly, while the tobacco was grabbed and appropriated by leaves or handfuls.

Next day we proceeded to formal business. His majesty
called a regular "palaver" of his chiefs and headmen, before
whom I stated my *dantica* and announced the terms. Very
soon several young folks were brought for sale, who, I am sure,
never dreamed at rising from last night's sleep, that they were
destined for Cuban slavery! My merchandise revived the memory of peccadilloes that had been long forgotten, and sentences
that were forgiven. Jealous husbands, when they tasted my rum,
suddenly remembered their wives' infidelities, and sold their better halves for more of the oblivious fluid. In truth I was exalt-

ed into a magician, unroofing the village, and baring its crime and wickedness to the eye of *justice*. Law became profitable, and virtue had never reached so high a price ! Before night the town was in a turmoil, for every man cudgelled his brain for an excuse to kidnap his neighbor, so as to share my commerce. As the village was too small to supply the entire gang of fifty, I had recourse to the neighboring settlements, where my " barkers," or agents, did their work in a masterly manner. Traps were adroitly baited with goods to lead the unwary into temptation, when the unconscious pilferer was caught by his ambushed foe, and an hour served to hurry him to the beach as a slave for ever. In fact, five days were sufficient to stamp my image permanently on the Matacan settlements, and to associate my memory with any thing but blessings in at least fifty of their families !

I had heard, on the Rio Pongo, of a wonderful wizard who dwelt in this region, and took advantage of the last day of my detention to inquire his whereabouts. The impostor was renowned for his wonderful tricks of legerdemain, as well as for cures, necromancy, and fortune-telling. The ill came to him by scores; credulous warriors approached him with valuable gifts for *fetiches* against musket balls and arrows; while the humbler classes bought his charms against snakes, alligators, sharks, evil spirits, or sought his protection for their unborn children.

My interpreter had already visited this fellow, and gave such charming accounts of his skill, that all my people wanted their fates divined, for which I was, of course, obliged to advance merchandise to purchase at least a gratified curiosity. When they came back I found every one satisfied with his future lot, and so happy was the chief of my kroomen that he danced around his new *fetiche* of cock's feathers and sticks, and snapped his fingers at all the sharks, alligators, and swordfish that swam in the sea.

By degrees these reports tickled my own curiosity to such a degree, that, incontinently, I armed myself with a quantity of cotton cloth, a brilliant bandanna, and a lot of tobacco, wherewith I resolved to attack the soothsayer's den. My credulity was not involved in the expedition, but I was sincerely anxious to comprehend the ingenuity or intelligence by which a negro could control the imagination of African multitudes.

The wizard chose his abode with skilful and romantic taste. Quitting the town by a path which ascended abruptly from the river, the traveller was forced to climb the steep by a series of dangerous zig-zags among rocks and bushes, until he reached a deep cave in an elevated cliff that bent over the stream. As we approached, my conductor warned the inmate of our coming by several whoops. When we reached the entrance I was directed to halt until the demon announced his willingness to receive us. At length, after as much delay as is required in the antechamber of a secretary of state, a growl, like the cry of a hungry crocodile, gave token of the wizard's coming.

As he emerged from the deep interior, I descried an uncommonly tall figure, bearing in his arms a young and living leopard. I could not detect a single lineament of his face or figure, for he was covered from head to foot in a complete dress of monkey skins, while his face was hidden by a grotesque white mask. Behind him groped a delicate blind boy.

We seated ourselves on hides along the floor, when, at my bidding, the interpreter, unrolling my gifts, announced that I came with full hands to his wizardship, for the purpose of learning my fortune.

The impostor had trained his tame leopard to fetch and carry like a dog, so that, without a word, the docile beast bore the various presents to his master. Every thing was duly measured, examined, or balanced in his hands to ascertain its quality and weight. Then, placing a bamboo between his lips and the blind boy's ear, he whispered the words which the child repeated aloud. First of all, he inquired what I wished to know ? As one of his follower's boasts was the extraordinary power he possessed of speaking various languages, I addressed him in Spanish, but as his reply displayed an evident ignorance of what I said, I took the liberty to reprimand him sharply in his native tongue. He waved me off with an imperious flourish of his hand, and ordered me to wait, as he perfectly comprehended my

Spanish, but the magic power would not suffer him to answer save in regular rotation, word by word.

I saw his trick at once, which was only one of prompt and adroit *repetition*. Accordingly, I addressed him in his native dialect, and requested a translation of my sentence into Spanish. But this was a puzzler; though it required but a moment for him to assure me that a foreign language could only be spoken by wizards of his degree *at the full of the moon!*

I thought it time to shift the scene to fortune-telling, and begged my demon to begin the task by relating the past, in order to confirm my belief in his mastery over the future. But the nonsense he uttered was so insufferable, that I dropped the curtain with a run, and commanded "the hereafter" to appear. This, at least, was more romantic. As usual, I was to be immensely rich. I was to become a great prince. I was to have a hundred wives; but alas! before six months elapsed, my factory would be burnt and I should lose a vessel!

Presently, the interpreter proposed an exhibition of legerdemain, and in this I found considerable amusement to make up for the preceding buffoonery. He knotted a rope, and untied it with a jerk. He sank a knife deep in his throat, and poured in a vessel of water. Other deceptions followed this skilful trick, but the cleverest of all was the handling of red hot iron, which, after covering his hands with a glutinous paste, was touched in the most fearless manner. I have seen this trick performed by other natives, and whenever ignited coals or ardent metal was used, the hands of the operator were copiously anointed with the pasty unguent.

A valedictory growl, and a resumption of the leopard, gave token of the wizard's departure, and closed the evening's entertainments.

If the ease with which a man is amused, surprised, or deluded, is a fair measure of intellectual grade, I fear that African minds will take a very moderate rank in the scale of humanity. The task of self-civilization, which resembles the self-filtering of water, has done but little for Ethiopia in the ages that have passed simultaneously over her people and the progressive races of other lands. It remains to be seen what the *infused* civilization of Christianity and Islamism will effect among these benighted nations. JESUS, MAHOMET, and the FETICHE, will, perhaps, long continue to be their types of distinctive separation.

# CHAPTER XXXIV.

THE Esperanza's capture made it absolutely necessary that I should visit Cuba, so that, when the Feliz was preparing to depart, I began to put my factory and affairs in such order as would enable me to embark in her and leave me master of myself for a considerable time. I may as well record the fact here that the unlucky Esperanza was sent to Sierra Leone, where she was, of course, condemned as a slaver, while the officers and crew were despatched by order of the Admiralty, in irons, to *Lisbon*, where a tribunal condemned them to the galleys for five years. I understand they were subsequently released by the clemency of Don Pedro de Braganza when he arrived from Brazil.

Every thing was ready for our departure. My rice was stored and about to be sent on board; when, about three o'clock in the morning of the 25th of May, 1828, the voice of my servant roused me from pleasant dreams, to fly for life! I sprang from the cot with a bound to the door, where the flickering of a bright flame, reflected through the thick, misty air, gave token of fire. The roof of my house was in a blaze, and one hundred and fifty kegs of powder were close at hand beneath a thatch! They could not be removed, and a single spark from the frail and tinder-like materials might send the whole in an instant to the skies.

A rapid discharge from a double-barrelled gun brought my

people to the spot with alacrity, and enabled me to rescue the two hundred and twenty slaves stowed in the *barracoon*, and march them to a neighboring wood, where they would be secure under a guard. In my haste to rescue the slaves I forgot to warn my body servant of his peril from the powder. The faithful boy made several trips to the dwelling to save my personal effects, and after removing every thing he had strength to carry, returned to unchain the bloodhound that always slept beside my couch in Africa. But the dog was as ignorant of his danger as the youth. *He knew no friend but myself*, and tearing the hand that was exposed to save him, he forced his rescuer to fly. And well was it he did so. Within a minute, a tremendous blast shook the earth, *and the prediction of the Matacan wizard was accomplished!* Not even the red coals of my dwelling smouldered on the earth. Every thing was swept as by the breath of a whirlwind. My terrified boy, bleeding at nose and ears, was rescued from the ruins of a shallow well in which he fortunately fell. The bamboo sheds, barracoons, and hovels,—the *adobe* dwelling and the comfortable garden—could all spring up again in a short time, as if by enchantment,—but my rich stuffs, my cottons, my provisions, my arms, my ammunition, my capital, were dust.

In a few hours, friends crowded round me, according to African custom, with proffered services to rebuild my establishment; but the heaviest loss I experienced was that of the rice designed for the voyage, which I could not replace in consequence of the destruction of my merchandise. In my difficulty, I was finally obliged to swap some of my two hundred and twenty negroes for the desired commodity, which enabled me to despatch the Feliz, though I was, of course, obliged to abandon the voyage in her.

My mind was greatly exercised for some time in endeavors to discover the origin of this conflagration. The blaze was first observed at the top of one of the gable ends, which satisfied Ali-Ninpha as well as myself that it was the work of a malicious incendiary. We adopted a variety of methods to trace or trap the scoundrel, but our efforts were fruitless, until a strange negro exhibited one of my double-barrelled guns for sale at a neighboring village, whose chief happened to recognize it. When the seller was questioned about his possession of the weapon, he alleged that it was purchased from inland negroes in a distant town. His replies were so unsatisfactory to the inquisitive chief, that he arrested the suspected felon and sent him to Kambia.

I had but little remorse in adopting any means in my power to extort a confession from the negro, who very soon admitted that my gun was stolen by a runner from the wizard of Matacan, who was still hanging about the outskirts of our settlement. I offered a liberal reward and handsome bribes to get possession of the necromancer himself, but such was the superstitious awe surrounding his haunt, that no one dared venture to seize him in his sanctuary, or seduce him within reach of my revenge. This, however, was not the case in regard to his emissary. I was soon in possession of the actual thief, and had little difficulty in securing his execution on the ruins he had made. Before we launched him into eternity, I obtained his confession after an obstinate resistance, and found with considerable pain that a brother of Ormond, the suicide, was a principal mover in the affair. The last words of the Mongo had been reported to this fellow as an injunction of revenge against me, and he very soon learned from personal experience that Kambia was a serious rival, if not antagonist, to Bangalang. His African simplicity made him believe that the " red cock " on my roof-tree would expel me from the river. I was not in a position to pay him back at the moment, yet I made a vow to give the new Mongo a free passage in irons to Cuba before many moons. But this, like other rash promises, I never kept.

Sad as was the wreck of my property, the conflagration was fraught with a misfortune that affected my heart far more deeply than the loss of merchandise. Ever since the day of my landing at Ormond's factory, a gentle form had flitted like a fairy among my fortunes, and always as the minister of kindness and hope. Skilled in the ways of her double blood, she was my discreet counsellor in many a peril ; and, tender as a well-bred dame of civilized lands, she was ever disposed to promote my happiness by disinterested offices. But, when we came to number the survivors of the ruin, ESTHER was nowhere to be found, nor could I ever trace, among the scattered fragments, the slightest relic of the Pariah's form!

---

Of course, I had very little beside my domestics to leave in charge of any one at Kambia, and intrusting them to the care of Ali-Ninpha, I went in my launch to Sierra Leone, where I purchased a schooner that had been condemned by the Mixed Commission.

In 1829, vessels were publicly sold, and, with very little trouble, equipped for the coast of Africa. The captures in that region were somewhat like playing a hand,—taking the tricks, reshuffling the same cards, and dealing again to take more tricks! Accordingly, I fitted the schooner to receive a cargo of negroes immediately on quitting port. My crew was made up of men from all nations, captured in prizes; but I guardedly selected my officers from Spaniards exclusively.

We were slowly wafting along the sea, a day or two out of the British colony, when the mate fell into chat with a clever lad, who was hanging lazily over the helm. They spoke of voyages and mishaps, and this led the sailor to declare his recent escape from a vessel, then in the Rio Nunez, whose mate had poisoned the commander to get possession of the craft. She had been fitted, he said, at St. Thomas with the feigned design of coasting; but, when she sailed for Africa, her register was sent back to the island in a boat to serve some other vessel, while she ventured to the continent *without* papers.

I have cause to believe that the slave trade was rarely conducted upon the honorable principles between man and man, which, of course, are the only security betwixt owners, commanders and consignees whose commerce is exclusively contraband. There were men, it is true, engaged in it, with whom the " point of honor " was more omnipotent than the dread of law in regular trade. But innumerable cases have occurred in which the spend-thrifts who appropriated their owners' property on the coast of

Africa, availed themselves of such superior force as they happened to control, in order to escape detection, or assure a favorable reception in the West Indies. In fact, the slaver sometimes ripened into something very like a pirate!

In 1828 and 1829, severe engagements took place between Spanish slavers and this class of contrabandists. Spaniards would assail Portuguese when the occasion was tempting and propitious. Many a vessel has been fitted in Cuba for these adventures, and returned to port with a living cargo, purchased by cannon-balls and boarding-pikes exclusively.

Now, I confess that my notions had become at this epoch somewhat relaxed by my traffic on the coast, so that I grew to be no better than folks of my cloth. I was fond of excitement; my craft was sadly in want of a cargo ; and, as the mate narrated the helmsman's story, the Quixotic idea naturally got control of my brain that I was destined to become the *avenger* of the poisoned captain. I will not say that I was altogether stimulated by the noble spirit of justice ; for it is quite possible I would never have thought of the dead man had not the sailor apprised us that his vessel was half full of negroes!

As we drifted slowly by the mouth of my old river, I slipped over the bar, and, while I fitted the schooner with a splendid nine-pounder amidships, I despatched a spy to the Rio Nunez to report the facts about the poisoning, as well as the armament of the unregistered slaver. In ten days the runner verified the tale. She was still in the stream, with one hundred and eighty-five human beings in her hold, but would soon be off with an entire cargo of two hundred and twenty-five.

The time was extraordinarily propitious. Every thing favored my enterprise. The number of slaves would exactly fit my schooner. Such a windfall could not be neglected; and, on the fourth day, I was entering the Rio Nunez under the Portuguese flag, which I unfurled by virtue of a pass from Sierra Leone to the Cape de Verd Islands.

I cannot tell whether my spy had been faithless, but when I reached Furcaria, I perceived that my game had taken wing from her anchorage. Here was a sad disappointment. The schooner drew too much water to allow a further ascent, and, moreover, I was unacquainted with the river.

As it was important that I should keep aloof from strangers, I anchored in a quiet spot, and seizing the first canoe that passed, learned, for a small reward, that the object of my search was hidden in a bend of the river at the king's town of Kakundy, which I could not reach without the pilotage of a certain mulatto, who was alone fit for the enterprise.

I knew this half-breed as soon as his person was described, but I had little hope of securing his services, either by fair means or promised recompense. He owed me five slaves for dealings that took place between us at Kambia, and had always refused so strenuously to pay, that I felt sure he would be off to the woods as soon as he knew my presence on the river. Accordingly, I kept my canoemen on the schooner by an abundant supply of " bitters," and at midnight landed half a dozen, who proceeded to the mulatto's cabin, where he was seized *sans ceremonie.* The terror of this ruffian was indescribable when he found himself in my presence,—a captive, as he supposed, for the debt of flesh. But I soon relieved him, and offered a liberal reward for his prompt, secret and safe pilotage, to Kakundy. The mulatto was willing, but the stream was too shallow for my keel. He argued the point so convincingly, that in half an hour, I relinquished the attempt, and resolved to make " Mahomet come to the mountain."

The two boats were quickly manned, armed, and supplied with lanterns ; and, with muffled oars, guided by our pilot,— whose skull was kept constantly under the lee of my pistol,—we fell like vampyres on our prey in the darkness.

With a wild hurrah and a blaze of our pistols in the air, we leaped on board, driving every soul under hatches without striking a blow ! Sentries were placed at the cabin door, forecastle and hatchway. The cable was slipped, my launch took her in tow, the pilot and myself took charge of the helm, and, before daylight, the prize was alongside my schooner, transhipping one hundred and ninety-seven of her slaves, with their necessary supplies.

Great was the surprise of the captured crew when they saw their fate; and great was the agony of the poisoner, when he returned next morning to the vacant anchorage, after a night of debauch with the king of Kakundy. First of all, he imagined we were regular cruisers, and that the captain's death was about to be avenged. But when it was discovered that they had fallen into the grasp of *friendly slavers,* five of his seamen abandoned their craft and shipped with me.

We had capital stomachs for breakfast after the night's romance. Hardly was it swallowed, however, when three canoes came blustering down the stream, filled with negroes and headed by his majesty. I did not wait for a salutation, but, giving the warriors a dose of bellicose grape, tripped my anchor, sheeted home my sails, and was off like an albatross !

The feat was cleverly achieved; but, since then, I have very often been taxed by my conscience with doubts as to its strict morality ! The African slave trade produces singular notions of *meum and tuum* in the minds and hearts of those who dwell for any length of time on that blighting coast; and it is not unlikely that I was quite as prone to the infection as better men, who perished under the malady, while I escaped !

# CHAPTER XXXV.

It was a sweltering July, and the "rainy season" proved its tremendous power by almost incessant deluges. In the breathless calms that held me spell-bound on the coast, the rain came down in such torrents that I often thought the solid water would bury and submerge our schooner. Now and then, a south-wester and the current would fan and drift us along; yet the tenth day found us rolling from side to side in the longitude of the Cape de Verds.

Day broke with one of its customary squalls and showers. As the cloud lifted, my look-out from the cross-trees announced a sail under our lee. It was invisible from deck, in the folds of the retreating rain, but, in the dead calm that followed, the distant whistle of a boatswain was distinctly audible. Before I could deliberate, all my doubts were solved by a shot in our mainsail, and the crack of a cannon. There could be no question that the unwelcome visitor was a man-of-war.

It was fortunate that the breeze sprang up after the lull, and enabled us to carry every thing that could be crowded on our spars. We dashed away before the freshening wind, like a deer with the unleashed hounds pursuing. The slaves were shifted from side to side—forward or aft—to aid our sailing. Head-stays were slackened, wedges knocked off the masts, and every incumbrance cast from the decks into the sea. Now and then, a fruitless shot from his bow-chasers, reminded the fugitive that the foe was still on his scent. At last, the cruiser got the range of his guns so perfectly, that a well-aimed ball ripped away our rail and tore a dangerous splinter from the foremast, three feet from deck. It was now perilous to carry a press of sail on the same tack with the weakened spar, whereupon I put the schooner about, and, to my delight, found we ranged ahead a knot faster on this course than the former. The enemy " went about " as quickly as we did, but her balls soon fell short of us, and, before noon, we had crawled so nimbly to windward, that her top-gallants alone were visible above the horizon.

———

Our voyage was uncheckered by any occurrence worthy of recollection, save the accidental loss of the mate in a dark and stormy night, until we approached the Antilles. Here, where every thing on a slaver assumes the guise of pleasure and relief, I remarked not only the sullenness of my crew, but a disposition to disobey or neglect. The second mate,—shipped in the Rio Nunez, and who replaced my lost officer,—was noticed occasionally in close intercourse with the watch, while his deportment indicated dissatisfaction, if not mutiny.

A slaver's life on shore, as well as at sea, makes him wary when another would not be circumspect, or even apprehensive. The sight of land is commonly the signal for merriment, for a well-behaved cargo is invariably released from shackles, and allowed free intercourse between the sexes during daytime on deck. Water tanks are thrown open for unrestricted use. " The cat " is cast into the sea. Strict discipline is relaxed. The day of danger or revolt is considered over, and the captain enjoys a new and refreshing life till the hour of landing. Sailors, with proverbial generosity, share their biscuits and clothing with the blacks. The women, who are generally without garments, appear in costume from the wardrobes of tars, petty officers, mates, and even captains. Sheets, table-cloths, and spare sails, are torn to pieces for raiment, while shoes, boots, caps, oil-cloths, and monkey-jackets, contribute to the gay masquerade of the " emigrants."

It was my sincere hope that the first glimpse of the Antilles would have converted my schooner into a theatre for such a display ; but the moodiness of my companions was so manifest, that I thought it best to meet rebellion half way, by breaking the suspected officer, and sending him forward, at the same time that I threw his " dog-house " overboard.[1]

I was now without a reliable officer, and was obliged to call two of the youngest sailors to my assistance in navigating the schooner. I knew the cook and steward—both of whom messed aft—to be trustworthy ; so that, with four men at my back, and the blacks below, I felt competent to control my vessel. From that moment, I suffered no one to approach the quarter-deck nearer than the mainmast.

It was a sweet afternoon when we were floating along the shores of Porto Rico, tracking our course upon the chart. Suddenly, one of my new assistants approached, with the sociability common among Spaniards, and, in a quiet tone, asked whether I would take a *cigarillo*. As I never smoked, I rejected the offer with thanks, when the youth immediately dropped the twisted paper on my map. In an instant, I perceived the *ruse*, and discovered that the *cigarillo* was, in fact, a *billet* rolled to resemble one. I put it in my mouth, and walked aft until I could throw myself on the deck, with my head over the stern, so as to open the paper unseen. It disclosed the organization of a mutiny, under the lead of the broken mate. Our arrival in sight of St. Domingo was to be the signal of its rupture, and for my immediate landing on the island. Six of the crew were implicated with the villain, and the boatswain, who was ill in the slave-hospital, was to share my fate.

My resolution was promptly made. In a few minutes, I had

---

The forecastle and cabin of a slaver are given up to the living freight, while officers sleep on deck in kennels, technically known as "dog-houses."

cast a hasty glance into the arm-chest, and seen that our weapons were in order.    Then, mustering ten of the stoutest and cleverest of my negroes on the quarter-deck, I took the liberty to invent a little strategic fib, and told them, in the Soosoo dialect, that there were bad men on board, who wanted to run the schooner ashore among rocks and drown the slaves while below. At the same time, I gave each a cutlass from the arm-chest, and supplying my trusty whites with a couple of pistols and a knife apiece, without saying a word, I seized the ringleader and his colleagues !    Irons and double-irons secured the party to the mainmast or deck, while a drum-head court-martial, composed of the officers, and presided over by myself, arraigned and tried the scoundrels in much less time than regular boards ordinarily spend in such investigations.    During the inquiry, we ascertained beyond doubt that the death of the mate was due to false play. He had been wilfully murdered, as a preliminary to the assault on me, for his colossal stature and powerful muscles would have made him a dangerous adversary in the seizure of the craft.

There was, perhaps, a touch of the old-fashioned Inquisition in the mode of our judicial researches concerning this projected mutiny.    We proceeded very much by way of " confession," and, whenever the culprit manifested reluctance or hesitation, his memory was stimulated by a " cat."    Accordingly, at the end of the trial, the mutineers were already pretty well punished ;  so that we sentenced the six accomplices to receive an additional flagellation, and continue ironed till we reached Cuba.    But the fate of the ringleader was not decided so easily.    Some were in favor of dropping him overboard, as he had done with the mate ; others proposed to set him adrift on a raft, ballasted with chains ; but I considered both these punishments too cruel, notwithstanding his treachery, and kept his head beneath the pistol of a sentry till I landed him in shackles on Turtle Island, with three days food and abundance of water.

# CHAPTER XXXVI.

AFTER all these adventures, I was very near losing the schooner before I got to land, by one of the perils of the sea, for which I blame myself that I was not better prepared.

It was the afternoon of a fine day. For some time, I had noticed on the horizon a low bank of white cloud, which rapidly spread itself over the sky and water, surrounding us with an impenetrable fog. I apprehended danger; yet, before I could make the schooner snug to meet the squall, a blast—as sudden and loud as a thunderbolt—prostrated her nearly on her beam. The shock was so violent and unforeseen, that the unrestrained slaves, who were enjoying the fine weather on deck, rolled to leeward till they floundered in the sea that inundated the scuppers. There was no power in the tiller to "keep her away" before the blast, for the rudder was almost out of water; but, fortunately, our mainsail burst in shreds from the bolt-ropes, and, relieving us from its pressure, allowed the schooner to right under control of the helm. The West Indian squall abandoned us as rapidly as it assailed, and I was happy to find that our entire loss did not exceed two slave-children, who had been carelessly suffered to sit on the rail.

The reader knows that my voyage was an *impromptu* speculation, without papers, manifest, register, consignees, or destination. It became necessary, therefore, that I should exercise a very unusual degree of circumspection, not only in landing my human cargo, but in selecting a spot from which I might communicate with proper persons. I had never been in Cuba, save on the occasion already described, nor were my business transactions extended beyond the Regla association, by which I was originally sent to Africa.

The day after the "white squall" I found our schooner drifting with a leading breeze along the southern coast of Cuba, and as the time seemed favorable, I thought I might as well cut the gordian knot of dilemma by landing my cargo in a secluded cove that indented the beach about nine miles east of Sant' Iago. If I had been consigned to the spot, I could not have been more fortunate in my reception. Some sixty yards from the landing I found the comfortable home of a *ranchero* who proffered the hospitality usual in such cases, and devoted a spacious barn to the reception of my slaves while his family prepared an abundant meal.

As soon as the cargo was safe from the grasp of cruisers, I resolved to disregard the flagless and paperless craft that bore it safely from Africa, and being unacquainted in Sant' Iago, to cross the island towards the capital, in search of a consignee. Accordingly I mounted a spirited little horse, and with a *montero* guide, turned my face once more towards the " ever faithful city of Havana."

My companion had a thousand questions for " the captain," all of which I answered with so much *bonhommie*, that we soon became the best friends imaginable, and chatted over all the scandal of Cuba. I learned from this man that a cargo had recently been "run" in the neighborhood of Matanzas, and that its disposal was most successfully managed by a Señor * * *, from Catalonia.

I slapped my thigh and shouted *eureka!* It flashed through my mind to trust this man without further inquiry, and I confess that my decision was based exclusively upon his *sectional* nationality. I am partial to the Catalans.

Accordingly, I presented myself at the counting-room of my future consignee in due time, and "made a clean breast" of the whole transaction, disclosing the destitute state of my vessel. In a very short period, his Excellency the Captain General was made aware of my arrival and furnished a list of "the Africans,"—by which name the Bosal slaves are commmonly known in Cuba. Nor was the captain of the port neglected. A convenient blank page of his register was inscribed with the name of my vessel as having sailed from the port six months before, and this was backed by a register and muster-roll, in order to secure my unquestionable entry into a harbor.

Before nightfall every thing was in order with Spanish despatch when stimulated either by doubloons or the smell of African blood ;—and twenty-four hours afterwards, I was again at the landing with a suit of clothes and blanket for each of my "domestics." The schooner was immediately put in charge of a clever pilot, who undertook the formal duty and *name* of her commander, in order to elude the vigilance of all the minor officials whose conscience had not been lulled by the golden anodyne.

In the meanwhile every attention had been given to the slaves by my hospitable *ranchero*. The "head-money" once paid, no body,—civil, military, foreign, or Spanish—dared interfere with them. Forty-eight hours of rest, ablution, exercise and feeding, served to recruit the gang and steady their gait. Nor had the sailors in charge of the party omitted the performance of their duty as "*valets*" to the gentlemen and "*ladies' maids*" to the females ; so that when the march towards Sant' Iago began, the procession might have been considered as "respectable as it was numerous."

The brokers of the southern emporium made very little delay in finding purchasers at retail for the entire venture. The returns were, of course, in cash ; and so well did the enterprise turn out, that I forgot the rebellion of our mutineers, and allowed them to share my bounty with the rest of the crew. In fact, so pleased was I with the result on inspecting the balance sheet, that I resolved to divert myself with the *dolce far niente* of Cuban country life for a month at least.

But while I was making ready for this delightful repose, a slight breeze passed over the calmness of my mirror. I had given, perhaps imprudently, but certainly with generous motives, a double pay to my men in recompense of their perilous service on the Rio Nunez. With the usual recklessness of their craft, they lounged about Havana, boasting of their success, while a Frenchman of the party,—who had been swindled of his wages at cards,—appealed to his Consul for relief. By dint of cross questions the Gallic official extracted the tale of our voyage from his countryman, and took advantage of the fellow's destitution to make him a witness against a certain Don Téodore Canot, who *was alleged to be a native of France !* Besides this, the punishment of my mate was exaggerated by the recreant Frenchman into a most unjustifiable as well as cruel act.

Of course the story was promptly detailed to the Captain General, who issued an order for my arrest. But I was too wary and flush to be caught so easily by the guardian of France's lilies. No person bearing my name could be found in the island ; and as the schooner had entered port with Spanish papers, Spanish crew, and was regularly sold, it became manifest to the stupefied Consul that the sailor's " yarn " was an entire fabrication. That night a convenient press-gang, in want of recruits for the royal marine, seized the braggadocio crew, and as there were no witnesses to corroborate the Consul's complaint, it was forthwith dismissed.

Things are managed very cleverly in Havana—*when you know how !*

## CHAPTER XXXVII.

BEFORE I went to sea again, I took a long holiday with full pockets, among my old friends at Regla and Havana. I thought it possible that a residence in Cuba for a season, aloof from traders and their transactions, might wean me from Africa; but three months had hardly elapsed, before I found myself sailing out of the harbor of St. Jago de Cuba to take, in Jamaica, a cargo of merchandise for the coast, and then to return and refit for slaves in Cuba.

My voyage began with a gale, which for three days swept us along on a tolerably good course, but on the night of the third, after snapping my mainmast on a lee shore, I was forced to beach the schooner in order to save our lives and cargo from destruction. Fortunately, we effected our landing with complete success, and at dawn I found my gallant little craft a total wreck on an uninhabited key. A large tent or pavilion was quickly built from our sails, sweeps, and remaining spars, beneath which every thing valuable and undamaged was stored before nightfall. Parties were sent forth to reconnoitre, while our remaining foremast was unshipped, and planted on the highest part of the sandbank with a signal of distress. The scouts returned without consolation. Nothing had been seen except a large dog, whose neck was encircled with a collar; but as he could not be made to approach by kindness, I forbade his execution. Neither smoke

nor tobacco freed us of the cloudy swarms of mosquitoes that filled the air after sunset, and so violent was the irritation of their
innumerable stings, that a delicate boy among the crew became
utterly insane, and was not restored till long after his return to
Cuba.

Several sad and weary days passed over us on this desolate
key, where our mode of life brought to my recollection many a
similar hour spent by me in company with Don Rafael and his
companions.    Vessel after vessel passed the reef, but none took
notice of our signal.    At last, on the tenth day of our imprisonment, a couple of small schooners fanned their way in a noncha-
lant manner towards our island, and knowing that we were quite
at their mercy, refused our rescue unless we assented to the
most extravagant terms of compensation.    After a good deal of
chaffering, it was agreed that the salvors should land us and our
effects at Nassau, New Providence, where the average should be
determined by the lawful tribunal.    The voyage was soon accomplished, and our amiable liberators from the mosquitoes of our
island prison obtained a judicial award of seventy per cent. for
their extraordinary trouble !

The wreck and the wreckers made so formidable an inroad
upon my finances, that I was very happy when I reached Cuba
once more, to accept the berth of sailing-master in a slave brig
which was fitting out at St. Thomas's, under an experienced
Frenchman.

My new craft, the SAN PABLO, was a trim Brazil-built brig,
of rather more than 300 tons.    Her hold contained sixteen
twenty-four carronades, while her magazine was stocked with
abundance of ammunition, and her kelson lined, fore and aft,
with round shot and grape.    Captain * * *, who had been described as a Tartar and martinet, received me with much affa-
bility, and seemed charmed when I told him that I conversed fluently not only in French but in English.

I had hardly arrived and begun to take the dimensions of my
new equipage, when a report ran through the harbor that a Danish cruiser was about to touch at the island.    Of course, every
thing was instantly afloat, and in a bustle to be off.    Stores and

provisions were tumbled in pell-mell, tanks were filled with water during the night; and, before dawn, fifty-five ragamuffins of
all castes, colors, and countries, were shipped as crew. By " six
bells," with a coasting flag at our peak, we were two miles at sea
with our main-topsail aback, receiving six kegs of specie and several chests of clothing from a lugger.

When we were fairly on " blue water " I discovered that our
voyage, though a slaver's, was not of an ordinary character. On
the second day, the mariners were provided with two setts of
uniform, to be worn on Sundays or when called to quarters.
Gold-laced caps, blue coats with anchor buttons, single epau-
lettes, and side arms were distributed to the officers, while a brief
address from the captain on the quarter-deck, apprised all hands
that if the enterprise resulted well, *a bounty* of one hundred dollars would be paid to each adventurer.

That night our skipper took me into council and developed
his plan, which was to load in a port in the Mozambique channel. To effect his purpose with more security, he had provided
the brig with an armament sufficient to repel a man of war of
equal size—(a fancy I never gave way to)—and on all occasions,
except in presence of a French cruiser, he intended to hoist the
Bourbon lilies, wear the Bourbon uniform, and conduct the vessel in every way as if she belonged to the royal navy. Nor
were the officers to be less favored than the sailors in regard to
double salary, certificates of which were handed to me for myself and my two subordinates. A memorandum book was then
supplied, containing minute instructions for each day of the en-
suing week, and I was specially charged, as second in command,
to be cautiously punctual in all my duties, and severely just towards my inferiors.

I took some pride in acquitting myself creditably in this new
military phase of a slaver's life. Very few days sufficed to put
the rigging and sails in perfect condition; to mount my sixteen
guns; to drill the men with small arms as well as artillery; and
by paint and sea-craft, to disguise the Saint Paul as a very respectable cruiser.

In twenty-seven days we touched at the Cape de Verds for

provisions, and shaped our way southward without speaking a single vessel of the multitude we met, until off the Cape of Good Hope we encountered a stranger who was evidently bent upon being sociable. Nevertheless, our inhospitable spirit forced us to hold our course unswervingly, till from peak and main we saw the white flag and pennant of France unfurled to the wind.

Our drum immediately beat to quarters; while the flag chest was brought on deck. Presently, the French *transport* demanded our private signal; which out of our ample supply, was promptly answered, and the royal ensign of Portugal set at our peak.

As we approached the Frenchman every thing was made ready for all hazards;—our guns were double-shotted, our matches lighted, our small arms distributed. The moment we came within hail, our captain,—who claimed precedence of the lieutenant of a transport,—spoke the Fenchman; and, for a while, carried on quite an amiable chat in Portuguese. At last the stranger requested leave to send his boat aboard with letters for the Isle of France; to which we consented with the greatest pleasure, though our captain thought it fair to inform him that we dared not prudently invite his officers on deck, inasmuch as there were " several cases of small-pox among our crew, contracted, in all likelihood, at Angola ! "

The discharge of an unexpected broadside could not have struck our visitor with more dismay or horror. The words were hardly spoken when her decks were in a bustle,—her yards braced sharply to the wind,—and her prow boiling through the sea, without so much as the compliment of a " *bon voyage !* "

Ten days after this *ruse d'esclave* we anchored at Quillimane, among a lot of Portuguese and Brazilian slavers, whose sails were either clewed up or unbent as if for a long delay. We fired a salute of twenty guns and ran up the French flag. The salvo was quickly answered, while our captain, in the full uniform of a naval commander, paid his respects to the Governor. Meantime orders were given me to remain carefully in charge of the ship; to avoid all intercourse with others; to go through the complete routine and show of a man of war; to strike the yards, haul down

signal, and fire a gun at sunset; but especially to get underway
and meet the captain at a small beach off the port, the instant I
saw a certain flag flying from the fort.

I have rarely seen matters conducted more skilfully than they
were by this daring Gaul. Next morning early the Governor's
boat was sent for the specie; the fourth day disclosed the signal
that called us to the beach; the fifth, sixth, and seventh, supplied us with *eight hundred negroes ;* and, on the ninth, we were
underway for our destination.

The success of this enterprise was more remarkable because
fourteen vessels, waiting cargoes, were at anchor when we arrived,
some of which had been detained in port over fifteen months. To
such a pitch had their impatience risen, that the masters made
common cause against all new-comers, and agreed that each ves
sel should take its turn for supply according to date of arrival.
But the astuteness of my veteran circumvented all these plans.
His anchorage and non-intercourse *as a French man-of-war* lulled every suspicion or intrigue against him, and he adroitly took
advantage of his kegs of specie to win the heart of the authorities and factors who supplied the slaves.

But wit and cleverness are not all in this world. Our
captain returned in high spirits to his vessel; but we hardly
reached the open sea before he was prostrated with an ague which
refused to yield to ordinary remedies, and finally ripened into
fever, that deprived him of reason. Other dangers thickened
around us. We had been several days off the Cape of Good
Hope, buffeting a series of adverse gales, when word was brought
me after a night of weary watching, that several slaves were ill
of small-pox. Of all calamities that occur in the voyage of a
slaver, this is the most dreaded and unmanageable. The news appalled me. Impetuous with anxiety I rushed to the captain, and
regardless of fever or insanity, disclosed the dreadful fact. He
stared at me for a minute as if in doubt; then opening his bureau
and pointing to a long coil of combustible material, said that it
communicated through the decks with the powder magazine, and
ordered me to—" *blow up the brig !* "

The master's madness sobered his mate. I lost no time in

securing both the dangerous implement and its perilous owner, while I called the officers into the cabin for inquiry and consultation as to our desperate state.

The gale had lasted nine days without intermission, and during all this time with so much violence that it was impossible to take off the gratings, release the slaves, purify the decks, or rig the wind-sails. When the first lull occurred, a thorough inspection of the eight hundred was made, and *a death announced*. As life had departed during the tempest, a careful inspection of the body was made, and it was this that first disclosed the pestilence in our midst. The corpse was silently thrown into the sea, and the malady kept secret from crew and negroes.

When breakfast was over on that fatal morning, I determined to visit the slave deck myself, and ordering an abundant supply of lanterns, descended to the cavern, which still reeked horribly with human vapor, even after ventilation. But here, alas! I found nine of the negroes infected by the disease. We took counsel as to the use of laudanum in ridding ourselves speedily of the sufferers,—a remedy that is seldom and secretly used in *desperate* cases to preserve the living from contagion. But it was quickly resolved that it had already gone too far, when nine were prostrated, to save the rest by depriving them of life. Accordingly, these wretched beings were at once sent to the forecastle as a hospital, and given in charge to the vaccinated or innoculated as nurses. The hold was then ventilated and limed; yet before the gale abated, our sick list was increased to thirty. The hospital could hold no more. Twelve of the sailors took the infection, and fifteen corpses had been cast in the sea!

All reserve was now at an end. Body after body fed the deep, and still the gale held on. At last, when the wind and waves had lulled so much as to allow the gratings to be removed from our hatches, our consternation knew no bounds when we found that nearly all the slaves were dead or dying with the distemper. I will not dwell on the scene or our sensations. It is a picture that must gape with all its horrors before the least vivid imagination. Yet there was no time for languor or sentimental sorrow. Twelve of the stoutest survivors were ordered to drag out the dead from among the ill, and though they were constantly drenched with rum to brutalize them, still we were forced to aid the gang by reckless volunteers from our crew, who, arming their hands with tarred mittens, flung the fœtid masses of putrefaction into the sea!

One day was a counterpart of another; and yet the love of life, or, perhaps, the love of gold, made us fight the monster with a courage that became a better cause. At length death was satisfied, but not until the eight hundred beings we had shipped in high health had dwindled to four hundred and ninety-seven skeletons!

# CHAPTER XXXVIII.

THE San Pablo might have been considered entitled to a " clean bill of health " by the time she reached the equator. The dead left space, food, and water for the living, and very little restraint was imposed on the squalid remnant. None were shackled after the outbreak of the fatal plague, so that in a short time the survivors began to fatten for the market to which they were hastening. But such was not the fate of our captain. The fever and delirium had long left him, yet a dysenteric tendency, —the result of a former malady,—suddenly supervened, and the worthy gentleman rapidly declined. His nerves gave way so thoroughly, that from fanciful weakness he lapsed into helpless hypochondria. One of his pet ideas was that a copious dose of calomel would ensure his restoration to perfect health. Unfortunately, however, during the prevalence of the plague, our medicine chest had one day been accidentally left exposed, and our mercury was abstracted. Still there was no use to attempt calming him with the assurance that his *nostrum* could not be had. The more we argued the impossibility of supplying him, the more was he urgent and imperative for the sanative mineral.

In this dilemma I ordered a bright look-out to be kept for merchantmen from whom I hoped to obtain the desirable drug. At last a sail was reported two points under our lee, and as her canvas was both patched and dark, I considered her a harmless Briton who might be approached with impunity.

It proved to be a brig from Belfast, in Ireland; but when I overhauled the skipper and desired him to send a boat on board, he declined the invitation and kept his course. A second and third command shared the same fate. I was somewhat nettled by this disregard of my flag, pennant, and starboard epaulette, and ordering the brig to be run alongside, I made her fast to the recusant, and boarded with ten men.

Our reception was, of course, not very amicable, though no show of resistance was made by officers or crew. I informed the captain that my object in stopping him was entirely one of mercy, and repeated the request I had previously made through the speaking trumpet. Still, the stubborn Scotchman persisted in denying the medicine, though I offered him payment in silver or gold. Thereupon, I commanded the mate to produce his log-book, and, under my dictation, to note the visit of the San Pablo, my request, and its churlish denial. This being done to my satisfaction, I ordered two of my hands to search for the medicine chest, which turned out to be a sorry receptacle of stale drugs, though fortunately containing an abundance of calomel. I did not parley about appropriating a third of the mineral, for which I counted five silver dollars on the cabin table. But the metal was no sooner exhibited than my Scotchman refused it with disdain. I handed it, however, to the mate, and exacted a receipt, which was noted in the log-book.

As I put my leg over the taffrail, I tried once more to smooth the bristles of the terrier, but a snarl and a snap repaid me for my good humor. Nevertheless, I resolved " to heap coals of fire on the head " of the ingrate; and, before I cast off our lashings, threw on his deck a dozen yams, a bag of frijoles, a barrel of pork, a couple of sacks of white Spanish biscuits,—and, with a cheer, bade him adieu.

But there was no balm in calomel for the captain. Scotch physic could not save him. He declined day by day; yet the energy of his hard nature kept him alive when other men would have sunk, and enabled him to command even from his sick bed.

It was always our Sabbath service to drum the men to quarters and exercise them with cannons and small arms. One Sunday, after the routine was over, the dying man desired to inspect his crew, and was carried to the quarter-deck on a mattress. Each sailor marched in front of him and was allowed to take his hand; after which he called them around in a body, and announced his apprehension that death would claim him before our destination was reached. Then, without previously apprising us of his design, he proceeded to make a verbal testament, and enjoined it upon all as a duty to his memory to obey implicitly. If the San Pablo arrived safely in port, he desired that every officer and mariner should be paid the promised bounty, and that the proceeds of cargo should be sent to his family in Nantz. But, if it happened that we were attacked by a cruiser, and the brig was saved by the risk and valor of a defence,—then, he directed that one half the voyage's avails should be shared between officers and crew, while one quarter was sent to his friends in France, and the other given to me. His sailing-master and Cuban consignees were to be the executors of this salt-water document.

We were now well advanced north-westwardly on our voyage, and in every cloud could see a promise of the continuing trade-wind, which was shortly to end a luckless voyage. From deck to royal,—from flying-jib to ring-tail, every stitch of canvas that would draw was packed and crowded on the brig. Vessels were daily seen in numbers, but none appeared suspicious till we got far to the westward, when my glass detected a cruising schooner, jogging along under easy sail. I ordered the helmsman to keep his course; and taughtening sheets, braces, and halyards, went into the cabin to receive the final orders of our commander.

He received my story with his usual bravery, nor was he startled when a boom from the cruiser's gun announced her in chase. He pointed to one of his drawers and told me to take out its contents. I handed him three flags, which he carefully unrolled, and displayed the ensigns of Spain, Denmark, and Portugal, in each of which I found a set of papers suitable for the San Pablo. In a feeble voice he desired me to select a nationality; and, when I chose the Spanish, he grasped my hand, pointed to the door, and bade me not to surrender.

When I reached the deck, I found our pursuer gaining on us with the utmost speed. She outsailed us—two to one. Escape was altogether out of the question; yet I resolved to show the inquisitive stranger our mettle, by keeping my course, firing a gun, and hoisting my Spanish signals at peak and main.

At this time the San Pablo was spinning along finely at the rate of about six knots an hour, when a shot from the schooner fell close to our stern. In a moment I ordered in studding-sails alow and aloft, and as my men had been trained to their duty in man-of-war fashion, I hoped to impose on the cruiser by the style and perfection of the manœuvre. Still, however, she kept her way, and, in four hours after discovery, was within half gun-shot of the brig.

Hitherto I had not touched my armament, but I selected this moment to load under the enemy's eyes, and, at the word of command, to fling open the ports and run out my barkers. The act was performed to a charm by my well-drilled gunners; yet all our belligerent display had not the least effect on the schooner, which still pursued us. At last, within hail, her commander leaped on a gun, and ordered me to " heave to, or take a ball ! "

Now, I was prepared for this arrogant command, and, for half an hour, had made up my mind how to avoid an engagement. A single discharge of my broadside might have sunk or seriously damaged our antagonist, but the consequences would have been terrible if he boarded me, which I believed to be his aim.

Accordingly, I paid no attention to the threat, but taughtened my ropes and surged ahead. Presently, my racing chaser came up *under my lee* within pistol-shot, when a reiterated command to heave to or be fired on, was answered for the first time by a faint " *no intiendo*,"—" I don't understand you,"—while the man-of-war shot ahead of me.

*Then I had him !* Quick as thought, I gave the order to " square away," and putting the helm up, struck the cruiser near the bow, carrying away her foremast and bowsprit. Such was the stranger's surprise at my daring trick that not a musket was fired or boarder stirred, till we were clear of the wreck.    It was then too late.    The loss of my jib-boom and a few rope-yarns did not prevent me from cracking on my studding-sails, and leaving the lubber to digest his stupid *forbearance!*

This adventure was a fitting epitaph for the stormy life of our poor commander, who died on the following night, and was buried under a choice selection of the flags he had honored with his various nationalities.    A few days after the blue water had closed over him for ever, our cargo was safely ensconsed in the *hacienda* nine miles east of St. Jago de Cuba, while the San Pablo was sent adrift and burnt to the water's edge.

# CHAPTER XXXIX.

THE beneficent disposition of my late commander, though not a regular testament, was carried out in Cuba, and put me in possession of twelve thousand dollars as my share of the enterprise. Yet my restless spirit did not allow me to remain idle. Our successful voyage had secured me scores of friends among the Spanish slavers, and I received daily applications for a fresh command.

But the plans of my French friend had so bewitched me with a desire for imitation, that I declined subordinate posts and aspired to ownership. Accordingly, I proposed to the proprietor of a large American clipper-brig, that we should fit her on the same system as the San Pablo; yet, wishing to surpass my late captain in commercial success, I suggested the idea of fighting for our cargo, or, in plainer language, of relieving another slaver of her living freight, a project which promptly found favor with the owner of " LA CONCHITA." The vessel in question originally cost twelve thousand dollars, and I proposed to cover this value by expending an equal sum on her outfit, in order to constitute me half owner.

The bargain was struck, and the armament, sails, additional spars, rigging, and provisions went on board, with prudential secrecy. Inasmuch as we could not leave port without some show of a cargo, merchandise *in bond* was taken from the public warehouses, and, after being loaded in our hold during day, was smuggled ashore again at night. As the manœuvre was a trick of my accomplice, who privately gained by the operation, I took no notice of what was delivered or taken away.

Finally, all was ready. Forty-five men were shipped, and the Conchita cleared. Next day, at daybreak, I was to sail with the land-breeze.

A sailor's last night ashore is proverbial, and none of the customary ceremonies were omitted on this occasion. There was a parting supper with plenty of champagne; there was a visit to the *café ;* a farewell call here, another there, and a bumper every where. In fact, till two in the morning, I was busy with my adieus; but when I got home at last, with a thumping headache, I was met at the door by a note from my partner, stating that our vessel was seized, and an order issued for my arrest. He counselled me to keep aloof from the *alguaziles*, till he could arrange the matter with the custom-house and police.

I will not enlarge this chapter of disasters. Next day, my accomplice was lodged in prison for his fraud, the vessel confiscated, her outfit sold, and my purse cropped to the extent of twelve thousand dollars. I had barely time to escape before the officers were in my lodgings; and I finally saved myself from an acquaintance with the interior of a Cuban prison, by taking another name, and playing *ranchero* among the hills for several weeks.

---

My finances were at low-water mark, when I strolled one fine morning into Matanzas, and, after some delay, again obtained command of a slaver, through the secret influence of my old and trusty friends. The new craft was a dashing schooner, of one hundred and twenty tons, fresh from the United States, and intended for Whydah on the Gold Coast. It was calculated that we might bring home at least four hundred and fifty slaves, for whose purchase, I was supplied plentifully with rum, powder, English muskets, and rich cottons from Manchester.

In due time we sailed for the Cape de Verds, the usual

"port of despatch" on such excursions; and at Praya, ex-changed our flag for the Portuguese, before we put up our helm for the coast. A British cruiser chased us fruitlessly for two days off Sierra Leone, and enabled me not only to test the sailing qualities, but to get the *sailing trim* of the "Estrella," in perfection. So confident did I become of the speed and bottom of my gallant clipper, that I ventured, with a leading wind, to chase the first vessel I descried on the horizon, and was altogether deceived by the tri-color displayed at her peak. Indeed, I could not divine this novel nationality, till the speaking trumpet apprised us that the lilies of France had taken triple hues in the hands of Louis Philippe! Accordingly, before I squared away for Whydah, I saluted the *royal republican*, by lowering my flag thrice to the new divinity.

---

I consigned the Estrella to one of the most remarkable traders that ever expanded the African traffic by his genius.

Señor Da Souza,—better known on the coast and interior as Cha-cha,—was said to be a native mulatto of Rio Janeiro, whence he emigrated to Dahomey, after deserting the arms of his imperial master. I do not know how he reached Africa, but it is probable the fugitive made part of some slaver's crew, and fled from his vessel, as he had previously abandoned the military service in the delicious clime of Brazil. His parents were poor, indolent, and careless, so that Cha-cha grew up an illiterate, headstrong youth. Yet, when he touched the soil of Africa, a new life seemed infused into his veins. For a while, his days are said to have been full of misery and trouble, but the Brazillian slave-trade happened to receive an extraordinary impetus about that period ; and, gradually, the adventurous refugee managed to profit by his skill in dealing with the natives, or by acting as broker among his countrymen. Beginning in the humblest way, he stuck to trade with the utmost tenacity till he ripened into an opulent factor. The tinge of native blood that dyed his complexion, perhaps qualified him peculiarly for this enterprise. He loved the customs of the people. He spoke their language with the fluency of a native. He won the favor of chief after chief. He strove to be considered a perfect African among Africans ; though, among whites, he still affected the graceful address and manners of his country. In this way, little by little, Cha-cha advanced in the regard of all he dealt with, and secured the commissions of Brazil and Cuba, while he was regarded and protected as a prime favorite by the warlike king of Dahomey. Indeed, it is alleged that this noted sovereign formed a sort of devilish compact with the Portuguese factor, and supplied him with every thing he desired during life, in consideration of inheriting his wealth when dead.

But Cha-cha was resolved, while the power of enjoyment was still vouchsafed him, that all the pleasures of human life, accessible to money, should not be wanting in Whydah. He built a large and commodious dwelling for his residence on a beautiful spot, near the site of an abandoned Portuguese fort. He filled his establishment with every luxury and comfort that could please the fancy, or gratify the body. Wines, food, delicacies and raiment, were brought from Paris, London, and Havana. The finest women along the coast were lured to his settlement. Billiard tables and gambling halls spread their wiles, or afforded distraction for detained navigators. In fine, the mongrel Sybarite surrounded himself with all that could corrupt virtue, gratify passion, tempt avarice, betray weakness, satisfy sensuality, and complete a picture of incarnate slavery in Dahomey.

When he sallied forth, his walk was always accompanied by considerable ceremony. An officer preceded him to clear the path ; a fool or buffoon hopped beside him ; a band of native musicians sounded their discordant instruments, and a couple of singers screamed, at the top of their voices, the most fulsome adulation of the mulatto.

Numbers of vessels were, of course, required to feed this African nabob with doubloons and merchandise. Sometimes, commanders from Cuba or Brazil would be kept months in his perilous nest, while their craft cruised along the coast, in expectation of human cargoes. At such seasons, no expedient was left untried for the entertainment and pillage of wealthy or trusted idlers. If Cha-cha's board and wines made them drunkards, it was no fault of his. If *rouge et noir*, or *monte*, won their doubloons and freight at his saloon, he regretted, but dared not interfere with the amusements of his guests. If the sirens of his harem betrayed a cargo for their favor over cards, a convenient fire destroyed the frail warehouse after its merchandise was secretly removed!

Cha-cha was exceedingly desirous that I should accept his hospitality. As soon as I read my invoice to him,—for he could not do it himself,—he became almost irresistible in his *empressement*. Yet I declined the invitation with firm politeness, and took up my quarters on shore, at the residence of a native *man-fuca*, or broker. I was warned of his allurements before I left Matanzas, and resolved to keep myself and property so clear of his clutches, that our contract would either be fulfilled or remain within my control. Thus, by avoiding his table, his "hells," and the society of his dissipated sons, I maintained my business relations with the slaver, and secured his personal respect so effectually, that, at the end of two months, four hundred and eighty prime negroes were in the bowels of La Estrella. [1]

[1] Da Souza died in May, 1849. Commander Forbes, R. N., in his book on Dahomey, says that a boy and girl were decapitated and buried with him, and that three men were sacrificed on the beach at Whydah. He alleges that, although this notorious slaver died in May, the funeral honors to his memory were not yet closed in October. "The town," he says, "is still in a ferment. Three hundred of the Amazons are daily in the square, firing and dancing; bands of Fetiche people parade the streets, headed by guinea-fowls, fowls, ducks, goats, pigeons, and pigs, on poles, alive, for sacrifice. Much rum is distributed, and all night there is shouting, firing and dancing."—*Dahomey and the Dahomans*, vol. i, 49.

# CHAPTER XL.

IF I had dreamed that these recollections of my African career would ever be made public, it is probable I should have taxed my memory with many events and characteristic anecdotes, of interest to those who study the progress of mankind, and the singular manifestations of human intellect in various portions of Ethiopia.

During my travels on that continent, I always found the negro a believer in some superior creative and controlling power, except among the marshes at the mouth of the Rio Pongo, where the Bagers, as I already stated, imagine that death is total annihilation. The Mandingoes and Fullahs have their Islamism and its Koran; the Soosoo has his good spirits and bad; another nation has its "pray-men" and "book-men," with their special creeds; another relies on the omnipotence of *juju* priests and *fetiche* worship;[1] some believe in the immortality of spirit; while others confide in the absolute translation of body. The Mahometan tribes adore the Creator, with an infinitude of ablutions, genuflexions, prayers, fasts, and by strictly adhering to the laws of the Prophet; while the heathen nations resort to their adroit priests, who shield them from the devil by charms of various degree, which are exclusively in their gift, and may consequently be imposed on the credulous for enormous prices.

[1] From the Portuguese *feitiço*—witchcraft.

At Whydah I found the natives addicted to a very grovelling species of idolatry. It was their belief that the Good as well as the Evil spirit existed in living Iguanas. In the home of the *man-fuca*, with whom I dwelt, several of these animals were constantly fed and cherished as *dii penates*, nor was any one allowed to interfere with their freedom, or to harm them when they grew insufferably offensive. The death of one of these crawling deities is considered a calamity in the household, and grief for the reptile becomes as great as for a departed parent.

Whilst I tarried at Whydah, an invitation came from the King of Dahomey, soliciting the presence of Cha-cha and his guests at the yearly sacrifice of human beings, whose blood is shed not only to appease an irritated god but to satiate the appetite of departed kings. I regret that I did not accompany the party that was present at this dreadful festival. Cha-cha despatched several of the captains who were waiting cargoes, under the charge of his own interpreters and the royal *manfucas;* and from one of these eye-witnesses, whose curiosity was painfully satiated, I received a faithful account of the horrid spectacle.

For three days our travellers passed through a populous region, fed with abundant repasts prepared in the native villages by Cha-cha's cooks, and resting at night in hammocks suspended among the trees. On the fourth day the party reached the great capital of Abomey, to which the king had come for the bloody festival from his residence at Cannah. My friends were comfortably lodged for repose, and next morning presented to the sovereign. He was a well built negro, dressed in the petticoat-trowsers of a Turk, with yellow morocco boots, while a profusion of silk shawls encircled his shoulders and waist, and a lofty *chapeau*, with trailing plumes, surmounted his wool. A vast body-guard of *female* soldiers or amazons, armed with lances and muskets, surrounded his majesty. Presently, the *manfucas* and interpreters, crawling abjectly on their hands and knees to the royal feet, deposited Cha-cha's tribute and the white men's offering. The first consisted of several pieces of crape, silks, and taffeta, with a large pitcher and basin of silver; while the latter was a trifling gift of twenty muskets and one hundred pieces of

blue *dungeree.* The present was gracefully accepted, and the do-
nors welcomed to the sacrifice, which was delayed on account of
the scarcity of victims, though orders had been given to storm a
neighboring tribe to make up three hundred slaves for the festival. In the mean while, a spacious house, furnished in European style, and altogether better than the ordinary dwellings of
Africa, was assigned to the strangers. Liberty was also given
them to enter wherever they pleased, and take what they wished,
inasmuch as all his subjects, male and female, were slaves whom
he placed at the white men's disposal.

The sixth of May was announced as the beginning of the sa-
crificial rites, which were to last five days. Early in the morning, two hundred females of the amazonian guard, naked to the
waist, but richly ornamented with beads and rings at every
joint of their oiled and glistening limbs, appeared in the area
before the king's palace, armed with blunt cutlasses. Very
soon the sovereign made his appearance, when the band of warriors began their manœuvres, keeping pace, with rude but not un-
martial skill, to the native drum and flute.

A short distance from the palace, within sight of the square,
a fort or inclosure, about nine feet high, had been built of *adobé,*
and surrounded by a pile of tall, prickly briers. Within this
barrier, secured to stakes, stood fifty captives who were to be
immolated at the opening of the festival. When the drill of the
amazons and the royal review were over, there was, for a considerable time, perfect silence in the ranks and throughout the vast
multitude of spectators. Presently, at a signal from the king,
one hundred of the women departed at a run, brandishing their
weapons and yelling their war-cry, till, heedless of the thorny
barricade, they leaped the walls, lacerating their flesh in crossing
the prickly impediment. The delay was short. Fifty of these
female demons, with torn limbs and bleeding faces, quickly returned, and offered their howling victims to the king. It was now
the duty of this personage to begin the sacrifice with his royal
hand. Calling the female whose impetuous daring had led her
foremost across the thorns, he took a glittering sword from her
grasp, and in an instant the head of the first victim fell to tho

dust. The weapon was then returned to the woman, who, handing it to the white men, desired them to unite in the brutal deed! The strangers, however, not only refused, but, sick at heart, abandoned the scene of butchery, which lasted, they understood, till noon, when the amazons were dismissed to their barracks, reeking with rum and blood.

I have limited the details of this barbarity to the initial cruelties, leaving the reader's imagination to fancy the atrocities that followed the second blow. It has always been noticed that the sight of blood, which appals a civilized man, serves to excite and enrage the savage, till his frantic passions induce him to mutilate his victims, even as a tiger becomes furious after it has torn the first wound in its prey. For five days the strangers were doomed to hear the yells of the storming amazons as they assailed the fort for fresh victims. On the sixth the sacrifice was over:—the divinity was appeased, and quiet reigned again in the streets of Abomey.

Our travellers were naturally anxious to quit a court where such abominations were regarded as national and religious duties; but before they departed, his majesty proposed to accord them a parting interview. He received the strangers with ceremonious politeness, and called their attention to the throne or royal seat upon which he had coiled his limbs. The chair is said to have been an heir-loom of at least twenty generations. Each leg of the article rests on the skull of some native king or chief, and such is the fanatical respect for the brutal usages of antiquity, that every three years the people of Dahomey are obliged to renew the steadiness of the stool by the fresh skulls of some noted princes!

———

I was not long enough at Whydah to observe the manners and customs of the natives with much care, still, as well as I now remember, there was great similarity to the habits of other tribes. The male lords it over the weaker sex, and as a man is valued according to the quantity of his wives; polygamy, even among civilized residents, is carried to a greater excess than elsewhere. Female chastity is not insisted on as in the Mandingo and Soosoo districts, but the husband contents himself with the seeming continence of his mistresses. Sixty or seventy miles south of Whydah, the adulterous wife of a chief is stabbed in the presence of her relations. Here, also, superstition has set up the altar of human sacrifice, but the divinity considers the offering of a single virgin sufficient for all its requirements.

Some years after my visit to Whydah, it happened that my traffic called me to Lagos at the season of this annual festival, so that I became an unwilling witness of the horrid scene.

When the slender crescent of the November moon is first observed, an edict goes forth from the king that his *Juju-man*, or high-priest, will go his annual round through the town, and during his progress it is strictly forbidden for any of his subjects to remain out of doors after sunset. Such is the terror with which the priests affect to regard the sacred demon, that even the fires are extinguished in their houses.

Towards midnight the *Juju-man* issued from a sacred *gree-gree* bush or grove, the entrance to which is inhibited to all negroes who do not belong to the religious brotherhood. The costume of the impostor is calculated to inspire his countrymen with fear. He was clad in a garment that descended from his waist to his heels like a petticoat or skirt, made of long black fur; a cape of the same material was clasped round his neck and covered his elbows; a gigantic hood which bristled with all the ferocity of a grenadier's cap, covered his head; his hands were disguised in tiger's paws, while a frightful mask, with sharp nose, thin lips, and white color, concealed his face. He was accompanied by ten stout barbarians, dressed and masked like himself, each sounding some discordant instrument. Every door, by law, is required to be left ajar for the free access of the *Juju*, but as soon as the horrid noise is heard approaching from the *tabooed grove*, each inhabitant falls to the ground, with eyes in the dust, to avoid even a look from the irritated spirit.

A victim is always agreed upon by the priests and the authorities before they leave the *gree-gree bush*, yet to instil a greater degree of superstitious terror, the frightful *Juju*, as if in doubt, promenades the town till daylight, entering a house now and then, and sometimes committing a murder or two to augment the panic. At dawn the home of the victim,—who, of course, is always the handsomest virgin in the settlement,—is reached, and the *Juju* immediately seizes and carries her to a place of concealment. Under pain of death her parents and friends are denied the privilege of uttering a complaint, or even of lifting their heads from the dust. Next day the unfortunate mother must seem ignorant of her daughter's doom, or profess herself proud of the *Juju's* choice. Two days pass without notice of the victim. On the third, at the river side, the king meets his fanatical subjects, clad in their choicest raiment, and wearing their sweetest smiles. A band of music salutes the sovereign, and suddenly the poor victim, *no longer a virgin and perfectly denuded*, is brought forward by a wizard, who is to act the part of executioner. The living sacrifice moves slowly with measured steps, but is no more to be recognized even by her nearest relatives, for face, body, and limbs, are covered thickly with chalk. As soon as she halts before the king, her hands and feet are bound to a bench near the trunk of a tree. The executioner then takes his stand, and with uplifted eyes and arms, seems to invoke a blessing on the people, while with a single blow of his blade, her head is rolled into the river. The bleeding trunk, laid carefully on a mat, is placed beneath a large tree to remain till a spirit shall bear it to the land of rest, and at night it is secretly removed by the priesthood.

It is gratifying to know that these *Jujus*, who in Africa assume the prerogatives of divinity, are only the principals of a religious fraternity who from time immemorial have constituted a secret society in this part of Ethiopia, for the purpose of sustaining their kings and ruling the people through their superstition. By fear and fanaticism these brutal priests exact confessions from ignorant negroes, which, in due time, are announced to the public as divinations of the oracle. The members of the society are the depositories of many secrets, tricks, and medical preparations, by which they are enabled to paralyze the body as well as affect the mind of their victim.    The king and his chiefs are generally supreme in this brotherhood of heathen superstition, and the purity of the sacrificed virgin, in the ceremony just described, was unquestionably yielded to her brutal prince.

# CHAPTER XLI.

I HAVE always regretted that I left Whydah on my homeward voyage without interpreters to aid in the necessary intercourse with our slaves. There was no one on board who understood a word of their dialect. Many complaints from the negroes that would have been dismissed or satisfactorily adjusted, had we comprehended their vivacious tongues and grievances, were passed over in silence or hushed with the lash. Indeed, the whip alone was the emblem of La Estrella's discipline; and in the end it taught me the saddest of lessons.

From the beginning there was manifest discontent among the slaves. I endeavored at first to please and accommodate them by a gracious manner; but manner alone is not appreciated by untamed Africans. A few days after our departure, a slave leaped overboard in a fit of passion, and another choked himself during the night. These two suicides, in twenty-four hours, caused much uneasiness among the officers, and induced me to make every preparation for a revolt.

We had been at sea about three weeks without further disturbance, and there was so much merriment among the gangs that were allowed to come on deck, that my apprehensions of danger began gradually to wear away. Suddenly, however, one fair afternoon, a squall broke forth from an almost cloudless sky;

and as the boatswain's whistle piped all hands to take in sail, a simultaneous rush was made by the confined slaves at all the after-gratings, and amid the confusion of the rising gale, they knocked down the guard and poured upon deck.   The sentry at the *fore-hatch* seized the cook's axe, and sweeping it round him like a scythe, kept at bay the band that sought to emerge from below him.   Meantime, the women in the cabin were not idle.   Seconding the males, they rose in a body, and the helmsman was forced to stab several with his knife before he could drive them below again.

About forty stalwart devils, yelling and grinning with all the savage ferocity of their wilderness, were now on deck, armed with staves of broken water-casks, or billets of wood, found in the hold.   The suddenness of this outbreak did not appal me, for, in the dangerous life of Africa, a trader must be always admonished and never off his guard.   The blow that prostrated the first white man was the earliest symptom I detected of the revolt; but, in an instant, I had the arm-chest open on the quarter-deck, and the mate and steward beside me to protect it. Matters, however, did not stand so well forward of the mainmast.   Four of the hands were disabled by clubs, while the rest defended themselves and the wounded as well as they could with handspikes, or whatever could suddenly be clutched.   I had always charged the cook, on such an emergency, to distribute from his coppers a liberal supply of scalding water upon the belligerents; and, at the first sign of revolt, he endeavored to baptize the heathen with his steaming slush.   But dinner had been over for some time, so that the lukewarm liquid only irritated the savages, one of whom laid the unfortunate " doctor " bleeding in the scuppers.

All this occurred in perhaps less time than I have taken to tell it; yet, rapid as was the transaction, I saw that, between the squall with its flying sails, and the revolt with its raving blacks, we would soon be in a desperate plight, unless I gave the order *to shoot*.   Accordingly, I told my comrades *to aim low and fire at once.*

Our carabines had been purposely loaded with buck-shot, to

suit such an occasion, so that the first two discharges brought several of the rebels to their knees. Still, the unharmed neither fled nor ceased brandishing their weapons. Two more discharges drove them forward amongst the mass of my crew, who had retreated towards the bowsprit; but, being reinforced by the boatswain and carpenter, we took command of the hatches so effectually, that a dozen additional discharges among the ebony legs, drove the refractory to their quarters below.

It was time; for sails, ropes, tacks, sheets, and blocks, were flapping, dashing, and rolling about the masts and decks, threatening us with imminent danger from the squall. In a short time, every thing was made snug, the vessel put on our course, and attention paid to the mutineers, who had begun to fight among themselves in the hold !

I perceived at once, by the infuriate sounds proceeding from below, that it would not answer to venture in their midst by descending through the hatches. Accordingly, we discharged the women from their quarters under a guard on deck, and sent several resolute and well-armed hands to remove a couple of boards from the bulk-head, that separated the cabin from the hold. When this was accomplished, a party entered, on hands and knees, through the aperture, and began to press the mutineers forward towards the bulk-head of the forecastle. Still, the rebels were hot for fight to the last, and boldly defended themselves with their staves against our weapons.

By this time, our lamed cook had rekindled his fires, and the water was once more boiling. The hatches were kept open but guarded, and all who did not fight were suffered to come singly on deck, where they were tied. As only about sixty remained below engaged in conflict, or defying my party of sappers and miners, I ordered a number of auger-holes to be bored in the deck, as the scoundrels were forced forward near the forecastle, when a few buckets of boiling water, rained on them through the fresh apertures, brought the majority to submission. Still, however, two of the most savage held out against water as well as fire. I strove as long as possible to save their lives, but their resistance was so prolonged and perilous, that we were obliged to disarm them *for ever* by a couple of pistol shots.

So ended the sad revolt of " La Estrella," in which two of my men were seriously wounded, while twenty-eight balls and buck shot were extracted, with sailors' skill, from the lower limbs of the slaves. One woman and three men perished of blows received in the conflict ; but none were deliberately slain except the two men, who resisted unto death.

I could never account for this mutiny, especially as the blacks from Ayudah and its neighborhood are distinguished for their humble manners and docility. There can be no doubt that the entire gang was not united or concerned in the original outbreak, else we should have had harder work in subduing them, amid the risk and turmoil of a West Indian squall.

# CHAPTER XLII.

THERE was very little comfort on board La Estrella, after the suppression of this revolt. We lived with a pent-up volcano beneath us, and, day and night, we were ceaselessly vigilant. Terror reigned supreme, and the lash was its sceptre.

At last, we made land at Porto Rico, and were swiftly passing its beautiful shores, when the inspector called my attention to the appearance of one of our attendant slaves, whom we had drilled as a sort of cabin-boy. He was a gentle, intelligent child, and had won the hearts of all the officers.

His pulse was high, quick and hard; his face and eyes red and swollen; while, on his neck, I detected half a dozen rosy pimples. He was sent immediately to the forecastle, free from contact with any one else, and left there, cut off from the crew, till I could guard against pestilence. It was small-pox!

The boy passed a wretched night of fever and pain, developing the malady with all its horrors. It is very likely that I slept as badly as the sufferer, for my mind was busy with his *doom*. Daylight found me on deck in consultation with our veteran boatswain, whose experience in the trade authorized the highest respect for his opinion. Hardened as he was, the old man's eyes filled, his lips trembled, and his voice was husky, as he whispered the verdict in my ear. I guessed it before he said a word; yet I hoped he would have counselled against the dread alternative. As we went aft to the quarter-deck, all eyes were bent upon us, for every one conjectured the malady and feared the result, yet none dared ask a question.

I ordered a general inspection of the slaves, yet when a *favorable* report was made, I did not rest content, and descended to examine each one personally. It was true; the child was *alone* infected!

For half an hour, I trod the deck to and fro restlessly, and caused the crew to subject themselves to inspection. But my sailors were as healthy as the slaves. There was no symptom that indicated approaching danger. I was disappointed again. A single case—a single sign of peril in any quarter, would have spared the poison!

That evening, in the stillness of night, a trembling hand stole forward to the afflicted boy with a potion that knows no waking. In a few hours, all was over. Life and the pestilence were crushed together; for a necessary murder had been committed, and the poor victim was beneath the blue water!

----

I am not superstitious, but a voyage attended with such calamities could not end happily. Incessant gales and head winds, unusual in this season and latitude, beset us so obstinately, that it became doubtful whether our food and water would last till we reached Matanzas. To add to our risks and misfortunes, a British corvette espied our craft, and gave chase off Cape Maize. All day long she dogged us slowly, but, at night, I tacked off shore, with the expectation of eluding my pursuer. Day dawn, however, revealed her again on our track, though this time we had unfortunately fallen to leeward. Accordingly, I put La Estrella directly before the wind, and ran till dark with a fresh breeze, when I again dodged the cruiser, and made for the Cuban coast. But the Briton seemed to scent my track, for sunrise revealed him once more in chase.

The wind lulled that night to a light breeze, yet the red

clouds and haze in the east betokened a gale from that quarter before meridian. A longer pursuit must have given considerable advantage to the enemy, so that my best reliance, I calculated, was in making the small harbor near St. Jago, now about twenty miles distant, where I had already landed two cargoes. The corvette was then full ten miles astern.

My resolution to save the cargo and lose the vessel was promptly made;—orders were issued to strike from the slaves the irons they had constantly worn since the mutiny; the boats were made ready; and every man prepared his bag for a rapid launch.

On dashed the cruiser, foaming at the bows, under the impetus of the rising gale, which struck him some time before it reached us. We were not more than seven miles apart when the first increased pressure on our sails was felt, and every thing was set and braced to give it the earliest welcome. Then came the tug and race for the beach, three miles ahead. But, under such circumstances, it was hardly to be expected that St. George could carry the day. Still, every nerve was strained to effect the purpose. Regardless of the gale, reef after reef was let out while force pumps moistened his sails; yet nothing was gained. Three miles against seven were too much odds;—and, with a slight move of the helm, and "letting all fly," as we neared the line of surf, to break her headway, La Estrella was fairly and safely *beached*.

The sudden shock snapped her mainmast like a pipe-stem, but, as no one was injured, in a twinkling the boats were overboard, crammed with women and children, while a stage was rigged from the bows to the strand, so that the males, the crew and the luggage were soon in charge of my old *haciendado*.

Prompt as we were, we were not sufficiently so for the cruiser. Half our cargo was ashore when she backed her top-sails off the mouth of the little bay, lowered her boats, filled them with boarders, and steered towards our craft. The delay of half a mile's row gave us time to cling still longer to the wreck, so that, when the boats and corvette began to fire, we wished them joy of their bargain over the remnant of our least valuable ne-

groes.   The rescued blacks are now, in all likelihood, citizens of
Jamaica ; but, under the influence of the gale, La Estrella made
a very picturesque bonfire, as we saw it that night from the
*azotéa* of our landlord's domicile.

# CHAPTER XLIII.

DISASTROUS as was this enterprise, both on the sea and in the counting-house, a couple of months found me on board a splendid clipper,—born of the famous waters of the Chesapeake,—delighting in the name of " AGUILA DE ORO," or " Golden Eagle," and spinning out of the Cape de Verds on a race with a famous West Indian privateer.

The " Montesquieu " was the pride of Jamaica for pluck and sailing, when folks of her character were not so unpopular as of late among the British Islands; and many a banter passed between her commander and myself, while I was unsuccessfully waiting till the governor resolved his conscientious difficulties about the *exchange of flags.* At last I offered a bet of five hundred dollars against an equal sum ; and next day a bag with the tempting thousand was tied to the end of my mainboom, with an invitation for the boaster to " follow and take." It was understood that, once clear of the harbor, the " Aguila " should have five minutes' start of the Montesquieu, after which we were to crowd sail and begin the race.

The contest was quickly noised throughout the port, and the captains smacked their lips over the *déjeuner* promised by the boaster out of the five hundred dollars won from the " Yankee nutshell." Accordingly, when all was ready and the breeze favored, the eastern cliffs of the Isle were crowded with spectators to witness the regatta.

As we were first at sea and clear of the harbor, we delayed for our antagonist; and without claiming the conceded start of five minutes, did not shoot ahead till our rival was within musket shot. But *then* the tug began with a will; and as the Aguila led, I selected her most favorable trim and kept her two points free. The Montesquieu did the same, but confident of her speed, did not spread all her canvas that would draw. The error, however, was soon seen. Our Chesapeake clipper crawled off as if her opponent was at anchor; and in a jiffy every thing that could be carried was sheeted home and braced to a hair. The breeze was steady and strong. Soon the island was cleared entirely; and by keeping away another point, I got out of the Aguila her utmost capacity as a racer. As she led off, the Montesquieu followed,—but glass by glass, and hour by hour, the distance between us increased, till at sunset the boaster's hull was below the horizon, and my bag taken in as a lawful prize.

I did not return to Praya after this adventure, but keeping on towards the coast, in four days entered the Rio Salum, an independent river between the French island of Goree and the British possessions on the Gambia. No slaver had haunted this stream for many a year, so that I was obliged to steer my mosquito pilot-boat full forty miles in the interior, through mangroves and forests, till I struck the trading ground of "the king."

After three days' parley I had just concluded my bargain with his breechless majesty, when a "barker" greeted me with the cheerless message that the "Aguila" was surrounded by man-of-war boats! It was true; but the mate refused an inspection of his craft *on neutral ground*, and the naval folks departed. Nevertheless, a week after, when I had just completed my traffic, I was seized by a gang of the treacherous king's own people; delivered to the second lieutenant of a French corvette—"La Bayonnaise;"—and my lovely little Eagle caged as her lawful prey!

I confess I have never been able to understand the legal merits of this seizure, so far as the act of the French officers was concerned, as no treaty existed between France and Spain for the suppression of slavery. The reader will not be surprised to learn, therefore, that there was a very loud explosion of wrath among my men when they found themselves prisoners; nor was their fury diminished when our whole band was forced into a dungeon at Goree, which, for size, gloom, and closeness, vied with the celebrated black hole of Calcutta.

For three days were we kept in this filthy receptacle, in a burning climate, without communication with friends or inhabitants, and on scanty fare, till it suited the local authorities to transfer us to San Luis, on the Senegal, in charge of a file of marines, *on board our own vessel!*

San Luis is the residence of the governor and the seat of the colonial tribunal, and here again we were incarcerated in a military *cachôt*, till several merchants who knew me on the Rio Pongo, interfered, and had us removed to better quarters in the military hospital. I soon learned that there was trouble among the natives. A war had broken out among some of the Moorish tribes, some two hundred miles up the Senegal, and my Aguila was a godsend to the Frenchmen, who needed just such a light craft to guard their returning flotilla with merchandise from Gatam. Accordingly, the craft was armed, manned, and despatched on this expedition *without waiting the decree of a court as to the lawfulness of her seizure!*

Meanwhile, the sisters of charity—those angels of devoted mercy, who do not shun even the heats and pestilence of Africa, —made our prison life as comfortable as possible; and had we not seen gratings at the windows, or met a sentinel when we attempted to go out, we might have considered ourselves valetudinarians instead of convicts.

A month oozed slowly away in these headquarters of suffering, before a military sergeant apprised us that he had been elevated to the dignity of the long-robe, and appointed our counsel in the approaching trial. No other lawyer was to be had in the colony for love or money, and, perhaps, our military man might have acquitted himself as well as the best, had not his superiors often imposed silence on him during the argument.

By this time the nimble Aguila had made two most service-able trips under the French officers, and proved so valuable to the Gallic government that no one dreamed of recovering her. The colonial authorities had two alternatives under the circumstances, —either to pay for or condemn her,—and as they knew I would not be willing to take the craft again after the destruction of my voyage, the formality of a trial was determined to legalize the condemnation. It was necessary, however, even in Africa, to show that I had violated the territory of the French colony by trading in slaves, and that the Aguila had been caught in the act.

I will not attempt a description of the court scene, in which my military friend was browbeaten by the prosecutor, the prosecutor by the judge, and the judge by myself. After various outrages and absurdities, a Mahometan *slave* was allowed to be sworn as a witness against me ; whereupon I burst forth with a torrent of argument, defence, abuse, and scorn, till a couple of soldiers were called to keep my limbs and tongue in forensic order.

But the deed was done. The foregone conclusion was formally announced. The Aguila de Oro became King Louis Philippe's property, while my men were condemned to two, my officers to five, and Don Téodor himself, to ten years' confinement in the central prisons of *la belle France !*

Such was the style of colonial justice in the reign of *le roi bourgeois !*

My sentence aroused the indignation of many respectable merchants at San Luis; and, of course, I did not lack kindly visits in the stronghold to which I was reconducted. It was found to be entirely useless to attack the sympathy of the tribunal, either to procure a rehearing of the cause or mitigation of the judgment. Presently, a generous friend introduced *a saw* suitable to discuss the toughness of iron bars, and hinted that on the night when my window gratings were severed, a boat might be found waiting to transport me to the opposite shore of the river, whence an independent chief would convey me on camels to Gambia.

I know not how it was that the government got wind of my

projected flight, but it certainly did, and we were sent on board a station ship lying in the stream. Still, my friends did not abandon me. I was apprised that a party,—bound on a shooting frolic down the river on the first *foggy* morning,—would visit the commander of the hulk,—a noted *bon-vivant*,—and while the vessel was surrounded by a crowd of boats, I might slip overboard amid the confusion. Under cover of the dense mist that shrouds the surface of an African river at dawn, I could easily elude even a ball if sent after me, and when I reached the shore, a canoe would be ready to convey me to a friendly ship.

The scheme was peculiarly feasible, as the captain happened to be a good fellow, and allowed me unlimited liberty about his vessel. Accordingly, when the note had been duly digested, I called my officers apart, and proposed their participation in my escape. The project was fully discussed by the fellows; but the risk of swimming, even in a fog, under the muzzles of muskets, was a danger they feared encountering. I perceived at once that it would be best to free myself entirely from the encumbrance of such chicken-hearted lubbers, so I bade them take their own course, but divided three thousand francs in government bills among the gang, and presented my gold pocket chronometer to the mate.

Next morning an impervious fog laid low on the bosom of the Senegal, but through its heavy folds I detected the measured beat of approaching oars, till five boats, with a sudden rush, dashed alongside us with their noisy and clamorous crews.

Just at this very moment a friendly hand passed through my arm, and a gentle tone invited me to a quarter-deck promenade. It was our captain!

There was, of course, no possibility of declining the proffered civility, for during the whole of my detention on board, the commander had treated me with the most assiduous politeness.

" *Mon cher Canot,*" said he, as soon as we got aft,—" you seem to take considerable interest in these visitors of ours, and I wish from the bottom of my heart that you could join the sport; *but, unfortunately for you, these gentlemen will not effect their purpose!* "

As I did not entirely comprehend,—though I rather guessed,—his precise meaning, I made an evasive answer; and, arm in arm I was led from the deck to the cabin.  When we were perfectly alone, he pointed to a seat, and frankly declared that I had been betrayed by a Judas to his sergeant of marines!  I was taken perfectly aback, as I imagined myself almost free, yet the loss of liberty did not paralyze me as much as the perfidy of my men.  Like a stupid booby, I stood gazing with a fixed stare at the captain, when the cabin door burst open, and with a shout of joyous merriment the hunters rushed in to greet their comrade.

My dress that morning was a very elaborate *negligé.*  I had purposely omitted coat, braces, stockings and shoes, so that my privateer costume of trowsers and shirt was not calculated for the reception of strangers.  It was natural, therefore, that the first sally of my friendly liberators should be directed against my toilette; I parried it, however, as adroitly as my temper would allow, by reproaching them with their "unseasonable visit, before I could complete the *bath* which they saw I was prepared for!"

The hint was understood; but the captain thought proper to tell the entire tale.  No man, he said, would have been happier than he, had I escaped before the treachery.  My friends were entreated not to risk further attempts, which might subject me to severe restraints; and my base comrades were forthwith summoned to the cabin, where, in presence of the merchants, they were forced to disgorge the three thousand francs and the chronometer.

" But this," said Captain Z———, " is not to be the end of the comedy,—*en avant, messieurs!* " as he led the way to the mess-room, where a sumptuous *déjeuner* was spread for officers and huntsmen, and over its fragrant fumes my disappointment was, for a while, forgotten.

## CHAPTER XLIV.

FOR fifteen days more the angry captive bit his thumbs on the taffrail of the guard-ship, and gazed either at vacancy or the waters of the Senegal. At the end of that period, a gunboat transferred our convict party to the frigate Flora, whose first lieutenant, to whom I had been privately recommended, separated me immediately from my men. The scoundrels were kept close prisoners during the whole voyage to France, while my lot was made as light as possible, under the severe sentence awarded at San Luis.

The passage was short. At Brest, they landed me privately, while my men and officers were paraded through the streets at mid-day, under a file of *gens d'armes*. I am especially grateful to the commander of this frigate, who alleviated my sufferings by his generous demeanor in every respect, and whose representations to the government of France caused my sentence to be subsequently modified to simple imprisonment.

I have so many pleasant recollections of this voyage as a convict in the Flora, that I am loth to recount the following anecdote; yet I hardly think it ought to be omitted, for it is characteristic in a double aspect. It exhibits at once the chivalric courtesy and the coarse boorishness of some classes in the naval service of France, at the period I am describing.

On board our frigate there were two Sisters of Charity, who were returning to their parent convent in France, after five years of colonial self-sacrifice in the pestilential marshes of Africa. These noble women lodged in a large state-room, built expressly for their use and comfort on the lower battery-deck, and, according to the ship's rule, were entitled to mess with the lieutenants in their wardroom. It so happened, that among the officers, there was one of those vulgar dolts, whose happiness consists in making others as uncomfortable as possible, both by bullying manners and lewd conversation. He seemed to delight in losing no opportunity to offend the ladies while at table, by ridiculing their calling and piety; yet, not content with these insults, which the nuns received with silent contempt, he grew so bold on one occasion, in the midst of dinner, as to burst forth with a song so gross, that it would have disgraced the orgies of a *cabaret*. The Sisters instantly arose, and, next morning, refused their meals in the wardroom, soliciting the steward to supply them a sailor's ration in their cabin, where they might be free from dishonor.

But the charitable women were soon missed from mess, and when the steward's report brought the dangerous idea of a court-martial before the terrified imagination of the vulgarians, a prompt resolve was made to implore pardon for the indecent officer, before the frigate's captain could learn the outrage. It is needless to add that the surgeon—who was appointed ambassador—easily obtained the mercy of these charitable women, and that, henceforth, our lieutenants' wardroom was a model of social propriety.

---

## THE PRISON OF BREST.

I was not very curious in studying the architecture of the strong stone lock-up, to which they conducted me in the stern and ugly old rendezvous of Brest. I was sick as soon as I beheld it from our deck. The entrance to the harbor, through the long, narrow, rocky strait, defended towards the sea by a frowning castle, and strongly fortified towards the land, looked to me like passing through the throat of a monster, who was to swallow me for ever. But I had little time for observation or reflection on external objects,—my business was with *interiors :* and when the polite midshipman with whom I landed bade farewell, it was only to transfer me to the *concièrge* of a prison within the royal arsenal. Here I was soon joined by the crew and officers. For a while, I rejected their penitence; but a man who is suddenly swept from the wild liberty of Africa, and doomed for ten years to penitential seclusion, becomes wonderfully forgiving when loneliness eats into his heart, and eternal silence makes the sound of his own voice almost insupportable. One by one, therefore, was restored at least to sociability ; so that, when I embraced the permission of our keeper to quit my cell, and move about the prison bounds, I found myself surrounded by seventy or eighty marines and seamen, who were undergoing the penalties of various crimes. The whole establishment was under the *surveillance* of a naval commissary, subject to strict regulations. In due time, two spacious rooms were assigned for my gang, while the jailer, who turned out to be an amphibious scamp,—half sailor, half soldier,—assured us, " on the honor of a *vieux militaire,*" that his entire jurisdiction should be our limits so long as we behaved with propriety.

Next day I descended to take exercise in a broad court-yard, over whose lofty walls the fresh blue sky looked temptingly ; and was diligently chewing the cud of bitter fancies, when a stout elderly man, in shabby uniform, came to a military halt before me, and, abruptly saluting in regulation style, desired the favor of a word.

" *Pardon, mon bráve !* " said the intruder, " but I should be charmed if *Monsieur le capitaine* will honor me by the information whether it has been his lot to enjoy the accommodations of a French prison, prior to the unlucky mischance which gives us the delight of his society ! "

" No," said I, sulkily.

" *Encore,*" continued the questioner, " will it be disagreeable, if I improve this opportunity, by apprising Monsieur *le capitaine*, on the part of our companions and comrades, of the regulations of this royal institution ? "

" By no means," returned I, somewhat softer.

" Then, *mon chèr*, the sooner you are initiated into the mysteries of the craft the better, and no one will go through the ceremony more explicitly, briefly and satisfactorily, than myself —*le Caporal Blon*. First of all, *mon brâve*, and most indispensable, as your good sense will teach you, it is necessary that every new comer is bound to pay his footing among the " *government boarders ;* " and as you, Monsieur le capitaine, seem to be the honored *chèf* of this charming little squadron, I will make bold to thank you for a *Louis d'or*, or a *Napoleon*, to insure your welcome."

The request was no sooner out than complied with.

" *Bien !* " continued the corporal, " *c'est un bon enfant, parbleu !* Now, I have but one more *mystère* to impart, and that is a regulation which no clever chap disregards. We are companions in misery ; we sleep beneath one roof ; we eat out of one kettle ;—in fact, *nous sommes frères*, and the *secrets of brothers are sacred, within these walls, from jailers and turn-keys !* "

As he said these words, he pursed up his mouth, bent his eyes scrutinizingly into mine, and laying his finger on his lip, brought his right hand once more, with a salute, to the oily remnant of a military cap.

I was initiated. I gave the required pledge for my party, and, in return, was assured that, in any enterprise undertaken for our escape,—which seemed to be the great object and concern of every body's prison-life,—we should be assisted and protected by our fellow-sufferers.

Most of this day was passed in our rooms, and, at dark, after being mustered and counted, we were locked up for the night. For some time we moped and sulked, according to the fashion of all *new* convicts, but, at length, we sallied forth in a body to the court-yard, determined to take the world as it went, and make the best of a bad bargain.

I soon fell into a pleasant habit of chatting familiarly with

old Corporal Blon, who was grand chamberlain, or master of ceremonies, to our penal household, and turned out to be a good
fellow, though a frequent offender against "*le coq de France.*"
Blon drew me to a seat in the sunshine, which I enjoyed, after
shivering in the cold apartments of the prison; and, stepping off
among the prisoners, began to bring them up for introduction to
Don Téodor, separately. First of all, I had the honor of receiving Monsieur Laramie, a stout, stanch, well-built marine,
who professed to be *maître d'armes* of our "royal boarding-
house," and tendered his services in teaching me the use of
rapier and broadsword, at the rate of a *franc* per week. Next
came a burly, beef-eating bully, half sailor, half lubber, who approached with a swinging gait, and was presented as *frère* Zouche,
teacher of single stick, who was also willing to make me skilful
in my encounters with foot-pads for a reasonable salary. Then
followed a dancing-master, a tailor, a violin-teacher, a shoe-
maker, a letter-writer, a barber, a clothes-washer, and various
other useful and reputable tradespeople or professors, all of
whom expressed anxiety to inform my mind, cultivate my taste,
expedite my correspondence, delight my ear, and improve my
appearance, for weekly stipends.

I did not, at first, understand precisely the object of all their
ceremonious appeals to my purse, but I soon discovered from
Corporal Blon,—*who desired an early discount of his note,*—
that I was looked on as a sort of Don Magnifico from Africa,
who had saved an immense quantity of gold from ancient traffic,
all of which I could command, in spite of imprisonment.

So I thought it best not to undeceive the industrious wretches,
and, accordingly, dismissed each of them with a few kind words,
and promised to accept their offers when I became a little more
familiar with my quarters.

After breakfast, I made a tour of the corridors, to see
whether the representations of my morning courtiers were true;
and found the shoemakers and tailors busy over toeless boots
and patchwork garments. One alcove contained the violinist
and dancing-master, giving lessons to several scapegraces in the
*terpsichorean* art; in another was the letter-writer, laboriously

adorning a sheet with cupids, hearts, flames, and arrows, while a love-lorn booby knelt beside him, dictating a message to his mistress; in a hall I found two pupils of Monsieur Laramie at *quart* and *tièrce;* in the corridors I came upon a string of tables, filled with cigars, snuff, writing-paper, ink, pens, wax, wafers, needles and thread; while, in the remotest cell, I discovered a pawn-broker and gambling-table. Who can doubt that a real Gaul knows how to kill time, when he is unwillingly converted into a " government boarder," and transfers the occupations, amusements, and vices of life, to the recesses of a prison!

---

Very soon after my incarceration at Brest, I addressed a memorial to the Spanish consul, setting forth the afflictions of twenty-two of his master's subjects, and soliciting the interference of our ambassador at Paris. We were promptly visited by the consul and an eminent lawyer, who asserted his ability to stay proceedings against the ratification of our sentence; but, as the Spanish minister never thought fit to notice our misfortunes, the efforts of the lawyer and the good will of our consul were ineffectual. Three months glided by, while I lingered at Brest; yet my heart did not sink with hope delayed, for the natural buoyancy of my spirit sustained me, and I entered with avidity upon all the schemes and diversions of our stronghold.

Blon kept me busy discounting his twenty *sous* notes, which I afterwards always took care to lose to him at cards. Then I patronized the dancing-master; took two months' lessons with Laramie and Zouche; caused my shoes to be thoroughly mended; had my clothes repaired and scoured; and, finally, patronized all the various industries of my comrades, to the extent of two hundred francs.

Suddenly, in the midst of these diversions, an order came for our immediate transfer to the *civil prison* of Brest, a gloomy tower in the walled *chateau* of that detestable town.

# CHAPTER XLV.

I was taken from one prison to the other in a boat, and once more spared the mortification of a parade through the streets, under a guard of soldiers.

A receipt was given for the whole squad to the *brigadier* who chaperoned us. My men were summarily distributed by the jailer among the cells already filled with common malefactors; but, as the appearance of the *officers* indicated the possession of cash, the turnkey offered " *la salle de distinction* " for our use, provided we were satisfied with a monthly rent of ten *francs*. I thought the French government was bound to find suitable accommodations for an involuntary guest, and that it was rather hard to imprison me first, and make me pay board afterwards; but, on reflection, I concluded to accept the offer, hard as it was, and, accordingly, we took possession of a large apartment, with two grated windows looking upon a narrow and sombre court-yard.

We had hardly entered the room, when a buxom woman followed with the deepest curtseys, and declared herself "most happy to have it in her power to supply us with beds and bedding, at ten sous per day." She apprised us, moreover, that the daily prison fare consisted of two pounds and a half of black bread, with water *à discretion*, but if we wished, she might intro duce the *vivandière* of the regiment, stationed in the chateau, who would supply our meals twice a day from the mess of the petty officers.

My money had not been seriously moth-eaten during our previous confinement, so that I did not hesitate to strike a bargain with Madame Sorret, and to request that *la vivandière* might make her appearance on the theatre of action as soon as possible. Presently, the door opened again, and the dame reappeared accompanied by two Spanish women, wives of musicians in the corps, who had heard that several of their countrymen had that morning been incarcerated, and availed themselves of the earliest chance to visit and succor them.

For the thousandth time I blessed the noble heart that ever beats in the breast of a Spanish woman when distress or calamity appeals, and at once proceeded to arrange the diet of our future prison life. We were to have two meals a day of three dishes, for each of which we were to pay fifteen *sous in advance*. The bargain made, we sat down on the floor for a chat.

My brace of Catalan visitors had married in this regiment when the Duke d'Angoulême marched his troops into Spain; and like faithful girls, followed their husbands in all their meanderings about France since the regiment's return. As two of my officers were Catalonians by birth, a friendship sprang up like wildfire between us, and from that hour, these excellent women not only visited us daily, but ran our errands, attended to our health, watched us like sisters, and procured all those little comforts which the tender soul of the sex can alone devise.

I hope that few of my readers have personal knowledge of the treatment or fare of civil prisons in the provinces of France during the republican era of which I am writing. I think it well to set down a record of its barbarity.

As I before said, the *regular ration* consisted exclusively of black bread and water. Nine pounds of straw were allowed weekly to each prisoner for his *lair*. Neither blankets nor covering were furnished, even in the winter, and as the cells are built without stoves or chimneys, the wretched convicts were compelled to huddle together in heaps to keep from perishing.

Besides this, the government denied all supplies of fresh raiment, so that the wretches who were destitute of friends or means, were alive and hideous with vermin in a few days after incarceration. No amusement was allowed in the fresh air save twice a week, when the prisoners were turned out on the flat roof of the tower, where they might sun themselves for an hour or two under the muzzle of a guard.

Such was the treatment endured by twelve of my men during the year they continued in France. There are some folks who may be charitable enough to remark—*that slavers deserved no better !*

I believe that convicts in the central prisons of France, where they were either made or allowed to work, fared better in every respect than in the provincial lock-ups on the coast. There is no doubt, however, that the above description at the epoch of my incarceration, was entirely true of all the smaller jurisdictions, whose culprits were simply doomed to confinement without labor.

Often did my heart bleed for the poor sailors, whom I aided to the extent of prudence from my slender means, when I knew not how long it might be my fate to remain an inmate of the chateau. After these unfortunate men had disposed of all their spare garments to obtain now and then a meagre soup to moisten their stony loaves, they were nearly a year without tasting either meat or broth! Once only,—on the anniversary of St. Philippe,—the Sisters of Charity gave them a pair of bullock's heads to make a *festival* in honor of the Good King of the French !

# CHAPTER XLVI.

As the apartment rented by us from the jailer was the only one in the prison he had a right to dispose of for his own benefit, several other culprits, able to pay for comfortable lodgings, were from time to time locked up in it. These occasional visitors afforded considerable entertainment for our seclusion, as they were often persons of quality arrested for petty misdemeanors or political opinions, and sometimes *chevaliers d'industrie*, whose professional careers were rich with anecdote and adventure.

It was probably a month after we began our intimacy with this "government boarding-house" that our number was increased by a gentleman of cultivated manners and foppish costume. He was, perhaps, a little too much over-dressed with chains, trinkets, and perfumed locks, to be perfectly *comme il faut*, yet there was an intellectual power about his forehead and eyes, and a bewitching smile on his lips, that insinuated themselves into my heart the moment I beheld him. He was precisely the sort of man who is considered by nine tenths of the world as a very "fascinating individual."

Accordingly, I welcomed the stranger most cordially in French, and was still more bewitched by the retiring shyness of his modest demeanor. As the jailer retired, a wink signified his desire to commune with me apart in his office, where I learn-

ed that the new comer had been arrested under a charge of *coun-
terfeiting*, but on account of his genteel appearance and blood, was
placed in our apartment. I had no doubt that neither appearance
nor blood had been the springs of sympathy in the jailer's heart,
but that the artificial money-maker had judiciously used certain
lawful coins to insure better quarters. Nevertheless, I did not
hesitate to approve the turnkey's disposal of the suspected felon,
and begged him to make no apologies or give himself concern as
to the quality of the article that could afford us a moment's
amusement in our dreary den.

I next proceeded to initiate my gentleman into the mysteries
of the *chateau ;* and as dinner was about serving, I suggested that
the most important of our domestic rites on such occasions, impe-
ratively required three or four bottles of first rate claret.

By this time we had acquired a tolerable knack of " slaugh-
tering the evening." Our Spanish girls supplied us with guitars
and violins, which my comrades touched with some skill. We
were thus enabled to give an occasional *soirée dansante*, assisted
by la Vivandière, her companions Dolorescita, Concha, Madame
Sorret, and an old maid who passed for her sister. The arrival
of the counterfeiter enabled us to make up a full cotillon without
the musicians. Our *soirées*, enlivened by private contributions
and a bottle or two of wine, took place on Thursdays and Sundays, while the rest of the week was passed in playing cards,
reading romances, writing petitions, flirting with the girls, and
cursing our fate and the French government. Fits of wrath
against the majesty of Gaul were more frequent in the early
morning, when the pleasant sleeper would be suddenly roused
from happy dreams by the tramp of soldiers and grating bolts,
which announced the unceremonious entrance of our inspector to
count his cattle and sound our window gratings.

But time wastes one's cash as well as one's patience in prison.
The more we grumbled, danced, drank, and eat, the more we spent
or lavished, so that my funds looked very like a thin sediment
at the bottom of the purse, when I began to reflect upon means of
replenishing. I could not beg; I was master of no handicraft;
nor was I willing to descend among the vermin of the common

chain-gang. Shame prevented an application to my relatives in France or Italy; and when I addressed my old partner or former friends in Cuba, I was not even favored with a reply. At last, my little trinkets and gold chronometer were sacrificed to pay the lawyer for a *final memorial* and to liquidate a week's lodging in advance.

"Now, *mon enfant,*" said Madame Sorret, as she took my money,—trimming her cap, and looking at me with that thrifty interest that a Frenchwoman always knows how to turn to the best account;—"now, mon enfant,—this is your last *franc* and your last week in my apartment, you say;—your last week in a room where you and I, and Babette, Dolorescita, and Concha, and *Monsieur,* have had such good times! *Mais pourquoi, mon cher?* why shall it be your last week? Come let us think a bit. Won't it be a thousand times better; won't it do you a vast deal more good,—if instead of *sacré*-ing *le bon Louis Philippe,*— paying lawyers for memorials that are never read,—hoping for letters from the Spanish envoy which never come, and eating your heart up in spite and bitterness—you look the matter plump in the face like a man, and not like a *polisson,* and turn to account those talents which it has pleased *le bon Dieu* to give you? *Voyez vous, Capitaine Téodore,*—you speak foreign languages like a native; and it was no longer than yesterday that Monsieur Randanne, your advocate, as he came down from the last interview with you, stopped at my bureau, and—'Ah! Madame Sorret,' said he, 'what a linguist poor Canot is,—how delightfully he speaks English, and how glad I should be if he had any place in which he could teach my sons the noble tongue of the great SKATSPEER!'

"Now, *mon capitaine,*" continued she, "what the good Randanne said, has been growing in my mind ever since, like the salad seed in the box that is sunned in our prison yard. In fact, I have fixed the matter perfectly. You shall have my bedroom for a schoolhouse; and, if you will, you may begin to-morrow with my two sons for pupils, at fifteen *francs* a month!"

Did I not bless the wit and heart of woman again and again

in my joy of industrial deliverance ! The heart of woman—that noble heart ! burn it in the fire of Africa ; steep it in the snow of Sweden ; lap it in the listless elysium of Indian tropics ; cage it in the centre of dungeons, as the palpitating core of that stony rind,—yet every where and always, throughout my wild career, has it been the last sought—but surest, sweetest, and truest of devoted friends !

*Aide toi, et Dieu t'aidera !*—was my motto from that moment. For years it was the first lesson of intellectual power and self-reliance that had checkered a life of outlawry, in which adventurous impatience preferred the gambling risks of fortune to the slow accretions of regular toil. I was a schoolmaster !

Madame Sorret's plan was perfectly successful. In less than a week I was installed in her chamber, with a class formed of my lady's lads, a son and friend of my lawyer, and a couple of sons of officers in the chateau ; the whole producing a monthly income of fifty francs. As I assumed my vocation with the spirit of a needy professor, I gained the good will of all the parents by assiduous instruction of their children. Gradually I extended the sphere of my usefulness, by adding penmanship to my other branches of tuition ; and so well did I please the parents, that they volunteered a stipend of eighteen *francs* more.

I would not dare affirm, that my pupils made extraordinary progress ; yet I am sure the children not only acquired cleverly, but loved me as a companion. My scheme of instruction was not modelled upon that of other pedagogues ; for I simply contented myself, in the small class, with reasoning out each lesson thoroughly, and never allowing the boys to depart till they comprehended every part of their task. After this, it was my habit to engage their interest *in language*, by familiar dialogues, which taught them the names of furniture, apparel, instruments, implements, animals, occupations, trades ; and thus I led them insensibly from the most simple nomenclature to the most abstract. I deprived the interview, as much as I could, of task-like formality ; and invariably closed the school with a story from my travels or adventures. I may not have ripened my scholars into classical Anglo-Saxons, but I have the happiness to know that I earned an honest living, supported my companions, and obtained the regard of my pupils to such a degree, that the little band accompanied me with tears to the ship, when, long afterwards, I was sent a happy exile from France.

# CHAPTER XLVII.

I HAVE said that our genteel felon was not only refined in manners but shy towards his new companions; nor, for several weeks, could all our efforts rub off his reserve. I was not surprised that he kept aloof from the coarser inmates, but I was not prepared to find that all my own advances to confidence and companionship, were repulsed with even more decision than those of my officers. At last, some passing event disclosed my *true* character to him, when I learned for the first time that he had mistaken me for *a government spy;* inasmuch as he could not otherwise account for my intimacy with Madame Sorret and her spouse.

Our first move towards confidence was owing to the following circumstance. I had been engaged one forenoon in writing a letter to my mother, when Madame Sorret sent for me to see the Sisters of Charity, who were making their rounds with a few comforts for the convicts. I made my toilette and repaired to the parlor, where the charitable women, who heard many kind things of me from the landlady, bestowed a liberal donation of books. Returning quickly to my letter, which I had left open on the table, confident that no one in the room read Italian, I again took up my pen to finish a paragraph. But, as I observed the page, it seemed that I had not written so much, yet the sheet was nearly full of words, and all in my handwriting. I reperused the document and found several lines, which, though in perfect keeping with the sense and context of the composition, were certainly not in my natural style. I was sure I had not used the complimentary language, to which I am always so averse. Still I read the page again—again—and again! I got up; walked about the room; took the paper to the window; put it down; walked about again, and then reperused the letter. For my life, I could not detect the precise difficulty that puzzled me. The paper was, perhaps, bewitched! It was mine, and yet it was not! In my dilemma, I rolled out a round Spanish *carramba* or two; and, with an *Ave Maria* of utter bewilderment, began to put up my writing materials.

My companions, who had been huddled in a corner, watching my actions, could stand it no longer, but bursting into peals of hearty laughter, announced that Monsieur Germaine had taken the liberty to add a postscript, while I was deep in literature with the Sisters of Charity!

The ice was broken! Monsieur Germaine was not yet convicted, so we gave him the benefit of the British law, and resolving to "consider the fellow innocent till proved to be guilty," we raised him to the dignity of companionship. His education was far superior to mine, and his conversational powers were wonderful. He seemed perfectly familiar with Latin and Greek, and had a commanding knowledge of history, theology, mathematics, and astronomy. I never met his equal in penmanship, drawing, and designing.

A few days of sociability sufficed to win a mutual confidence, and to demand the mutual stories of our lives.

Germaine was born so high up on those picturesque borders of Piedmont, that it was difficult to say whether the Swiss or Italian predominated in his blood. The troubles and wars of the region impoverished his parents, who had been gentlefolks in better times; yet they managed to bestow the culture that made him the accomplished person I have described. No opportunity offered, however, for his advancement as he reached maturity, and it was thought best that he should go abroad in search of fortune. For a while the quiet and modest youth was successful in the humbler employments to which he stooped for bread; but his address and talents, and especially his skill in designing and penmanship, attracted the notice of a sharper, with whom he accidentally became intimate; so that, before he knew it, the adroit scrivener was both *used* and *compromised* by the knave. In truth, I do not suppose that Germaine's will was made of stern and tough materials. Those soft and gentle beings are generally disposed to grasp the pleasures of life without labor; and whenever a relaxed conscience has once allowed its possessor to tamper with crime, its success is not only a stimulant but a motive for farther enterprise. Germaine was soon a successful forger. He amassed twenty or thirty thousand *francs* by practices so perfect in their execution, that he never dreamed of detection. But, at last, a daring speculation made him our companion in the tower.

Three days before his introduction to the *chateau* of Brest, and a few hours before the regular departure of the Paris mail, Germaine called on an exchange broker with seventeen thousand *francs* in gold, with which he purchased a sight draft on the capital. Soon after he called a second time on the broker, and exhibiting a letter of orders, bearing a regular post-mark, from his principals, who were alleged to be oil merchants at Marseilles, desired to countermand the transaction, and receive back his gold for the bill of exchange which he tendered. The principal partner of the brokers did not happen to be within at the moment, and the junior declined complying till his return. *En attendant,* Monsieur Germaine sallied forth, and offered a neighboring broker an additional half per cent. on the current value of gold for the cash. He expressed, as the cause of this sacrifice, extreme anxiety to depart by the four o'clock *diligence,* but the urgency aroused the broker's suspicion, and led him to request Germaine's return in half an hour, which he required to collect the specie.

The incautious forger went off to his hotel with the promise in his ear, while the wary broker dropped in on the drawers of the draft to compare notes. The result of the interview was a visit to the *bureau de police,* whence a couple of officers were despatched to Germaine's hotel. They entered the dandy's room in disguise, but they were not quick enough to save from destruction several *proof impressions* of blank drafts, which the counterfeiter cast into the fire the moment he heard a knock at his door. In his trunks, they found engraving tools, a small press, various acids and a variety of inks ; all of which were duly noted and preserved, while Monsieur Germaine was committed to the *chateau.*

In those days there were no electric wires, and as the weather became thick and cloudy, the old-fashioned semaphore or telegraph was useless in giving notice to the Parisian police to stop the payment of a suspected draft, and arrest the forger's accomplice in the capital.

Soon after the mail *of that day* from Brest reached the metropolis, a lady of most respectable appearance, clad in mourning, presented herself at the counter of the broker's Parisian correspondent, and exhibiting an unquestionable draft, drew seventeen thousand francs. From the rapidity with which the whole of this adroit scheme was accomplished in Brest and Paris, it seems that Germaine required but four hours to copy, engrave, print and fill up the forged bill ; and yet, so perfectly did he succeed, that when the discharged draft came back to Brest, neither drawers, brokers, nor police could distinguish between the true one and the false ! No one had seen Germaine at work, or could prove complicity with the lady. The mourning dame was nowhere to be found in Paris, Brest or Marseilles ; so that when I finally quitted the *chateau,* the adroit *chevalier* was still an inmate, but detained only *on suspicion !*

# CHAPTER XLVIII.

THIS charming young soldier of fortune was our room-mate for nine months, and engaged in several of our enterprises for escape. But Germaine was more a man of *finesse* than action, and his imprisonment was the first mishap of that nature in his felonious career; so that I cannot say I derived much advantage, either from his contrivances or suggestions.

---

I always cultivated a sneaking fondness for the sex, and was, perhaps, especially devoted to those who *might* aid me if they pleased, when I got into difficulties. Into this category, under existing circumstances, fell that very worthy person, Mademoiselle Babette, whom I have heretofore rather ungallantly reported as an "antique virgin." It is true that Babette was, perhaps, not as young as she had been; but an unmarried Frenchwoman is unquestionably possessed of an elixir against age,—some *eau restoratif*,—with which she defies time, preserves her outlines, and keeps up that elastic gayety of heart, which renders her always the most delightful of companions. Now, I do not pretend, when I flirted with Babette, and sometimes made downright love to the damsel, that I ever intended leading her to any of the altars of Brest, when it should please the "king of the barricades" to release me from prison. No such design ever possessed my mind, at the age of twenty-seven, towards a maid of thirty. Yet, I confess that Babette bewitched the sting and memory from many an hour of prison-life, and played the comedy of love *à la Francaise* to such perfection, that I doubt not her heart rebounded from the encounter as scarless as my own.

Germaine joked me very often about the tender passion, the danger of trifling with youthful hearts, and the risk I ran from encounters with such glittering eyes; till, one day, he suggested that we should take advantage of the flirtation, by turning it to our benefit in flight. Sorret and his wife often went out in the afternoon, and left the gate and the keys solely in charge of Babette, who improved their absence by spending half the time in our apartment. Now, Germaine proposed that, during one of these absences, I should, in my capacity as teacher, feign some excuse to leave our room, and, if I found the lieutenant porteress unwilling to yield the keys to my passionate entreaty, we would unhesitatingly seize, gag, and muffle the damsel so securely, that, with the keys in our possession, we might open the gates, and pass without question the only sentinels who guarded the exterior corridor. Germaine was eloquent upon the merit of his scheme, while, to my mind, it indicated the bungling project of a beginner, and was promptly rejected, because I would not injure with violence the innocent girl I had trifled with, and because I would not dishonor the kindness of Sorret and his wife, by compromising their *personal* vigilance.

Next morning, Germaine turned over to me long before daylight, and whispered his delight that I had discarded his scheme, for it "never could have been perfected without passports to quit the town!" This deficiency, he said, had absorbed his mind the livelong night, and, at last, a bright thought suggested the supply.

"Babette," continued the forger, "is *not* to be molested in any way, so you may make your mind easy about your sweet heart, though I am afraid she will not be able to accompany us in our enterprise. First and foremost, we must have a visit

from our Spanish girls to-morrow, and, as you enjoy more influence than I, it will be best for you to prepare them. Dolores,
who is by far the cleverest of the party, is to go with Concha
boldly to the prefecture of police, and demand passports for
Paris. These, in all likelihood, will be furnished without question. The passports once in hand, our *demoiselles* must be off
to an apothecary's for such acids as I shall prescribe; and then,
*mon capitaine*, leave the rest to me!"

I turned the matter over in my mind, pretending to finish a
morning nap, and, while we were dressing, assented. The Spanish women, who never refused their countrymen a favor, daringly
obtained the passports, and smuggled them into prison with the
required acids. Before night the deed was done; the gender
of the documents was changed; Germaine was metamorphosed
into "*Pietro Nazzolini*," a tailor, and I was turned into a certain "*Dominico Antonetti*," by trade a carpenter!

How to escape was our next concern. This could not be
effected without breaking prison,—a task of some enterprise, as
our apartment was above a store-room, always closed, barred, and
locked. The door of our room opened on a long passage, broken
at intervals by several iron gates before the main portal was
reached; so that our only hope was the single window, that illuminated our apartment and looked into a small yard, guarded
after sunset by a sentinel. This court, moreover, was entirely
hemmed in by a wall, which, if successfully escaladed, would
lead us to the parade ground of the *chateau.*

Days passed, while my dull brain and the kindled fancy of
the new Nazzolini were inventing plans. Pietro had schemes
enough, for his imagination was both vivid and ceaseless; but
whenever he came to reduce them to words, it was always found
that they required a little more "*polishing* in certain links,"
which he forthwith retired to perform.

One of our greatest difficulties was, how to deal with my
officers, who had proved so false on the Senegal. We debated
the matter for a long time; but, considering that they were sick
of long confinement and bereft of future comfort without my
labor we resolved to let them partake our flight, though, once

outside the chateau, we would abandon them to their own resources.

Accordingly, we imparted our scheme, which was eagerly embraced; and, through the kindness of our Spanish girls, we secretly despatched all our spare garments, so that we might not issue bare into the censorious world.

All being prepared, it was proposed by *Signore Pietro* that New Year, which was at hand, should be signalized by our enterprise. As I had carefully kept and secreted the saw received from my Goree friends, we possessed a most valuable implement; so that it was resolved to attack a bar the moment we had been mustered and locked up on that auspicious night. At eleven, a descent into the court beneath the window was to be commenced, and, if this proved successful, there was no doubt we could reach the beach across the parade. But the sentinel still required "polishing" out of the court-yard! This was a tremendous obstacle; still, Germaine once more put on his fancy-wings, and recommended that our fair Catalans, whose occupation made them familiar with the whole regiment, should ascertain the sentinels for the night in question, and, as it was a festival, they might easily insinuate a few bottles of brandy into the guard-house, and prepare the soldiery for sleep instead of vigilance. But the success and merit of this plan were considered so doubtful, that another scheme was kept in reserve to silence the soldier whose duty required a continual march beneath our window. If the women failed to accomplish our wishes with liquor, and if the sentry persisted in a vigilant promenade, it was proposed, as soon as the bar parted, to drop the noose of a *lazo* quietly over his head, and dragging him with a run to the window-sill, knock out his brains, if necessary, with the iron.

The last days of December were at hand; every body was busy with hope or preparation; the women carried off our garments; then they brought us an abundance of fishing lines, hidden beneath their petticoats; and, finally, a rope, strong enough to hang a man, was spun in darkness by the whole detachment.

The wished-for day at length came, with the jollity, merri-

ment, and drunkenness, that attend it almost universally throughout *la belle France*.   But there was not so sober a party in the
kingdom as that which was anxiously gathered together over a
wineless meal in the chateau of Brest.   We trembled lest a
word, a traitor, or an accident, should frustrate our hope of life
and freedom.

In the afternoon, our Spanish women, gay with fresh apparel,
dashing ribbons, and abundant claret, visited their fluttering
birds in the cage, and *assured* success.   The sergeant of the
guard was married to one of their intimate friends, and, *in her*
company, they were confident, on such a night, of reaching the
guard-room.   A long embrace, perhaps a kiss, and a most affectionate farewell!

Supper was over.   Muster passed.   Oh! how slowly was
drawn the curtain of darkness over that shortest of days.   Would
night *never* come?   It did.   By eight o'clock the severed bar
hung by threads, while the well-greased *lazo* lay coiled on the
sill.   Nine o'clock brought the sentinel, who began his customary
tramp with great regularity, but broke forth in a drinking song
as soon as the sergeant was out of hearing.

So impatient were my comrades for escape, that they declined
waiting till the appointed hour of eleven, and, at ten, ranged
themselves along the floor, with the end of the rope firmly
grasped, ready for a strong and sudden pull, while the intrepid
Germaine stood by, bar in hand, ready to strike, if necessary.
At a signal from me, after I had dropped the *lazo*, they were to
haul up, make fast, and follow us through the aperture by a
longer rope, which was already fastened for our descent.

Softly the sash was opened, and, stretching my neck into the
darkness, I distinctly saw, by a bright star-light, the form of the
sentinel, pacing, with staggering strides, beneath the casement.
Presently, he came to a dead halt, at the termination of a *roulade*
in his song, and, in a wink, the *lazo* was over him.   A kick with
my heel served for signal to the halliards, and up flew the pendant against the window-sill.   But, alas! it was not the sentinel.
The noose had not slipped or caught with sufficient rapidity, and
escaping the soldier's neck, it only grasped and secured his *chako*

and musket. In an instant, I saw the fatal misfortune, and, clearing the weapon, dropped it, *plumb*, on the head of the tipsy and terrified guardsman. Its fall must have stunned and prostrated the poor fellow, for not a word or groan escaped from the court-yard.

# CHAPTER XLIX.

Silent as was the sentinel after the restoration of his musket, it was, nevertheless, unanimously voted that our enterprise was a failure. Accordingly, the bar was replaced, the window closed, our implements stowed in the mattresses, and ourselves packed beneath the blankets, in momentary expectation of a visit from the jailer and military commander. We passed the night in feverish expectation, but our bolts remained undrawn.

Bright and early, with a plenteous breakfast, appeared our spirited Spaniards, and, as the turnkey admitted and locked them in, they burst into a fit of uproarious laughter at our maladroit adventure. The poor sentinel, they said, was found, at the end of his watch, stretched on the ground in a sort of fainting fit and half frozen. He swore, in accounting for a bleeding skull, that an invisible hand from the store-room beneath us, had dealt him a blow that felled him to the earth! His story was so silly and maudlin, that the captain of the guard, who remembered the festival and knew the tipsiness of the entire watch, gave no heed to the tale, but charged it to the account of New Year and *eau de vie*. We were sadly jeered by the lasses for our want of pluck, in forsaking the advantage fortune had thrown in our way, and I was specially charged to practise my hand more carefully with the *lazo*, when I next got a chance on the plantations of Cuba, or among the *vaqueros* of Mexico.

As we expected the daily visit from the punctual inspector, to try our bars with his iron rod, we hastened to secure our window, and stuffing all the fissures with straw and rags, so as almost to exclude light, we complained bitterly to the official of the cold wind to which the apertures exposed us, and thus prevented him from touching the sash. Besides this precaution, we thought it best to get rid of our tools and cord in the same way we received them ; and thus terminated our project of escape.

Soon after, I heard from a relative in Paris, that my petition had been presented to Louis Philippe, whose reception of it encouraged a hope for my pardon. The news somewhat restored us to the good humor that used to prevail in our party, but which had been sadly dashed since our failure. Even Monsieur Germaine, saw in our anticipated liberation, a phantom of encouragement for himself, and began to talk confidentially of his plans. He fancied that I had been gradually schooled *into a taste for misdemeanor*, so that he favored me with innumerable anecdotes of swindling, and countless schemes of future robbery. By making me an incipient accomplice, he thought to secure my aid either for his escape or release.

I will take the liberty to record a single specimen of Germaine's prolific fancy in regard to the higher grades of elegant felony, and will leave him to the tender mercy of the French government, which allows no *bail* for such *chevaliers* but chastises their crime with an iron hand.

We had scarcely recovered from our trepidation, when the forger got up one morning, with a radiant face, and whispered that the past night was fruitful to his brain, for he had planned an enterprise which would yield a fortune for *any two* who were wise and bold enough to undertake it.

Germaine was a philosophic felon. It was perhaps the trick of an intellect naturally astute, and of a spirit originally refined, to reject the vulgar baseness of common pilfering. Germaine never stole or defrauded ;—he only outwitted and outgeneralled. If he spoke of the world, either in politics or trade, he insisted that shams, forgeries, and counterfeits were quite as much played off in the language, address and dealings of statesmen, merchants, parsons, doctors, and lawyers, as they were by himself and his accomplices. The only difference between the felon and the jury, he alleged, existed in the fact that the jury was in the majority and the felon in the vocative. He advocated the worst forms of liberty and equality; he was decidedly in favor of a division of property, which he was sure would end what *the law called* crime, because all would be supplied on the basis of a common balance. Whenever he told his ancient exploits or suggested new ones, he glossed them invariably with a rhetorical varnish about the laws of nature, social contracts, human rights, *meum and tuum*; and concluded, to his perfect satisfaction, with a favorite axiom, that " he had quite as much *right* to the world's goods as they who possessed them."

A hypocritical farrago of this character always prefaced one of Germaine's tales, so that I hardly ever interrupted the rogue when he became fluent about social theories, but waited patiently, in confidence that I was shortly to be entertained with an adventure or enterprise.

The forger began his story on this occasion with a most fantastical and exaggerated account of the celebrated *Santissima Casa* of Loretto, which he imagined was still endowed with all the treasures it possessed anterior to its losses during the pontificate of Pius VI. He asserted that it was the richest tabernacle in Europe, and that the adornments of the altar were valued at several millions of crowns,—the votive offerings and legacies of devotees during a long period of time.

This holy and opulent shrine, the professor of politico-economico-equality proposed to rob at some convenient period; and, to effect it, he had "polished" the following plan during the watches of the night.

On some stormy day of winter, he proposed to leave Ancona, as a traveller from South America, and approaching the convent attached to the church of the Madonna of Loretto, demand hospitality for a penitent who had made the tiresome pilgrimage on a vow to the Virgin. There could be no doubt of his admission.

For three days he would most devoutly attend *matins* and vespers, and crave permission to serve as an *acolyte* at the altar, the duties of which he perfectly understood. When the period of his departure arrived, he would be seized with sudden illness, and, in all likelihood, the brethren would lodge him in their infirmary. As his malady increased, he would call a confessor, and, pouring into the father's credulous ear a tale of woes, sorrows, superstition and humbug, he would make the convent a donation of *all his estates in South America*, and pray for a remission of his sins !

When this comedy was over, convalescence should supervene; but he would adhere with conscientious obstinacy to his dying gift, and produce documents showing the immense value of the bequeathed property. Presently, he would be suddenly smitten with a love for monastic life ; and, on his knees, the Prior was to be interceded for admission to the brotherhood. All this, probably, would require time, as well as playacting of the adroitest character ; yet he felt confident he could perform the drama.

At last, when a vow had sealed his novitiate, no one of the fraternity should exceed him in fervent piety and bodily mortification. Every hour would find him at the altar before the Virgin, missal in hand, *and eyes intent on the glittering image.* This incessant and unwatched devotion, he calculated, would enable him in two months to take an impression of all the locks in the *sacristy ;* and, as his confederate would call every market-day at the convent gate, in the guise of a pedler, he could easily cause the keys to be fabricated in different villages by common locksmiths.

Germaine considered it indispensable that his colleague in this enterprise should be *a sailor ;* for the flight with booty was to be made over sea from Ancona. As soon, therefore, as the keys were perfected, and in the hands of the impostor, the mariner was to cause a *felucca* to cruise off shore, in readiness for immediate departure. Then, at a fixed time, the pedler should lurk near the convent, with a couple of mules ; and, in the dead of night, the sacrilege would be accomplished.

When he finished his story, the pleasant villain rubbed his hands with glee, and skipping about the floor like a dancing-master, began to whistle "*La Marseillaise.*" That night, he retired earlier than usual, "to polish," as he said; but before dawn he again aroused me, with a pull, and whispered a sudden fear that his "Loretto masterpiece" would prove an abortion!

"I have considered," said he, "that the Virgin's jewels are probably nothing but false stones and waxen pearls in pinchbeck gold! Surely, those cunning monks would never leave such an amount of property idle, simply to adorn a picture or statue! No, I am positive they must have sold the gems, substituted imitations, and bought property for their opulent convents!"— As I felt convinced of this fact, and had some inkling of a recollection about losses during a former reign, I was happy to hear that the swindler's fancy had "polished" the crime to absolute annihilation.

And now that I am about to leave this forging philosopher in prison, to mature, doubtless, some greater act of villany, I will merely add, that when I departed, he was constructing a new scheme, in which the Emperor of Russia was to be victim and paymaster. As my liberation occurred before the finishing touches were given by the artist, I am unable to say how it fared with Nicholas; but I doubt, exceedingly, whether the galleys of Brest contained a greater scoundrel, both in deeds and imaginings, than the metaphysical dandy—Monsieur Germaine.[1]

At length, my pardon and freedom came; but this was the sole reparation I received at the hands of Louis Philippe, for the unjust seizure and appropriation of my vessel in the neutral waters of Africa. When Sorret rushed in, followed by his wife, Babette, and the children, to announce the glorious news, the

---

[1] I know not what was his fate; but he has probably long since realized his dream of equality, though, in all likelihood, it was the equality described by old Patris of Caen:

> Ici tous sont egaux; je ne te dois plus rien:
> Je suis sur mon *fumier* comme toi sur le tien!"

good fellow's emotion was so great, that he stood staring at me like a booby, and for a long while could not articulate. Then came La Vivandière Dolores, and my pretty Concha. Next arrived Monsieur Randanne, with the rest of my pupils ; so that, in an hour, I was overwhelmed with sunshine and tears. I can still feel the grasp of Sorret's hand, as he led me beyond the bolts and bars, to read the act of royal grace. May we not feel a *spasm* of regret at leaving even a prison ?

Next day, an affectionate crowd of friends and pupils followed the emancipated slaver to a vessel, which, by order of the king, was to bear me, a willing exile, from France for ever.

## CHAPTER L.

I said, at the end of the last chapter, that my friends bade adieu on the quay of Brest to an "emancipated *slaver;*" for *slaver* I was determined to continue, notwithstanding the capture of my vessel, and the tedious incarceration of my body. Had the seizure and sentence been justly inflicted for a violation of local or international law, I might, perhaps, have become penitent for early sins, during the long hours of reflection afforded me in the *chateau.* But, with all the fervor of an ardent and thwarted nature, I was much more disposed to rebel and revenge myself when opportunity occurred, than to confess my sins with a lowly and obedient heart. Indeed, most of my time in prison had been spent in cursing the court and king, or in reflecting how I should get back to Africa in the speediest manner, if I was ever lucky enough to elude the grasp of the model monarch.

The vessel that bore me into perpetual banishment from France, was bound to Lisbon; but, delaying in Portugal only long enough to procure a new passport, under an assumed name, I spat upon Louis Philippe's "eternal exile," and took shipping for his loyal port of Marseilles! Here I found two vessels fitting for the coast of Africa; but, in consequence of the frightful prevalence of cholera, all mercantile adventures were temporarily suspended. In fact, such was the panic, that no one dreamed of despatching the vessel in which I was promised a passage, until the pestilence subsided. Till this occurred, as my means were of the scantiest character, I took lodgings in an humble hotel.

The dreadful malady was then apparently at its height, and nearly all the hotels were deserted, for most of the regular inhabitants had fled; while the city was unfrequented by strangers except under pressing duty. It is altogether probable that the lodging-houses and hotels would have been closed entirely, so slight was their patronage, had not the prefect issued an order, depriving of their licenses, for the space of two years, all who shut their doors on strangers. Accordingly, even when the scourge swept many hundred victims daily to their graves, every hotel, caffé, grocery, butcher shop, and bakery, was regularly opened in Marseilles; so that a dread of famine was not added to the fear of cholera.

Of course, the lowly establishment where I dwelt was not thronged at this epoch; most of its inmates or frequenters had departed for the country before my arrival, and I found the house tenanted alone by three boarders and a surly landlord, who cursed the authorities for their compulsory edict. My reception, therefore, was by no means cordial. I was told that the proclamation had not prevented the *cook* from departing; and that I must be content with whatever the master of the house could toss up for my fare.

A sailor—especially one fresh from the *chateau* of Brest,—is not apt to be over nice in the article of cookery, and I readily accompanied my knight of the rueful countenance to his *table d'hôte*, which I found to be a long oval board, three fourths bare of cloth and guests, while five human visages clustered around its end.

I took my seat opposite a trim dashing brunette, with the brightest eyes and rosiest cheeks imaginable. Her face was so healthily refreshing in the midst of malady and death, that I altogether forgot the cholera under the charm of her ardent gaze. Next me sat a comical sort of fellow, who did not delay in scraping an acquaintance, and jocularly insisted on introducing all the company.

" It's a case of emergency," said the droll, " we have no time to lose or to stand on the ceremony of fashionable etiquette. Here to-day, gone to-morrow—is the motto of Marseilles! *Hola! Messieurs,* shall we not make the most of new acquaintances when they may be so brief?"

I thanked him for his hospitality. I had so little to lose in this world, either of property or friends, that I feared the cholera quite as slightly as any of the company. "A thousand thanks," said I, "Monsieur, for your politeness; I'll bury you to-morrow, if it is the cholera's pleasure, with ten times more pleasure now that I have had the honor of an introduction. A fashionable man hardly cares to be civil to a stranger—even if he happens to be a corpse!"

There was so hearty a cheer at this sally, that, in spite of the shallow soundings of my purse, I called for a fresh bottle, and pledged the party in a bumper all round.

"And now," continued my neighbor, "as it may be necessary for some one of us to write your epitaph in a day or two, or, at least, to send a message of condolence and sympathy to your friends; pray let us know a bit of your history, and what the devil brings you to Marseilles when the cholera thermometer is up to 1000 degrees per diem?"

Very few words were necessary to impart such a name and tale as I chose to invent for the company's edification. "Santiago Ximenes," and my tawny skin betokened my nationality and profession, while my threadbare garments spoke louder than words that I was at suit with Fortune.

Presently, after a lull in the chat, a dapper little prig of a dandy, who sat on my left, volunteered to inform me that he was no less a personage than *le Docteur* Du Jean, a medical practitioner fresh from Metropolitan hospitals, who, in a spirit of the loftiest philanthropy, visited this provincial town at his own expense to succor the poor.

"*C'est une belle dame, notre vis à vis, n'est elle pas mon cher?*" said he pointing to our patron saint opposite.

I admitted without argument that she was the most charming woman I ever saw out of Cuba.

"*C'est ma chère amie,*" whispered he confidentially in my

ear, strongly emphasizing the word " friend " and nodding very knowingly towards the lady herself.  " At the present moment the dear little creature is exclusively under my charge and protection, for she is *en route* to join her husband, a captain in the army at Algiers ; but, alas !  *grâce à Dieu*, there's no chance of a transport so long as this cursed pestilence blockades Marseilles !  Do you know the man on your right ?—No !  *Bien !* that's the celebrated S——, the oratorical advocate about whom the papers rang when Louis Philippe began his assault on the press.  He's on his way to Algiers too, and will be more successful in liberalizing the Arabs than the French.  That old chap over yonder with the snuffy nose, the snuffy wig, and snuffy coat, is a grand speculator in horses, on his way to the richest cavalry corps of the army ; and, as for our *maître d'hotel* at the head of this segment, *pauvre diable*, you see what he is without a revelation.  The pestilence has nearly used him up.   He sits half the day in his bureau on the stairs looking for guests who never come, reading the record which adds no name, cursing the cholera, counting a penitential *ave* and *pater* on his rosary, and flying from the despair of silence and desertion to his pans to stew our wretched fare.  *Voila mon cher, la carte de la table !  le Cholera et ses Convives !*

If there is a creature I detest in the world it is a flippant, intrusive, voluntary youth who thrusts his coversation and affairs upon strangers, and makes bold to monopolize their time with his unasked confidence.  Such persons are always silly and vulgar pretenders ; and before Doctor Du Jean got through his description of the lady, I had already classified him among my particular aversions.

When the doctor nodded so patronizingly to the dame, and spoke of his friendly protectorate, I thought I saw that the quick-witted woman not only comprehended his intimation, but denied it by the sudden glance she gave me from beneath her thin and arching eyebrows.  So, when dinner was over, without saying a word to the doctor, I made a slight inclination of the head to Madame Duprez, and rising before the other guests, passed to her side and tendered my arm for a promenade on the balcony.

" *Mon docteur*," said I as we left the room, " life, you know, is too short and precarious to suffer a monoply of such blessings," —looking intently into the lady's eyes,—" besides which, we sailors, in defiance of you landsmen, go in for the most ' perfect freedom of the seas.' "

Madame Duprez declared I was entirely right ; that I was no pirate.—" Mais, mon capitaine," said the fair one, as she leaned with a fond pressure on my arm, " I'd have no objection if you were, so that you'd capture me from that frightful gallipot ! Besides, you sailors are always so gallant towards the ladies, and tell us such delightful stories, and bring us such charming presents when you come home, and love us so much while you're in port, because you see so few when you are away ! Now is'nt that a delightful *catalogue raisonné* of arguments why women should love *les mâtelots ?* "

" Pity then, madame," said I, " that you married a *soldier*."

" Ah ! " returned the ready dame, " *I* didn't ;—that was my mother's match. In France, you know, the old folks marry us ; but we take the liberty to *love* whomsoever we please ! "

" But, what of *Monsieur le capitaine*, in the present instance ? " interrupted I inquiringly.

" Ah ! *fi donc !* " said Madame, " what bad taste to speak of an *absent* husband when you have the liberty to talk with a *present* wife ! "

In fact, the lovely Helen of this tavern-Troy was the dearest of coquettes, whose fence of tongue was as beautiful a game of thrust and parry as I ever saw played with Parisian foils. Du Jean had been horribly mortified by the contemptuous manner in which the threadbare Spaniard bore off his imaginary prize ; and would probably have assailed me on the spot, before he knew my temper or quality, had not the lawyer drawn him aside on a plea of medical advice and given his inflamed honor time to cool.

But the wit of Madame Duprez was not so satisfied by a single specimen of our mutual folly, as to allow the surgeon to resume the undisputed post of *cavaliere serviente* which he occupied before my arrival. It was her delight to see us at logger-heads for her favor, and though we were both aware of her arrant coquetry, neither had moral courage enough, in that dismal time, to desist from offering the most servile courtesies. We mined and counter-mined, marched and counter-marched, deceived and re-deceived, for several days, without material advantage to either, till, at last, the affair ended in a battle.

The prefecture's bulletin announced at dinner-time twelve hundred deaths! but, in spite of the horror, or perhaps to drown its memory, our undiminished party called for several more bottles, and became uproariously gay.

The conversation took a physiological turn; and gradually the modern science of phrenology, which was just then becoming fashionable, came on the carpet. Doctor Du Jean professed familiarity with its mysteries. Spurzheim, he said, had been his professor in Paris. He could read our characters on our skulls as if they were written in a book. Powers, passions, propensities, and even thoughts, could not be hidden from him ;—and, " who dared try his skill ? "

" *C'est moi!* " said Madame Duprez, as she drew her chair to the centre of the room, and accepting the challenge, cast loose her beautiful hair, which fell in a raven torrent over snowy neck and shoulders, heightening tenfold every charm of face and figure.

Du Jean was nothing loth to commence his tender manipulation of the charming head, whose wicked mouth and teasing eyes shot glances of defiance at me. Several organs were disclosed and explained to the company ; but then came others which he ventured to whisper in her ears alone, and, as he did so, I noticed that his mouth was pressed rather deeper than I thought needful among the folds of her heavy locks. I took the liberty to hint rather jestingly that the doctor " *cut quite too deep* with his lips ; " but the coquette at once saw my annoyance, and persisted with malicious delight in making Du Jean whisper—heaven knows what—in her ear. In fact, she insisted that some of the organs should be repeated to her three or four times over, while, at each rehearsal, the doctor grew bolder in his dives among the curls, and the lady louder and redder in her merriment.

At last, propriety required that the scene should be closed, and no one knew better than this arch coquette the precise limit of decency's bounds. Next came the lawyer's cranium; then followed the horse-jockey and tavern-keeper; and finally, it was *my* turn to take the stool.

I made every objection I could think of against submitting to inspection, for I was sure the surgeon had wit enough not to lose so good a chance of quizzing or ridiculing me; but a whispered word from Madame forced an assent, with the stipulation that Du Jean should allow *me* to examine his skull afterwards, pretending that if he had studied with Spurzheim, I had learned the science from Gall.

The doctor accepted the terms and began his lecture. First of all my Jealousy was enormous, and only equalled by my Conceit and Envy. I was altogether destitute of Love, Friendship, or the Moral sentiments. I was an immoderate wine-bibber; extremely avaricious; passionate, revengeful, and blood-thirsty; in fine, I was a monstrous conglomerate of every thing devilish and dreadful. The first two or three essays of the doctor amused the company and brought down a round of laughter; but as he grew coarser and coarser, I saw the increasing disgust of our comrades by their silence, though I preserved my temper most admirably till he was done. Then I rose slowly from the seat, and pointing the doctor silently to the vacant chair,—for I could not speak with rage,—I took my stand immediately in front of him, gazing intently into his eyes. The company gathered eagerly round, expecting I would retaliate wittily, or pay him back in his coin of abuse.

After a minute's pause I regained my power of speech, and inquired whether the phrenologist was ready. He replied affirmatively; whereupon my right hand discovered the bump of impudence with a tremendous slap on his left cheek, while my left hand detected the organ of blackguardism with equal prominence on his right!

It was natural that this new mode of scientific investigation was as novel and surprising as it was disagreeable to poor Du Jean; for, in an instant, we were exchanging blows with intense zeal, and would probably have borrowed a couple of graves from

the cholera, had not the boarders interfered.   All hands, however, were unanimous in my favor, asserting that Du Jean had
provoked me beyond endurance ; and, as *la belle Duprez* joined
heartily in the verdict, the doctor gave up the contest, and, ever
after, " cut " the lady.

## CHAPTER LI.

In the first lull of the pestilence, the French merchantman was despatched from Marseilles, and, in twenty-seven days, I had the pleasure to shake hands with the generous friends, who, two years before, labored so hard for my escape. The colonial government soon got wind of my presence notwithstanding my disguise, and warning me from Goree, cut short the joys of an African welcome.

I reached Sierra Leone in time to witness the arbitrary proceeding of the British government towards Spanish traders and coasters, by virtue of the treaty for the suppression of the slave trade. *Six months* after this compact was signed and ratified in London and Madrid, it was made known with the proverbial despatch of Spain, in the Islands of Cuba and Porto Rico. Its stipulations were such as to allow very considerable latitude of judgment in captures; and when prizes were once within the grasp of the British lion, that amiable animal was neither prompt to release nor anxious to acquit. Accordingly, when I reached Sierra Leone, I beheld at anchor under government guns, some thirty or forty vessels seized by cruisers, several of which I have reason to believe were captured in the "Middle Passage," bound from Havana to Spain, but entirely free from the taint or design of slavery.

I was not so inquisitive or patriotic in regard to treaty rights and violations, as to dally from mere curiosity in Sierra Leone. My chief object was employment.  At twenty-eight, after trials, hazards, and chances enough to have won half a dozen fortunes, I was utterly penniless.  The Mongo of Kambia,—the Mahometan convert of Ahmah-de-Bellah,—the pet of the Ali-mami of Footha Yallon,—the leader of slave caravans,—the owner of barracoons, —and the bold master of clippers that defied the British flag, was reduced to the humble situation of coast-pilot and interpreter on board an American brig bound to the celebrated slave mart of Gallinas!  We reached our destination safely; but I doubt exceedingly whether the "Reaper's" captain knows to this day that his brig was guided by a marine adventurer, who knew nothing of the coast or port save the little he gleaned in half a dozen chats with a Spaniard, who was familiar with this notorious resort and its surroundings.

In the history of African servitude, no theatre of Spanish, Portuguese, British, or American action has been the scene of more touching, tragic, and *profitable* incidents than the one to which fortune had now directed my feet.

Before the generous heart and far-seeing mind of America perceived *in Colonization* the true secret of Africa's hope, the whole of its coast, from the Rio Gambia to Cape Palmas, without a break except at Sierra Leone, was the secure haunt of daring slavers.  The first impression on this lawless disposal of full fifteen hundred miles of beach and continent, was made by the bold establishment of Liberia; and, little by little has its power extended, until treaty, purchase, negotiation, and influence, drove the trade from the entire region.  After the firm establishment of this colony, the slave trade on the windward coast, north and west of Cape Palmas, was mainly confined to Portuguese settlements at Bissaos, on the Rios Grande, Nunez, and Pongo, at Grand and Little Bassa, New Sestros and Trade-town; but the lordly establishment at Gallinas was the heart of the slave marts, to which, in fact, Cape Mesurado was only second in importance.

Our concern is now with Gallinas.  Nearly one hundred

miles northwest of Monrovia, a short and sluggish river, bearing this well-known name, oozes lazily into the Atlantic; and, carrying down in the rainy season a rich alluvion from the interior, sinks the deposit where the tide meets the Atlantic, and forms an interminable mesh of spongy islands. To one who approaches from sea, they loom up from its surface, covered with reeds and mangroves, like an immense field of *fungi*, betokening the damp and dismal field which death and slavery have selected for their grand metropolis. A spot like this, possessed, of course, no peculiar advantages for agriculture or commerce; but its dangerous bar, and its extreme desolation, fitted it for the haunt of the outlaw and slaver.

Such, in all likelihood, were the reasons that induced Don Pedro Blanco, a well-educated mariner from Malaga, to select Gallinas as the field of his operations. Don Pedro visited this place originally in command of a slaver; but failing to complete his cargo, sent his vessel back with one hundred negroes, whose value was barely sufficient to pay the mates and crew. Blanco, however, remained on the coast with a portion of the Conquistador's cargo, and, on its basis, began a trade with the natives and slaver-captains, till, four years after, he remitted his owners the product of their merchandise, and began to flourish on his own account. The honest return of an investment long given over as lost, was perhaps the most active stimulant of his success, and for many years he monopolized the traffic of the Vey country, reaping enormous profits from his enterprise.

Gallinas was not in its prime when I came thither, yet enough of its ancient power and influence remained to show the comprehensive mind of Pedro Blanco. As I entered the river, and wound along through the labyrinth of islands, I was struck, first of all, with the vigilance that made this Spaniard stud the field with look-out seats, protected from sun and rain, erected some seventy-five or hundred feet above the ground, either on poles or on isolated trees, from which the horizon was constantly swept by telescopes, to announce the approach of cruisers or slavers. These telegraphic operators were the keenest men on the islands, who were never at fault, in discriminating between friend and foe.

About a mile from the river's mouth we found a group of islets, on each of which was erected the factory of some particular slave-merchant belonging to the grand confederacy. Blanco's establishments were on several of these marshy flats. On one, near the mouth, he had his place of business or trade with foreign vessels, presided over by his principal clerk, an astute and clever gentleman. On another island, more remote, was his residence, where the only white person was a sister, who, for a while, shared with Don Pedro his solitary and penitential domain. Here this man of education and refined address surrounded himself with every luxury that could be purchased in Europe or the Indies, and dwelt in a sort of oriental but semi-barbarous splendor, that suited an African prince rather than a Spanish grandee. Further inland was another islet, devoted to his seraglio, within whose recesses each of his favorites inhabited her separate establishment, after the fashion of the natives. Independent of all these were other islands, devoted to the barracoons or slave-prisons, ten or twelve of which contained from one hundred to five hundred slaves in each. These barracoons were made of rough staves or poles of the hardest trees, four or six inches in diameter, driven five feet in the ground, and clamped together by double rows of iron bars. Their roofs were constructed of similar wood, strongly secured, and overlaid with a thick thatch of long and wiry grass, rendering the interior both dry and cool. At the ends, watch-houses—built near the entrance—were tenanted by sentinels, with loaded muskets. Each barracoon was tended by two or four Spaniards or Portuguese; but I have rarely met a more wretched class of human beings, upon whom fever and dropsy seemed to have emptied their vials.

Such were the surroundings of Don Pedro in 1836, when I first saw his slender figure, swarthy face, and received the graceful welcome, which I hardly expected from one who had passed fifteen years without crossing the bar of Gallinas ! Three years after this interview, he left the coast for ever, with a fortune of near a million. For a while, he dwelt in Havana, engaged in commerce ; but I understood that family difficulties induced him to retire altogether from trade ; so that, if still alive, he is prob ably a resident of "Genova la Superba," whither he went from the island of Cuba.

The power of this man among the natives is well known; it far exceeded that of Cha-cha, of whom I have already spoken. Resolved as he was to be successful in traffic, he left no means untried, with blacks as well as whites, to secure prosperity. I have often been asked what was the character of a mind which could voluntarily isolate itself for near a lifetime amid the pestilential swamps of a burning climate, trafficking in human flesh, exciting wars, bribing and corrupting ignorant negroes; totally without society, amusement, excitement, or change; living, from year to year, the same dull round of seasons and faces; without companionship, save that of men at war with law; cut loose from all ties except those which avarice formed among European outcasts who were willing to become satellites to such a luminary as Don Pedro? I have always replied to the question, that this African enigma puzzled *me* as well as those orderly and systematic persons, who would naturally be more shocked at the tastes and prolonged career of a resident slave-factor in the marshes of Gallinas.

I heard many tales on the coast of Blanco's cruelty, but I doubt them quite as much as I do the stories of his pride and arrogance. I have heard it said that he shot a sailor for daring to ask him for permission to light his cigar at the *puro* of the Don. Upon another occasion, it is said that he was travelling the beach some distance from Gallinas, near the island of Sherbro, where he was unknown, when he approached a native hut for rest and refreshment. The owner was squatted at the door, and, on being requested by Don Pedro to hand him fire to light his cigar, deliberately refused. In an instant Blanco drew back, seized a carabine from one of his attendants, and slew the negro on the spot. It is true that the narrator apologized for Don Pedro, by saying, that to deny a Castilian *fire for his tobacco* was the gravest insult that can be offered him; yet, from my knowledge of the person in question, I cannot believe that he carried etiquette to so frightful a pitch, even among a class whose lives are considered of trifling value *except in market*. On several occasions, during our subsequent intimacy, I knew him to chastise with rods, even to the brink of death, servants who ventured to infringe the sacred limits of his *seraglio.* But, on the other hand, his generosity was proverbially ostentatious, not only among the natives, whom it was his interest to suborn, but to the whites who were in his employ, or needed his kindly succor. I have already alluded to his mental culture, which was decidedly *soigné* for a Spaniard of his original grade and time. His memory was remarkable. I remember one night, while several of his *employés* were striving unsuccessfully to repeat the Lord's prayer in Latin, upon which they had made a bet, that Don Pedro joined the party, and taking up the wager, went through the petition without faltering. It was, indeed, a sad parody on prayer to hear its blessed accents fall perfectly from such lips on a bet; but when it was won, the slaver insisted on receiving *the slave which was the stake,* and immediately bestowed him in charity on a captain, who had fallen into the clutches of a British cruiser !

Such is a rude sketch of the great man-merchant of Africa, the Rothschild of slavery, whose bills on England, France, or the United States, were as good as gold in Sierra Leone and Monrovia !

# CHAPTER LII.

THE day after our arrival within the realm of this great spider,—
who, throned in the centre of his mesh, was able to catch almost
every fly that flew athwart the web,—I landed at one of the
minor factories, and sold a thousand quarter kegs of powder to
Don José Ramon.  But, next day, when I proceeded in my capacity of interpreter to the establishment of Don Pedro, I found
his Castilian plumage ruffled, and, though we were received with
formal politeness, he declined to purchase, because we had failed
to address *him* in advance of any other factor on the river.

The folks at Sierra Leone dwelt so tenderly on the generous
side of Blanco's character, that I was still not without hope that
I might induce him to purchase a good deal of our rum and
tobacco, which would be drugs on our hands unless he consented
to relieve us.  I did not think it altogether wrong, therefore, to
concoct a little *ruse* whereby I hoped to touch the pocket through
the breast of the Don.   In fact, I addressed him a note, in which
I truly related my recent mishaps, adventures, and imprison-
ments ; but I concluded the narrative with a hope that he would
succor one so destitute and unhappy, by allowing him to win an
honest *commission* allowed by the American captain on any sales
I could effect.  The bait took ; a prompt, laconic answer re-

turned ; I was bidden to come ashore with the invoice of our
cargo ; and, *for my sake*, Don Pedro purchased from the Yankee
brig $5000 worth of rum and tobacco, all of which was paid by
drafts on London, *of which slaves were, of course, the original
basis !* My imaginary commissions, however, remained in the
purse of the owners.

An accident occurred in landing our merchandise, which will
serve to illustrate the character of Blanco. While the hogs-
heads of tobacco were discharging, our second mate, who suffered
from *strabismus* more painfully than almost any cross-eyed man
I ever saw, became excessively provoked with one of the native
boatmen who had been employed in the service. It is probable
that the negro was insolent, which the mate thought proper to
chastise by throwing staves at the Krooman's head. The negro
fled, seeking refuge on the other side of his canoe ; but the enraged officer continued the pursuit, and, in his double-sighted
blundering, ran against an oar which the persecuted black suddenly lifted in self-defence. I know not whether it was rage or
blindness, or both combined, that prevented the American from
seeing the blade, but on he dashed, rushing impetuously against
the implement, severing his lip with a frightful gash, and knocking four teeth from his upper jaw.

Of course, the luckless negro instantly fled to " the bush ; "
and, that night, in the agony of delirium, caused by fever and
dreaded deformity, the mate terminated his existence by laudanum.

The African law condemns the man who *draws blood* to a
severe fine in slaves, proportioned to the harm that may have
been inflicted. Accordingly, the culprit Krooman, innocent as
he was of premeditated evil, now lay heavily loaded with irons in
Don Pedro's barracoon, awaiting the sentence which the whites
in his service already declared *should be death*. " He struck a
white ! " they said, and the wound he inflicted was reported to
have caused that white man's ruin. But, luckily, before the sentence was executed, *I* came ashore, and, as the transaction occurred in my presence, I ventured to appeal from the verdict of
public opinion to Don Pedro, with the hope that I might excul

pate the Krooman. My simple and truthful story was sufficient. An order was instantly given for the black's release, and, in spite of native chiefs and grumbling whites, who were savagely greedy for the fellow's blood, Don Pedro persisted in his judgment and sent him back on board the "Reaper."

The character manifested by Blanco on this occasion, and the admirable management of his factory, induced me to seize a favorable moment to offer my services to the mighty trader. They were promptly accepted, and in a short time I was employed as *principal* in one of Don Pedro's branches.

The Vey natives on this river and its neighborhood were not numerous before the establishment of Spanish factories, but since 1813, the epoch of the arrival of several Cuban vessels with rich merchandise, the neighboring tribes flocked to the swampy flats, and as there was much similarity in the language and habits of the natives and emigrants, they soon intermarried and mingled in ownership of the soil.

In proportion as these upstarts were educated in slave-trade under the influence of opulent factors, they greedily acquired the habit of hunting their own kind and abandoned all other occupations but war and kidnapping. As the country was prolific and the trade profitable, the thousands and tens of thousands annually sent abroad from Gallinas, soon began to exhaust the neighborhood ; but the appetite for plunder was neither satiated nor stopped by distance, when it became necessary for the neighboring natives to extend their forays and hunts far into the interior. In a few years war raged wherever the influence of this river extended. The slave factories supplied the huntsmen with powder, weapons, and enticing merchandise, so that they fearlessly advanced against ignorant multitudes, who, too silly to comprehend the benefit of alliance, fought the aggressors singly, and, of course, became their prey

Still, however, the demand increased. Don Pedro and his satellites had struck a vein richer than the gold coast. His flush barracoons became proverbial throughout the Spanish and Portuguese colonies, and his look-outs were ceaseless in their signals of approaching vessels. New factories were established, as branches, north and south of the parent den.  Mana-Rock, Sherboro, Sugarei, Cape Mount, Little Cape Mount, and even Digbay, at the door of Monrovia, all had depots and barracoons of slaves belonging to the whites of Gallinas.

But this prosperity did not endure.  The torch of discord, in a civil war which was designed for revengeful murder rather than slavery, was kindled by a black Paris, who had deprived his uncle of an Ethiopian Helen.  Every bush and hamlet contained its Achilles and Ulysses, and every town rose to the dignity of a Troy.

The geographical configuration of the country, as I have described it, isolated almost every family of note on various branches of the river, so that nearly all were enabled to fortify themselves within their islands or marshy flats.  The principal parties in this family feud were the Amarars and Shiakars.  Amarar was a native of Shebar, and, through several generations, had Mandingo blood in his veins;—Shiakar, born on the river, considered himself a noble of the land, and being aggressor in this conflict, disputed his prize with the wildest ferocity of a savage. The whites, who are ever on the watch for native quarrels, wisely refrained from partisanship with either of the combatants, but continued to purchase the prisoners brought to their factories by both parties.  Many a vessel bore across the Atlantic two inveterate enemies shackled to the same bolt, while others met on the same deck a long-lost child or brother who had been captured in the civil war.

I might fill a volume with the narrative of this horrid conflict before it was terminated by the death of Amarar.  For several months this savage had been blockaded in his stockade by Shiakar's warriors.  At length a sortie became indispensable to obtain provisions, but the enemy were too numerous to justify the risk.  Upon this, Amarar called his soothsayer, and required him to name a propitious moment for the sally.  The oracle retired to his den, and, after suitable incantations, declared that the effort should be made as soon as the hands of Amarar were stained in the blood of his own son.  It is said that the prophet intended the victim to be a youthful son of Amarar, who had joined his mother's family, and was then distant; but the impatient and superstitious savage, seeing a child of his own, two years old, at hand, when the oracle announced the decree, snatched the infant from his mother's arms, threw it into a rice mortar, and, with a pestle, mashed it to death!

The sacrifice over, a sortie was ordered. The infuriate and starving savages, roused by the oracle and inflamed by the bloody scene, rushed forth tumultuously. Amarar, armed with the pestle, still warm and reeking with his infant's blood, was foremost in the onset. The besiegers gave way and fled; the town was re-provisioned; the fortifications of the enemy demolished, and the soothsayer rewarded with a slave for his barbarous prediction!

At another time, Amarar was on the point of attacking a strongly fortified town, when doubts were intimated of success. Again the wizard was consulted, when the mysterious oracle declared that the chief "*could not conquer till he returned once more to his mother's womb!*" That night Amarar committed the blackest of incests; but his party was repulsed, and the false prophet stoned to death!

These are faint incidents of a savage drama which lasted several years, until Amarar, in his native town, became the prisoner of Shiakar's soldiery. Mana, his captor, caused him to be decapitated; and while the blood still streamed from the severed neck, the monster's head was thrust into the fresh-torn bowels of his mother!

# CHAPTER LIII.

THE first expedition upon which Don Pedro Blanco despatched me revealed a new phase of Africa to my astonished eyes. I was sent in a small Portuguese schooner to Liberia for tobacco; and here the trader who had never contemplated the negro on the shores of his parent country except as a slave or a catcher of slaves, first beheld the rudiments of an infant state, which in time may become the wedge of Ethiopian civilization. The comfortable government house, neat public warerooms, large emigration home, designed for the accommodation of the houseless; clean and spacious streets, with brick stores and dwellings; the twin churches with their bells and comfortable surroundings; the genial welcome from well dressed negroes; the regular wharves and trim craft on the stocks, and last of all, a visit from a colored collector with a *printed* bill for twelve dollars "anchor dues," all convinced me that there was, in truth, something more in these ebony frames than an article of commerce and labor. I paid the bill eagerly,—considering that a document *printed in Africa by Negroes*, under North American influence, would be a curiosity among the infidels of Gallinas!

My engagements with Blanco had been made on the basis of familiarity with the slave-trade in all its branches, but my independent spirit and impatient temper forbade, from the first, the acceptance of any subordinate position at Gallinas. Accordingly, as soon as I returned from the new Republic, Don Pedro desired me to prepare for the establishment of a branch factory, under my exclusive control, at New Sestros, an independent principality in the hands of a Bassa chief.

I lost no time in setting forth on this career of comparative independence, and landed with the trading cargo provided for me, at the Kroomen's town, where I thought it best to dwell till a factory could be built.

An African, as well as a white man, must be drilled into the traffic. It is one of those things that do not " come by nature : " yet its mysteries are acquired, like the mysteries of commerce generally, with much more facility by some tribes than others. I found this signally illustrated by the prince and people of New Sestros, and very soon detected their great inferiority to the Soosoos, Mandingoes, and Veys. For a time their conduct was so silly, arrogant, and trifling, that I closed my chests and broke off communication. Besides this, the slaves they offered were of an inferior character and held at exorbitant prices. Still, as I was commanded to purchase rapidly, I managed to collect about seventy-five negroes of medium grades, all of whom I designed sending to Gallinas in the schooner that was tugging at her anchor off the beach.

At the proper time I sent for the black prince *to assist me in shipping the slaves*, and to receive the head money which was his export duty on my cargo. The answer to my message was an illustration of the character and insolence of the ragamuffins with whom I had to deal. " The prince," returned my messenger, " don't like your sauciness, Don Teodore, *and won't come till you beg his pardon by a present !* "

It is very true that after my visit to their republic, I began to entertain a greater degree of respect than was my wont, for black men, yet my contempt for the original, unmodified race was so great, that when the prince's son, a boy of sixteen, delivered this reply on behalf of his father, I did not hesitate to cram it down his throat by a back-handed blow, which sent the sprig of royalty bleeding and howling home.

It may be easily imagined what was the condition of the native town when the boy got back to the "palace," and told his tale of Spanish boxing. In less than ten minutes, another messenger arrived with an order for my departure from the country "before next day at noon;"—an order which, the envoy declared, would be *enforced* by the outraged townsfolk unless I willingly complied.

Now, I had been too long in Africa to tremble before a negro prince, and though I really hated the region, I determined to disobey in order to teach the upstart a lesson of civilized manners. Accordingly, I made suitable preparations for resistance, and, when my hired servants and *barracooniers* fled in terror at the prince's command, I landed some whites from my schooner, to aid in protecting our slaves.

By this time, my house had been constructed of the frail bamboos and matting which are exclusively used in the buildings of the Bassa country. I had added a cane verandah or piazza to mine, and protected it from the pilfering natives, by a high palisade, that effectually excluded all intruders. Within the area of this inclosure was slung my hammock, and here I ate my meals, read, wrote, and received "Princes" as well as the mob.

At nightfall, I loaded twenty-five muskets, and placed them *inside my sofa*, which was a long trade-chest. I covered the deal-table with a blanket, beneath whose pendent folds I concealed a keg of powder *with the head out.* Hard by, under a broad-brimmed *sombrero*, lay a pair of double-barrelled pistols. With these dispositions of my volcanic armory, I swung myself asleep in the hammock, and leaving the three whites to take turns in watching, never stirred till an hour after sunrise, when I was roused by the war-drum and bells from the village, announcing the prince's approach.

In a few minutes my small inclosure of palisades was filled with armed and gibbering savages, while his majesty, in the red coat of a British drummer, but without any trowsers, strutted pompously into my presence. Of course, I assumed an air of humble civility, and leading the potentate to one end of the guarded piazza, where he was completely isolated from his people, I stationed myself between the table and the *sombrero*. Some of the prince's relations attempted to follow him within my inclosure, but, according to established rules, they dared not advance beyond an assigned limit.

When the formalities were over, a dead silence prevailed for some minutes. I looked calmly and firmly into the prince's eyes, and waited for him to speak. Still he was silent. At last, getting tired of dumb-show, I asked the negro if he had "come to assist me in shipping my slaves; the sun is getting rather high," said I, "and we had better begin without delay!"

"Did you get my message?" was his reply, "and why haven't you gone?"

"Of course I received your message," returned I, "but as I came to New Sestros at my leisure, I intend to go away when it suits me. Besides this, Prince Freeman, I have no fear that you will do me the least harm, especially as I shall be *before* you in any capers of that sort."

Then, by a sudden jerk, I threw off the blanket that hid the exposed powder, and, with pistols in hand, one aimed at the keg and the other at the king, I dared him to give an order for my expulsion.

It is inconceivable how *moving* this process proved, not only to Freeman, but to the crowd comprising his body-guard. The poor blusterer, entirely cut off from his companions, was in a laughable panic. His tawny skin became ashen, as he bounded from his seat and rushed to the extremity of the piazza; and, to make a long story short, in a few minutes he was as penitent and humble as a dog.

I was, of course, not unforgiving, when Freeman advanced to the rail, and warning the blacks that he had "changed his mind," ordered the odorous crowd out of my inclosure. Before the negroes departed, however, I made him swear eternal fidelity and friendship in their presence, after which I sealed the compact with a couple of demijohns of New-England rum.

Before sunset, seventy-five slaves were shipped for me in his canoes, and ever after, Prince Freeman was a model monument of the virtues of gunpowder physic!

## CHAPTER LIV.

THE summary treatment of this ebony potentate convinced the Kroo and Fishmen of New Sestros that they would find my break-fast parties no child's play. Bold *bravado* had the best effect on the adjacent inland as well as the immediate coast. The free blacks not only treated my person and people with more respect, but began to supply me with better grades of negroes; so that when Don Pedro found my success increasing, he not only resolved to establish a permanent factory, but enlarged my commission to ten slaves for every hundred I procured. Thereupon, I at once com-menced the erection of buildings suitable for my personal comfort and the security of slaves. I selected a pretty site closer to the beach. A commodious two-story house, surrounded by double verandahs, was topped by a look-out which commanded an ocean-view of vast extent, and flanked by houses for all the necessities of a first-rate factory. There were stores, a private kitchen, a rice house, houses for domestic servants, a public workshop, a depot for water, a slave-kitchen, huts for single men, and sheds under which gangs were allowed to recreate from time to time during daylight. The whole was surrounded by a tall hedge-fence, thick-ly planted, and entered by a double gate, on either side of which were long and separate *barracoons* for males and females. The entrance of each slave-pen was commanded by a cannon, while in the centre of the square, I left a vacant space, whereon I have

often seen seven hundred slaves, guarded by half a dozen musketeers, singing, drumming and dancing, after their frugal meals.

It is a pleasant fancy of the natives, who find our surnames
rather difficult of pronunciation, while they know very little of
the Christian calendar, to baptize a new comer with some title,
for which, any chattel or merchandise that strikes their fancy, is
apt to stand godfather. My exploit with the prince christened
me "Powder" on the spot; but when they saw my magnificent
establishment, beheld the wealth of my warehouse, and heard the
name of "store," I was forthwith whitewashed into "*Storee.*"

And "*Storee,*" without occupying a legislative seat in Africa,
was destined to effect a rapid change in the motives and prospects of that quarter. In a few months, New Sestros was alive.
The isolated beach, which before my arrival was dotted with half
a dozen Kroo hovels, now counted a couple of flourishing towns,
whose inhabitants were supplied with merchandise and labor in
my factory. The neighboring princes and chiefs, confident of
selling their captives, struggled to the sea-shore through the track-
less forest; and in a very brief period, Prince Freeman, who "no
likee war" over my powder-keg, sent expedition after expedition
against adjacent tribes, to redress imaginary grievances, or to settle
old bills with his great-grandfather's debtors. There was no absolute idea of "extending the area of freedom, or of territorial
annexation," but it was wonderful to behold how keen became the
sovereign's sensibility to national wrongs, and how patriotically
he labored to vindicate his country's rights. It is true, this African metamorphosis was not brought about without some sacrifice
of humanity; still I am confident that during my stay, greater
strides were made towards modern civilization than during the
visit of any other factor. When I landed among the handful of
savages I found them given up to the basest superstition. All
classes of males as well as females, were liable to be accused upon
any pretext by the *ju-ju-men* or priests, and the dangerous *saucy-
wood* potion was invariably administered to test their guilt or innocence. It frequently happened that accusations of witchcraft
or evil practices were purchased from these wretches in order to
get rid of a sick wife, an imbecile parent, or an opulent relative;

and, as the poisonous draught was mixed and graduated by the *ju-ju-man*, it rarely failed to prove fatal when the drinker's death was necessary.*  Ordeals of this character occurred almost daily in the neighboring country, of course destroying numbers of innocent victims of cupidity or malice.  I very soon observed the frequency of this abominable crime, and when it was next attempted in the little settlement that clustered around my factory, I respectfully requested that the accused might be locked up *for safety in my barracoon*, till the fatal liquid was prepared and the hour for its administration arrived.

It will be readily understood that the saucy-wood beverage, like any other, may be prepared in various degrees of strength, so that the operator has entire control of its noxious qualities.   If the accused has friends, either to pay or tamper with the medicator, the draft is commonly made weak enough to insure its harmless rejection from the culprit's stomach; but when the victim is friendless, time is allowed for the entire venom to exude, and the drinker dies ere he can drink the second bowl.

Very soon after the offer of my *barracoon* as a prison for the accused, a Krooman was brought to it, accused of causing his nephew's death by fatal incantations.  The *ju-ju* had been consulted and confirmed the suspicion; whereupon the luckless negro was seized, ironed, and delivered to my custody. /

Next day early the *ju-ju-man* ground his bark, mixed it with water, and simmered the potion over a slow fire to extract the poison's strength.  As I had reason to believe that especial enmity was entertained against the imprisoned uncle, I called at the *ju-ju's* hovel while the medication was proceeding, and, with the bribe of a bottle, requested him to impart triple power to the noxious draught.  My own *ju-ju*, I said, had nullified his by pronouncing the accused innocent, and I was exceedingly anxious to test the relative truth of our soothsayers.

The rascal promised implicit compliance, and I hastened back

---

* *Saucy-wood* is the reddish bark of the *gedu* tree, which when ground and mixed with water, makes a poisonous draught, believed to be infallible in the detection of crime.  It is, in fact, "a trial by ordeal;" if the drinker survives he is innocent, if he perishes, guilty.

to the *barracoon* to await the fatal hour. Up to the very moment of the draught's administration, I remained alone with the culprit, and administering a double dose of tartar-emetic just before the gate was opened, I led him forth loaded with irons. The daring negro, strong in his truth, and confident of the white man's superior witchcraft, swallowed the draught without a wink, and in less than a minute, the rejected venom established his innocence, and covered the African wizard with confusion.

This important trial and its results were of course noised abroad throughout so superstitious and credulous a community. The released Krooman told his companions of the " white-man-saucy wood," administered by me in the *barracoon;* and, ever afterwards, the accused were brought to my sanctuary where the conflicting charm of my emetic soon conquered the native poison and saved many a useful life. In a short time the malicious practice was discontinued altogether

---

During the favorable season, I had been deprived of three vessels by British cruisers, and, for as many months, had not shipped a single slave,—five hundred of whom were now crowded in my *barracoons*, and demanded our utmost vigilance for safe keeping. In the gang, I found a family consisting of a man, his wife, three children and a sister, all sold under an express obligation of exile and slavery among Christians. The luckless father was captured by my blackguard friend Prince Freeman in person, and the family had been secured when the parents' village was subsequently stormed. Barrah was an outlaw and an especial offender in the eyes of an African, though his faults were hardly greater than the deeds that bestowed honor and knighthood in the palmy days of our ancestral feudalism. Barrah was the discarded son of a chief in the interior, and had presumed to blockade the public path towards the beach, and collect duties from transient passengers or caravans. This interfered with Freeman and his revenues; but, in addition to the pecuniary damage, the alleged robber ventured on several occasions to defeat and plunder the prince's vagabonds, so that, in time, he became rich and strong enough to build a town and fortify it with a regular stockade, *directly on the highway!*   All these offences were so heinous in the sight of my beach prince, that no foot was suffered to cool till Barrah was captured.   Once within his power, Freeman would not have hesitated to kill his implacable enemy as soon as delivered at New Sestros; but the interference of friends, and, perhaps, the laudable conviction that a live negro was worth more than a dead one, induced his highness to sell him under pledge of Cuban banishment.

Barrah made several ineffectual attempts to break my *barracoon* and elude the watchfulness of my guards, so that they were frequently obliged to restrict his liberty, deprive him of comforts, or add to his shackles.   In fact, he was one of the most formidable savages I ever encountered, even among the thousands who passed in terrible procession before me in Africa. One day he set fire to the bamboo-matting with which a portion of the *barracoon* was sheltered from the sun, for which he was severely lashed ; but next day, when allowed, under pretence of ague, to crawl with his heavy irons to the kitchen fire, he suddenly dashed a brand into the thatch, and, seizing another, sprang towards the powder-house, which his heavy shackles did not allow him to reach before he was felled to the earth.

Freeman visited me soon afterwards, and, in spite of profit and liquor, insisted on taking the brutal savage back; but, in the mean time, the Bassa chief, to whom my prince was subordinate, heard of Barrah's attempt on my magazine, and demanded the felon to expiate his crime, according to the law of his country, at the stake.   No argument could appease the infuriate judges, who declared that a cruel death would alone satisfy the people whose lives had been endangered by the robber.   Nevertheless, I declined delivering the victim for such a fate, so that, in the end, we compromised the sentence by shooting Barrah in the presence of all the slaves and townsfolk,—the most unconcerned spectators among whom were his wife and sister !

# CHAPTER LV.

THERE is no river at the New Sestros settlement, though geographers, with their usual accuracy in African outlines, have often projected one on charts and maps. Two miles from the short and perilous beach where I built my *barracoons*, there was a slender stream, which, in consequence of its shallow bed, and narrow, rock-bound entrance, the natives call " Poor River; " but my factory was at New Sestros *proper ;* and there, as I have said, there was no water outlet from the interior; in fact, nothing but an embayed strand of two hundred yards, flanked by dangerous cliffs. Such a beach, open to the broad ocean and for ever exposed to the full rage of its storms, is of course more or less dangerous at all times for landing; and, even when the air is perfectly calm, the common surf of the sea pours inward with tremendous and combing waves, which threaten the boats of all who venture among them without experienced skill. Indeed, the landing at New Sestros would be impracticable were it not for the dexterous Kroomen, whose canoes sever and surmount the billows in spite of their terrific power.

Kroomen and Fishmen are different people from the Bushmen. The two former classes inhabit the seashore exclusively, and living apart from other African tribes, are governed by their elders under a somewhat democratic system. The Bushmen do not suffer the Kroos and Fishes to trade with the interior; but, in recompense for the monopoly of traffic with the strongholds of Africa's heart, these expert boatmen maintain despotic sway along the beach in trade with the shipping.  As European or Yankee boats cannot live in the surf I have described, the Kroo and Fishmen have an advantage over their brothers of the Bush, as well as over the whites, which they are not backward in using to their profit.   In fact, the Bushmen fight, travel, steal and trade, while the Kroos and Fishes, who for ages have fringed at least seven hundred miles of African coast, constitute the mariners, without whose skill and boldness slaves would be drugs in caravans or *barracoons*.  And this is especially the case since British, French, and American cruisers have driven the traffic from every nook and corner of the west coast that even resembled *a harbor*, and forced the slavers to lay in wait in open roadsteads for their prey.

The Kroo canoe, wedge-like at both ends, is hollowed from the solid trunk of a tree to the thickness of an inch.  Of course they are so light and buoyant that they not only lie like a feather on the surface of the sea, so as to require nothing but freedom from water for their safety, but a canoe, capable of containing four people, may be borne on the shoulders of one or two to any reasonable distance.  Accordingly, Kroomen and Fishmen are the prime pets of all slavers, traders, and men-of-war that frequent the west coast of Africa; while no one dwelling on the shore, engaged in commerce, is particularly anxious to merit or receive their displeasure.

When I landed at New Sestros, I promptly supplied myself with a little fleet of these amphibious natives; and, as the news of my liberality spread north and south along the shore, the number of my retainers increased with rapidity.   Indeed, in six months a couple of rival towns,—one of Kroos and the other of Fishes,—hailed me severally as their " Commodore " and " Consul."  With such auxiliaries constantly at hand, I rarely feared the surf when the shipment of slaves was necessary.  At Gallinas, under the immediate eye of Don Pedro, the most elaborate care was taken to secure an ample supply of these people and their boats, and I doubt not that the multitude employed in the establishment's prime, could, at a favorable moment, despatch at least a thousand slaves within the space of four hours. Yet I have heard from Kroomen at Gallinas the most harrowing tales of disaster connected with the shipment of negroes from that perilous bar. Even in the dry season, the mouth of this river is frequently dangerous, and, with all the adroitness they could display, the Kroos could not save boat load after boat load from becoming food for the ravenous sharks !

I was quite afloat at New Sestros on the tide of success, when the cruiser that for a while had annoyed me with a blockade, became short of food, and was obliged to bear away for Sierra Leone. My well paid spy—a Krooman who had been employed by the cruiser—soon apprised me of the brig's departure and its cause; so that in an hour the beach was in a bustle, despatching a swift canoe to Gallinas with a message to Don Pedro :—" The coast is clear :—send me a vessel :—relieve my plethora ! "

Forty-eight hours were hardly over when the twin masts of a clipper brig were seen scraping along the edge of the horizon, with the well-known signal for " embarkation." I was undoubtedly prepared to welcome my guest, for Kroos, Fishes, Bushmen, Bassas and all, had been alert since daybreak, ready to hail the craft and receive their fees. There had been a general embargo on all sea-going folks for a day before, so that there was not a fish to be had for love or money in the settlement. Minute precautions like these are absolutely necessary for all prudent slavers, for it was likely that the cruiser kept a spy in her pay among *my* people, as well as I did among *hers* !

All, therefore, was exceedingly comfortable, so far as ordinary judgment could foresee; but alas! the moon was full, and the African surf at such periods is fearfully terrific. As I listened from my piazza or gazed from my *bellevue*, it roared on the strand like the charge of interminable cavalry. My watchful enemy had been several days absent, and I expected her return from hour to hour. The shipment, though extremely perilous, was, therefore indispensable; and four short hours of daylight alone remained to complete it. I saw the risk, yet, taking counsel with the head Kroo and Fishmen, I persuaded them, under the provocation of triple reward, to attempt the enterprise with the smallest skiffs and stoutest rowers, while a band of lusty youths stood by to plunge in whenever the breakers capsized a canoe.

We began with females, as the most difficult cargo for embarkation, and seventy reached the brig safely.   Then followed the stronger sex; but by this time a sea breeze set in from the south-west like a young gale, and driving the rollers with greater rapidity, upset almost every alternate cockleshell set adrift with its living freight.   It was fortunate that our sharks happened that evening to be on a frolic elsewhere, so that negro after negro was rescued from the brine, though the sun was rapidly sinking when but two thirds of my slaves were safely shipped.

I ran up and down the beach, in a fever of anxiety, shouting, encouraging, coaxing, appealing, and *refreshing* the boatmen and swimmers; but as the gangs came ashore, they sank exhausted on the beach, refusing to stir.   Rum, which hitherto roused them like electricity, was now powerless.   Powder they did not want, nor muskets, nor ordinary trade stuff, for they never engaged in kidnapping or slave wars.

As night approached the wind increased.   *There* was the brig with topsails aback, signalling impatiently for despatch; but never was luckless factor more at fault!   I was on the eve of giving up in despair, when a bright flash brought to recollection a quantity of Venetian beads of mock coral which I had stowed in my chest.   They happened, at that moment, to be the rage among the girls of our beach, and were of course irresistible keys to the heart of every belle.   Now the smile of a lip has the same magical power in Africa as elsewhere; and the offer of a coral bunch for each head embarked, brought all the dames and damsels of Sestros to my aid.   Such a shower of chatter was never heard out of a canary cage.   Mothers, sisters, daughters, wives, sweethearts, took charge of the embarkation by coaxing or commanding their respective gentlemen; and, before the sun's rim dipped below the horizon, a few strands of false coral, or the kiss of a negro wench, sent one hundred more of the Africans into Spanish slavery.

But this effort exhausted my people.   The charm of beads

and beauty was over : Three slaves found a tomb in the sharks, or a grave in the deep, while the brig took flight in the darkness without the remaining one hundred and twenty I had designed for her hold.

Next morning the cruiser loomed once more in the offing, and, in a fit of impetuous benevolence, I hurried a Krooman aboard, with the offer of my compliments, and a *sincere* hope that I could render some service !

# CHAPTER LVI.

ABOUT this time, a Spanish vessel from the Canaries, laden with fruit, the greater part of which had been sold at Goree, Sierra Leone, Gallinas, and Cape Mesurado, dropped anchor opposite my little roadstead with a letter from Blanco. The Spaniard had been chartered by the Don to bring from the Grain Coast a cargo of rice, which he was to collect under my instructions.

My *barracoons* happened to be just then pretty bare, and as the season did not require my presence in the factory for trade, it struck me that I could not pass a few weeks more agreeably, and ventilate my jaded faculties more satisfactorily, than by throwing my carpet-bag on the Brilliant, and purchasing the cargo myself.

In the prosecution of this little adventure, I called along the coast with cash at several English factories, where I obtained rice ; and on my return anchored off the river to purchase sea-stores. Here I found Governor Findley, chief of the colony, laboring under a protracted illness which refused yielding to medicine, but might, probably, be relieved by a voyage, even of a few days, in the pure air of old Neptune. Slaver as I was, I contrived never to omit a civility to gentlemen on the coast of Africa; and I confess I was proud of the honorable service, when Governor Findley accepted the Brilliant for a trip along the coast. He proposed visiting Monrovia and Bassa; and after landing at some port in that quarter to await the captain's return from windward.

I fanned along the coast as slowly as I could, to give the Governor every possible chance to recruit his enervated frame by change of air; but, as I looked in at New Sestros in passing, I found three trading vessels with cargoes of merchandise to my consignment, so that I was obliged to abandon my trip and return to business. I left the Governor, however, in excellent hands, and directed the captain to land him at Bassa, await his pleasure three days, and finally, to bear him to Monrovia, the last place he desired visiting.

The Rio San Juan or Grand Bassa, is only fourteen miles north-west of New Sestros, yet it was near nightfall when the Brilliant approached the river landing. The Spaniard advised his guest not to disembark till next morning, but the Governor was so restless and anxious about delay, that he declined our captain's counsel, and went ashore at a native town, with the design of crossing on foot the two miles of beach to the American settlement.

As Findley went over the Brilliant's side into the Krooman's canoe, the jingle of silver was heard in his pocket; and warning was given him either to hide his money or leave it on board. But the Governor smiled at the caution, and disregarding it entirely, threw himself into the African skiff.

Night fell. The curtain of darkness dropped over the coast and sea. Twice the sun rose and set without word from the Governor. At last, my delayed mariner became impatient if not anxious, and despatched one of my servants who spoke English, in search of Mr. Findley at the American Settlement. *No one had seen or heard of him!* But, hurrying homeward from his fruitless errand, my boy followed the winding beach, and half way to the vessel found a human body, its head gashed with a deep wound, floating and beating against the rocks. He could not recognize the features of the battered face; but the well remembered garments left no doubt on the servant's mind that the corpse was Findley's.

The frightful story was received with dismay on the Bril·

liant, whose captain, unfamiliar with the coast and its people, hesitated to land, with the risk of treachery or ambush, even to give a grave to the dust of his wretched passenger. In this dilemma he thought best to run the fourteen miles to New Sestros, where he might counsel with me before venturing ashore.

Whatever personal anxiety may have flashed athwart my mind when I heard of the death of a colonial governor while enjoying the hospitality of myself,—a slaver,—the thought vanished as quickly as it was conceived. In an instant I was busy with detection and revenge.

It happened that the three captains had already landed the cargoes to my consignment, so that their empty vessels were lying at anchor in the roads, and the officers ready to aid me in any enterprise I deemed feasible. My colleagues were from three nations :—one was a Spaniard, another a Portuguese, and the last American.

Next morning I was early aboard the Spaniard, and sending for the Portuguese skipper, we assembled the crew. I dwelt earnestly and heartily on the insult the Castilian flag had received by the murder of an important personage while protected by its folds. I demonstrated the necessity there was for prompt chastisement of the brutal crime, and concluded by informing the crowd, that their captains had resolved to aid me in vindicating our banner. When I ventured to hope that *the men* would not hesitate to back their officers, a general shout went up that they were ready to land and punish the negroes.

As soon as the enterprise was known on board the American, her captain insisted on volunteering in the expedition; and by noon, our little squadron was under way, with fifty muskets in the cabins.

The plan I roughly proposed, was, under the menacing appearance of this force, to demand the murderer or murderers of Governor Findley, and to execute them, either on his grave, or the spot where his corpse was found. Failing in this, I intended to land portions of the crews, and destroy the towns nearest the theatre of the tragedy.

The sun was still an hour or more high, when we sailed in

line past the native towns along the fatal beach, and displayed our flags and pennants. Off the Rio San Juan, we tacked in man-of-war fashion, and returning southward, each vessel took post opposite a different town as if to command it.

While I had been planning and executing these manœuvres, the colonial settlers had heard of the catastrophe, and found poor Findley's mangled corpse. At the moment of our arrival off the river's mouth, an anxious council of resolute men was discussing the best means of chastising the savages. When my servant inquired for the governor he had spoken of him as a passenger in the Spanish craft, so that the parade of our vessels alongshore and in front of the native towns, betokened, they thought, co-operation on the part of the Mongo of New Sestros.

Accordingly, we had not been long at anchor before Governor Johnson despatched a Krooman to know whether I was aboard a friendly squadron; and, if so, he trusted I would land at once, and unite with his forces in the intended punishment.

In the interval, however, the cunning savages who soon found out that we had no cannons, flocked to the beach, and as they were beyond musket shot, insulted us by gestures, and defied a battle.

Of course no movement was made against the blacks that night, but it was agreed in council at the American settlement, that the expedition, supported by a field piece, should advance next day by the beach, where I could reinforce it with my seamen a short distance from the towns.

Punctual to the moment, the colonial flag, with drum and fife, appeared on the sea-shore at nine in the morning, followed by some forty armed men, dragging their cannon. Five boats, filled with sailors instantly left our vessels to support the attack, and, by this time, the colonists had reached a massive rock which blocked the beach like a bulwark, and was already possessed by the natives. My position, in flank, made my force most valuable in dislodging the foe, and of course I hastened my oars to open the passage. As I was altogether ignorant of the numbers that might be hidden and lurking in the dense jungle that was not more than fifty feet from the water's edge, I kept my men afloat within musket shot, and, with a few rounds of ball cartridge purged the rock of its defenders, though but a single savage was mortally wounded.

Upon this, the colonists advanced to the vacant bulwark, and were joined by our reinforcement. Wheeler, who commanded the Americans, proposed that we should march in a compact body to the towns, and give battle to the blacks if they held out in their dwellings. But his plan was not executed, for, before we reached the negro huts, we were assailed from the bushes and jungle. Their object was to keep hidden within the dense underwood; to shoot and run; while we, entirely exposed on the open shore, were obliged to remain altogether on the defensive by dodging the balls, or to fire at the smoke of an unseen enemy. Occasionally, large numbers of the savages would appear at a distance beyond musket range, and tossing their guns and lances, or brandishing their cutlasses, would present their naked limbs to our gaze, slap their shining flanks, and disappear! But this diverting exercise was not repeated very often. A sturdy colonist, named Bear, who carried a long and heavy old-fashioned *rifle*, took rest on my shoulder, and, when the next party of annoying jokers displayed their personal charms, laid its leader in the dust by a Yankee ball. Our cannon and blunderbusses were next brought into play to scour the jungle and expel the marksmen, who, confident in the security of their impervious screen, began to fire among us with more precision than was desirable. A Krooman of our party was killed, and a colonist severely wounded. Small sections of our two commands advanced at a run, and fired a volley into the bushes, while the main body of the expedition hastened along the beach towards the towns. By repeating this process several times, we were enabled, without further loss, to reach the first settlement.

Here, of course, we expected to find the savages arrayed in force to defend their roof-trees, but when we entered the place cautiously, and crept to the first dwelling in the outskirt, it was empty. So with the second, third, fourth,—until we overran the whole settlement and found it utterly deserted;—its furniture, stock, implements, and even *doors* carried off by the deliberate fugitives. The guardian *fetiche* was alone left to protect their abandoned hovels. But the superstitious charm did not save them. The brand was lighted; and, in an hour, five of these bamboo confederacies were given to the flames.

We discovered while approaching the towns, that our assault had made so serious an inroad on the slim supply of ammunition, that it was deemed advisable to send a messenger to the colony for a reinforcement. By neglect or mishap, the powder and ball never reached us; so that when the towns were destroyed, no one dreamed of penetrating the forest to unearth its vermin with the remnant of cartridges in our chest and boxes. I never was able to discover the cause of this unpardonable neglect, or the officer who permitted it to occur in such an exigency; but it was forthwith deemed advisable to waste no time in retreating after our partial revenge.

Till now, the Africans had kept strictly on the defensive, but when they saw our faces turned towards the beach, or colony, every bush and thicket became alive again with aggressive foes. For a while, the cannon kept them at bay, but its grape soon gave out; and, while I was in the act of superintending a fair division of the remaining ball cartridges, I was shot in the right foot with an iron slug. At the moment of injury I scarcely felt the wound, and did not halt, but, as I trudged along in the sand and salt-water, my wound grew painful, and the loss of blood which tracked my steps, soon obliged me to seek refuge in the canoe of my Kroomen.

The sight of my bleeding body borne to the skiff, was hailed with shouts and gestures of joy and contempt by the savages. As I crossed the last breaker and dropped into smooth water, my eyes reverted to the beach, where I heard the exultant war drum and war bells, while the colonists were beheld in full flight, leaving their artillery in the hands of our foe! It was subsequently reported that the commander of the party had been panic struck by the perilous aspect of affairs, and ordered the precipitate and fatal retreat, which that very night emboldened the negroes to revenge the loss of their towns by the conflagration of Bassa-Cove.

Next day, my own men, and the volunteers from our Spanish, Portuguese and American vessels, were sent on board, eight of them bearing marks of the fray, which fortunately proved neither fatal nor dangerous. The shameful flight of my comrades not only gave heart to the blacks, but spread its cowardly panic among the resident colonists. The settlement, they told me, was in danger of attack, and although my wound and the disaster both contributed to excite me against the fugitives, I did not quit the San Juan without reinforcing Governor Johnson with twenty muskets and some kegs of powder.

I have dwelt rather tediously perhaps on this sad occurrence —but I have a reason. Governor Findley's memory was, at this time, much vilified on the coast, because that functionary had accepted the boon of a passage in the Brilliant, which was falsely declared to be " a Spanish slaver." There were some among the overrighteous who even went so far as to proclaim his death " a judgment for venturing on the deck of such a vessel ! "

As no one took the trouble to investigate the facts and contradict the malicious lie, I have thought it but justice to tell the entire story, and exculpate a gentleman who met a terrible death in the bold prosecution of his duty.

# CHAPTER LVII.

I took the earliest opportunity to apprise Don Pedro Blanco of the mishap that had befallen his factor's limb, so that I might receive the prompt aid of an additional clerk to attend the more active part of our business. Don Pedro's answer was extremely characteristic. The letter opened with a draft for five hundred dollars, which he authorized me to bestow on the widow and orphans of Governor Findley, if he left a family. The slaver of Gallinas then proceeded to comment upon my Quixotic expedition; and, in gentle terms, intimated a decided censure for my immature attempt to chastise the negroes. He did not disapprove my *motives;* but considered any revengeful assault on the natives unwise, unless every precaution had previously been taken to insure complete success. Don Pedro hoped that, henceforth, I would take things more coolly, so as not to hazard either my life or his property; and concluded the epistle by superscribing it:

" To
" *Señor* Powder,
" *at his Magazine,*
" New Sestros."

--------

The slug that struck the upper part of my foot, near the

ankle joint, tore my flesh and tendons with a painfully danger-gerous wound, which, for nine months, kept me a prisoner on crutches.  During the long and wearying confinement which almost broke my restless heart, I had little to do save to superintend the general fortunes of our factory.  Now and then, an incident occurred to relieve the monotony of my sick chair, and make me forget, for a moment, the pangs of my crippled limb.  One of these events flashes across my memory as I write, in the shape of a letter which was mysteriously delivered at my landing by a coaster, and came from poor Joseph, my ancient partner on the Rio Pongo.  Coomba's spouse was in trouble ! and the ungrate-ful scamp, though forgetful of my own appeals from the *Chateau of Brest*, did not hesitate to claim my brotherly aid.  Captured in a Spanish slaver, and compromised beyond salvation, Joseph had been taken into Sierra Leone, where he was now under sen-tence of transportation.  The letter hinted that a liberal sum might purchase his escape, even from the tenacious jaws of the British lion ; and when I thought of old times, the laughable marriage ceremony, and the merry hours we enjoyed at Kambia, I forgave his neglect.  A draft on Don Pedro was readily cashed at Sierra Leone, notwithstanding the paymaster was a slaver and the jurisdiction that of St. George and his Cross.  The trans-action, of course, was " purely commercial," and, therefore, sin-less ;  so that, in less than a month, Joseph and the bribed turnkey were on their way to the Rio Pongo.

By this time the sub-factory of New Sestros was somewhat renowned in Cuba and Porto Rico.  Our dealings with comman-ders, the character of my cargoes, and the rapidity with which I despatched a customer and his craft were proverbial in the islands.  Indeed, the third year of my lodgment had not rolled over, be-fore the slave-demand was so great, that in spite of rum, cottons, muskets, powder, kidnapping and Prince Freeman's wars, the country could not supply our demand.

To aid New Sestros, I had established several *nurseries*, or junior factories, at Little Bassa and Digby ; points a few miles from the limits of Liberia.  These " chapels of ease " furnished my parent *barracoons* with young and small negroes, mostly kidnapped, I suppose, in the neighborhood of the beach.

When I was perfectly cured of the injury I sustained in my first philanthropic fight, I loaded my spacious cutter with a choice collection of trade-goods, and set sail one fine morning for this outpost at Digby. I designed, also, if advisable, to erect another receiving *barracoon* under the lee of Cape Mount.

But my call at Digby was unsatisfactory. The pens were vacant, and our merchandise squandered *on credit*. This put me in a very uncomfortable passion, which would have rendered an interview between " Mr. Powder " and his agent any thing but pleasant or profitable, had that personage been at his post. Fortunately, however, for both of us, he was abroad carousing with " a *king;* " so that I refused landing a single yard of merchandise, and hoisted sail for the next village.

There I transacted business in regular " ship-shape." Our rum was plenteously distributed and established an *entente cordiale* which would have charmed a diplomatist at his first dinner in a new capital. The naked blackguards flocked round me like crows, and I clothed their loins in parti-colored calicoes that enriched them with a plumage worthy of parrots. I was the prince of good fellows in " every body's " opinion; and, in five days, nineteen newly-" *conveyed* " darkies were exchanged for London muskets, Yankee grog, and Manchester cottons ! "

My cutter, though but twenty-seven feet long, was large enough to stow my gang, considering that the voyage was short, and the slaves but boys and girls; so I turned my prow homeward with contented spirit and promising skies. Yet, before night, all was changed. Wind and sea rose together. The sun sank in a long streak of blood. After a while, it rained in terrible squalls; till, finally, darkness caught me in a perfect gale. So high was the surf and so shelterless the coast, that it became utterly impossible to make a lee of any headland where we might ride out the storm in safety. Our best hope was in the cutter's ability to keep the open sea without swamping ; and, accordingly, under the merest patch of sail, I coasted the perilous breakers, guided by their roar, till day dawn. But, when the sun lifted over the horizon,—peering for an instant through a rent in the

storm-cloud, and then disappearing behind the gray vapor,—I
saw at once that the coast offered no chance of landing our
blacks at some friendly town.  Every where the bellowing shore
was lashed by surf, impracticable even for the boats and skill of
Kroomen.  On I dashed, therefore, driving and almost burying
the cutter, with loosened reef, till we came opposite Monrovia ;
where, safe in the absence of cruisers, I crept at dark under the
lee of the cape, veiling my cargo with our useless sails.

Sunset "killed the wind," enabling us to be off again at
dawn ; yet hardly were we clear of the cape, when both gale and
current freshened from the old quarter, holding us completely
in check.  Nevertheless, I kept at sea till evening, and then
sneaked back to my protecting anchorage.

By this time, my people and slaves were wellnigh famished,
for their sole food had been a scant allowance of raw *cassava*.
Anxiety, toil, rain, and drenching spray, broke their spirits.
The blacks, from the hot interior, and now for the first time off
their mother earth, suffered not only from the inclement weather,
but groaned with the terrible pangs of sea-sickness.  I resolved,
therefore, if possible, to refresh the drooping gang by a hot meal ;
and, beneath the shelter of a tarpaulin, contrived to cook a mess
of rice.  Warm food comforted us astonishingly ; but, alas ! the
next day was a picture of the past !  A slave—cramped and
smothered amid the crowd that soaked so long in the salt water
at our boat's bottom—died during the darkness.  Next morning,
the same low, leaden, coffin-lid sky, hung like a pall over sea and
shore.  Wind in terrific blasts, and rain in deluging squalls,
howled and beat on us.  Come what might, I resolved not to
stir !  All day I kept my people beneath the sails, with orders
to move their limbs as much as possible, in order to overcome the
benumbing effect of moisture and packed confinement.  The incessant drenching from sea and sky to which they had been so
long subjected, chilled their slackened circulation to such a degree, that death from torpor seemed rapidly supervening.  Motion, motion, motion, was my constant command ; but I hoarded
my alcohol for the last resource.

I saw that no time was to be lost, and that nothing but a

bold encounter of hazard would save either lives or property. Before dark my mind was made up as to the enterprise. I would land in the neighborhood of the colony, and cross its territory during the shadow of night!

I do not suppose that the process by which I threw my stiffened crew on the beach, and revived them with copious draughts of brandy, would interest the reader; *but midnight did not strike before my cargo, under the escort of Kroo guides, was boldly marched through the colonial town, and safe on its way to New Sestros!* Fortunately for my dare-devil adventure, the tropical rain poured down in ceaseless torrents, compelling the unsuspicious colonists to keep beneath their roofs. Indeed, no one dreamed of a forced march by human beings on that dreadful night of tempest, else it might have gone hard had I been detected in the desecration of colonial soil. Still I was prepared for all emergencies. I never went abroad without the two great keys of Africa—gold and firearms; and had it been my lot to encounter a colonist, he would either have learned the value of silence, or have been carried along, under the muzzle of a pistol, till the gang was in safety.

While it was still dark, I left the caravan advancing by an interior path to Little Bassa, where one of my branches could furnish it with necessaries to cross the other colony of Bassa San Juan, so as to reach my homestead in the course of three days. Meanwhile I retraced my way to Monrovia, and, reaching it by sunrise, satisfied the amiable colonists that I had just taken shelter in their harbor, and was fresh from my dripping cutter. It is very likely that no one in the colony to the present day knows the true story of this adventure, or would believe it unless *confessed* by me.

It was often my fate in Africa, and elsewhere, to hear gossips declare that colonists were no better than others who dwelt amid coast temptations, and that they were sometimes even willing to back a certain Don Theodore Canot, if not absolutely to share his slave trade! I never thought it prudent to exculpate those honorable emigrants who were consolidating the first colonial lodgments from the United States; for I believed that *my* denial would only add sarcastic venom to the scandal of vilifiers. But now that my African career is over, and the slave trade a mere tradition in the neighborhood of Liberia, I may assure the friends of colonization, that, in all my negro traffic, no American settler gave assistance or furnished merchandise which I could not have obtained at the most loyal establishments of Britain or France. I think it will be granted by unprejudiced people, that the colonist who sold me a few pieces of cloth, lodged me in travelling, or gave me his labor for my flesh-colored gold, participated no more in the African slave trade than the European or American supercargo who sold assorted cargoes, selected with the most deliberate judgment in London, Paris, Boston, New-York, Philadelphia, or Baltimore, expressly to suit the well-known cupidity of my warriors, kidnappers, and slave merchants.

Commerce is sometimes an adroit metaphysican—but a bad moralist!

# CHAPTER LVIII.

IT was my invariable custom whenever a vessel made her appearance in the roadstead of New Sestros, to despatch my canoe with " Captain Canot's compliments ; " nor did I omit this graceful courtesy when his Britannic Majesty's cruisers did me the honor of halting in my neighborhood to watch or destroy my operations.   At such times I commonly increased the politeness by an offer of my services, and a tender of provisions, or of any commodity the country could supply !

I remember an interesting rencounter of this sort with the officers of the brig of war Bonito.   My note was forwarded by a trusty Krooman, even before her sails were furled, but the courteous offer was respectfully declined "*for the present.*"   The captain availed himself, however, of my messenger's return, to announce that the " commodore in command of the African squadron had specially deputed the Bonito *to blockade* New Sestros, for which purpose she was provisioned for *six months*, and ordered not to budge from her anchorage till relieved by a cruiser ! "

This formidable announcement was, of course, intended to

strike me with awe.  The captain hoped in conclusion, that I would see the folly of prosecuting my abominable traffic in the face of such a disastrous *vis à vis ;* nor could he refrain from intimating his surprise that a man of my reputed character and ability, would consent to manacle and starve the unfortunate negroes who were now suffering in my *barracoons.*

I saw at once from this combined attack of fear and flattery, backed by blockade, that his majesty's officer had either been grossly misinformed, or believed that a scarcity of rice prevailed in my establishment as well as elsewhere along the coast.

The suspicion of *starving blacks in chains*, was not only pathetic but mortifying!  It was part of the sentimental drapery of British reports and despatches, to which I became accustomed in Africa.  I did not retort upon my dashing captain with a sneer at his ancestors who had taught the traffic to Spaniards, yet I resolved not to let his official communications reach the British admiralty with a fanciful tale about *my* barracoons and starvation.  Accordingly, without more ado, I sent a second *billet* to the Bonito, desiring her captain or any of her officers to visit New Sestros, and ascertain personally the condition of my establishment.

Strange to tell, my invitation was accepted ; and at noon a boat with a white flag, appeared on the edge of the surf, conveying two officers to my beach.  The surgeon and first lieutenant were my visitors.  I welcomed them most cordially to my cottage, and as soon as the customary refreshments were despatched, proposed a glance at the dreadful *barracoons.*

As well as I now remember, there must have been at least five hundred slaves in my two pens, sleek in flesh, happy in looks, and ready for the first customer who could outwit the cruiser.  I quietly despatched a notice of our advent to the *barracooniers*, with directions as to their conduct, so that the moment my naval friends entered the stanch inclosures, full two hundred and fifty human beings, in each, rose to their feet and saluted the strangers with long and reiterated clapping.  This sudden and surprising demonstration somewhat alarmed my guests at its outburst, and made them retreat a pace towards the door,—perhaps in fear of treachery;—but when they saw the smiling faces and heard the pleased chatter of my people, they soon came forward to learn that the compliment was worth a customary *demijohn of rum.*

The adventure was a fortunate one for the reputation of New Sestros, Don Pedro my employer, and Don Téodor, his clerk. Our establishment happened just then to be at a summit of material comfort rarely exceeded or even reached by others. My pens were full of slaves; my granary, of rice; my stores, of merchandise.

From house to house,—from hut to hut,—the sailor and saw-bones wandered with expressions of perfect admiration, till the hour for dinner approached. I ordered the meal to be administered with minute attention to all our usual ceremonies. The washing, singing, distribution of food, beating time, and all the prandial *etceteras* of comfort, were performed with the utmost precision and cleanliness. They could not believe that such was the ordinary routine of slave life in *barracoons,* but ventured to hint that I must have got up the drama for their special diversion, and that it was impossible for such to be the ordinary drill and demeanor of Africans. Our dapper little surgeon, with almost dissective inquisitiveness, pried into every nook and corner; and at length reached the slave kitchen, where a caldron was full and bubbling with the most delicious rice. Hard by stood a pot, simmering with meat and soup, and in an instant the doctor had a morsel between his fingers and brought his companion to follow his example.

Now, in sober truth, this was no casual display got up for effect, but the common routine of an establishment conducted with prudent foresight, for the profit of its owners as well as the comfort of our people. And yet, such was the fanatical prepossession of these Englishmen, whose idea of Spanish *factories* and *barracoons* was formed exclusively from exaggerated reports, that I could not satisfy them of my truth till I produced our journal, in which I noted minutely every item of daily expenditure. It must be understood, however, that it was not my habit to give the slaves *meat* every day of the week. Such a diet would not be prudent, because it is not habitual with the majority of negroes. Two bullocks were slaughtered each week for the use of my *factory*, while the hide, head, blood, feet, neck, tail, and entrails, were appropriated for broth in the *barracoons*. It happended that my visitors arrived on the customary day of our butchering.

A stinging appetite was the natural result of our review, and while the naval guests were whetting it still more, I took the opportunity to slip out of my verandah with orders for our harbor pilot to report the beach "impracticable for boats,"—a report which no prudent sailor on the coast ever disregards. Meanwhile, I despatched a Krooman with a note to the Bonito's captain, notifying that personage of the marine hazard that prevented his officers' immediate return, and fearing they might even find it necessary to tarry over night. This little *ruse* was an *impromptu* device to detain my inspectors, and make us better acquainted over the African *cuisine*, which, by this time was smoking in tureens and dishes flanked by spirited sentinels, in black uniform, of claret and eau de vie.

Our dinner-chat was African all over : slavery, cruisers, prize-money, captures, war, negro-trade, and philanthropy ! The surgeon melted enough under the blaze of the bottle to admit, *as a philosopher*, that Cuffee was happier in the hands of white men than of black, and that he would even support the institution if it could be carried on with a little more humanity and less bloodshed. The lieutenant saw nothing, even through the "Spiritual Medium " of our flagons, save prize-money and obedience to the Admiral ; while Don Téodor became rather tart on the service, and confessed that his incredulity of British philanthropy would never cease till England abandoned her Indian wars, her opium smuggling, and her persecution of the Irish !

In truth, these loyal subjects of the King, and the Spanish slaver became most excellent friends before bed-time, and ended the evening by a visit to Prince Freeman, who forthwith got up a negro dance and jollification for our special entertainment.

I have not much recollection after the end of this savage frolic till my " look-out " knocked at the door with the news that our brig was firing for her officers, while a suspicious sail flitted along the horizon.

All good sailors sleep with one eye and ear open, so that in a twinkling the lieutenant was afoot making for the beach, and calling for the surgeon to follow. " A canoe ! a canoe! a canoe ! " shouted the gallant blade, while he ran to and fro on the edge of the surf, beholding signal after signal from his vessel. But alas ! for the British navy,—out of all the Kroo spectators not one stirred hand or foot for the royal officer. Next came the jingle of dollars, and the offer of twenty to the boatmen who would launch their skiff and put them on board. " No savez ! No savez ! ax Commodore ! ax Consul ! "

" Curse your Commodore and Consul ! " yelled the lieutenant, as the surgeon came up with the vociferous group : " put us aboard and be paid, or I'll——"

" Stop, stop ! " interposed my pacific saw-bones, " no swearing and no threats, lieutenant. One's just as useless as the other. First of all, the Bonito's off about her business;—and next, my dear fellow, the chase she's after is one of Canot's squadron, and, of course, there's an embargo on every canoe along this beach ! The Commodore's altogether *too cute*, as the Yankees say, to reinforce his enemy with officers ! "

During this charming little episode of my *blockade*, I was aloft in my bellevieu, watching the progress of the chase ; and as both vessels kept steadily northward they soon disappeared behind the land.

By this time it was near breakfast, and, with a good appetite, I descended to the verandah, with as unconcerned an air as if nothing had occurred beyond the ordinary routine of factory life. But, not so, alas ! my knight of the single epaulette.

" This is a pretty business, sir ; " said the lieutenant, fixing a look on me which was designed to annihilate ; striding up and down the piazza, " a *very* pretty business, I repeat ! " Pray, Commodore, Consul, Don, Señor, Mister, Monsieur, Theodore Canot, or whatever the devil else you please to call yourself, how long do you intend to keep British officers prisoners in your infernal slave den ? "

Now it is very likely that some years before, or if I had not contrived the plot of this little naval *contre temps*, I might have burst forth in a beautiful rage, and given my petulant and foiled visitor a specimen of my Spanish vocabulary, which would not have rested pleasantly in the memory of either party. But as *he* warmed *I* cooled. His rage, in fact, was a fragment of my practical satire, and I took special delight in beholding the contortions caused by my physic.

"Sit down, sit down, lieutenant!" returned I very composedly, "we're about to have coffee, and you are my *guest*. Nothing, lieutenant, ever permits me to neglect the duties of hospitality in such an out-of-the-way and solitary place as Africa. Sit down, doctor! Calm yourselves, gentlemen. Take example by *me!* Your Bonito is probably playing the devil with one of Don Pedro's craft by this time; but that don't put me out of temper, or *make me unmannerly* to gentlemen who honor my bamboo hut with their presence!" I laid peculiar stress, by way of accent, on the word "unmannerly," and in a moment I saw the field was in my hands.

"Yes, gentlemen," continued I, "I comprehend very well both your duty and responsibility; but, now that I see you are calmer, have the kindness to say *in what* I am to blame? Did you not come here to "blockade" New Sestros, with a brig and provisions for half a year? And do I prevent your embarkation, if you can find any Krooman willing to take you on board? Nay, did either of you apprise me, as is customary when folks go visiting, that you designed leaving my quarters at so early an hour as to afford me the pleasure of seeing every thing in order for your accommodation? Come now, my good fellows, New Sestros is *my* flagship, as the Bonito is *yours!* No body stirs from this beach without the wink from its Commodore; and I shall be much surprised to hear such excellent disciplinarians dispute the propriety of my rule. Nevertheless, as you feel anxious to be gone on an independent cruise, you shall be furnished with a canoe *instanter!*"

"An offer," interjected the surgeon, "which it would be d—d nonsense to accept! Have done with your infernal sneering, Don Téodor; strike your flag, Mr. Lieutenant; and let the darkies bring in the breakfast!"

I have narrated this little anecdote to show that Spanish slavers sometimes ventured to have a little fun with the British lion,
and that when we got him on his haunches, his mouth full of beef
and his fore paws in air, he was by no means the unamiable beast
he is described to be, when, in company with the *unicorn*, he
goes

"a-fighting for the crown!"

# CHAPTER LIX.

THE balance of life vibrated considerably on the African coast. Sometimes Mr. Bull's scale ascended and sometimes the Slaver's. It was now the turn of the former to be exalted for a while by way of revenge for my forced hospitality.

Our friends of the Bonito held on with provoking pertinacity in front of my factory, so that I was troubled but little with company from Cuba for several months. At last, however, it became necessary that I should visit a neighboring colony for supplies, and I took advantage of a Russian trader along the coast to effect my purpose. But when we were within sight of our destination, a British cruiser brought us to and visited the " Galopsik." As her papers were in order, and the vessel altogether untainted, I took it for granted that Lieutenant Hill would make a short stay and be off to his "Saracen." Yet, a certain "slave deck," and an unusual quantity of water-casks, aroused the officer's suspicions, so that instead of heading for our port, we were unceremoniously favored with a prize crew, and ordered to Sierra Leone!

I did not venture to protest against these movements, inasmuch as I had no interest whatever in the craft, but I ventured to suggest that " as I was only a *passenger*, there could be no objection to my landing before the new voyage was commenced."

" By no means, sir," was the prompt reply, "*your presence is a material fact for the condemnation of the vessel !*"   Indeed, I soon found out that I was recognized by some of the Kroomen on the cruiser, and my unlucky reputation was a hole in the bottom of our Russian craft!

At Sierra Leone matters became worse. The Court did not venture to condemn the Russian, but resolved on ordering her to England; and when I re-stated my reasonable appeal for release, I was told that I must accompany the vessel on her visit to Great Britain.

This arbitrary decision of our captors sadly disconcerted my plans. A voyage to England would ruin New Sestros. My *barracoons* were alive with blacks, but I had not a month's provisions in my stores. The clerk, temporarily in charge, was altogether unfit to conduct a factory during a prolonged absence,—and all my personal property, as well as Don Pedro's, was at the hazard of his judgment during a period of considerable difficulty.

I resolved to take "French leave."

Three men of war were anchored astern and on our bows. No boats were allowed to approach us from shore; at night two marines and four sailors paraded the deck, so that it was a thing of some peril to dream of escape in the face of such Arguses. Yet there was no help for it. I could not afford an Admiralty or Chancery suit in England, while my *barracoons* were foodless in Africa.

No one had been removed from the Russian since her seizure, nor were we denied liberty of motion and intercourse so long as suspicion had not ripened into legal condemnation. The captain, by birth a Spaniard, was an old acquaintance, while the steward and boatswain were good fellows who professed willingness to aid me in any exploit I might devise for my liberty.

I hit upon the plan of a regular carouse; and at once decided that my Spanish skipper was bound to keep his birth-day with commendable merriment and abundant grog. There was to be no delay; one day was as good as another for his festival, while all that we needed, was time enough to obtain the requisite supplies of food and fluid.

This was soon accomplished, and the "fatted pig" slaughtered for the feast. As I never left home unprovided with gold, means were not wanting to stock our pantry with champagne as well as brandy.

Every thing went off to a charm. We fed like gluttons and drank like old-fashioned squires. Bumper after bumper was quaffed to the captain. Little by little, the infection spread, as it always does, from the ward-room to the cabin, and "goodfellow-ship" was the watchword of the night. Invitations were given and accepted by our prize crew. Bull and the Lion again relaxed under the spell of beef and brandy, so that by sundown every lip had tasted our *eau de vie*, and watered for more. The "first watch" found every soul on board, with the exception of our corporal of marines, as happy as lords.

This corporal was a regular "character;" and, from the first, had been feared as our stumbling-block. He was a perfect mar-tinet; a prim, precise, black-stock'd, military, Miss Nancy. He neither ate nor drank, neither talked nor smiled, but paraded the deck with a grim air of iron severity, as if resolved to preserve his own "discipline" if he could not control that of any one else. I doubt very much whether her Majesty has in her service a more dutiful loyalist than Corporal Blunt, if that excellent functionary has not succumbed to African malaria.

I hoped that something would occur to melt the corporal's heart during the evening, and had prepared a little vial in my pocket, which, at least, would have given him a stirless nap of twenty-four hours. But nothing broke the charm of his spell-bound sobriety. There he marched, to and fro, regular as a drum tap, hour after hour, stiff and inexorable as a ramrod!

But who, after the fall of Corporal Blunt, shall declare that there is a living man free from the lures of betrayal? And yet, he only surrendered to an enemy in disguise!

"God bless me, corporal," said our prize lieutenant, "in the name of all that's damnable, why don't you let out a reef or two from those solemn cheeks of yours, and drink a bumper to Captain Gaspard and Don Téodor? You ain't afraid of *cider*, are you?"

"*Cider*, captain?" said the corporal, advancing to the front and throwing up his hand with a military salute.

"Cider and be d—d to you!" returned the lieutenant. "Cider—of course, corporal; what other sort of pop can starving wretches like us drink in Sary-loney?"

"Well, lieutenant," said the corporal, "if so be as how them fizzing bottles which yonder Spanish gentleman is a pourin down is *only cider ;* and if cider ain't agin rules after · eight bells;' and if you, lieutenant, orders me to handle my glass,—I don't see what right I have to disobey the orders of my superior!"

"Oh! blast your sermon and provisos," interjected the lieutenant, filling a tumbler and handing it to the corporal, who drained it at a draught. In a moment the empty glass was returned to the lieutenant, who, instead of receiving it from the subaltern, refilled the tumbler.

"Oh, I'm sure I'm a thousand times obliged, lieutenant," said Blunt, with his left hand to his cap, "a thousand, thousand times, lieutenant,—but I'd rather take no more, if it's all the same to your honor."

"But it ain't, Blunt, by any means; the rule is universal among gentlemen on ship and ashore, that whenever a fellow's glass is filled, he must drink it to the dregs, though he may leave a drop in the bottom to pour out on the table in honor of his sweetheart;—so, down with the cider! And now Blunt, my boy, that you've calked your *first* nail-head, I insist upon a bumper all round to that sweetheart you were just talking of!"

"*Me*, lieutenant?"

"*You*, corporal!"

"I wasn't talking about any sweetheart, as I remembers, lieutenant;—'pon the honor of a soldier, I haven't had no such a thing this twenty years, since one warm summer's afternoon, when Jane——"

"Now, corporal, you don't pretend to contradict your superior officer, I hope. You don't intend to be the first man on this ship to show a mutinous example!"

"Oh! God bless me, lieutenant, the thought never entered my brain!"

But the third tumbler of champaigne *did*, in the apple-blossom disguise of "*cider ;*" and, in half an hour, there wasn't an odder figure on deck than the poor corporal, whose vice-like stock steadied his neck, though there was nothing that could make him toe the plank which he pertinaciously insisted on promenading. Blunt the immaculate, was undeniably drunk!

In fact,—though I say it with all possible respect for her Majesty's naval officers, *while on duty*,—there was, by this time, hardly a sober man on deck or in the cabin except myself and the Spanish captain, who left me to engage the prize-officer in a game of backgammon or dominoes. The crew was dozing about the decks, or nodding over the taffrail, while my colleague, the boatswain, prepared an oar on the forecastle to assist me in reaching the beach.

It was near midnight when I stripped in my state-room, leaving my garments in the berth, and hanging my watch over its pillow. In a small bundle I tied a flannel shirt and a pair of duck pantaloons, which I fastened behind my neck as I stood on the forecastle ; and then, placing the oar beneath my arm, I glided from the bows into the quiet water.

The night was not only very dark, but a heavy squall of wind and rain, accompanied by thunder, helped to conceal my escape and free the stream from sharks. I was not long in reaching a native town, where a Krooman from below, who had known me at Gallinas, was prepared for my reception and concealment.

Next morning, the cabin-boy, who did not find me as usual on deck, took my coffee to the state-room, where, it was supposed, I still rested in comfortable oblivion of last night's carouse. But the bird had flown! There were my trunk, my garments, my watch,—undisturbed as I left them when preparing for bed. There was the linen of my couch turned down and tumbled during repose. The inquest had no doubt of my fate :—*I had fallen overboard during the night*, and was doubtless, by this time, well digested in the bowels of African sharks! Folks shook their heads with surprise when it was reported that the notorious slaver, Canot, had fallen a victim to *mania à potu!*

The *report* of my death soon reached shore ; the British townsfolk believed it, but I never imagined for a moment that the warm-hearted tar who commanded the prize had been deceived by such false signals.

During eight days I remained hidden among the friendly negroes, and from my loop-hole, saw the Russian vessel sail under the Saracen's escort. I was not, however, neglected in my concealment by the worthy tradesmen of the British colony, who knew I possessed money as well as credit. This permitted me to receive visits and make purchases for the factory, so that I was enabled, on the eighth day, with a full equipment of all I desired, to quit the British jurisdiction in a Portuguese vessel.

On our way to New Sestros, I made the skipper heave his main-yard aback at Digby, while I embarked thirty-one " darkies," and a couple of stanch canoes with their Kroomen, to land my human freight in case of encountering a cruiser.

And well was it for me that I took this precaution. Night fell around us, dark and rainy,—the wind blowing in squalls, and sometimes dying away altogether. It was near one o'clock when the watch announced two vessels on our weather bow; and, of course, the canoes were launched, manned, filled with twenty of the gang, and set adrift for the coast, ere our new acquaintances could honor us with their personal attention. Ten of the slaves still remained on board, and as it was perilous to risk them in our own launch, we capsized it over the squad, burying the fellows in its bowels under the lee of a sailor's pistol to keep them quiet if we were searched.

Our lights had hardly been extinguished in cabin and binnacle, when we heard the measured stroke of a man-of-war oar In a few moments more the boat was alongside, the officer on deck, and a fruitless examination concluded. The blacks beneath the launch were as silent as death ; nothing was found to render the " Maria " suspicious ; and we were dismissed with a left-handed blessing for rousing gentlemen from their bunks on so comfortless a night. Next morning at dawn we reached New Sestros, where my ten lubbers were landed without delay.

But our little comedy was not yet over. Noon had not struck before the " Dolphin " cast anchor within hail of the " Maria," and made so free as to claim her for a prize ! In the darkness and confusion of shipping the twenty slaves who were first of all despatched in canoes, one of them slipped overboard with a paddle, and sustained himself till daylight, when he was picked up by the cruiser whose jaws we had escaped during the night! The negro's story of our trick aroused the ire of her commander, and the poor " Maria " was obliged to pay the for- feit by revisiting Sierra Leone in custody of an officer.

There were great rejoicings on my return to New Sestros. The coast was full of odd and contradictory stories about our capture. When the tale of my death at Sierra Leone by drown- ing, in a fit of drunkenness, was told to my patron Don Pedro, that intelligent gentleman denied it without hesitation, because, in the language of the law, " *it proved too much.*" It was *possible*, he said, that I might have been drowned; but when they told him I had come to my death by strong drink, they declared what was not only improbable, but altogether out of the question. Accordingly, he would take the liberty to discredit the entire story, being sure that I would turn up before long.

But poor Prince Freeman was not so clever a judge of nature as Don Pedro  Freeman had heard of my death; and, imbued as he was with the superstitions of his country, nobody could make him credit my existence till he despatched a committee to my factory, headed by his son, to report the facts. But then, on the instant, the valiant prince paid me a visit of congratulation. As I held out both hands to welcome him, I saw the fellow shrink with distrust.

" Count your fingers ! " said Freeman.

" Well," said I, " what for ?—here they are—one—two— three—four—five—six—seven—eight—nine—ten ! "

" Good—good ! " shouted the prince, as he clasped my digits. " White men tell too many lies 'bout the commodore ! White man say, John Bull catch commodore, and cut him fingers all off, so commodore no more can ' makee book ' for makee fool of John Bull ! " Which, being translated into English, signifies that it was reported my fingers had been cut off by my British captors to prevent me from writing letters by which the innocent natives believed I so often bamboozled and deceived the cruisers of her Majesty.

During my absence, a French captain, who was one of our

most attentive friends, had left a donkey which he brought from the Cape de Verds for my especial delectation, by way of an occasional *promenade à cheval!* I at once resolved to bestow the "long-eared convenience" on Freeman, not only as a type, but a testimonial; yet, before a week was over, the unlucky quadruped reappeared at my quarters, with a message from the prince that it might do well enough for a bachelor like me, but its infernal voice was enough to cause the miscarriage of an entire harem, if not of every honest woman throughout his jurisdiction! The superstition spread like wildfire. The women were up in arms against the beast; and I had no rest till I got rid of its serenades by despatching it to Monrovia, where the dames and damsels were not afraid of donkeys of any dimensions.

# CHAPTER LX.

It was my habit to employ at New Sestros a clerk, storekeeper, and four seamen, all of whom were whites of reliable character, competent to aid me efficiently in the control of my *barracoons.*

One of these sailors died of dropsy while in my service; and, as I write, the memory of his death flashes across my mind so vividly, that I cannot help recording it among the characteristic events of African coast-life.

Sanchez, I think, was by birth a Spaniard; at least his perfect familiarity with the language, as well as name and appearance, induced me to believe that the greater part of his life must have been spent under the shield of Saint Iago. The poor fellow was ill for a long time, but in Africa, existence is so much a long-drawn malady, that we hardly heeded his bloated flesh or cadaverous skin, as he sat, day after day, musket in hand, at the gate of our barracoon. At last, however, his confinement to bed was announced, and every remedy within our knowledge applied for relief. This time, however, the summons was peremptory; the sentence was final; there was no reprieve.

On the morning of his death, the sufferer desired me to be called, and, sending away the African nurse and the two old comrades who watched faithfully at his bedside, explained that he felt his end approaching, yet could not depart without easing his soul by *confession !*

"Here, Don Téodor," said he, "are five ounces of gold—all I have saved in this world,—the lees of my life,—which I want you to take care of, and when I am dead send to my sister, who is married to ——, in Matanzas. Will you promise?"

I promised.

"And now, Don Téodor," continued he, "I must *confess!*"

I could not repress a smile as I replied,—"But, José, I am no *padre*, you know; a *clerigo* is no part of a slave factory; I cannot absolve your sins; and, as for my *prayers*, poor fellow, alas! what can they do for your sins when I fear they will hardly avail for my own!"

"It's all one, *mi capitan*," answered the dying man; "it makes not the least difference, Don Téodor, if you are a clergyman or any thing else; it is the law of our church; and when confession is over, a man's soul is easier under canvas, even if there's no regular *padre* at hand to loosen the ropes, and let one's sins fly to the four winds of heaven. Listen,—it will be short.

"It is many years since I sailed from Havana with that notorious slaver, Miguel ——, whose murder you may have heard of on the coast. Our vessel was in capital order for speed as well as cargo, and we reached Cape Mount after a quick voyage. The place, however, was so bare of slaves, that we coasted the reefs till we learned from a Mesurado Krooman that, in less than a month, the supply at Little Bassa would be abundant. We shipped the savage with his boatman, and next day reached our destination.

"Miguel was welcomed warmly by the chiefs, who offered a choice lot of negroes for a portion of our cargo, inviting the captain to tarry with the rest of his merchandise and establish a factory. He assented; our brig was sent home with a short cargo, while I and two others landed with the captain, to aid in the erection and defence of the requisite buildings.

"It did not take long to set up our bamboo houses and open a trade, for whose supply Miguel began an intercourse with Cape Mesurado, paying in doubloons and receiving his merchandise in vessels manned by American blacks.

" Our captain was no niggard in housekeeping. Bountiful meals every day supplied his friends and factory. No man went from his door hungry or dissatisfied. When the colonists came up in their boats with goods, or walked the beach from the Cape to our settlement, Miguel was always alert with a welcome. A great intimacy, of course, ensued ; and, among the whole crowd of traffickers, none were higher in our chief's estimation than a certain T———, who rarely visited the *barracoons* without a gift from Miguel, in addition to his stipulated pay.

" In due time the brig returned from Havana, with a cargo of rum, tobacco, powder, and *a box of doubloons;* but she was ordered to the Cape de Verds to change her flag. In the interval, the Mesurado colonists picked a quarrel with the Trade-Town chiefs, and, aided by an American vessel, under Colombian colors, landed a division of colonial troops and destroyed the Spanish barracoons.*

" The ruin of a Spanish factory could not be regarded by our captain with any other feeling than that of resentment. Still, he manifested his sensibility by coolness towards the colonists, or by refraining from that *profitable* welcome to which they had hitherto been accustomed. But the Monrovians were not to be rebuffed by disdain. They had heard, I suppose, of the box of doubloons, and Miguel was " a good fellow," in spite of his frigidity. They were *his* friends for ever, and all the harm that had been done his countrymen was attributable alone to their Colombian foes, and not to the colonists. Such were the constant declarations of the Monrovians, as they came, singly and in squads, to visit us after the Trade-Town plunder. T———, in particular, was loud in his protestations of regard ; and such was the earnestness of his manner, that Miguel, by degrees, restored him to confidence.

" Thus, for a while, all things went smoothly, till T——— reached our anchorage, with several passengers in his craft, bound, as they said, to Grand Bassa. As usual on such visits, the whole party dined with Miguel at four in the afternoon, and,

---

* The reader will recollect this is not CANOT's story, but the sailor's.

at six, retired towards their vessel, with a gift of provisions and liquor for their voyage.

"About eight o'clock, a knocking at our gates—closed invariably at dark, according to custom—gave notice that our recent guests had returned. They craved hospitality for the night. They had dallied a couple of hours on the beach, with the hope of getting off, but the surf was so perilous that no Kroomen would venture to convey them through the breakers.

"Such an appeal was, of course, enough for the heart of a courteous Spaniard,—and, on the coast, you know, it is imperative. Miguel opened the door, and, in an instant, fell dead on the threshold, with a ball in his skull. Several guns were discharged, and the house filled with colonists. At the moment of attack I was busy in the *barracoon;* but, as soon as I came forth, the assailants approached in such numbers that I leaped the barriers and hid myself in the forest till discovered by some friendly natives.

"I remained with these Africans several weeks, while a canoe was summoned from Gallinas for my rescue. From thence I sailed to Cuba, and was the first to apprise our owners of the piratical onslaught by which the factory had been destroyed.

"After this, I made several successful voyages to the coast; and, at last, sauntering one evening along the *paséo* at Havana, I met Don Miguel's brother, who, after a sorrowful chat about the tragedy, offered me a quarter-master's berth in a brig he was fitting out for Africa. It was accepted on the spot.

"In a month we were off Mesurado, and cruised for several days from the cape to Grand Bassa, avoiding every square-rigged vessel that loomed above the horizon. At length, we espied a small craft beating down the coast. We bore the stranger company for several hours, till, suddenly taking advantage of her long tack out to sea, we gave chase and cut off her return towards land.

"It was a fine afternoon, and the sun was yet an hour in the sky when we intercepted the schooner. As we ran alongside, I thought I recognized the faces of several who, in days of old, were familiar in our factory,—but what was my surprise, when

T——— himself came to the gangway, and hailed us in Spanish!

" I pointed out the miscreant to my comrade, and, in an instant, he was in our clutches. We let the sun go down before we contrived a proper death for the felon. His five companions, double-ironed, were nailed beneath the hatches in the hold. After this, we riveted the murderer, in chains, to the mainmast, and, for better security, fastened his spread arms to the deck by spikes through his hands. Every sail was then set on the craft, two barrels of tar were poured over the planks, and a brand was thrown in the midst of the combustible materials. For a while, the schooner was held by a hawser till we saw the flames spread from stern to cut-water, and then, with a cheer, *adios!* It was a beautiful sight,—that *auto-da-fé* on the sea, in the darkness!

" My confession, Don Téodor, is over. From that day, I have never been within a church or alongside a *padre;* but I could not die without sending the gold to my sister, and begging a mass in some parish for the rest of my soul! "

I felt very conscious that I was by no means the person to afford ghostly consolation to a dying man under such circumstances, but while I promised to fulfil his request carefully, I could not help inquiring whether he sincerely repented these atrocious deeds?

" Ah! yes, Don Téodor, a thousand times! Many a night, when alone on my watch at sea, or in yonder stockade, marching up and down before the *barracoon*, I have wept like a child for the innocent crew of that little schooner; but, as for the murderer of *Don Miguel*— ! " He stared wildly for a minute into my eyes—shuddered—fell back—was dead!

I have no doubt the outlaw's story contained exaggerations, or fell from a wrecked mind that was drifting into eternity on the current of delirium. I cannot credit his charge against the Monrovian colonists; yet I recount the narrative as an illustration of many a bloody scene that has stained the borders of Africa.

## CHAPTER LXI.

During my first visit to Digby, I promised my trading friends—perhaps rather rashly—that I would either return to their settlement, or, at least, send merchandise and a clerk to establish a factory. This was joyous news for the traffickers, and, accordingly, I embraced an early occasion to despatch, in charge of a clever young sailor, such stuffs as would be likely to tickle the negro taste.

There were two towns at Digby, governed by cousins who had always lived in harmony. My mercantile venture, however, was unhappily destined to be the apple of discord between these relatives. The establishment of so important an institution as a slave-factory within the jurisdiction of the younger savage, gave umbrage to the elder. His town could boast neither of " merchandise " nor a " white man; " there was no profitable tax to be levied from foreign traffic; and, in a very short time, this unlucky partiality ripened the noble kinsmen into bitter enemies.

It is not the habit in Africa for negroes to expend their wrath in harmless words, so that preparations were soon made in each settlement for defence as well as hostility. Both towns were stockaded and carefully watched by sentinels, day and night. At times, forays were made into each other's suburbs, but as the chiefs were equally vigilant and alert, the extent of harm was the occasional capture of women or children, as they wandered to the forest and stream for wood and water.

This dalliance, however, did not suit the ardor of my angry favorite. After wasting a couple of months, he purchased the aid of certain *bushmen*, headed by a notorious scoundrel named Jen-ken, who had acquired renown for his barbarous ferocity throughout the neighborhood. Jen-ken and his chiefs were *cannibals*, and never trod the war-path without a pledge to return laden with human flesh to gorge their households.

Several assaults were made by this savage and his *bushmen* on the dissatisfied cousin, but as they produced no significant results, the barbarians withdrew to the interior. A truce ensued. Friendly proposals were made by the younger to the elder, and again, a couple of months glided by in seeming peace.

Just at this time business called me to Gallinas. On my way thither I looked in at Digby, intending to supply the displeased chieftain with goods and an agent if I found the establishment profitable.

It was sunset when I reached the beach; too late, of course, to land my merchandise, so that I postponed furnishing both places until the morning. As might fairly be expected, there was abundant joy at my advent. The neglected rival was wild with satisfaction at the report that he, too, at length was favored with a "white-man." His "town" immediately became a scene of unbounded merriment. Powder was burnt without stint. Gallons of rum were distributed to both sexes; and dancing, smoking and carousing continued till long after midnight, when all stole off to maudlin sleep.

About three in the morning, the sudden screams of women and children aroused me from profound torpor! Shrieks were followed by volleys of musketry. Then came a loud tattoo of knocks at my door, and appeals from the negro chief to rise and fly. "The town was besieged:—the head-men were on the point of escaping:—resistance was vain:—they had been betrayed:—there were no fighters to defend the stockade!"

I was opening the door to comply with this advice, when my Kroomen, who knew the country's ways even better than I, dissuaded me from departing, with the confident assurance that our assailants were unquestionably composed of the rival townsfolk, who had only temporarily discharged the bushmen to deceive my entertainer. The Kroos insisted that I had nothing to fear. We might, they said, be seized and even imprisoned; but after a brief detention, the captors would be glad enough to accept our ransom. If we fled, we might be slaughtered by mistake.

I had so much confidence in the sense and fidelity of the band that always accompanied me,—partly as boatmen and partly as body guard,—that I experienced very little personal alarm when I heard the shouts as the savages rushed through the town murdering every one they encountered. In a few moments our own door was battered down by the barbarians, and Jen-ken, torch in hand, made his appearance, claiming us as prisoners.

Of course, we submitted without resistance, for although fully armed, the odds were so great in those ante-revolver days, that we would have been overwhelmed by a single wave of the infuriated crowd. The barbarian chief instantly selected our house for his headquarters, and despatched his followers to complete their task. Prisoner after prisoner was thrust in. At times the heavy mash of a war club and the cry of strangling women, gave notice that the work of death was not yet ended. But the night of horror wore away. The gray dawn crept through our hovel's bars, and all was still save the groans of wounded captives, and the wailing of women and children.

By degrees, the warriors dropped in around their chieftain. A *palaver-house*, immediately in front of my quarters, was the general rendezvous; and scarcely a *bushman* appeared without the body of some maimed and bleeding victim. The mangled but living captives were tumbled on a heap in the centre, and soon, every avenue to the square was crowded with exulting savages. Rum was brought forth in abundance for the chiefs. Presently, slowly approaching from a distance, I heard the drums, horns, and war-bells; and, in less than fifteen minutes, a procession of women, whose naked limbs were smeared with chalk and ochre, poured into the palaver-house to join the beastly rites. Each of these devils was armed with a knife, and bore in her hand some cannibal trophy. Jen-ken's wife,—a corpulent wench of forty-five,—dragged along the ground, by a single limb, the

THE MASSACRE AT DIGBY.

slimy corpse of an infant ripped alive from its mother's womb. As her eyes met those of her husband the two fiends yelled forth a shout of mutual joy, while the lifeless babe was tossed in the air and caught as it descended on the point of a spear. Then came the *refreshment*, in the shape of rum, powder, and blood, which was quaffed by the brutes till they reeled off, with linked hands, in a wild dance around the pile of victims. As the women leaped and sang, the men applauded and encouraged. Soon, the ring was broken, and, with a yell, each female leaped on the body of a wounded prisoner and commenced the final sacrifice with the mockery of lascivious embraces!

In my wanderings in African forests I have often seen the tiger pounce upon its prey, and, with instinctive thirst, satiate its appetite for blood and abandon the drained corpse; but these African negresses were neither as decent nor as merciful as the beast of the wilderness. Their malignant pleasure seemed to consist in the invention of tortures, that would agonize but not slay. There was a devilish spell in the tragic scene that fascinated my eyes to the spot. A slow, lingering, tormenting mutilation was practised on the living, as well as on the dead; and, in every instance, the brutality of the women exceeded that of the men. I cannot picture the hellish joy with which they passed from body to body, digging out eyes, wrenching off lips, tearing the ears, and slicing the flesh from the quivering bones; while the queen of the harpies crept amid the butchery gathering the brains from each severed skull as a *bonne bouche* for the approaching feast!

After the last victim yielded his life, it did not require long to kindle a fire, produce the requisite utensils, and fill the air with the odor of *human flesh*. Yet, before the various messes were half broiled, every mouth was tearing the dainty morsels with shouts of joy, denoting the combined satisfaction of revenge and appetite! In the midst of this appalling scene, I heard a fresh cry of exultation, as a pole was borne into the apartment, on which was impaled the living body of the conquered chieftain's wife. A hole was quickly dug, the stave planted and fagots supplied; but before a fire could be kindled the wretched woman was dead, so that the barbarians were defeated in their hellish scheme of burning her alive.

I do not know how long these brutalities lasted, for I remember very little after this last attempt, except that the bushmen packed in plantain leaves whatever flesh was left from the orgie, to be conveyed to their friends in the forest. This was the first time it had been my lot *to behold the most savage development of African nature under the stimulus of war.* The butchery made me sick, dizzy, paralyzed. I sank on the earth benumbed with stupor; nor was I aroused till nightfall, when my Kroomen bore me to the conqueror's town, and negotiated our redemption for the value of twenty slaves.

# CHAPTER LXII.

I HOPE that no one will believe I lingered a moment in Digby, or ever dealt again with its miscreants, after the dreadful catastrophe I have described in the last chapter.    It is true that this tragedy might never have happened within the territory of the rival kinsmen had not the temptations of slave-trade been offered to their passionate natures ; yet the event was so characteristic, not only of slave-war but of indigenous barbarity, that I dared not withhold it in these sketches of my life.

Light was not gleaming over the tops of the forest next morning before I was on the beach ready to embark for Gallinas. But the moon was full, and the surf so high that my boat could not be launched.    Still, so great were my sufferings and disgust that I resolved to depart at all hazards ; and divesting myself of my outer garments, I stepped into a native canoe with one man only to manage it, and dashed through the breakers.    Our provisions consisted of three bottles of gin, a jug of water, and a basket of raw cassava, while a change of raiment and my accounts were packed in an air-tight keg.    Rough as was the sea, we succeeded in reaching the neighborhood of Gallinas early next morning.    My Spanish friends on shore soon detected me with their excellent telescopes, by my well-known cruising dress of red flannel shirt and Panama hat ; but, instead of running to the beach with a welcome, they hoisted the black flag, which is ever a signal of warning to slavers.

My Krooman at once construed the telegraphic despatch as an intimation that the surf was impassable. Indeed, the fact was visible enough even to an uninstructed eye, as we approached the coast. For miles along the bar at the river's mouth, the breakers towered up in tall masses, whitening the whole extent of beach with foam. As our little canoe rose on the top of the swell, outside the rollers, I could see my friends waving their hats towards the southward, as if directing my movements towards Cape Mount.

In my best days on the coast I often swam in perilous seasons a far greater distance than that which intervened betwixt my boat and the shore. My companions at Gallinas well knew my dexterity in the water, and I could not comprehend, therefore, why they forbade my landing, with so much earnestness. In fact, their zeal somewhat nettled me, and I began to feel that dare-devil resistance which often goads us to acts of madness which make us heroes if successful, but fools if we fail.

It was precisely this temper that determined me to hazard the bar; yet, as I rose on my knees to have a better view of the approaching peril, I saw the black flag thrice lowered in token of adieu. Immediately afterward it was again hoisted *over the effigy of an enormous shark !*

In a twinkling, I understood the *real* cause of danger, which no alacrity or courage in the water could avoid, and comprehended that my only hope was in the open sea. A retreat to Cape Mount was a toilsome task for my weary *Krooman*, who had been incessantly at work for twenty-four hours. Yet, there were but two alternatives,—either to await the subsidence of the surf, or the arrival of some friendly vessel. In the mean time, I eat my last morsel of cassava, while the *Krooman* stretched himself in the bottom of the canoe,—half in the water and half in the glaring sun,—and went comfortably to sleep.

I steered the boat with a paddle, as it drifted along with tide and current, till the afternoon, when a massive pile of clouds in the south-east gave warning of one of those tornadoes which deluge the coast of Africa in the months of March and April. A stout punch in the Krooman's ribs restored him to consciousness from his hydropathic sleep; but he shivered as he looked at the sky and beheld a token of that greatest misfortune that can befall a negro,—a wet skin at sea from a shower of rain.

We broached our last bottle to battle the chilling element. Had we been in company with other canoes, our first duty would have been to lash the skiffs together so as to breast the gusts and chopping sea with more security; but as I was entirely alone, our sole reliance was on the expert arm and incessant vigilance of my companion.

I will not detain the reader by explaining the simple process that carried us happily through the deluge. By keeping the canoe bow on, we nobly resisted the shock of every wave, and gradually fell back under the impulse of each undulation. Thus we held on till the heavy clouds discharged their loads, beating down the sea and half filling the canoe with rain water. While the Krooman paddled and steered, I conducted the bailing, and as the African dipper was not sufficient to keep us free, I pressed my Panama hat into service as an extra hand.

These savage squalls on the African coast, at the beginning of the rainy season, are of short duration, so that our anxiety quickly left us to the enjoyment of soaking skins. A twist at my red flannel relieved it of superabundant moisture, but as the negro delighted in no covering except his flesh, an additional kiss of the bottle was the only comfort I could bestow on his shivering limbs.

This last dram was our forlorn hope, but it only created a passing comfort, which soon went off leaving our bodies more chill and dejected than before. My head swam with feverish emptiness. I seemed suddenly possessed by a feeling of wild independence—seeing nothing, fearing nothing. Presently, this died away, and I fell back in utter helplessness, wholly benumbed.

I do not remember how long this stupor lasted, but I was aroused by the Krooman with the report of a land breeze, and a sail which he declared to be a cruiser. It cost me considerable effort to shake off my lethargy, nor do I know whether I would have succeeded had there not been a medical magic in the idea of a man-of-war, which flashed athwart my mind a recollection of the slave accounts in our keg!

I had hardly time to throw the implement overboard before the craft was within hail; but instead of a cruiser she turned out to be a slaver, destined, like myself, for Gallinas. A warm welcome awaited me in the cabin, and a comfortable bed with plenty of blankets restored me for a while to health, though in all likelihood my perilous flight from Digby and its horrors, will ache rheumatically in my limbs till the hour of my death.

It was well that I did not venture through the breakers on the day that the dead shark was hoisted *in terrorem* as a telegraph. Such was the swarm of these monsters in the surf of Gallinas, that more than a hundred slaves had been devoured by them in attempting a shipment a few nights before!

# CHAPTER LXIII.

"Don Pedro Blanco had left Gallinas,—a retired *millionnaire!*"
When I heard this announcement at the factory, I could with
difficulty restrain the open expression of my sorrow.  It confirmed me in a desire that for some time had been strengthening
in my mind.  Years rolled over my head since, first of all, I
plunged accidentally into the slave trade. My passion for a roving
life and daring adventure was decidedly cooled.  The late barbarities inflicted on the conquered in a war of which I was the involuntary cause, appalled me with the traffic; and humanity called
louder and louder than ever for the devotion of my remaining
days to honest industry.

As I sailed down the coast to restore a child to his father,—
the King of Cape Mount,—I was particularly charmed with the
bold promontory, the beautiful lake, and the lovely islands, that
are comprised in this enchanting region.  When I delivered the
boy to his parent, the old man's gratitude knew no bounds for
his offspring's redemption from slavery.  Every thing was tendered for my recompense; and, as I seemed especially to enjoy the
delicious scenery of his realm, he offered me its best location as a
gift, if I desired to abandon the slave trade and establish a *lawful* factory.

I made up my mind on the spot that the day should come
when I would be lord and master of Cape Mount; and, nestling
under the lee of its splendid headland, might snap my fingers at

the cruisers.   Still I could not, at once, retreat from my establishment at New Sestros.   Don Pedro's departure was a sore disappointment, because it left my accounts unliquidated and my release from the trade dependent on circumstances.   Nevertheless,
I resolved to risk his displeasure by quitting the factory for a
time, and visiting him at Havana after a trip to England.

----

It was in the summer of 1839 that I arranged my affairs for
a long absence, and sailed for London in the schooner Gil Blas.
We had a dull passage till we reached the chops of the British
Channel, whence a smart south-wester drove us rapidly towards our
destination.

Nine at night was just striking from the clocks of Dover when
a bustle on deck, a tramping of feet, a confused sound of alarm,
orders, obedience and anxiety, was followed by a tremendous crash
which prostrated me on the cabin floor, whence I bounded, with a
single spring, to the deck.   "A steamer had run us down ! "
Aloft, towered a huge black wall, while the intruder's cut-water
pressed our tiny craft almost beneath the tide.   There was no
time for deliberation.   The steamer's headway was stopped.   The
Gil Blas, like her scapegrace godfather, was in peril of sinking;
and as the wheels began to revolve and clear the steamer from
our wreck, every one scrambled in the best way he could on board
the destroyer.

Our reception on this occasion by the British lion was not
the most respectful or hospitable that might be imagined.   In fact,
no notice was taken of us by these " hearts of oak," till a clever
Irish soldier, who happened to be journeying to Dublin, invited
us to the forward cabin.   Our mate, however, would not listen to
the proposal, and hastening to the quarter-deck, coarsely upbraided the steamer's captain with his misconduct, and demanded suitable accommodations for his wounded commander and passengers.

In a short time the captain of the Gil Blas and I were conducted to the "gentlemen's cabin," and as I was still clad in the

thin cotton undress in which I was embarking for the land of dreams, when the accident occurred, a shirt and trowsers were handed me fresh from the slop-shop. When my native servant appeared in the cabin, a shower of coppers greeted him from the passengers.

Next morning we were landed at Cowes, and as the steward claimed the restitution of a pair of slippers in which I had encased my toes, I was forced to greet the loyal earth of England with bare feet as well as uncovered head. Our sailors, however, were better off. In the forecastle they had fallen into the hands of Samaritans. A profusion of garments was furnished for all their wants, while a subscription, made up among the soldiers and women, supplied them with abundance of coin for their journey to London.

---

An economical life in Africa, and a series of rather profitable voyages, enabled me to enjoy my wish to see London, "above stairs as well as below."

I brought with me from Africa a body servant named Lunes, an active youth, whose idea of city-life and civilization had been derived exclusively from glimpses of New Sestros and Gallinas. I fitted him out on my arrival in London as a fashionable "tiger," with red waistcoat, corduroy smalls, blue jacket and gold band; and trotted him after me wherever I went in search of diversion. It may be imagined that I was vastly amused by the odd remarks and the complete amazement, with which this savage greeted every object of novelty or interest. After he became somewhat acquainted with the streets of London, Lunes occasionally made explorations on his own account, yet he seldom came back without a tale that showed the African to have been quite as much a curiosity to the cockneys as the cockneys were to the darkey.

It happened just at this time that "Jim Crow" was the rage at one of the minor theatres, and as I felt interested to know how the personification would strike the boy, I sent him one night to the gallery with orders to return as soon as the piece was concluded. But the whole night passed without the appearance of my valet. Next morning I became anxious about his fate, and, after waiting in vain till noon, I employed a reliable officer to search for the negro, without disclosing the fact of his servitude.

In the course of a few hours poor Lunes was brought to me in a most desolate condition. His clothes were in rags, and his gold-lace gone. It appeared that " Jim Crow " had outraged his sense of African character so greatly that he could not restrain his passion ; but vented it in the choicest *billingsgate* with which his vocabulary had been furnished in the forecastle of the " Gil Blas." His criticism of the real Jim was by no means agreeable to the patrons of the fictitious one. In a moment there was a row ; and the result was, that Lunes after a thorough dilapidation of his finery, departed in custody of the police, more, however, for the negro's protection than his chastisement.

The loss of his dashing waistcoat, and the sound thrashing he received at the hands of a London mob while asserting the dignity of his country, and a night in the station house, spoiled my boy's opinion of Great Britain. I could not induce him afterwards to stir from the house without an escort, nor would he believe that every policeman was not specially on the watch to apprehend him. I was so much attached to the fellow, and his sufferings became so painful, that I resolved to send him back to Africa ; nor shall I ever forget his delight when my decision was announced. The negro's joy, however, was incomprehensible to my fellow-lodgers, and especially to the gentle dames, who could not believe that an African, whose liberty was assured in England, would *voluntarily* return to Africa and slavery !

One evening, just before his departure, Lunes was sternly tried on this subject in my presence in the parlor, yet nothing could make him revoke his trip to the land of palm-trees and *malaria*. London was too cold for him ;—he hated stockings ;— shoes were an abomination !

" Yet, tell me, Lunes," said one of the most bewitching of my fair friends,—" how is it that you go home to be a slave, when you may remain in London as a freeman ? "

I will repeat his answer—divested of its native gibberish :

" Yes, Madam, I go—because I like my country best; if I

am to be a slave or work, I want to do so for a true *Spaniard*. I don't like this thing, Miss,"—pointing to his shirt collar,—" it cuts my ears ;—I don't like this thing "—pointing to his trowsers; " I like my country's fashion better than yours ; "—and, taking out a large handkerchief, he gave the inquisitive dame a rapid demonstration of African economy in concealing nakedness, by twisting it round those portions of the human frame which modesty is commonly in the habit of hiding !

There was a round of applause and a blaze of blushes at this extemporaneous pantomime, which Lunes concluded with the assurance that he especially loved his master, because, —" when he grew to be a proper man, I would give him plenty of wives !"

I confess that my valet's philanthropic audience was not exactly prepared for this edifying culmination in favor of Africa ; but, while my friends were busy in obliterating the red and the wrinkles from their cheeks, I took the liberty to enjoy, from behind the shadow of my tea cup, the manifest disgust they felt for the bad taste of poor Lunes !

## CHAPTER LXIV.

By this time my curiosity was not only satiated by the diversions of the great metropolis, but I had wandered off to the country and visited the most beautiful parts of the islands. Two months thus slipped by delightfully in Great Britain when a sense of duty called me to Havana; yet, before my departure, I resolved, if possible, to secure the alliance of some opulent Englishman to aid me in the foundation and maintenance of lawful commerce at Cape Mount. Such a person I found in Mr. George Clevering Redman, of London, who owned the Gil Blas, which, with two other vessels, he employed in trade between England and Africa.

I had been introduced to this worthy gentleman as " a lawful trader on the coast," still, as I did not think that business relations ought to exist between us while he was under so erroneous an impression, I seized an early opportunity to unmask myself. At the same time, I announced my unalterable resolution to abandon a slaver's life for ever; to establish a trading post at some fortunate location; and, while I recounted the friendship and peculiar bonds between the king and myself, offered to purchase Cape Mount from its African proprietor, if such an enterprise should be deemed advisable.

Redman was an enterprising merchant. He heard my proposal with interest, and, after a few days' consideration, assented to a negotiation, as soon as I gave proofs of having abandoned the slave traffic for ever. It was understood that no contract was to be entered into, or document signed, till I was at liberty to withdraw completely from Don Pedro Blanco and all others concerned with him. This accomplished, I was to revisit England and assume my lawful functions.

----

When I landed in the beautiful Queen of the Antilles I found Don Pedro in no humor to accede to these philanthropic notions. The veteran slaver regarded me, no doubt, as a sort of cross between a fool and zealot. An American vessel had been recently chartered to carry a freight to the coast; and, accordingly, instead of receiving a release from servitude, I was ordered on board the craft as supercargo of the enterprise! In fact, on the third day after my arrival at Havana, I was forced to re-embark for the coast without a prospect of securing my independence.

The reader may ask why I did not burst the bond, and free myself at a word from a commerce with which I was disgusted? The question is *natural*—but the reply is *human*. I had too large an unliquidated interest at New Sestros, and while it remained so, I was not entitled to demand from my employer a final settlement for my years of labor. In other words *I was in his power*, so far as my means were concerned, and my services were too valuable to be surrendered by him voluntarily.

A voyage of forty-two days brought me once more to New Sestros, accompanied by a couple of negro women, who paid their passage and were lodged very comfortably in the steerage. The elder was about forty and extremely corpulent, while her companion was younger as well as more comely.

This respectable dame, after an absence of twenty-four years, returned to her native Gallinas, on a visit to her father, king Shiakar. At the age of fifteen, she had been taken prisoner and sent to Havana. A Cuban confectioner purchased the likely girl, and, for many years, employed her in hawking his cakes and pies. In time she became a favorite among the townsfolk, and, by degrees, managed to accumulate a sufficient amount to purchase her freedom. Years of frugality and thrift made her proprietor of a house in the city and an egg-stall in the market, when chance threw in her way a cousin, lately imported from Africa, who gave her news of her father's family. A quarter of a century had not extinguished the natural fire in this negro's heart, and she immediately resolved to cross the Atlantic and behold once more the savage to whom she owed her birth.

I sent these adventurous women to Gallinas by the earliest trader that drifted past New Sestros, and learned that they were welcomed among the islands with all the ceremony common among Africans on such occasions. Several canoes were despatched to the vessel, with flags, tom-toms, and horns, to receive and welcome the ladies. On the shore, a procession was formed, and a bullock offered to the captain in token of gratitude for his attention.

When her elder brother was presented to the retired egg-merchant, he extended his arms to embrace his kinswoman; but, to the amazement of all, she drew back with a mere offer of her hand, refusing every demonstration of affection *till he should appear dressed with becoming decency.* This rebuke, of course, kept the rest of her relatives at bay, for there was a sad deficiency of trowsers in the gang, and it was the indispensable garment that caused so unsisterly a reception.

But Shiakar's daughter, travelled as she was, could neither set the fashions nor reform the tastes of Gallinas. After a sojourn of ten days, she bade her kindred an eternal adieu, and returned to Havana, disgusted with the manners and customs of her native land.

# CHAPTER LXV.

ON my return to New Sestros, I found that the colonial authorities of Liberia had been feeling the pulse of my African friend,
Freeman, in order to secure the co-operation of that distinguished
personage in the suppression of the slave traffic.  Freeman professed his willingness to conclude a treaty of commerce and
amity with Governor Buchanan, but respectfully declined to
molest the factories within his domain.

Still, Buchanan was not to be thwarted by a single refusal,
and enlisted the sympathy of an officer in command of a United
States cruiser, who accompanied the governor to the anchorage
at New Sestros.  As soon as these personages reached their destination, a note was despatched to the negro potentate, desiring
him to expel from his territory all Spaniards who were possessed
of factories.  To this, it is said, the chief returned a short and
tart rebuke for the interference with his independence ; whereupon the following singular missive was immediately delivered
to the Spaniards :—

"U. S. BRIG DOLPHIN,
"NEW SESTROS, *March* 6, 1840.

" SIR :

"I address you in consequence of having received a
note from you a few evenings since ; but I wish it to be under-

stood that this communication is intended for all or any persons who are now in New Sestros, engaged in the slave-trade.

" I have received information that you now have, in your establishments on shore, several hundred negroes confined in barracoons, waiting for an opportunity to ship them. Whether you are Americans, English, French, Spaniards, or Portuguese, you are acting in violation of the established laws of your respective countries, and, therefore, are not entitled to any protection from your governments. You have placed yourselves beyond the protection of any civilized nation, as you are engaged in a traffic which has been made *piracy* by most of the Christian nations of the world.

" As I have been sent by my government to root out, if possible, this traffic on and near our settlements on the coast, I must now give you notice, that you must break up your establishment at this point, in two weeks from this date; failing to do so, I shall take such measures as I conceive necessary to attain this object. I will thank you to send a reply to this communication immediately, stating your intentions, and also sending an account of the number of slaves you have on hand.

" I am, &c., &c., &c.,

" CHARLES R. BELL,

"*Lieut. Com. U. S. Naval Forces, Coast of Africa.*

"To Mr. A. DEMER and others,

   "NEW SESTROS, *Coast of Africa.*"

I do not know what reply was made to this communication, as a copy was not retained; but when my clerk handed me the original letter from Lieutenant Bell, on my arrival from Cuba I lost no time in forwarding the following answer to Col. Hicks, at Monrovia, to be despatched by him to the American officer :

"To CHARLES R. BELL, ESQ.,

" *Lieut. Com. of the U. S. Forces, Coast of Africa, Monrovia.*

"NEW SESTROS, *April* 2, 1840.

" SIR :

" Your letter of the 6th March, directed to the white residents of New Sestros, was handed me on my return to this country, and I am sorry I can make but the following short answer.

" First, sir, you seem to assume a supremacy over the most civilized nations of the world, and, under the doubtful pretext of your nation's authority, threaten to land and destroy our property on these neutral shores.  Next, you are pleased to inform us that all Christian nations have declared the slave-trade *piracy*, and that we are not entitled to any protection from our government.  Why, then, do the Southern States of your great confederacy allow slavery, public auctions, transportation from one State to another,—not only of civilized black native subjects, —but of nearly white, American, Christian citizens ?  Such is the case in your free and independent country ; and, though the slave trade is carried on in the United States of America with more brutality than in any other colony, I still hope you are a Christian !

" To your third article, wherein you observe, having " been sent by your government to root out this traffic, if possible, near your own settlements on the coast,"—allow me to have my doubts of such orders.  Your government could not have issued them without previously making them publicly known ;—and, permit me to say, those Christian nations you are pleased to mention, are not aware that your nation had set up colonies on the coast of Africa.  They were always led to believe that these Liberian settlements were nothing but Christian beneficial societies, humanely formed by private philanthropists, to found a refuge for the poor blacks born in America, who cannot be protected in their native country by the free and independent laws and institutions of the United States.

" If my argument cannot convince you that you are not justified in molesting a harmless people on these desolate shores, allow me to inform you that, should you put your threats in execution and have the advantage over us, many factories would suffer by your unjust attack, which would give them an indisputable right to claim high damages from your government.

" Most of the white residents here, are, and have been, friendly to Americans at large ; some have been educated in your country, and it would be the saddest day of their lives, if obliged to oppose by force of arms the people of a nation they love as much as their own countrymen. The undersigned, in particular, would wish to observe that the same spirit that led him to avenge Governor Findley's murder, will support him in defence of his property, though much against his inclination.

> " I remain, very respectfully,
>> " Your obedient servant,
>>> " THEODORE CANOT."

This diplomatic encounter terminated the onslaught. Buchanan, who was over hasty with military display on most occasions, made a requisition for volunteers to march against New Sestros. But the troops were never set in motion. In the many years of my residence in the colonial neighborhood, this was the only occasion that menaced our friendship or verged upon hostilities.

———

Whilst I was abroad in England and Cuba, my *chargé d'affaires* at New Sestros sent off a cargo of three hundred negroes, nearly all of whom were safely landed in the West Indies, bringing us a profit of nine thousand dollars. There were, however, still one hundred and fifty in our *barracoons* to be shipped; and, as the cargo from the Crawford was quickly exchanged with the natives for more slaves, in two months' time, I found my pens surcharged with six hundred human beings. Two other neighboring factories were also crammed; while, unfortunately, directly in front of us, a strong reinforcement of British men-of war kept watch and ward to prevent our depletion.

No slaver dared show its topsails above the horizon. The season did not afford us supplies from the interior. Very few coasters looked in at New Sestros; and, as our stock of grain and provisions began to fail, the horrors of famine became the sole topic of conversation among our alarmed factors.

It will readily be supposed that every effort was made, not only to economize our scanty stores, but to increase them through the intervention of boats that were sent far and wide to scour the coast for rice and cassava.  Double and triple prices were offered for these articles, yet our agents returned without the required supplies.  In fact, the free natives themselves were in danger of starvation, and while they refused to part with their remnants, even under the temptation of luxuries, they sometimes sent deputations to my settlement in search of food.

By degrees I yielded to the conviction that I must diminish my mouths.  First of all, I released the old and feeble from the *barracoon*.  This, for a few days, afforded ample relief; but, as I retained only the staunchest, the remaining appetites speedily reduced our rations to a single meal *per diem*.  At last, the steward reported, that even this allowance could be continued for little more than a week.  In twelve days, at farthest, my resources would be utterly exhausted.

In this extremity I summoned a council of neighboring chiefs, and exposing my situation, demanded their opinion as to a fitting course on the dreaded day.  I had resolved to retain my blacks till the last measure was distributed, and then to liberate them to shift for themselves.

But the idea of releasing six hundred famishing foemen struck the beach people with horror.  It would, they said, be a certain source of war and murder; and they implored me not to take such a step till they made every effort to ease my burden.  As a beginning, they proposed at once relieving the *barracoon* of a large portion of females and of all the male youths, who were to be fed and guarded by them, on my account, till better times.

By this system of colonizing I got rid of the support of two hundred and twenty-five negroes; and, as good luck would have it, a visit from a friendly coaster enabled me, within ten days, to exchange my beautiful cutter "Ruth" for a cargo of rice from the colony at Cape Palmas.

It was fortunate that in a week after this happy relief the

British cruisers left our anchorage for a few days. No sooner were they off, than a telegraph of smoke, which, in those days, was quite as useful on the African coast, as the electric is on ours, gave notice to the notorious " Volador." There was joy in the teeming factories when her signal was descried in the offing ; and, before the following dawn, seven hundred and forty-nine human beings, packed within her one hundred and sixty-five tons, were on their way to Cuba.

*This was the last cargo of slaves I ever shipped !*

# CHAPTER LXVI.

WHEN the thought struck me of abandoning the slave-trade, and I had resolved to follow out the good impulse, I established a store in the neighborhood of my old *barracoons* with the design of trafficking in the produce of industry alone. This concern was intrusted to the management of a clever young colonist.

It was about this time that the British brig of war Termagant held New Sestros in permanent blockade, forbidding even a friendly boat to communicate with my factory. Early one morning I was called to witness a sturdy chase between my scolding foe and a small sail which was evidently running for the shore in order to save her crew by beaching. The British bull dog, however, was not to be deterred by the perils of the surf; and, holding on with the tenacity of fate, pursued the stranger, till he discovered that a large reinforcement of armed natives was arrayed on the strand ready to protect the fugitives. Accordingly, the Englishmen refrained from assailing the mariners, and confined their revenge to the destruction of the craft.

As this affray occurred within gunshot of my lawful factory, I hastened to the beach under the belief that some of my *employés* had unluckily fallen into a difficulty with the natives. But on my arrival I was greeted by a well-known emissary from our headquarters at Gallinas, who bore a missive imparting the Volador's arrival in Cuba with six hundred and eleven of her people. The letter furthermore apprised me that Don Pedro, who persisted in sending merchandise to my slave factory, still declined my resignation as his agent, but acknowledged a credit in his chest of thirteen thousand dollars for my commissions on the Volador's slaves.  Here, then, were Confidence and Temptation, both resolutely proffered to lure me back to my ancient habits !

I was busily engaged on the sands, enforcing from the negroes a restitution of clothes to the plundered postman, when the crack of a cannon, higher up the beach, made me fear that an aggression was being committed against my homestead.    Before I could depart, however, two more shots in the same quarter, left me no room to doubt that the Termagant was talking most shrewishly with my factory at New Sestros.

I reached the establishment with all convenient speed, only to find it full of natives, who had been brought to the spot from the interior by the sound of a cannonade.  The following letter from the captain of the man-of-war, it seems, had been landed in a fishing canoe very soon after my departure in the morning, and the shots, I suppose, were discharged to awake my attention to its contents.

> "HER BRITANNIC MAJESTY'S SHIP TERMAGANT,
> "*Off* NEW SESTROS, *Nov.* 5, 1840.

" SIR :

" The natives or Kroomen of your settlement having this day fired on the boats of Her B. M. ship under my command, while in chase of a Spanish boat with seven men going to New Sestros, I therefore demand the persons who fired on the boats, to answer for the same; and, should this demand not be complied with, I shall take such steps as I deem proper to secure satisfaction.

" I have addressed you on this occasion, judging by the interference of those blacks in your behalf, that they are instigated by you.

" I have the honor to be, sir, your obed't serv't,

> " H. F. SEAGRAM,
> " *Lieut. Com.*

"To MR. T. CANOT,
    NEW SESTROS."

When this cartel fell into my hands it lacked but an hour of sunset.  The beach was alive with angry rollers, while the Termagant was still under easy sail, hovering up and down the coast before my factory, evidently meditating the propriety of another pill to provoke my notice.

I sat down at once and wrote a sort of model response, promising to come on board bodily next morning to satisfy the lieutenant of my innocence; but when I inquired for a Mercury to bear my message, there was not a Krooman to be found willing to face either the surf or the British sailor.  Accordingly, there was no alternative but to suffer my bamboo *barracoons* and factory to be blown about my ears by the English vixen, or to face the danger, in person, and become the bearer of my own message.

The proposal sounded oddly enough in the ears of the Kroomen, who, in spite of their acquaintance with my hardihood, could scarcely believe I would thrust my head into the very jaws of the lion.  Still, they had so much confidence in the judgment displayed by white men on the coast, that I had little difficulty in engaging the boat and services of a couple of sturdy chaps; and, stripping to my drawers, so as to be ready to swim in the last emergency, I committed myself to their care.

We passed the dangerous surf in safety, and in a quarter of an hour were alongside the Termagant, whose jolly lieutenant could not help laughing at the drenched *uniform* in which I saluted him at the gangway.  Slaver as I was, he did not deny me the rites of hospitality.  Dry raiment and a consoling glass were speedily supplied; and with the reassured stamina of my improved condition, it may readily be supposed I was not long in satisfying the worthy Mr. Seagram that I had no concern in the encounter betwixt the natives and his boats.  To clinch the argument I assured the lieutenant that I was not only guiltless of the assault, *but had made up my mind irrevocably to abandon the slave trade!*

I suppose there was as much rejoicing that night on board the Termagant over the redeemed slaver, as there is in most churches over a rescued sinner.  It was altogether too late and too dark for me to repeat the perils of the surf and sharks, so that I willingly accepted the offer of a bed, and promised to accompany Seagram in the morning to the prince.

Loud were the shouts of amazement and fear when the negroes saw me landing next day, side by side, in pleasant chat, with an officer, who, eighteen hours before, had been busy about my destruction. It was beyond their comprehension how an Englishman could visit my factory under such circumstances, nor could they divine how I escaped, after my voluntary surrender on board a cruiser. When the prince saw Seagram seated familiarly under my verandah, he swore that I must have some powerful *fetiche* or *juju* to compel the confidence of enemies; but his wonder became unbounded when the officer proposed his entire abandonment of the slave trade, *and I supported the lieutenant's proposal!*

I have hardly ever seen a man of any hue or character, so sorely perplexed as our African was by this singular suggestion. To stop the slave trade, unless by compulsion, was, in his eyes, the absolute abandonment of a natural appetite or function. At first, he believed we were joking. It was inconceivable that I, who for years had carried on the traffic so adroitly, could be serious in the idea. For half an hour the puzzled negro walked up and down the verandah, muttering to himself, stopping, looking at both of us, hesitating, and laughing,—till at last, as he afterwards confessed, he concluded that I was only "*deceiving the Englishman*," and came forward with an offer to sign a treaty on the spot for the extinction of the traffic.

Now the reader must bear in mind that I allowed the prince to mislead himself through his natural duplicity on this occasion, as I was thereby enabled to bring him again in contact with Seagram, and secure the support of British officers for my own purposes.

In a few days the deed was done. The slave trade at New Sestros was formally and for ever abolished by the prince and myself. As I was the principal mover in the affair, I voluntarily surrendered to the British officer on the day of signature, one hundred slaves; *in return for which I was guarantied the safe removal of my valuable merchandise and property from the settlement.*

It was a very short time after I had made all snug at New Sestros that misfortune fell suddenly on our parent nest at Gallinas. The Hon. Joseph Denman, who was senior officer of the British squadron on the coast, unexpectedly landed two hundred men, and burnt or destroyed all the Spanish factories amid the lagunes and islets. By this uncalculated act of violence, the natives of the neighborhood were enabled to gorge themselves with property that was valued, I understand, at a very large sum. An event like this could not escape general notice along the African coast, and in a few days I began to hear it rumored and discussed among the savages in *my* vicinity.

For a while it was still a mystery why *I* escaped while Gallinas fell; but at length the sluggish mind of Prince Freeman began to understand my diplomacy, and, of course, to repent the sudden contract that deprived him of a right to rob me. Vexed by disappointment, the scoundrel assembled his minor chiefs, and named a day during which he knew the Termagant would be absent, to plunder and punish me for my interference with the welfare and " institutions " of his country. The hostile meeting took place without my knowledge, though it was disclosed to all my domestics, whose silence the prince had purchased. Indeed, I would have been completely surprised and cut off, *had it not been for the friendly warning of the negro whose life 1 had saved from the saucy-wood ordeal.*

I still maintained in my service five white men, and four sailors who were wrecked on the coast and awaited a passage home. With this party and a few household negroes on whom reliance might be placed, I resolved at once to defend my quarters. My cannons were loaded, guards placed, muskets and cartridges distributed, and even the domestics supplied with weapons ; yet, on the very night after the warning, every slave abandoned my premises, while even Lunes himself,—the companion of my journey to London, and pet of the ladies,—decamped with my favorite fowling piece.

When I went my rounds next morning, I was somewhat disheartened by appearances ; but my spirits were quickly restored by the following letter from Seagram :

"HER B. M. BRIG TERMAGANT, OFF TRADE-TOWN,
*23d January,* 1841.

" Sir,

" In your letter of yesterday, you request protection for your property, and inform me that you are in danger from the princes. I regret, indeed, that such should be the case, more especially as they have pledged me their words, and signed a *" book "* to the effect that they would never again engage in the slave traffic. But, *as I find you have acted in good faith since I commenced to treat with you on the subject,* I shall afford you every assistance in my power, and will land an armed party of twenty men before daylight on Monday.

" I am, Sir, your obt. servt.,

" H. F. SEAGRAM, Lieut. Com'g."

The Termagant's unlooked-for return somewhat dismayed the prince and his ragamuffins, though he had contrived to assemble quite two thousand men about my premises. Towards noon, however, there were evident signs of impatience for the expected booty ; still, a wholesome dread of my cannon and small-arms, together with the cruiser's presence, prevented an open attack. After a while I perceived an attempt to set my stockade on fire, and as a conflagration would have given a superb opportunity to rob, I made the concerted signal for our British ally. In a twinkling, three of the cruiser's boats landed an officer with twenty-five musketeers, and before the savages could make the slightest show of resistance, I was safe under the bayonets of Saint George!

It is needless to set forth the details of my rescue. The prince and his poltroons were panic-struck ; and in three or four days my large stock of powder and merchandise was embarked without loss for Monrovia.

# CHAPTER LXVII.

My *barracoons* and trading establishments were now totally destroyed, and I was once more afloat in the world. It immediately occurred to me that no opportunity would, perhaps, be more favorable to carry out my original designs upon Cape Mount, and when I sounded Seagram on the subject, he was not only willing to carry me there in his cruiser, but desired to witness my treaty with the prince for a cession of territory.

Our adieus to New Sestros were not very painful, and on the evening of the same day the Termagant hove to off the bold and beautiful hills of Cape Mount. As the breeze and sun sank together, leaving a brilliant sky in the west, we descried from deck a couple of tall, raking masts relieved like cobwebs against the azure. From aloft, still more of the craft was visible, and from our lieutenant's report after a glance through his glass, there could be no doubt that the stranger was a slaver.

Light as was the breeze, not a moment elapsed before the cruiser's jib was turned towards her natural enemy. For a while an ebb from the river and the faint night wind off shore, forced us seaward, yet at daylight we had gained so little on the chase, that she was still full seven miles distant.

They who are familiar with naval life will appreciate the annoying suspense on the Termagant when dawn revealed the calm sea, quiet sky, and tempting but unapproachable prize. The well-known *pluck* of our British tars was fired by the alluring vision, and nothing was heard about decks but prayers for a puff and whistling for a breeze. Meanwhile, Seagram, the surgeon, and purser were huddled together on the quarter, cursing a calm which deprived them of prize-money if not of promotion. Our master's-mate and passed midshipman were absent in some of the brig's boats cruising off Gallinas or watching the roadstead of New Sestros.

The trance continued till after breakfast, when our officers' impatience could no longer withstand the bait, and, though short of efficient boats, the yawl and lieutenant's gig were manned for a hazardous enterprise. The former was crammed with six sailors, two marines, and a supernumerary mate; while the gig, a mere fancy craft, was packed with five seamen and four marines under Seagram himself. Just as this flotilla shoved off, a rough boatswain begged leave to fit out my nutshell of a native canoe; and embarking with a couple of Kroomen, he squatted amidships, armed with a musket and cutlass !

This expedition exhausted our stock of *nautical* men so completely, that as Seagram crossed the gangway he commended the purser and surgeon to *my care, and left Her Majesty's brig in charge of the reformed slaver !*

No sooner did the chase perceive our manœuvre, than, running in her sweeps, she hoisted a Spanish flag and fired a warning cartridge. A faint hurrah answered the challenge, while our argonauts kept on their way, till, from deck, they became lost below the horizon. Presently, however, the boom of another gun, followed by repeated discharges, rolled through the quiet air from the Spaniard, and the look-out aloft reported our boats in retreat. Just at this moment, a light breeze gave headway to the Termagant, so that I was enabled to steer towards the prize, but before I could overhaul our warriors, the enemy had received the freshening gale, and, under every stitch of canvas, stood rapidly to sea.

When Seagram regained his deck, he was bleeding profusely from a wound in the head received from a handspike while at tempting to board. Besides this, two men were missing, while three had been seriously wounded by a shot that sunk the yawl. My gallant boatswain, however, returned unharmed, and, if I may believe the commander of the " Serea,"—whom I encountered some time after,—this daring sailor did more execution with his musket than all the marines put together. The *Kroo* canoe dashed alongside with the velocity of her class, and, as a petty officer on the Spaniard bent over to sink the skiff with a ponder-ous top-block, our boatswain cleft his skull with a musket-ball, and brought home the block as a trophy !  In fact, Seagram con-fessed that the Spaniard behaved magnanimously; for the moment our yawl was sunk, Olivares cut adrift his boat, and bade the struggling swimmers return in it to their vessel.

I have described this little affray not so much for its interest, but because it illustrates the vicissitudes of coast-life and the ra-pidity of their occurrence.  Here was I, on the deck of a British man-of-war, in charge of her manœuvres while in chase of a Span-iard, who, for aught I knew, might have been consigned to me for slaves !  I gave my word to Seagram as he embarked, to manage his ship, and had I attained a position that would have enabled me to sink the " Serea," I would not have shrunk from my duty.  Yet it afforded me infinite satisfaction to see the chase escape, for my heart smote me at taking arms against men who had probably broken bread at my board.

# CHAPTER LXVIII.

NEXT day we recovered our anchorage opposite Cape Mount, and wound our way eight or ten miles up the river to the town of Toso, which was honored with the residence of King Fana-Toro. It did not require long to satisfy his majesty of the benefits to be derived from my plan. The news of the destruction of Gallinas, and of the voluntary surrender of my quarters at New Sestros, had spread like wildfire along the coast; so that when the African princes began to understand they were no longer to profit by unlawful traffic, they were willing enough not to lose *all* their ancient avails, by compromising for a *legal* commerce, under the sanction of national flags. I explained my projects to Fana-Toro in the fullest manner, offering him the most liberal terms. My propositions were forcibly supported by Prince Gray; and a cession of the Mount and its neighboring territory was finally made, under a stipulation that the purchase-money should be paid in presence of the negro's council, and the surrender of title witnessed by the Termagant's officers.[1]

---

[1] As the document granting this beautiful headland and valuable trading post is of some interest, I have added a copy of the instrument:

"KNOW ALL MEN BY THESE PRESENTS, that I, FANA-TORO, King of Cape Mount and its rivers, in the presence, and with the full consent and approbation of my principal chiefs in council assembled, in considera-

As soon as the contract was fully signed, sealed, and delivered, making Mr. Redman and myself proprietors, in fee-simple, of this beautiful region, I hastened in company with my

tion of a mutual friendship existing between George Clavering Redman, Theodore Canot & Co., British subjects, and myself, the particulars whereof are under-written, do, for myself, my heirs and successors, give and grant unto the said George Clavering Redman, Theodore Canot & Co., their heirs and assigns in perpetuity, all land under the name of Cape Mount, extending, on the south and east sides, to *Little Cape Mount,* and on the northwest side to *Sugarie River,* comprised with the islands, lakes, brooks, forests, trees, waters, mines, minerals, rights, members, and appurtenances thereto belonging or appertaining, and all wild and tame beasts and other animals thereon; TO HAVE AND TO HOLD the said cape, rivers, islands, with both sides of the river and other premises hereby granted unto the said G. Clavering Redman, T. Canot & Co., their heirs and assigns for ever, subject to the authority and dominion of Her Majesty the Queen of Great Britain, her heirs and successors.

"And I, also, give and grant unto the said G. C. Redman, T. Canot & Co., the sole and exclusive rights of traffic with my Nation and People, and with all those tributary to me, and I hereby engage to afford my assistance and protection to the said party, and to all persons who may settle on the said cape, rivers, islands, lakes, and both sides of the river, by their consent, wishing peace and friendship between my nation and all persons belonging to the said firm.

> "Given under my hand and seal, at the town of Fanama, this twenty-third day of February, one thousand eight hundred and forty-one.

his
" King  X  Fana-Toro.    (L. S.)
mark.

his
" Prince X Gray.    (L. S.)
mark.

" Witnesses,

    " Hy. Frowd Seagram, R. N.     ⎫ *of Her Majesty's*
    " Geo. D. Noble, Clerk in Charge. ⎬ *brig Termagant."*
    " Thos. Crawford, Surgeon.      ⎭

I paid King Fana-Toro and his chiefs in council the following merchandise in exchange for his territory: six casks of rum; twenty muskets; twenty quarter-kegs powder; twenty pounds tobacco; twenty pieces white cottons; thirty pieces blue cottons; twenty iron bars; twenty cutlasses; twenty wash-basins; and twenty *each* of several other articles of trifling value.

naval friends to explore my little principality for a suitable town-site. We launched our boat on the waters of the noble lake Plitzogee at Toso, and after steering north-eastwardly for two hours under the pilotage of Prince Gray, entered a winding creek and penetrated its thickets of mangrove and palm, till the savage landed us on decayed steps and pavement made of *English brick*. At a short distance through the underwood, our con-ductor pointed out a denuded space which had once served as the foundation of an *English slave factory;* and when my com-panions hesitated to believe the prince's dishonorable charge on their nation, the negro confirmed it by pointing out, deeply carved in the bark of a neighboring tree, the name of :—

## T. WILLIAMS,

### 1 8 0 4.

I took the liberty to compliment Seagram and the surgeon on the result of our exploration ; and, after a hearty laugh at the denouement of the prince's search for a *lawful* homestead, we plunged still deeper in the forest, but returned without finding a location to my taste. Next day we recommenced our explora-tion by land, and, in order to obtain a comprehensive view of my dominion, as far as the eye would reach, I proposed an ascent of the promontory of the Cape which lifts its head quite twelve hun-dred feet above the sea. A toilsome walk of hours brought us to the summit, but so dense was the foliage and so lofty the mag-nificent trees, that, even by climbing the tallest, my scope of vision was hardly increased. As we descended the slopes, how-ever, towards the strait between the sea and lake, I suddenly came upon a rich, spacious level, flanked by a large brook of delicious water, and deciding instantly that it was an admirable spot for intercourse with the ocean as well as interior, I resolved that it should be the site of my future home. A tar was at hand to climb the loftiest palm, to strip its bushy head, and hoist the union-jack. Before sundown, I had taken solemn terri-torial possession, and baptized the future town "New Florence," in honor of my Italian birthplace.

My next effort was to procure laborers, for whom I invoked the aid of Fana-Toro and the neighboring chiefs. During two days, forty negroes, whom I hired for their food and a *per diem* of twenty cents, wrought faithfully under my direction; but the constant task of felling trees, digging roots, and clearing ground, was so unusual for savages, that the entire gang, with the exception of a dozen, took their pay in rum and tobacco and quitted me. A couple of days more, devoted to such endurance, drove off the remaining twelve, so that on the fifth day of my philanthropic enterprise I was left in my solitary hut with a single attendant. I had, alas! undertaken a task altogether unsuited to people whose idea of earthly happiness and duty is divided between palm-oil, concubinage, and sunshine!

I found it idle to remonstrate with the king about the indolence of his subjects. Fana-Toro entertained very nearly the same opinion as his slaves. He declared,—and perhaps very sensibly,—that white men were fools to work from sunrise to sunset every day of their lives; nor could he comprehend how negroes were expected to follow their example; nay, it was not the "fashion of Africa;" and, least of all, could his majesty conceive how a man possessed of so much merchandise and property, would voluntarily undergo the toils I was preparing for the future!

The king's censure and surprise were not encouraging; yet I had so long endured the natural indolence of negrodom, that I hardly expected either a different reply or influential support from his majesty. Nevertheless, I was not disheartened. I remembered the old school-boy maxim, *non vi sed sæpe cadendo*, and determined to effect by degrees what I could not achieve at a bound. For a while I tried the effect of higher wages; but an increase of rum, tobacco, and coin, could not string the nerves or cord the muscles of Africa. Four men's labor was not equivalent to one day's work in Europe or America. The negro's philosophy was both natural and self-evident:—*why should he work for pay when he could live without it?—labor could not give him more sunshine, palm-oil, or wives; and, as for grog and tobacco, they might be had without the infringement of habits which had almost the sacredness of religious institutions.*

With such slender prospects of prosperity at New Florence, I left a man in charge of my hut, and directing him to get on as well as he could, I visited Monrovia, to look after the merchandise that had been saved from the wreck of New Sestros.

# CHAPTER LXIX.

I MIGHT fairly be accused of ingratitude if I passed without notice the Colony of Liberia and its capital, whose hospitable doors
were opened widely to receive an exile, when the barbarians of
New Sestros drove me from that settlement.

It is not my intention to tire the reader with an account of
Liberia, for I presume that few are unacquainted with the thriv-
ing condition of those philanthropic lodgments, which hem the
western coast of Africa for near eight hundred miles.

In my former visits to Monrovia, I had been regarded as a
dangerous intruder, who was to be kept for ever under the vigilant
eyes of government officials. When my character as an established slaver was clearly ascertained, the port was interdicted to my
vessels, and my appearance in the town itself prohibited. Now,
however, when I came as a fugitive from violence, and with the
acknowledged relinquishment of my ancient traffic, every hand
was extended in friendship and commiseration. The governor
and council allowed the landing of my rescued slave-goods on
deposit, while the only two servants who continued faithful were
secured to me as apprentices by the court. Scarcely more than
two months ago, the people of this quiet village were disturbed
from sleep by the roll of drums beating for recruits to march
against "*the slaver Canot;*" to-day I dine with the chief of the
colony and am welcomed as a brother! This is another of those
remarkable vicissitudes that abound in this work, and which the
critics, in all likelihood, may consider too often repeated. To

my mind, however, it is only another illustration of the probability of the odd and the strangeness of *truth !*

I had no difficulty in finding all sorts of workmen in Monrovia, for the colonists brought with them all the mechanical ingenuity and thrift that characterize the American people. In four months, with the assistance of a few carpenters, sawyers and blacksmiths, I built a charming little craft of twenty-five tons, which, in honor of my British protector, I dubbed the "Termagant." I notice the construction of this vessel, merely to show that the colony and its people were long ago capable of producing every thing that may be required by a commercial state in the tropics. When my cutter touched the water, she was indebted to foreign countries for nothing but her copper, chains and sails, every thing else being the product of Africa and *colonial* labor. Had nature bestowed a better harbor on the Mesurado river, and afforded a safer entrance for large vessels, Monrovia would now be second only to Sierra Leone. Following the beautiful border of the Saint Paul's, a few miles from Monrovia the eye rests on extensive plains teeming with luxurious vegetation. The amplest proof has been given of the soil's fertility in the production of coffee, sugar, cotton and rice. I have frequently seen cane fourteen feet high, and as thick as any I ever met with in the Indies. Coffee trees grow much larger than on this side of the Atlantic ; single trees often yielding sixteen pounds, which is about seven more than the average product in the West Indies.* Throughout the entire jurisdiction

---

* I wish to confirm and fortify this statement in regard to the value of coffee culture in the colonies, by the observation of Dr. J. W. Lugenbeel, late colonial physician and United States agent in Liberia. The Doctor gave "particular attention to observations and investigations respecting coffee culture in Liberia." "I have frequently seen," he says, "isolated trees growing in different parts of Liberia, which yielded from ten to twenty pounds of clean dry coffee at one picking ; and, however incredible it may appear, it is a fact that one tree in Monrovia yielded four and a half bushels of coffee in the hull, at one time, which, when dried and shelled, weighed thirty-one pounds. This is the largest quantity I ever heard of, and the largest tree I ever saw, being upwards of twenty feet high and of proportionate dimensions."

The Doctor is of opinion, however, that as the coffee tree begins to bear

between Cape Mount and Cape Palmas, to the St. Andrew's, the soil is equally prolific.  Oranges, lemons, cocoanuts, pine-apples, mangoes, plums, granadillas, sour and sweet sop, plantains, bananas, guyavas, tamarinds, ginger, sweet potatoes, yams, cassava, and corn, are found in abundance; while the industry of American settlers has lately added the bread-fruit, rose apple, patanga, cantelope, water-melon, aguacate and mulberry.  Garden culture produces every thing that may be desired at the most luxurious table.

Much has been said of the "pestilential climate of Africa," and the certain doom of those who venture within the spell of its miasma.  I dare not deny that the coast is scourged by dangerous maladies, and that nearly all who take up their abode in the colonies are obliged to undergo the ordeal of a fever which assails them with more or less virulence, according to the health, constitution, or condition of the patient.  Yet I think, if the colonization records are read with a candid spirit, they will satisfy unprejudiced persons that the mortality of emigrants has diminished nearly one half, in consequence of the sanitary care exercised by the colonial authorities during the period of acclimation.  The colonies are now amply supplied with lodgings for new comers, where every thing demanded for comfort, cure, or alleviation, is at hand in abundance.  Colored physicians, who studied their art in America, have acquainted themselves with the local distempers, and proved their skill by successful practice.  Nor is there now the difficulty or expense which, twelve years ago, before the destruction of the neighboring slave marts, made it almost impossible to furnish convalescents with that delicate nourishment which was needed to re-establish their vigor.

---

It may not be amiss if I venture to hope that these colonial experiments, which have been fostered for the civilization of Africa

at the end of its fourth year, an *average* yield at the end of the sixth year may be calculated on of at least four pounds.  Three hundred trees may be planted on an acre, giving each twelve feet, and in six years the culture will become profitable as well as easy.

as well as for the amelioration of the American negro's lot, will continue to receive the support of all good men. Some persons assert that the race is incapable of self-government beyond the tribal state, and *then* only through fear; while others allege, that no matter what care may be bestowed on African intellect, it is unable to produce or sustain the highest results of modern civilization. It would not be proper for any one to speak oracularly on this mooted point; yet, in justice to the negroes who never left their forests, as well as to those who have imbibed, for more than a generation, the civilization of Europe or America, I may unhesitatingly say, that the colonial trial has thus far been highly promising. I have often been present at difficult councils and "*palavers*" among the *wild* tribes, when questions arose which demanded a calm and skilful judgment, and in almost every instance, the decision was characterized by remarkable good sense and equity. In most of the *colonies* the men who are intrusted with local control, a few years since were either slaves in America, or employed in menial tasks which it was almost hopeless they could escape. Liberia, at present, may boast of several individuals, who, but for their caste, might adorn society; while they who have personally known Roberts, Lewis, Benedict, J. B. McGill, Teage, Benson of Grand Bassa, and Dr. McGill of Cape Palmas, can bear testimony that nature has endowed numbers of the colored race with the best qualities of humanity.

Nevertheless, the prosperity, endurance and influence of the colonies, are still problems. I am anxious to see the second generation of the colonists in Africa. I wish to know what will be the force and development of the negro mind on its native soil,—civilized, but cut off from all instruction, influence, or association with the white mind. I desire to understand, precisely, whether the negro's faculties are original or imitative, and consequently, whether he can stand alone in absolute independence, or is only respectable when reflecting a civilization that is cast on him by others.

If the descendants of the present colonists, increased by an immense immigration *of all classes and qualities* during the next twenty-five years, shall sustain the young nation with that industrial energy and political dignity that mark its population in our day, we shall hail the realized fact with infinite delight. We will rejoice, not only because the emancipated negro may thenceforth possess a realm wherein his rights shall be sacred, but because the civilization with which the colonies must border the African continent, will, year by year, sink deeper and deeper into the heart of the interior, till barbarism and Islamism will fade before the light of Christianity.

But the test and trial have yet to come. The colonist of our time is an exotic under glass,—full, as yet, of sap and stamina drawn from his native America, but nursed with care and exhibited as the efflorescence of modern philanthropy. Let us hope that this wholesome guardianship will not be too soon or suddenly withdrawn by the parent societies; but that, while the state of pupilage shall not be continued till the immigrants and their children are emasculated by lengthened dependence, it will be upheld until the republic shall exhibit such signs of manhood as cannot deceive the least hopeful.

# CHAPTER LXX.

I RETURNED to Cape Mount from the colony with several American mechanics and a fresh assortment of merchandise for traffic
with the natives. During my absence, the agent I left in charge
had contrived, with great labor, to clear a large space in the
forest for my projected establishment, so that with the aid of my
Americans, I was soon enabled to give the finishing touch to
New-Florence. While the buildings were erecting, I induced a
number of natives, by force of double pay and the authority of
their chiefs, to form and cultivate a garden, comprising the
luxuries of Europe and America as well as of the tropics, which,
in after days, secured the admiration of many a naval commander.

As soon as my dwelling was nicely completed, I removed my
furniture from the colony; and, still continuing to drum through
the country for business with the Africans, I despatched my
Kroomen and pilots on board of every cruiser that appeared in the
offing, to supply them with provisions and refreshments.

An event took place about this time which may illustrate the
manner in which a branch of the slave trade is carried on along
the coast. Her Britannic Majesty's sloop of war L—— was

in the neighborhood, and landed three of her officers at my
quarters to spend a day or two in hunting the wild boars with
which the adjacent country was stocked.  But the rain poured
down in such torrents, that, instead of a hunt, I proposed a
dinner to my jovial visitors.  Soon after our soup had been despatched on the piazza, there was a rush of natives into the yard,
and I was informed that one of our Bush chiefs had brought in a
noted gambler, whom he threatened either to sell or kill.

It struck me instantly that this would be a good opportunity
to give my British friends a sight of native character, at the
same time that they might be enabled, if so disposed, to do a
generous action.  Accordingly, I directed my servant to bring
the Bushman and gambler before us; and as the naked victim,
with a rope round his neck, was dragged by the savage to our
table, I perceived that it was Soma, who had formerly been in
my service on the coast.  The vagabond was an excellent interpreter and connected with the king, but I had been obliged to discharge him in consequence of his dissipated habits, and especially
for having gambled away his youngest sister, whose release from
Gallinas I had been instrumental in securing.

" I have brought Soma to your store-keeper," said the Bushman, " and I want him to buy the varlet.  Soma has been half
the day gambling with me.  First of all he lost his gun, then his
cap, then his cloth, then his right leg, then his left, then his arms,
and, last of all, his head.  I have given his friends a chance to
redeem the dog, but as they had bought him half a dozen times
already, there's not a man in the town that will touch him.
Soma *never* pays his debts; and now, Don Téodore, I have
brought him here, and if *you* don't buy him, I'll take him to the
water-side and *cut his throat !* "

There,—with an imploring countenance, bare as he came into
the world, a choking cord round his throat, and with pinioned
arms,—stood the trembling gambler, as I glanced in vain from
the Bushman to the officers, in expectation of his release by those
philanthropists !  As Soma spoke English, I told him in our
language, that I had no pity for his fate, and that he must take
the chances he had invoked.  Twenty dollars would have saved

his life, and yet the British did not melt ! " Take him off, said I sternly, to the Bushman, " and use him as you choose ! "— but at the same moment, a wink to my interpreter sufficed, and the Bushman returned to the forest with tobacco and rum, while Soma was saved from slaughter. It is by no means improbable that the gambler is now playing *monté* on some plantation in Cuba.

---

I continued my labors at New-Florence without intermission for several months, but when I cast up my account, I found the wages and cost of building so enormous, that my finances would soon be exhausted. Accordingly, by the advice of my friend Seagram, as well as of Captain Tucker, who commanded on the station, I petitioned Lord Stanley to grant me one hundred recaptured Africans to till my grounds and learn the rudiments of agricultural industry. Some time elapsed before an answer was sent, but when it came, my prospects were dashed to the earth.

"GOVERNMENT HOUSE, SIERRA LEONE,
*28th October,* 1843.

" SIR :
I beg to acknowledge the receipt of your letter dated August last, inclosing the copy of a petition, the original of which you had transmitted to the acting Lieutenant Governor Ferguson, for the purpose of having it forwarded to her Majesty's Government.

" In reply, I have to acquaint you, that by the receipt of a despatch from the Rt. Hon. Lord Stanley, Secretary of State for the Colonies, bearing date 8th April 1842, his Lordship states that he cannot sanction a compliance with your request to have a number of liberated Africans, as apprentices, in tilling your grounds; and further, that he could not recognize the purchase of Cape Mount, as placing that district under the protection and sovereignty of the British crown.

" I beg to add, that I am glad to be informed by Captain

Oake that the vessel, alluded to in your letter, which you had been unable to despatch for want of a license, had obtained one for that purpose from the governor of Monrovia."

"I am, sir, your obedient servant,

"G. MAC DONALD,

"*To* MR. THEODORE CANOT."                              "*Governor.*"

The picture that had been painted by my imagination with so many bright scenes and philanthropic hopes, fell as I finished this epistle. It not only clouded my future prospects of lawful commerce, but broke off, at once, the correspondence with my generous friend Redman in London. As I dropped the missive on the table, I ordered the palm tree on which I had first unfurled the British flag to be cut down; and next day, on a tall pole, in full view of the harbor, I hoisted a tri-colored banner, adorned by a central star, which I caused to be baptized, in presence of Fana-Toro, with a salvo of twenty guns.

I am not naturally of a mischievous or revengful temper, but I can scarcely find language to express the mortification I experienced when Lord Stanley thwarted my honest intentions, by his refusal to protect the purchase whereon I had firmly resolved to be an ally and friend, in concentrating a lawful commerce. I was especially disgusted by this mistrust, or mistake, after the flattering assurances with which my design had, from the first, been cherished by the British officers on the station. I may confess that, for a moment, I almost repented the confidence I had reposed in the British lion, and was at a loss whether to abandon Cape Mount and return to my former traffic, or to till the ground and play waterman to the fleet.

After proper deliberation, however, I resolved to take the plough for my device; and before Christmas, I had already ordered from England a large supply of agricultural implements and of every thing requisite for elaborate husbandry. After this, I purchased forty youths to be employed on a coffee plantation, and to drag my ploughs till I obtained animals to replace them. In a short time I had abundance of land cleared, and an overseer's house erected for an old barracoonier, who, I am grieved to say, turned out but a sorry farmer. He had no idea of systematic labor or discipline save by the lash, so that in a month, four of his gang were on the sick list, and five had deserted. I replaced the Spaniard by an American colored man, who, in turn, made too free with my people and neglected the plantations. My own knowledge of agriculture was so limited, that unless I fortified every enterprise by constant reference to books, I was unable to direct my hands with skill; and, accordingly, with all these mishaps to my commerce and tillage, I became satisfied that it was easier to plough the ocean than the land.

Still I was not disheartened. My trade, on a large scale, with the interior, and my agriculture had both failed; yet I resolved to try the effect of traffic in a humble way, combined with such *mechanical* pursuits as would be profitable on the coast. Accordingly, I divided a gang of forty well drilled negroes into two sections, retaining the least intelligent on the farm, while the brighter youths were brought to the landing. Here I laid out a shipyard, blacksmith's shop, and sawpit, placing at the head of each, a Monrovian colonist to instruct my slaves. In the mean time the neighboring natives, as well as the people some distance in the interior, were apprised by my runners of the new factory I was forming at Cape Mount.

By the return of the dry season our establishment gave signs of renewed vitality. Within the fences of New Florence there were already twenty-five buildings and a population of one hundred, and nothing was wanting but a stock of cattle, which I soon procured from the Kroo country.

Thus, for a long time all things went on satisfactorily, not only with the natives, but with foreign traders and cruisers, till a native war embarrassed my enterprise, and brought me in contact with the enemies of King Fana-Toro, of whose realm and deportment I must give some account.

# CHAPTER LXXI.

THE Africans who cluster about the bold headland of Cape Mount,—which, in fair weather, greets the mariner full thirty miles at sea,—belong to the Vey tribe, and are in no way inferior to the best classes of natives along the coast.   Forty or fifty families constitute " a town," the government of which is generally in the hands of the oldest man, who administers justice by a " palaver " held in public, wherein the seniors of the settlement are alone consulted.   These villages subject themselves voluntarily to the protectorate of larger towns, whose chief arbitrates as sovereign without appeal in all disputes among towns under his wardship ; yet, as his judgments are not always pleasing, the dissatisfied desert their huts, and, emigrating to another jurisdiction, build their village anew within its limits.

The Veys of both sexes are well built, erect, and somewhat stately.   Their faith differs but little from that prevalent among the Soosoos of the Rio Pongo.   They believe in a superior power that may be successfully invoked through *gree-grees* and *fetiches*, but which is generally obstinate or mischievous.   It is their idea that the good are rewarded after death by transformation into some favorite animal ; yet their entire creed is not subject to any definite description, for they blend the absurdities of Mahometan-ism with those of paganism, and mellow the whole by an acknow-ledgment of a supreme deity.

The Vey, like other *uncontaminated* Ethiopians, is brought up in savage neglect by his parents, crawling in perfect naked-ness about the villages, till imitation teaches him the use of rai-ment, which, in all likelihood, he first of all obtains by theft. There is no difference between the sexes during their early years.   A sense of shame or modesty seems altogether un-known or disregarded; nor is it unusual to find ten or a dozen of both genders huddled promiscuously beneath a roof whose walls are not more than fifteen feet square.

True to his nature, a Vey bushman rises in the morning to swallow his rice and cassava, and crawls back to his mat which is invariably placed in the sunshine, where he *simmers* till noon-tide, when another wife serves him with a second meal.   The re-mainder of daylight is passed either in gossip or a second *siesta*, till, at sundown, his other wives wash his body, furnish a third meal, and stretch his wearied limbs before a blazing fire to re-fresh for the toils of the succeeding day.   In fact, the slaves of a household, together with its females, form the entire working class of Africa, and in order to indoctrinate the gentler sex in its future toils and duties, there seems to be a sort of national semi-nary which is known as the Gree-gree-bush.

The Gree-gree-bush is a secluded spot or grove of consider-able extent in the forest, apart from dwellings and cultivated land though adjacent to villages, which is considered as consecrated ground and forbidden to the approach of men.   The establishment within this precinct consists of a few houses, with an extensive area for exercise.   It is governed chiefly by an old woman of superior skill and knowledge, to whose charge the girls of a vil-lage are intrusted as soon as they reach the age of ten or twelve. There are various opinions of the use and value of this institu-tion in the primitive polity of Africa.   By some writers it is treated as a religious cloister for the protection of female chas-tity, while by others it is regarded as a school of licentiousness. From my own examination of the establishment, I am quite satisfied that a line drawn between these extremes will, most probably, characterize the " bush " with accuracy, and that what was originally a conservative seclusion, has degenerated greatly under the lust of tropical passions.

As the procession of novices who are about to enter the grove approaches the sanctuary, music and dancing are heard and seen on every side. As soon as the maidens are received, they are taken by the *gree-gree* women to a neighboring stream, where they are washed, and undergo an operation which is regarded as a sort of circumcision. Anointed from head to foot with palm oil, they are next reconducted to their home in the gree-gree bush. Here, under strict watch, they are maintained by their relatives or those who are in treaty for them as wives, until they reach the age of puberty. At this epoch the important fact is announced by the gree-gree woman to the purchaser or future husband, who, it is expected, will soon prepare to take her from the retreat. Whenever his *new* house is ready for the bride's reception, it is proclaimed by the ringing of bells and vociferous cries during night. Next day search is made by females through the woods, to ascertain whether intruders are lurking about, but when the path is ascertained to be clear, the girl is forthwith borne to a rivulet, where she is washed, anointed, and clad in her best attire. From thence she is borne, amid singing, drumming, shouting, and firing, in the arms of her female attendants, till her unsoiled feet are deposited on the husband's floor.[1]

I believe this institution exists throughout a large portion of Africa, and such is the desire to place females within the bush, that poor parents who cannot pay the initiatory fee, raise subscriptions among their friends to obtain the requisite slave whose gift entitles their child to admission. Sometimes, it is said, that this *human ticket is stolen* to effect the desired purpose, and that no native power can recover the lost slave when once within the sacred precincts.

The gree-gree-bush is not only a resort of the virgin, but of

---

[1] See Maryland Colonization Journal, vol. i., n. s., p. 212.

the wife, in those seasons when approaching maternity indicates need of repose and care.   In a few hours, the robust mother issues with her new-born child, and after a plunge into the nearest brook, returns to the domestic drudgery which I have already described.

————

In the time of Fana-Toro, Toso was the royal residence where his majesty played sovereign and protector over six towns and fifteen villages.   His government was generally considered patriarchal.   When I bought Cape Mount, the king numbered " seventy-seven rains," equivalent to so many years;—he was small, wiry, meagre, erect, and proud of the respect he universally commanded.   His youth was notorious among the tribes for intrepidity, and I found that he retained towards enemies a bitter resentment that often led to the commission of atrocious cruelties.

It was not long after my instalment at the Cape, that I accidentally witnessed the ferocity of this chief.   Some trifling " country affair " caused me to visit the king; but upon landing at Toso I was told he was abroad.   The manner of my informant, however, satisfied me that the message was untrue ; and accordingly, with the usual confidence of a " white man " in Africa, I searched his premises till I encountered him in the " palaver-house."   The large inclosure was crammed with a mob of savages, all in perfect silence around the king, who, in an infuriate manner, with a bloody knife in his hand, and a foot on the dead body of a negro, was addressing the carcass.   By his side stood a pot of hissing oil, in which the heart of his enemy was frying !

My sudden and, perhaps, improper entrance, seemed to exasperate the infidel, who, calling me to his side, knelt on the corpse, and digging it repeatedly with his knife, exclaimed with trembling passion, that it was his bitterest and oldest foe's !   For twenty years he had butchered his people, sold his subjects, violated his daughters, slain his sons, and burnt his towns;—and with each charge, the savage enforced his assertion by a stab.

I learned that the slaughtered captive was too brave and wary to be taken alive in open conflict.   He had been kidnapped by treachery, and as he could not be forced to walk to Toso, the king's trappers had cooped him in a huge basket, which they bore on their shoulders to the Cape. No sooner was the brute in his captor's presence, than he broke a silence of three days by imprecations on Fana-Toro. In a short space, his fate was decided in the scene I had witnessed, while his body was immediately burnt to prevent it from taking the form of some ferocious beast which might vex the remaining years of his royal executioner!

This was the only instance of Fana-Toro's barbarity that came under my notice, and in its perpetration he merely followed the example of his ancestors in obedience to African ferocity. Yet, of his intrepidity and nobler endurance, I will relate an anecdote which was told me by reliable persons. Some twenty years before my arrival at the Cape, large bands of mercenary bushmen had joined his enemies along the beach, and after desolating his territory, sat down to beleaguer the stockade of Toso. For many a day thirst and hunger were quietly suffered under the resolute command of the king, but at length, when their pangs became unendurable, and the people demanded a surrender, Fana-Toro strode into the " palaver house," commanding a *sortie* with his famished madmen. The warriors protested against the idea, for their ammunition was exhausted. Then arose a wild shout for the king's deposition and the election of a chief to succeed him. A candidate was instantly found and installed; but no sooner had he been chosen, than Fana-Toro,—daring the new prince to prove a power of *endurance* equal to his own,—plunged his finger in a bowl of boiling oil, and held it over the fire, without moving a muscle, till the flesh was crisped to the bone.

It is hardly necessary to say that the sovereign was at once restored to his rights, or that, availing himself of the fresh enthusiasm, he rushed upon his besiegers, broke their lines, routed the mercenaries, and compelled his rival to sue for peace. Until the day of his death, that mutilated hand was the boast of his people.

The Vey people mark with some ceremony the extremes of human existence—birth and death. Both events are honored with feasting, drinking, dancing, and firing; and the descendants of the dead sometimes impoverish, and even ruin themselves, to inter a venerable parent with pomp.

Prince Gray, the son of Fana-Toro, whom I have already mentioned, died during my occupation of Cape Mount. I was at Mesurado when the event happened, but, as soon as I heard it, I resolved to unite with his relations in the last rites to his memory. Gray was not only a good negro and kind neighbor but, as my fast friend in "country.matters," his death was a personal calamity.

The breath was hardly out of the prince's body, when his sons, who owned but little property and had no slaves for sale, hastened to my agent, and pledged their town of Fanama for means to defray his funeral. In the mean time, the corpse, swathed in twenty large country sheets, and wrapped in twenty pieces of variegated calico, was laid out in a hut, where it was constantly watched and *smoked* by three of the favorite widows.

After two months devotion to moaning and *seasoning*, notice was sent forty miles round the country, summoning the tribes to the final ceremony. On the appointed day the corpse was brought from the hut, *a perfect mass of bacon*. As the procession moved towards the palaver-house, the prince's twenty wives—almost entirely denuded, their heads shaved, and their bodies smeared with dust—were seen following his remains. The eldest spouse appeared covered with self-inflicted bruises, burns, and gashes—all indications of sorrow and future uselessness.

The crowd reached the apartment, singing the praises of the defunct in chorus, when the body was laid on a new mat, covered with his war shirt, while the parched lump that indicated his head was crowned with the remains of a fur hat. All the amulets, charms, gree-grees, fetiches and flummery of the prince were duly bestowed at his sides. While these arrangements were making within, his sons stood beneath an adjoining verandah, to receive the condolences of the invited guests, who, according to custom, made their bows and deposited a tribute of rice, palm-oil, palm-wine, or other luxuries, to help out the merry-making.

When I heard of the prince's death at Monrovia, I resolved not to return without a testimonial of respect for my ally, and ordered an enormous coffin to be prepared without delay. In due time the huge chest was made ready, covered with blue cotton, studded with brass nails, and adorned with all the gilded ornaments I could find in Monrovia. Besides this splendid sarcophagus, my craft from the colony was ballasted with four bullocks and several barrels of rum, as a contribution to the funeral.

I had timed my arrival at Fanama, so as to reach the landing about ten o'clock on the morning of burial; and, after a salute from my brazen guns, I landed the bullocks, liquor, and coffin, and marched toward the princely gates.

The unexpected appearance of the white friend of their father, lord, and husband, was greeted by the family with a loud wail, and, as a mark of respect, I was instantly lifted in the arms of the weeping women, and deposited on the mat beside the corpse. Here I rested, amid cries and lamentations, till near noon, when the bullocks were slaughtered, and their blood offered in wash-bowls to the dead. As soon as this was over, the shapeless mass was stowed in the coffin without regard to position, and borne by six carriers to the beach, where it was buried in a cluster of cotton-woods.

On our return to Fanama from the grave, the eldest son of the deceased was instantly saluted as prince. From this moment the festivities began, and, at sundown, the twenty widows reappeared upon the ground, clad in their choicest raiment, their shaven skulls anointed with oil, and their limbs loaded with every bead and bracelet they could muster. Then began the partition of these disconsolate relicts among the royal family. Six were selected by the new prince, who divided thirteen among his brothers and kinsmen, but gave his mother to his father-in-law. As soon as the allotment was over, his highness very courteously offered me the choice of his *six*, in return for my gifts ; but as I never formed a family tie with natives, I declined the honor, as altogether too overwhelming !

# CHAPTER LXXII.

WHEN I was once comfortably installed at my motley establishment, and, under the management of Colonists, had initiated the
native workmen into tolerable skill with the adze, saw, sledge-
hammer and forge, I undertook to build a brig of one hundred
tons. In six months, people came from far and near to behold the mechanical marvels of Cape Mount. Meanwhile, my
plantation went on slowly, while my *garden* became a matter of
curiosity to all the intelligent coasters and cruisers, though I
could never enlighten the natives as to the value of the " foreign
grass " which I cultivated so diligently.   They admired the symmetry of my beds, the richness of my pine-apples, the luxurious
splendor of my sugar-cane, the abundance of my coffee, and the
cool fragrance of the arbors with which I adorned the lawn; but
they would never admit the use of my exotic vegetables.   In
order to water my premises, I turned the channel of a brook,
surrounding the garden with a perfect canal; and, as its sides
were completely laced with an elaborate wicker-work of willows,
the aged king and crowds of his followers came to look upon the
Samsonian task as one of the wonders of Africa.   " What is it,"
exclaimed Fana-Toro, as he beheld the deflected water-course,
" that a white man cannot do ! "   After this, his majesty in-

spected all my plants, and shouted again with surprise at the toil we underwent to satisfy our appetites. The use or worth of *flowers*, of which I had a rare and beautiful supply, he could never divine; but his chief amazement was still devoted to our daily expenditure of time, strength, and systematic toil, when rice and palm-oil would grow wild while we were sleeping!

It will be seen from this sketch of my domestic comforts and employment, that New Florence prospered in every thing but *farming* and *trade*. At first it was my hope, that two or three years of perseverance would enable me to open a lawful traffic with the interior; but I soon discovered that the slave-trade was alone thought of by the natives, who only bring the neighboring produce to the beach, when their captives are ready for a market. I came, moreover, to the conclusion that the interior negroes about Cape Mount had no commerce with Eastern tribes except for slaves, and consequently that its small river will never create marts like those which have direct communications by water with the heart of a rich region, and absorb its gold, ivory, wax, and hides. To meet these difficulties, I hastened the building of my vessel *as a coaster*.

About this time, an American craft called the A——, arrived in my neighborhood. She was loaded with tobacco, calicoes, rum, and powder. Her captain who was unskilled in coast-trade, and ignorant of Spanish, engaged me to act as supercargo for him to Gallinas. In a very short period I disposed of his entire investment. The trim and saucy rig of this Yankee clipper bewitched the heart of a Spanish trader who happened to be among the *lagunes*, and an offer was forthwith made, through me, for her purchase. The bid was accepted at once, and the day before Christmas fixed as the period of her delivery, after a trip to the Gaboon.

In contracting to furnish this slaver with a craft and the necessary apparatus for his cargo, it would be folly for me to deny that I was dipping once more into my ancient trade; yet, on reflection, I concluded that in covering the vessel for a moment with my name, I was no more amenable to rebuke, than the respectable merchants of Sierra Leone and elsewhere who passed hardly a day without selling, to notorious slavers, such merchandise as could be used *alone* in slave-wars or slave-trade. It is probable that the sophism soothed my conscience at the moment, though I could never escape the promise that sealed my agreement with Lieutenant Seagram.

The appointed day arrived, and my smoking semaphores announced the brigantine's approach to Sugarei, three miles from Cape Mount. The same evening the vessel was surrendered to me by the American captain, who landed his crew and handed over his flag and papers. As soon as I was in charge, no delay was made to prepare for the reception of freight; and by sunrise I resigned her to the Spaniard, who immediately embarked seven hundred negroes, and landed them in Cuba in twenty-seven days.

Till now the British cruisers had made Cape Mount their friendly rendezvous, but the noise of this shipment in my neighborhood, and my refusal to explain or converse on the subject, gave umbrage to officers who had never failed to supply themselves from my grounds and larder. In fact I was soon marked as an enemy of the squadron, while our intercourse dwindled to the merest shadow. In the course of a week, the Commander on the African station, himself, hove to off the Cape, and summoning me on board, concluded a petulant conversation by remarking that " a couple of men like Monsieur Canot would make work enough in Africa for the whole British squadron ! "

I answered the compliment with a profound *salaam*, and went over the Penelope's side satisfied that my friendship was at an end with her Majesty's cruisers.

---

The portion of Cape Mount whereon I pitched my tent, had been so long depopulated by the early wars against Fana-Toro, that the wild beasts re-asserted their original dominion over the territory. The forest was full of leopards, wild cats, cavallis or wild boars, and ourang-outangs.

Very soon after my arrival, a native youth in my employ had been severely chastised for misconduct, and in fear of repetition, fled to the mount after supplying himself with a basket of cassava. As his food was sufficient for a couple of days, we thought he might linger in the wood till the roots were exhausted, and then return to duty. But three days elapsed without tidings from the truant. On the fourth, a diligent search disclosed his corpse in the forest, every limb dislocated and covered with bites apparently made by human teeth. It was the opinion of the natives that the child had been killed by ourang-outangs, nor can I doubt their correctness, for when I visited the scene of the murder, the earth for a large space around, was covered with the footprints of the beast and scattered with the skins of its favorite esculent.

I was more annoyed, however, at first, by leopards than any other animal. My cattle could not stray beyond the fences, nor could my laborers venture abroad at any time without weapons. I made use of spring-traps, pit-falls, and various expedients to purify the forest; but such was the cunning or agility of our nimble foes that they all escaped. The only mode by which I succeeded in freeing the *homestead* of their ravages, was by arming the muzzle of a musket with a slice of meat which was attached by a string to the trigger, so that the load and the food were discharged into the leopard's mouth at the same moment. Thus, by degrees as my settlement grew, the beasts receded from the promontory and its adjacent grounds; and in a couple of years, the herds were able to roam where they pleased without danger.

Cape Mount had long been deserted by elephants, but about forty miles from my dwelling, on the upper forests of the lake, the noble animal might still be hunted; and whenever the natives were fortunate enough to " bag " a specimen, I was sure to be remembered in its division. If the prize proved a male, I received the feet and trunk, but if it turned out of the gentler gender, I was honored with the udder, as a royal *bonne-bouche.*

In Africa a slaughtered elephant is considered public property by the neighboring villagers, all of whom have a right to

AN ELEPHANT HUNT.

carve the giant till his bones are bare. A genuine sportsman claims nothing but the ivory and tail, the latter being universally a perquisite of the king. Yet I frequently found that associations were made among the natives to capture this colossal beast and his valuable tusks. Upon these occasions, a club was formed on the basis of a whaling cruise, while a single but well known hunter was chosen to do execution. One man furnished the muskets, another supplied the powder, a third gave the iron bolts for balls, a fourth made ready the provender, while a fifth despatched a bearer with the armament. As soon as the outfit was completed, the huntsman's *ju-ju* and *feitiche* were invoked for good luck, and he departed under an escort of wives and associates.

An African elephant is smaller, as well as more cunning and wild, than the Asiatic. Accordingly, the sportsman is often obliged to circumvent his game during several days, for it is said that in populous districts, its instincts are so keen as to afford warning of the neighborhood of fire-arms, even at extraordinary distances. The common and most effectual mode of enticing an elephant within reach of a ball, is to strew the forest for several miles with *pine apples*, whose flavor and fragrance infallibly bewitch him. By degrees, he tracks and nibbles the fruit from slice to slice, till, lured within the hunter's retreat, he is despatched from the branches of a lofty tree by repeated shots at his capacious forehead.

Sometimes it happens that four or five discharges with the wretched powder used in Africa fail to slay the beast, who escapes from the jungle and dies afar from the encounter. When this occurs, an attendant is despatched for a reinforcement, and I have seen a whole settlement go forth *en masse* to search for the monster that will furnish food for many a day. Sometimes the crowd is disappointed, for the wounds have been slight and the animal is seen no more. Occasionally, a dying elephant will linger a long time, and is only discovered by the buzzards hovering above his body. Then it is that the bushmen, guided by the vultures, haste to the forest, and fall upon the putrid flesh with more avidity than birds of prey. Battles have been fought on the carcass of an elephant, and many a slave, captured in the conflict, has been marched from the body to the beach.

# CHAPTER LXXIII.

THE war, whose rupture I mentioned at the end of the seventieth chapter, spread rapidly throughout our borders; and absorbing the entire attention of the tribe, gave an impulse to slavery which had been unwitnessed since my advent to the Cape. The reader may readily appreciate the difficulty of my position in a country, hemmed in by war which could only be terminated by slaughter or slavery. Nor could I remain neutral in New Florence, which was situated on the same side of the river as Toso, while the enemies of Fana-Toro were in complete possession of the opposite bank.

When I felt that the rupture between the British and myself was not only complete but irreparable, I had less difficulty in deciding my policy as to the natives; and, chiefly under the impulse of self-protection, I resolved to serve the cause of my ancient ally. I made whatever fortifications could be easily defended in case of attack, and, by way of show, mounted some cannon on a boat which was paraded about the waters in a formidable way. My judgment taught me from the outset that it was folly to think of joining actively in the conflict; for, while I had but three white men in my quarters, and the colonists had returned to Monrovia, my New Sestros experience taught me the value of bondsmen's backing.

Numerous engagements and captures took place by both parties, so that my doors were daily beseiged by a crowd of wretches sent by Fana-Toro to be purchased *for shipment.* I declined the contract with firmness and constancy, but so importunate was the chief that I could not resist his desire that a Spanish factor might come within my limits with merchandise from Gallinas to purchase his prisoners. " He could do nothing with his foes," he said, " when in his grasp, but slay or sell them." The king's enemy, on the opposite shore, disposed of his captives to Gallinas, and obtained supplies of powder and ball, while Fana-Toro, who had no vent for his prisoners, would have been destroyed without my assistance.

Matters continued in this way for nearly two years, during which the British kept up so vigilant a blockade at Cape Mount and Gallinas, that the slavers had rarely a chance to enter a vessel or run a cargo. In time, the *barracoons* became so gorged, that the slavers began to build their own schooners. When the A—— was sold, I managed to retain her long-boat in my service, but such was now the value of every egg-shell on the coast, that her owner despatched a carpenter from Gallinas, who, in a few days, decked, rigged, and equipped her for sea. She was twenty-three feet long, four feet deep, and five feet beam, so that, when afloat, her measurement could not have exceeded four tons. Yet, on a dark and stormy night, she dropped down the river, and floated out to sea through the besieging lines, with thirty-three black boys, two sailors, and a navigator. In less than forty days she transported the whole of her living freight across the Atlantic to Bahia. The negroes almost perished from thirst, but the daring example was successfully followed during the succeeding year, by skiffs of similar dimensions.

-----

I can hardly hope that a narrative of my dull routine, while I lingered on the coast, entirely aloof from the slave-trade, would either interest or instruct the general reader. The checkered career I have already exposed, has portrayed almost every phase of African life. If I am conscious of any thing during my domicile at Cape Mount, it is of a sincere desire to prosper by lawful and honorable thrift. But, between the native wars, the turmoil of intruding slavers, and the suspicions of the English, every thing went wrong. The friendship of the colonists at Cape Palmas and Monrovia was still unabated; appeals were made by missionaries for my influence with the tribes; coasters called on me as usual for supplies; yet, with all these encouragements for exertion, I must confess that my experiment was unsuccessful.

Nor was this all. I lost my cutter, laden with stores and merchandise for my factory. A vessel, filled with rice and lumber for my ship-yard, was captured *on suspicion*, and, though sent across the Atlantic for adjudication, was dismissed uncondemned. The sudden death of a British captain from Sierra Leone, deprived me of three thousand dollars. Fana-Toro made numerous assaults on his foes, all of which failed; and, to cap the climax of my ills, on returning after a brief absence, I found that a colonist, whom I had rescued from misery and employed in my forge, had fled to the enemy, carrying with him a number of my most useful servants.

It was about this time that circumstances obliged me to make a rapid voyage to New York and back to Africa, where the blind goddess had another surprise in store for me. During my absence, our ancient king was compelled to make a treaty with his rival, who, under the name of George Cain, dwelt formerly among the American colonists and acquired our language. It was by treachery alone that Fana-Toro had been dragooned into an arrangement, by which my *quondam* blacksmith, who married a sister of Cain, was elevated to the dignity of prince George's *premier!*

Both these scamps, with a troop of their followers, planted themselves on my premises near the beach, and immediately let me understand that they were my sworn enemies. Cain could not pardon the aid I gave to Fana-Toro in his earlier conflicts, nor would the renegade colonist forsake his kinsman or the African barbarism, into which he had relapsed.

By degrees, these varlets, whom I was unable, in my crippled condition, to dislodge, obtained the ears of the British commanders, and poured into them every falsehood that could kindle their ire. The Spanish factory of Fana-Toro's agent was reported to be *mine*. The shipment in the A—— and the adventure of her boat, were said to be *mine*. Another suspected clipper was declared to be *mine*. These, and a hundred lies of equal baseness, were adroitly purveyed to the squadron by the outlaws, and, in less than a month, my fame was as black as the skin of my traducers. Still, even at this distant day, I may challenge my worst enemy on the coast to prove that I participated, after 1839, in the purchase of a single slave for transportation beyond the sea !

From the moment that the first dwelling was erected at New Florence, I carefully enforced the most rigid decorum between the sexes throughout my jurisdiction. It was the boast of our friends at Cape Palmas and Monrovia, that my grounds were free from the debauchery, which, elsewhere in Africa, was unhappily too common. I have had the honor to entertain at my table at Cape Mount, not only the ordinary traders of the coast, but commodores of French squadrons, commanders of British and American cruisers, governors of colonies, white and colored missionaries, as well as innumerable merchants of the first respectability, and I have yet to meet the first of them, in any part of the world, who can redden my cheek with a blush.

But such was not the case at the Cape after Cain and Curtis became the pets of the cruisers, and converted the beach into a brothel.[1]

---

[1] I have spoken of visits and appeals from missionaries, and will here insert a letter of introduction, which I received by the hands of the Reverend Mr. Williams, whilst I inhabited Cape Mount. Mr. Williams had been a former governor of Liberia, and was deputed to Cape Mount by the Methodist Episcopal Mission, in Liberia.

"DEAR SIR:

"This will be handed you by the Rev. A. D. Williams, a minister of the M. E. Church, with whom you are so well acquainted that I hardly need introduce him. It is a matter of regret that I am so situated

After a brief sojourn at my quarters to repair " The Chan-cellor," in which I had come with a cargo from the United States, I hastened towards Gallinas to dispose of our merchan-

as to be unable to accompany Mr. Williams to Cape Mount. It would have afforded me pleasure to visit your establishment, and it might have facilitated our mission operations, could I have done so. Allow me, however, to be-speak for Mr. Williams your attention and patronage, both of which you have, in conversation, so kindly promised.

" Our object is to elevate the natives of Cape Mount; to establish a school for children; to have divine service regularly performed on the Sab-bath; and thus to endeavor to introduce among the people a knowledge of the only wise and true God and the blessings of Christianity. Such is the immense influence you have over the Cape Mount people, in consequence of your large territorial possessions, that a great deal of the success of our efforts will depend on you.

" To your endeavors, then, for our prosperity, we look very anxiously. In the course of a few months, should circumstances warrant the expense, I intend to erect suitable buildings for divine service, and for the occupa-tion of the missionary and his family. In this case, we shall have to intrude on your land for building room. I shall endeavor to visit Cape Mount as soon as possible.

" I remain, my dear sir,

"Yours truly,

" JOHN SEYS.

" To THEODORE CANOT, ESQ.,
   " *Cape Mount.*"

It would have afforded me sincere pleasure to gratify Messrs. Williams and Seys, but, unluckily, they had chosen the worst time imaginable for the establishment of a mission and school. The country was ravaged by war, and the towns were depopulated. The passions of the tribes were at their height. Still, as I had promised my co-operation, I introduced the Rev. Mr. Williams to the king, who courteously told the missionary all the dan-gers and difficulties of his position, but promised, should the conflict speed-ily end, to send him notice, when a "book-man" would be received with pleasure.

To give my reverend friend a proof of the scarcity of people *in the towns,* I sent messages to Toso, Fanama and Sugarei, for the inhabitants to assem-ble at New Florence on the next Sunday, to hear " God's palabra," (as they call sacred instruction;) but when the Sabbath came, the Rev. Mr. Wil-liams held forth to my clerk, mechanics and servants, alone!

I reported the mortifying failure to the Rev. Mr. Seys, and Mr. W. returned to Monrovia.

dise. We had been already boarded by an American officer, who reported us to his superior as a regular merchantman; yet, such were the malicious representations on the beach against the vessel and myself, that the Dolphin tarried a month at the anchorage to watch our proceedings. When I went to the old mart of Don Pedro, a cruiser dogged us; when I sailed to leeward of Cape Palmas for oil and ivory, another took charge of our movements,—anchoring where we anchored, getting under way when we did, and following us into every nook and corner. At Grand Buttoa, I took "The Chancellor" within a reef of rocks, and here I was left to proceed as I pleased, while the British cruiser returned to Cape Mount.

The fifteenth of March, eighteen hundred and forty-seven, is scored in my calendar with black. It was on the morning of that day that the commander who escorted me so warily as far as Buttoa, landed a lieutenant and sailors at New Florence, and unceremoniously proceeded to search my premises for slaves. As none were found, the valiant captors seized a couple of handcuffs, like those in use every where to secure refractory seamen, and carried them on board to their commander. Next day, several boats, with marines and sailors, led by a British captain and lieutenant, landed about noon, and, without notice, provocation, or even allowing my clerk to save his raiment, set fire to my brigantine, store-houses, and dwelling.

As I was absent, I cannot vouch for every incident of this transaction, but I have the utmost confidence in the circumstantial narrative which my agent, Mr. Horace Smith, soon after prepared under oath at Monrovia. The marines and Kroomen were permitted to plunder at will. Cain and Curtis revelled in the task of philanthropic destruction. While the sailors burnt my houses, these miscreants and their adherents devoted themselves to the ruin of my garden, fruit trees, plantations, and waterworks. My cattle, even, were stolen, to be sold to the squadron; and, ere night, New Florence was a smouldering heap!

I would gladly have turned the last leaf of this book without a murmur, had not this wanton outrage been perpetrated, not only while I was abroad, but without a shadow of justice. To this hour, I am ignorant of any lawful cause, or of any thing but suspicion, that may be alleged in palliation of the high-handed wrong. Not a line or word was left, whereby I could trace a pretext for my ruin.

Three days after the catastrophe, my ancient ally of Toso paid the debt of nature. In a month, his tribes awoke from their stupor with one of those fiery spasms that are not uncommon in Africa, and, missing their "white man" and his merchandise, rose in a mass, and, without a word of warning, sacrificed the twin varlets of the beach and restored their lawful prince.

**THE END.**

# A CATALOGUE OF SELECTED DOVER BOOKS
## IN ALL FIELDS OF INTEREST

# A CATALOGUE OF SELECTED DOVER BOOKS
## IN ALL FIELDS OF INTEREST

WHAT IS SCIENCE?, *N. Campbell*
The role of experiment and measurement, the function of mathematics, the nature of scientific laws, the difference between laws and theories, the limitations of science, and many similarly provocative topics are treated clearly and without technicalities by an eminent scientist. "Still an excellent introduction to scientific philosophy," H. Margenau in *Physics Today*. "A first-rate primer . . . deserves a wide audience," *Scientific American*. 192pp. 5⅜ x 8.

S43    Paperbound $1.25

THE NATURE OF LIGHT AND COLOUR IN THE OPEN AIR, *M. Minnaert*
Why are shadows sometimes blue, sometimes green, or other colors depending on the light and surroundings? What causes mirages? Why do multiple suns and moons appear in the sky? Professor Minnaert explains these unusual phenomena and hundreds of others in simple, easy-to-understand terms based on optical laws and the properties of light and color. No mathematics is required but artists, scientists, students, and everyone fascinated by these "tricks" of nature will find thousands of useful and amazing pieces of information. Hundreds of observational experiments are suggested which require no special equipment. 200 illustrations; 42 photos. xvi + 362pp. 5⅜ x 8.

T196    Paperbound $2.00

THE STRANGE STORY OF THE QUANTUM, AN ACCOUNT FOR THE GENERAL READER OF THE GROWTH OF IDEAS UNDERLYING OUR PRESENT ATOMIC KNOWLEDGE, *B. Hoffmann*
Presents lucidly and expertly, with barest amount of mathematics, the problems and theories which led to modern quantum physics. Dr. Hoffmann begins with the closing years of the 19th century, when certain trifling discrepancies were noticed, and with illuminating analogies and examples takes you through the brilliant concepts of Planck, Einstein, Pauli, Broglie, Bohr, Schroedinger, Heisenberg, Dirac, Sommerfeld, Feynman, etc. This edition includes a new, long postscript carrying the story through 1958. "Of the books attempting an account of the history and contents of our modern atomic physics which have come to my attention, this is the best," H. Margenau, Yale University, in *American Journal of Physics*. 32 tables and line illustrations. Index. 275pp. 5⅜ x 8.    T518    Paperbound $2.00

GREAT IDEAS OF MODERN MATHEMATICS: THEIR NATURE AND USE, *Jagjit Singh*
Reader with only high school math will understand main mathematical ideas of modern physics, astronomy, genetics, psychology, evolution, etc. better than many who use them as tools, but comprehend little of their basic structure. Author uses his wide knowledge of non-mathematical fields in brilliant exposition of differential equations, matrices, group theory, logic, statistics, problems of mathematical foundations, imaginary numbers, vectors, etc. Original publication. 2 appendixes. 2 indexes. 65 ills. 322pp. 5⅜ x 8.

T587    Paperbound $2.00

A SHORT ACCOUNT OF THE HISTORY OF MATHEMATICS,
**W. W. Rouse Ball**
Last previous edition (1908) hailed by mathematicians and laymen for lucid overview of math as living science, for understandable presentation of individual contributions of great mathematicians. Treats lives, discoveries of every important school and figure from Egypt, Phoenicia to late nineteenth century. Greek schools of Ionia, Cyzicus, Alexandria, Byzantium, Pythagoras; primitive arithmetic; Middle Ages and Renaissance, including European and Asiatic contributions; modern math of Descartes, Pascal, Wallis, Huygens, Newton, Euler, Lambert, Laplace, scores more. More emphasis on historical development, exposition of ideas than other books on subject. Non-technical, readable text can be followed with no more preparation than high-school algebra. Index. 544pp. 5⅜ x 8.     Paperbound $2.25

GREAT IDEAS AND THEORIES OF MODERN COSMOLOGY, **Jagjit Singh**
Companion volume to author's popular "Great Ideas of Modern Mathematics" (Dover, $2.00). The best non-technical survey of post-Einstein attempts to answer perhaps unanswerable questions of origin, age of Universe, possibility of life on other worlds, etc. Fundamental theories of cosmology and cosmogony recounted, explained, evaluated in light of most recent data: Einstein's concepts of relativity, space-time; Milne's a priori world-system; astrophysical theories of Jeans, Eddington; Hoyle's "continuous creation;" contributions of dozens more scientists. A faithful, comprehensive critical summary of complex material presented in an extremely well-written text intended for laymen. Original publication. Index. xii + 276pp. 5⅜ x 8½.     Paperbound $2.00

THE RESTLESS UNIVERSE, **Max Born**
A remarkably lucid account by a Nobel Laureate of recent theories of wave mechanics, behavior of gases, electrons and ions, waves and particles, electronic structure of the atom, nuclear physics, and similar topics. "Much more thorough and deeper than most attempts . . . easy and delightful," *Chemical and Engineering News*. Special feature: 7 animated sequences of 60 figures each showing such phenomena as gas molecules in motion, the scattering of alpha particles, etc. 11 full-page plates of photographs. Total of nearly 600 illustrations. 351pp. 6⅛ x 9¼.     Paperbound $2.00

PLANETS, STARS AND GALAXIES: DESCRIPTIVE ASTRONOMY FOR BEGINNERS, **A. E. Fanning**
What causes the progression of the seasons? Phases of the moon? The Aurora Borealis? How much does the sun weigh? What are the chances of life on our sister planets? Absorbing introduction to astronomy, incorporating the latest discoveries and theories: the solar wind, the surface temperature of Venus, the pock-marked face of Mars, quasars, and much more. Places you on the frontiers of one of the most vital sciences of our time. Revised (1966). Introduction by Donald H. Menzel, Harvard University. References. Index. 45 illustrations. 189pp. 5¼ x 8¼.     Paperbound $1.50

GREAT IDEAS IN INFORMATION THEORY, LANGUAGE AND CYBERNETICS, **Jagjit Singh**
Non-mathematical, but profound study of information, language, the codes used by men and machines to communicate, the principles of analog and digital computers, work of McCulloch, Pitts, von Neumann, Turing, and Uttley, correspondences between intricate mechanical network of "thinking machines" and more intricate neurophysiological mechanism of human brain. Indexes. 118 figures. 50 tables. ix + 338pp. 5⅜ x 8½.     Paperbound $2.00

THE MUSIC OF THE SPHERES: THE MATERIAL UNIVERSE — FROM ATOM TO QUASAR, SIMPLY EXPLAINED, *Guy Murchie*
Vast compendium of fact, modern concept and theory, observed and calculated data, historical background guides intelligent layman through the material universe. Brilliant exposition of earth's construction, explanations for moon's craters, atmospheric components of Venus and Mars (with data from recent fly-by's), sun spots, sequences of star birth and death, neighboring galaxies, contributions of Galileo, Tycho Brahe, Kepler, etc.; and (Vol. 2) construction of the atom (describing newly discovered sigma and xi subatomic particles), theories of sound, color and light, space and time, including relativity theory, quantum theory, wave theory, probability theory, work of Newton, Maxwell, Faraday, Einstein, de Broglie, etc. "Best presentation yet offered to the intelligent general reader," *Saturday Review*. Revised (1967). Index. 319 illustrations by the author. Total of xx + 644pp. 5⅜ x 8½.

Vol. 1 Paperbound $2.00, Vol. 2 Paperbound $2.00,
The set $4.00

FOUR LECTURES ON RELATIVITY AND SPACE, *Charles Proteus Steinmetz*
Lecture series, given by great mathematician and electrical engineer, generally considered one of the best popular-level expositions of special and general relativity theories and related questions. Steinmetz translates complex mathematical reasoning into language accessible to laymen through analogy, example and comparison. Among topics covered are relativity of motion, location, time; of mass; acceleration; 4-dimensional time-space; geometry of the gravitational field; curvature and bending of space; non-Euclidean geometry. Index. 40 illustrations. x + 142pp. 5⅜ x 8½.                                        Paperbound $1.35

HOW TO KNOW THE WILD FLOWERS, *Mrs. William Starr Dana*
Classic nature book that has introduced thousands to wonders of American wild flowers. Color-season principle of organization is easy to use, even by those with no botanical training, and the genial, refreshing discussions of history, folklore, uses of over 1,000 native and escape flowers, foliage plants are informative as well as fun to read. Over 170 full-page plates, collected from several editions, may be colored in to make permanent records of finds. Revised to conform with 1950 edition of Gray's Manual of Botany. xlii + 438pp. 5⅜ x 8½.                                                              Paperbound $2.00

MANUAL OF THE TREES OF NORTH AMERICA, *Charles Sprague Sargent*
Still unsurpassed as most comprehensive, reliable study of North American tree characteristics, precise locations and distribution. By dean of American dendrologists. Every tree native to U.S., Canada, Alaska; 185 genera, 717 species, described in detail—leaves, flowers, fruit, winterbuds, bark, wood, growth habits, etc. plus discussion of varieties and local variants, immaturity variations. Over 100 keys, including unusual 11-page analytical key to genera, aid in identification. 783 clear illustrations of flowers, fruit, leaves. An unmatched permanent reference work for all nature lovers. Second enlarged (1926) edition. Synopsis of families. Analytical key to genera. Glossary of technical terms. Index. 783 illustrations, 1 map. Total of 982pp. 5⅜ x 8.

Vol. 1 Paperbound $2.25, Vol. 2 Paperbound $2.25,
The set $4.50

IT's FUN TO MAKE THINGS FROM SCRAP MATERIALS,
*Evelyn Glantz Hershoff*
What use are empty spools, tin cans, bottle tops? What can be made from rubber bands, clothes pins, paper clips, and buttons? This book provides simply worded instructions and large diagrams showing you how to make cookie cutters, toy trucks, paper turkeys, Halloween masks, telephone sets, aprons, linoleum block- and spatter prints — in all 399 projects! Many are easy enough for young children to figure out for themselves; some challenging enough to entertain adults; all are remarkably ingenious ways to make things from materials that cost pennies or less! Formerly "Scrap Fun for Everyone." Index. 214 illustrations. 373pp. 5⅜ x 8½.                    Paperbound $1.50

SYMBOLIC LOGIC and THE GAME OF LOGIC, *Lewis Carroll*
"Symbolic Logic" is not concerned with modern symbolic logic, but is instead a collection of over 380 problems posed with charm and imagination, using the syllogism and a fascinating diagrammatic method of drawing conclusions. In "The Game of Logic" Carroll's whimsical imagination devises a logical game played with 2 diagrams and counters (included) to manipulate hundreds of tricky syllogisms. The final section, "Hit or Miss" is a lagniappe of 101 additional puzzles in the delightful Carroll manner. Until this reprint edition, both of these books were rarities costing up to $15 each. Symbolic Logic: Index. xxxi + 199pp. The Game of Logic: 96pp. 2 vols. bound as one. 5⅜ x 8.
Paperbound $2.00

MATHEMATICAL PUZZLES OF SAM LOYD, PART I
*selected and edited by M. Gardner*
Choice puzzles by the greatest American puzzle creator and innovator. Selected from his famous collection, "Cyclopedia of Puzzles," they retain the unique style and historical flavor of the originals. There are posers based on arithmetic, algebra, probability, game theory, route tracing, topology, counter and sliding block, operations research, geometrical dissection. Includes the famous "14-15" puzzle which was a national craze, and his "Horse of a Different Color" which sold millions of copies. 117 of his most ingenious puzzles in all. 120 line drawings and diagrams. Solutions. Selected references. xx + 167pp. 5⅜ x 8.
Paperbound $1.00

STRING FIGURES AND HOW TO MAKE THEM, *Caroline Furness Jayne*
107 string figures plus variations selected from the best primitive and modern examples developed by Navajo, Apache, pygmies of Africa, Eskimo, in Europe, Australia, China, etc. The most readily understandable, easy-to-follow book in English on perennially popular recreation. Crystal-clear exposition; step-by-step diagrams. Everyone from kindergarten children to adults looking for unusual diversion will be endlessly amused. Index. Bibliography. Introduction by A. C. Haddon. 17 full-page plates, 960 illustrations. xxiii + 401pp. 5⅜ x 8½.
Paperbound $2.00

PAPER FOLDING FOR BEGINNERS, *W. D. Murray and F. J. Rigney*
A delightful introduction to the varied and entertaining Japanese art of origami (paper folding), with a full, crystal-clear text that anticipates every difficulty; over 275 clearly labeled diagrams of all important stages in creation. You get results at each stage, since complex figures are logically developed from simpler ones. 43 different pieces are explained: sailboats, frogs, roosters, etc. 6 photographic plates. 279 diagrams. 95pp. 5⅜ x 8⅜. Paperbound $1.00

PRINCIPLES OF ART HISTORY,
*H. Wölfflin*

Analyzing such terms as "baroque," "classic," "neoclassic," "primitive," "picturesque," and 164 different works by artists like Botticelli, van Cleve, Dürer, Hobbema, Holbein, Hals, Rembrandt, Titian, Brueghel, Vermeer, and many others, the author establishes the classifications of art history and style on a firm, concrete basis. This classic of art criticism shows what really occurred between the 14th-century primitives and the sophistication of the 18th century in terms of basic attitudes and philosophies. "A remarkable lesson in the art of seeing," *Sat. Rev. of Literature.* Translated from the 7th German edition. 150 illustrations. 254pp. 6⅛ x 9¼. Paperbound $2.00

PRIMITIVE ART,
*Franz Boas*

This authoritative and exhaustive work by a great American anthropologist covers the entire gamut of primitive art. Pottery, leatherwork, metal work, stone work, wood, basketry, are treated in detail. Theories of primitive art, historical depth in art history, technical virtuosity, unconscious levels of patterning, symbolism, styles, literature, music, dance, etc. A must book for the interested layman, the anthropologist, artist, handicrafter (hundreds of unusual motifs), and the historian. Over 900 illustrations (50 ceramic vessels, 12 totem poles, etc.). 376pp. 5⅜ x 8. Paperbound $2.25

THE GENTLEMAN AND CABINET MAKER'S DIRECTOR,
*Thomas Chippendale*

A reprint of the 1762 catalogue of furniture designs that went on to influence generations of English and Colonial and Early Republic American furniture makers. The 200 plates, most of them full-page sized, show Chippendale's designs for French (Louis XV), Gothic, and Chinese-manner chairs, sofas, canopy and dome beds, cornices, chamber organs, cabinets, shaving tables, commodes, picture frames, frets, candle stands, chimney pieces, decorations, etc. The drawings are all elegant and highly detailed; many include construction diagrams and elevations. A supplement of 24 photographs shows surviving pieces of original and Chippendale-style pieces of furniture. Brief biography of Chippendale by N. I. Bienenstock, editor of *Furniture World.* Reproduced from the 1762 edition. 200 plates, plus 19 photographic plates. vi + 249pp. 9⅛ x 12¼. Paperbound $3.50

AMERICAN ANTIQUE FURNITURE: A BOOK FOR AMATEURS,
*Edgar G. Miller, Jr.*

Standard introduction and practical guide to identification of valuable American antique furniture. 2115 illustrations, mostly photographs taken by the author in 148 private homes, are arranged in chronological order in extensive chapters on chairs, sofas, chests, desks, bedsteads, mirrors, tables, clocks, and other articles. Focus is on furniture accessible to the collector, including simpler pieces and a larger than usual coverage of Empire style. Introductory chapters identify structural elements, characteristics of various styles, how to avoid fakes, etc. "We are frequently asked to name some book on American furniture that will meet the requirements of the novice collector, the beginning dealer, and . . . the general public. . . . We believe Mr. Miller's two volumes more completely satisfy this specification than any other work," *Antiques.* Appendix. Index. Total of vi + 1106pp. 7⅞ x 10¾.
Two volume set, paperbound $7.50

THE BAD CHILD'S BOOK OF BEASTS, MORE BEASTS FOR WORSE CHILDREN, and A MORAL ALPHABET, *H. Belloc*
Hardly and anthology of humorous verse has appeared in the last 50 years without at least a couple of these famous nonsense verses. But one must see the entire volumes — with all the delightful original illustrations by Sir Basil Blackwood — to appreciate fully Belloc's charming and witty verses that play so subacidly on the platitudes of life and morals that beset his day — and ours. A great humor classic. Three books in one. Total of 157pp. 5⅜ x 8.
Paperbound $1.00

THE DEVIL'S DICTIONARY, *Ambrose Bierce*
Sardonic and irreverent barbs puncturing the pomposities and absurdities of American politics, business, religion, literature, and arts, by the country's greatest satirist in the classic tradition. Epigrammatic as Shaw, piercing as Swift, American as Mark Twain, Will Rogers, and Fred Allen, Bierce will always remain the favorite of a small coterie of enthusiasts, and of writers and speakers whom he supplies with "some of the most gorgeous witticisms of the English language" (H. L. Mencken). Over 1000 entries in alphabetical order. 144pp. 5⅜ x 8. Paperbound $1.00

THE COMPLETE NONSENSE OF EDWARD LEAR.
This is the only complete edition of this master of gentle madness available at a popular price. *A Book of Nonsense, Nonsense Songs, More Nonsense Songs and Stories* in their entirety with all the old favorites that have delighted children and adults for years. The Dong With A Luminous Nose, The Jumblies, The Owl and the Pussycat, and hundreds of other bits of wonderful nonsense. 214 limericks, 3 sets of Nonsense Botany, 5 Nonsense Alphabets, 546 drawings by Lear himself, and much more. 320pp. 5⅜ x 8. Paperbound $1.00

THE WIT AND HUMOR OF OSCAR WILDE, *ed. by Alvin Redman*
Wilde at his most brilliant, in 1000 epigrams exposing weaknesses and hypocrisies of "civilized" society. Divided into 49 categories—sin, wealth, women, America, etc.—to aid writers, speakers. Includes excerpts from his trials, books, plays, criticism. Formerly "The Epigrams of Oscar Wilde." Introduction by Vyvyan Holland, Wilde's only living son. Introductory essay by editor. 260pp. 5⅜ x 8. Paperbound $1.00

A CHILD'S PRIMER OF NATURAL HISTORY, *Oliver Herford*
Scarcely an anthology of whimsy and humor has appeared in the last 50 years without a contribution from Oliver Herford. Yet the works from which these examples are drawn have been almost impossible to obtain! Here at last are Herford's improbable definitions of a menagerie of familiar and weird animals, each verse illustrated by the author's own drawings. 24 drawings in 2 colors; 24 additional drawings. vii + 95pp. 6½ x 6. Paperbound $1.00

THE BROWNIES: THEIR BOOK, *Palmer Cox*
The book that made the Brownies a household word. Generations of readers have enjoyed the antics, predicaments and adventures of these jovial sprites, who emerge from the forest at night to play or to come to the aid of a deserving human. Delightful illustrations by the author decorate nearly every page. 24 short verse tales with 266 illustrations. 155pp. 6⅝ x 9¼.
Paperbound $1.50

THE PRINCIPLES OF PSYCHOLOGY,
*William James*

The full long-course, unabridged, of one of the great classics of Western literature and science. Wonderfully lucid descriptions of human mental activity, the stream of thought, consciousness, time perception, memory, imagination, emotions, reason, abnormal phenomena, and similar topics. Original contributions are integrated with the work of such men as Berkeley, Binet, Mills, Darwin, Hume, Kant, Royce, Schopenhauer, Spinoza, Locke, Descartes, Galton, Wundt, Lotze, Herbart, Fechner, and scores of others. All contrasting interpretations of mental phenomena are examined in detail—introspective analysis, philosophical interpretation, and experimental research. "A classic," *Journal of Consulting Psychology.* "The main lines are as valid as ever," *Psychoanalytical Quarterly.* "Standard reading . . . a classic of interpretation," *Psychiatric Quarterly.* 94 illustrations. 1408pp. 5⅜ x 8.

Vol. 1 Paperbound $2.50, Vol. 2 Paperbound $2.50,
The set $5.00

VISUAL ILLUSIONS: THEIR CAUSES, CHARACTERISTICS AND APPLICATIONS,
*M. Luckiesh*

"Seeing is deceiving," asserts the author of this introduction to virtually every type of optical illusion known. The text both describes and explains the principles involved in color illusions, figure-ground, distance illusions, etc. 100 photographs, drawings and diagrams prove how easy it is to fool the sense: circles that aren't round, parallel lines that seem to bend, stationary figures that seem to move as you stare at them — illustration after illustration strains our credulity at what we see. Fascinating book from many points of view, from applications for artists, in camouflage, etc. to the psychology of vision. New introduction by William Ittleson, Dept. of Psychology, Queens College. Index. Bibliography. xxi + 252pp. 5⅜ x 8½. Paperbound $1.50

FADS AND FALLACIES IN THE NAME OF SCIENCE,
*Martin Gardner*

This is the standard account of various cults, quack systems, and delusions which have masqueraded as science: hollow earth fanatics, Reich and orgone sex energy, dianetics, Atlantis, multiple moons, Forteanism, flying saucers, medical fallacies like iridiagnosis, zone therapy, etc. A new chapter has been added on Bridey Murphy, psionics, and other recent manifestations in this field. This is a fair, reasoned appraisal of eccentric theory which provides excellent inoculation against cleverly masked nonsense. "Should be read by everyone, scientist and non-scientist alike," R. T. Birge, Prof. Emeritus of Physics, Univ. of California; Former President, American Physical Society. Index. x + 365pp. 5⅜ x 8. Paperbound $1.85

ILLUSIONS AND DELUSIONS OF THE SUPERNATURAL AND THE OCCULT,
*D. H. Rawcliffe*

Holds up to rational examination hundreds of persistent delusions including crystal gazing, automatic writing, table turning, mediumistic trances, mental healing, stigmata, lycanthropy, live burial, the Indian Rope Trick, spiritualism, dowsing, telepathy, clairvoyance, ghosts, ESP, etc. The author explains and exposes the mental and physical deceptions involved, making this not only an exposé of supernatural phenomena, but a valuable exposition of characteristic types of abnormal psychology. Originally titled "The Psychology of the Occult." 14 illustrations. Index. 551pp. 5⅜ x 8. Paperbound $2.25

FAIRY TALE COLLECTIONS, *edited by Andrew Lang*
Andrew Lang's fairy tale collections make up the richest shelf-full of traditional children's stories anywhere available. Lang supervised the translation of stories from all over the world—familiar European tales collected by Grimm, animal stories from Negro Africa, myths of primitive Australia, stories from Russia, Hungary, Iceland, Japan, and many other countries. Lang's selection of translations are unusually high; many authorities consider that the most familiar tales find their best versions in these volumes. All collections are richly decorated and illustrated by H. J. Ford and other artists.

THE BLUE FAIRY BOOK. 37 stories. 138 illustrations. ix + 390pp. 5⅜ x 8½.
Paperbound $1.50

THE GREEN FAIRY BOOK. 42 stories. 100 illustrations. xiii + 366pp. 5⅜ x 8½.
Paperbound $1.50

THE BROWN FAIRY BOOK. 32 stories. 50 illustrations, 8 in color. xii + 350pp. 5⅜ x 8½.
Paperbound $1.50

THE BEST TALES OF HOFFMANN, *edited by E. F. Bleiler*
10 stories by E. T. A. Hoffmann, one of the greatest of all writers of fantasy. The tales include "The Golden Flower Pot," "Automata," "A New Year's Eve Adventure," "Nutcracker and the King of Mice," "Sand-Man," and others. Vigorous characterizations of highly eccentric personalities, remarkably imaginative situations, and intensely fast pacing has made these tales popular all over the world for 150 years. Editor's introduction. 7 drawings by Hoffmann. xxxiii + 419pp. 5⅜ x 8½.
Paperbound $2.00

GHOST AND HORROR STORIES OF AMBROSE BIEPCE,
*edited by E. F. Bleiler*
Morbid, eerie, horrifying tales of possessed poets, shabby aristocrats, revived corpses, and haunted malefactors. Widely acknowledged as the best of their kind between Poe and the moderns, reflecting their author's inner torment and bitter view of life. Includes "Damned Thing," "The Middle Toe of the Right Foot," "The Eyes of the Panther," "Visions of the Night," "Moxon's Master," and over a dozen others. Editor's introduction. xxii + 199pp. 5⅜ x 8½.
Paperbound $1.25

THREE GOTHIC NOVELS, *edited by E. F. Bleiler*
Originators of the still popular Gothic novel form, influential in ushering in early 19th-century Romanticism. Horace Walpole's *Castle of Otranto*, William Beckford's *Vathek*, John Polidori's *The Vampyre*, and a *Fragment* by Lord Byron are enjoyable as exciting reading or as documents in the history of English literature. Editor's introduction. xi + 291pp. 5⅜ x 8½.
Paperbound $2.00

BEST GHOST STORIES OF LEFANU, *edited by E. F. Bleiler*
Though admired by such critics as V. S. Pritchett, Charles Dickens and Henry James, ghost stories by the Irish novelist Joseph Sheridan LeFanu have never become as widely known as his detective fiction. About half of the 16 stories in this collection have never before been available in America. Collection includes "Carmilla" (perhaps the best vampire story ever written), "The Haunted Baronet," "The Fortunes of Sir Robert Ardagh," and the classic "Green Tea." Editor's introduction. 7 contemporary illustrations. Portrait of LeFanu. xii + 467pp. 5⅜ x 8.
Paperbound $2.00

SOCIAL THOUGHT FROM LORE TO SCIENCE,
*H. E. Barnes and H. Becker*
An immense survey of sociological thought and ways of viewing, studying, planning, and reforming society from earliest times to the present. Includes thought on society of preliterate peoples, ancient non-Western cultures, and every great movement in Europe, America, and modern Japan. Analyzes hundreds of great thinkers: Plato, Augustine, Bodin, Vico, Montesquieu, Herder, Comte, Marx, etc. Weighs the contributions of utopians, sophists, fascists and communists; economists, jurists, philosophers, ecclesiastics, and every 19th and 20th century school of scientific sociology, anthropology, and social psychology throughout the world. Combines topical, chronological, and regional approaches, treating the evolution of social thought as a process rather than as a series of mere topics. "Impressive accuracy, competence, and discrimination . . . easily the best single survey," *Nation.* Thoroughly revised, with new material up to 1960. 2 indexes. Over 2200 bibliographical notes. Three volume set. Total of 1586pp. 5⅜ x 8.
Vol. 1 Paperbound $2.75, Vol. 2 Paperbound $2.75, Vol. 3 Paperbound $2.50
The set $8.00

A HISTORY OF HISTORICAL WRITING, *Harry Elmer Barnes*
Virtually the only adequate survey of the whole course of historical writing in a single volume. Surveys developments from the beginnings of historiography in the ancient Near East and the Classical World, up through the Cold War. Covers major historians in detail, shows interrelationship with cultural background, makes clear individual contributions, evaluates and estimates importance; also enormously rich upon minor authors and thinkers who are usually passed over. Packed with scholarship and learning, clear, easily written. Indispensable to every student of history. Revised and enlarged up to 1961. Index and bibliography. xv + 442pp. 5⅜ x 8½. Paperbound $2.50

JOHANN SEBASTIAN BACH, *Philipp Spitta*
The complete and unabridged text of the definitive study of Bach. Written some 70 years ago, it is still unsurpassed for its coverage of nearly all aspects of Bach's life and work. There could hardly be a finer non-technical introduction to Bach's music than the detailed, lucid analyses which Spitta provides for hundreds of individual pieces. 26 solid pages are devoted to the B minor mass, for example, and 30 pages to the glorious St. Matthew Passion. This monumental set also includes a major analysis of the music of the 18th century: Buxtehude, Pachelbel, etc. "Unchallenged as the last word on one of the supreme geniuses of music," John Barkham, *Saturday Review Syndicate.* Total of 1819pp. Heavy cloth binding. 5⅜ x 8.
Two volume set, clothbound $13.50

BEETHOVEN AND HIS NINE SYMPHONIES, *George Grove*
In this modern middle-level classic of musicology Grove not only analyzes all nine of Beethoven's symphonies very thoroughly in terms of their musical structure, but also discusses the circumstances under which they were written, Beethoven's stylistic development, and much other background material. This is an extremely rich book, yet very easily followed; it is highly recommended to anyone seriously interested in music. Over 250 musical passages. Index. viii + 407pp. 5⅜ x 8. Paperbound $2.00

THREE SCIENCE FICTION NOVELS,
*John Taine*
Acknowledged by many as the best SF writer of the 1920's, Taine (under the name Eric Temple Bell) was also a Professor of Mathematics of considerable renown. Reprinted here are *The Time Stream*, generally considered Taine's best, *The Greatest Game*, a biological-fiction novel, and *The Purple Sapphire*, involving a supercivilization of the past. Taine's stories tie fantastic narratives to frameworks of original and logical scientific concepts. Speculation is often profound on such questions as the nature of time, concept of entropy, cyclical universes, etc. 4 contemporary illustrations. v + 532pp. 5⅜ x 8⅜.

T1180　Paperbound $2.00

SEVEN SCIENCE FICTION NOVELS,
*H. G. Wells*
Full unabridged texts of 7 science-fiction novels of the master. Ranging from biology, physics, chemistry, astronomy, to sociology and other studies, Mr. Wells extrapolates whole worlds of strange and intriguing character. "One will have to go far to match this for entertainment, excitement, and sheer pleasure . . ."*New York Times*. Contents: The Time Machine, The Island of Dr. Moreau, The First Men in the Moon, The Invisible Man, The War of the Worlds, The Food of the Gods, In The Days of the Comet. 1015pp. 5⅜ x 8.

T264　Clothbound $5.00

28 SCIENCE FICTION STORIES OF H. G. WELLS.
Two full, unabridged novels, *Men Like Gods* and *Star Begotten*, plus 26 short stories by the master science-fiction writer of all time! Stories of space, time, invention, exploration, futuristic adventure. Partial contents: *The Country of the Blind, In the Abyss, The Crystal Egg, The Man Who Could Work Miracles, A Story of Days to Come, The Empire of the Ants, The Magic Shop, The Valley of the Spiders, A Story of the Stone Age, Under the Knife, Sea Raiders* etc. An indispensable collection for the library of anyone interested in science fiction adventure. 928pp. 5⅜ x 8.

T265　Clothbound $5.00

THREE MARTIAN NOVELS,
*Edgar Rice Burroughs*
Complete, unabridged reprinting, in one volume, of Thuvia, Maid of Mars; Chessmen of Mars; The Master Mind of Mars. Hours of science-fiction adventure by a modern master storyteller. Reset in large clear type for easy reading. 16 illustrations by J. Allen St. John. vi + 490pp. 5⅜ x 8½.

T39　Paperbound $2.50

AN INTELLECTUAL AND CULTURAL HISTORY OF THE WESTERN WORLD,
*Harry Elmer Barnes*
Monumental 3-volume survey of intellectual development of Europe from primitive cultures to the present day. Every significant product of human intellect traced through history: art, literature, mathematics, physical sciences, medicine, music, technology, social sciences, religions, jurisprudence, education, etc. Presentation is lucid and specific, analyzing in detail specific discoveries, theories, literary works, and so on. Revised (1965) by recognized scholars in specialized fields under the direction of Prof. Barnes. Revised bibliography. Indexes. 24 illustrations. Total of xxix + 1318pp.

T1275, T1276, T1277　Three volume set, paperbound $7.50

HEAR ME TALKIN' TO YA, *edited by Nat Shapiro and Nat Hentoff*
In their own words, Louis Armstrong, King Oliver, Fletcher Henderson, Bunk Johnson, Bix Beiderbecke, Billy Holiday, Fats Waller, Jelly Roll Morton, Duke Ellington, and many others comment on the origins of jazz in New Orleans and its growth in Chicago's South Side, Kansas City's jam sessions, Depression Harlem, and the modernism of the West Coast schools. Taken from taped conversations, letters, magazine articles, other first-hand sources. Editors' introduction. xvi + 429pp. 5⅜ x 8½. T1726 Paperbound $2.00

THE JOURNAL OF HENRY D. THOREAU
A 25-year record by the great American observer and critic, as complete a record of a great man's inner life as is anywhere available. Thoreau's Journals served him as raw material for his formal pieces, as a place where he could develop his ideas, as an outlet for his interests in wild life and plants, in writing as an art, in classics of literature, Walt Whitman and other contemporaries, in politics, slavery, individual's relation to the State, etc. The Journals present a portrait of a remarkable man, and are an observant social history. Unabridged republication of 1906 edition, Bradford Torrey and Francis H. Allen, editors. Illustrations. Total of 1888pp. 8⅜ x 12¼.
T312, T313 Two volume set, clothbound $25.00

A SHAKESPEARIAN GRAMMAR, *E. A. Abbott*
Basic reference to Shakespeare and his contemporaries, explaining through thousands of quotations from Shakespeare, Jonson, Beaumont and Fletcher, North's *Plutarch* and other sources the grammatical usage differing from the modern. First published in 1870 and written by a scholar who spent much of his life isolating principles of Elizabethan language, the book is unlikely ever to be superseded. Indexes. xxiv + 511pp. 5⅜ x 8½. T1582 Paperbound $2.75

FOLK-LORE OF SHAKESPEARE, *T. F. Thistelton Dyer*
Classic study, drawing from Shakespeare a large body of references to supernatural beliefs, terminology of falconry and hunting, games and sports, good luck charms, marriage customs, folk medicines, superstitions about plants, animals, birds, argot of the underworld, sexual slang of London, proverbs, drinking customs, weather lore, and much else. From full compilation comes a mirror of the 17th-century popular mind. Index. ix + 526pp. 5⅜ x 8½.
T1614 Paperbound $2.75

THE NEW VARIORUM SHAKESPEARE, *edited by H. H. Furness*
By far the richest editions of the plays ever produced in any country or language. Each volume contains complete text (usually First Folio) of the play, all variants in Quarto and other Folio texts, editorial changes by every major editor to Furness's own time (1900), footnotes to obscure references or language, extensive quotes from literature of Shakespearian criticism, essays on plot sources (often reprinting sources in full), and much more.

HAMLET, *edited by H. H. Furness*
Total of xxvi + 905pp. 5⅜ x 8½.
T1004, T1005 Two volume set, paperbound $5.25

TWELFTH NIGHT, *edited by H. H. Furness*
Index. xxii + 434pp. 5⅜ x 8½. T1189 Paperbound $2.75

LA BOHEME BY GIACOMO PUCCINI,
*translated and introduced by Ellen H. Bleiler*
Complete handbook for the operagoer, with everything needed for full enjoyment except the musical score itself. Complete Italian libretto, with new, modern English line-by-line translation—the only libretto printing all repeats; biography of Puccini; the librettists; background to the opera, Murger's La Boheme, etc.; circumstances of composition and performances; plot summary; and pictorial section of 73 illustrations showing Puccini, famous singers and performances, etc. Large clear type for easy reading. 124pp. 5⅜ x 8½.
T404    Paperbound $1.00

ANTONIO STRADIVARI: HIS LIFE AND WORK (1644-1737),
*W. Henry Hill, Arthur F. Hill, and Alfred E. Hill*
Still the only book that really delves into life and art of the incomparable Italian craftsman, maker of the finest musical instruments in the world today. The authors, expert violin-makers themselves, discuss Stradivari's ancestry, his construction and finishing techniques, distinguished characteristics of many of his instruments and their locations. Included, too, is story of introduction of his instruments into France, England, first revelation of their supreme merit, and information on his labels, number of instruments made, prices, mystery of ingredients of his varnish, tone of pre-1684 Stradivari violin and changes between 1684 and 1690. An extremely interesting, informative account for all music lovers, from craftsman to concert-goer. Republication of original (1902) edition. New introduction by Sydney Beck, Head of Rare Book and Manuscript Collections, Music Division, New York Public Library. Analytical index by Rembert Wurlitzer. Appendixes. 68 illustrations. 30 full-page plates. 4 in color. xxvi + 315pp. 5⅜ x 8½.
T425    Paperbound $2.25

MUSICAL AUTOGRAPHS FROM MONTEVERDI TO HINDEMITH,
*Emanuel Winternitz*
For beauty, for intrinsic interest, for perspective on the composer's personality, for subtleties of phrasing, shading, emphasis indicated in the autograph but suppressed in the printed score, the mss. of musical composition are fascinating documents which repay close study in many different ways. This 2-volume work reprints facsimiles of mss. by virtually every major composer, and many minor figures—196 examples in all. A full text points out what can be learned from mss., analyzes each sample. Index. Bibliography. 18 figures. 196 plates. Total of 170pp. of text. 7⅞ x 10¾.
T1312, T1313    Two volume set, paperbound $4.00

J. S. BACH,
*Albert Schweitzer*
One of the few great full-length studies of Bach's life and work, and the study upon which Schweitzer's renown as a musicologist rests. On first appearance (1911), revolutionized Bach performance. The only writer on Bach to be musicologist, performing musician, and student of history, theology and philosophy, Schweitzer contributes particularly full sections on history of German Protestant church music, theories on motivic pictorial representations in vocal music, and practical suggestions for performance. Translated by Ernest Newman. Indexes. 5 illustrations. 650 musical examples. Total of xix + 928pp. 5⅜ x 8½.
T1631, T1632    Two volume set, paperbound $4.50

THE METHODS OF ETHICS, *Henry Sidgwick*
Propounding no organized system of its own, study subjects every major methodological approach to ethics to rigorous, objective analysis. Study discusses and relates ethical thought of Plato, Aristotle, Bentham, Clarke, Butler, Hobbes, Hume, Mill, Spencer, Kant, and dozens of others. Sidgwick retains conclusions from each system which follow from ethical premises, rejecting the faulty. Considered by many in the field to be among the most important treatises on ethical philosophy. Appendix. Index. xlvii + 528pp. 5⅜ x 8½.
T1608    Paperbound $2.50

TEUTONIC MYTHOLOGY, *Jakob Grimm*
A milestone in Western culture; the work which established on a modern basis the study of history of religions and comparative religions. 4-volume work assembles and interprets everything available on religious and folkloristic beliefs of Germanic people (including Scandinavians, Anglo-Saxons, etc.). Assembling material from such sources as Tacitus, surviving Old Norse and Icelandic texts, archeological remains, folktales, surviving superstitions, comparative traditions, linguistic analysis, etc. Grimm explores pagan deities, heroes, folklore of nature, religious practices, and every other area of pagan German belief. To this day, the unrivaled, definitive, exhaustive study. Translated by J. S. Stallybrass from 4th (1883) German edition. Indexes. Total of lxxvii + 1887pp. 5⅜ x 8½.
T1602, T1603, T1604, T1605    Four volume set, paperbound $10.00

THE I CHING, *translated by James Legge*
Called "The Book of Changes" in English, this is one of the Five Classics edited by Confucius, basic and central to Chinese thought. Explains perhaps the most complex system of divination known, founded on the theory that all things happening at any one time have characteristic features which can be isolated and related. Significant in Oriental studies, in history of religions and philosophy, and also to Jungian psychoanalysis and other areas of modern European thought. Index. Appendixes. 6 plates. xxi + 448pp. 5⅜ x 8½.
T1062    Paperbound $2.75

HISTORY OF ANCIENT PHILOSOPHY, *W. Windelband*
One of the clearest, most accurate comprehensive surveys of Greek and Roman philosophy. Discusses ancient philosophy in general, intellectual life in Greece in the 7th and 6th centuries B.C., Thales, Anaximander, Anaximenes, Heraclitus, the Eleatics, Empedocles, Anaxagoras, Leucippus, the Pythagoreans, the Sophists, Socrates, Democritus (20 pages), Plato (50 pages), Aristotle (70 pages), the Peripatetics, Stoics, Sceptics, Neo-platonists, Christian Apologists, etc. 2nd German edition translated by H. E. Cushman. xv + 393pp. 5⅜ x 8.
T357    Paperbound $2.25

THE PALACE OF PLEASURE, *William Painter*
Elizabethan versions of Italian and French novels from *The Decameron,* Cinthio, Straparola, Queen Margaret of Navarre, and other continental sources — the very work that provided Shakespeare and dozens of his contemporaries with many of their plots and sub-plots and, therefore, justly considered one of the most influential books in all English literature. It is also a book that any reader will still enjoy. Total of cviii + 1,224pp.
T1691, T1692, T1693    Three volume set, paperbound $6.75

THE WONDERFUL WIZARD OF OZ, *L. F. Baum*
All the original W. W. Denslow illustrations in full color—as much a part of
"The Wizard" as Tenniel's drawings are of "Alice in Wonderland." "The
Wizard" is still America's best-loved fairy tale, in which, as the author expresses
it, "The wonderment and joy are retained and the heartaches and nightmares
left out." Now today's young readers can enjoy every word and wonderful picture of the original book. New introduction by Martin Gardner. A Baum
bibliography. 23 full-page color plates. viii + 268pp. 5⅜ x 8.
T691 Paperbound $1.75

THE MARVELOUS LAND OF OZ, *L. F. Baum*
This is the equally enchanting sequel to the "Wizard," continuing the adventures of the Scarecrow and the Tin Woodman. The hero this time is a little
boy named Tip, and all the delightful Oz magic is still present. This is the
Oz book with the Animated Saw-Horse, the Woggle-Bug, and Jack Pumpkin-
head. All the original John R. Neill illustrations, 10 in full color. 287pp.
5⅜ x 8.
T692 Paperbound $1.50

ALICE'S ADVENTURES UNDER GROUND, *Lewis Carroll*
The original *Alice in Wonderland*, hand-lettered and illustrated by Carroll
himself, and originally presented as a Christmas gift to a child-friend. Adults
as well as children will enjoy this charming volume, reproduced faithfully
in this Dover edition. While the story is essentially the same, there are slight
changes, and Carroll's spritely drawings present an intriguing alternative to
the famous Tenniel illustrations. One of the most popular books in Dover's
catalogue. Introduction by Martin Gardner. 38 illustrations. 128pp. 5⅜ x 8½.
T1482 Paperbound $1.00

THE NURSERY "ALICE," *Lewis Carroll*
While most of us consider *Alice in Wonderland* a story for children of all
ages, Carroll himself felt it was beyond younger children. He therefore provided this simplified version, illustrated with the famous Tenniel drawings
enlarged and colored in delicate tints, for children aged "from Nought to
Five." Dover's edition of this now rare classic is a faithful copy of the 1889
printing, including 20 illustrations by Tenniel, and front and back covers
reproduced in full color. Introduction by Martin Gardner. xxiii + 67pp.
6⅛ x 9¼.
T1610 Paperbound $1.75

THE STORY OF KING ARTHUR AND HIS KNIGHTS, *Howard Pyle*
A fast-paced, exciting retelling of the best known Arthurian legends for young
readers by one of America's best story tellers and illustrators. The sword
Excalibur, wooing of Guinevere, Merlin and his downfall, adventures of Sir
Pellias and Gawaine, and others. The pen and ink illustrations are vividly
imagined and wonderfully drawn. 41 illustrations. xviii + 313pp. 6⅛ x 9¼.
T1445 Paperbound $1.75

*Prices subject to change without notice.*

Available at your book dealer or write for free catalogue to Dept. Adsci,
Dover Publications, Inc., 180 Varick St., N.Y., N.Y. 10014. Dover publishes more
than 150 books each year on science, elementary and advanced mathematics,
biology, music, art, literary history, social sciences and other areas.